THE CUBAN REVOLUTION
AND THE NEW LEFT

Caribbean Crossroads:
Race, Identity, and Freedom Struggles

Edited by Michelle Chase and Isabella Cosse
Lillian Guerra, Devyn Spence Benson,
April Mayes, and Solsiree del Moral / *Series Editors*

The Cuban Revolution and the New Left

TRANSNATIONAL
HISTORIES OF
GENDER, SEXUALITY,
AND FAMILY

University of Florida Press / *Gainesville*

This book will be made open access within three years of publication thanks to Path to Open, a program developed in partnership between JSTOR, the American Council of Learned Societies (ACLS), University of Michigan Press, and The University of North Carolina Press to bring about equitable access and impact for the entire scholarly community, including authors, researchers, libraries, and university presses around the world. Learn more at https://about.jstor.org/path-to-open/

Publication of this work made possible by a Sustaining the Humanities through the American Rescue Plan grant from the National Endowment for the Humanities.

Copyright 2026 by Michelle Chase and Isabella Cosse
All rights reserved
Published in the United States of America

31 30 29 28 27 26   6 5 4 3 2 1

DOI: http://doi.org/10.5744/9781683405566

LIBRARY OF CONGRESS CATALOGING-IN-PUBLICATION DATA
Names: Chase, Michelle editor | Cosse, Isabella editor
Title: The Cuban Revolution and the new left : transnational histories of gender, sexuality, and family / edited by Michelle Chase and Isabella Cosse.
Other titles: Caribbean crossroads: race, identity, and freedom struggles
Description: Gainesville : University of Florida Press, 2026. | Series: Caribbean crossroads: race, identity, and freedom struggles | Includes index.
Identifiers: LCCN 2025029473 (print) | LCCN 2025029474 (ebook) | ISBN 9781683405566 hardback | ISBN 9781683405702 paperback | ISBN 9781683405924 ebook | ISBN 9781683405795 pdf
Subjects: LCSH: New Left—Cuba—History | Revolutions—Social aspects—Cuba | Gender identity—Cuba—History | Sexual minorities—Cuba—History | Families—Cuba—History | Transnationalism—Political aspects—Cuba | Solidarity—Political aspects—Cuba | Feminism—Cuba—History | Political culture—Cuba—History | Cuba—History—Revolution, 1959—Influence | Cuba—Foreign relations—Social aspects | Cuba—Social conditions—1959-
Classification: LCC F1788 .C827995 2026 (print) | LCC F1788 (ebook) | DDC 306.2097291—dc23/eng/20250908
LC record available at https://lccn.loc.gov/2025029473
LC ebook record available at https://lccn.loc.gov/2025029474

| UF PRESS |

University of Florida Press
2046 NE Waldo Road
Suite 2100
Gainesville, FL 32609
floridapress.org

GPSR EU Authorized Representative: Mare Nostrum Group B.V., Mauritskade 21D, 1091 GC Amsterdam, The Netherlands, gpsr@mare-nostrum.co.uk

CONTENTS

vii List of Figures

ix Acknowledgments

1 **INTRODUCTION** The Island and the World: Rethinking the Cuban Revolution Through Transnational and Sociocultural Histories *Michelle Chase and Isabella Cosse*

REVOLUTIONARY WOMEN

17 **ONE** "The Voice of the Skin": Racial Politics in Cuban-Angolan Cooperation, 1965–1967 *Rafael Cesar*

44 **TWO** The Heroic Example of the Vietnamese Woman: Gender and Solidarity in Cuba's Age of the Tricontinental *Michelle Chase*

67 **THREE** Angela Davis in Cuba as Symbol and Subject, 1960–1970s *Sarah J. Seidman*

SEXUALITY

93 **FOUR** The Orphans of the Sierra Maestra: Cuba and the Homosexual Movements in Latin America, 1960–1990 *Felipe Caro Romero*

117 **FIVE** Transgressing Che: Irina Layevska Echeverría Gaitán, Disability Politics, and Transgendering the New Man in Mexico, 1964–2001 *Robert Franco*

GENDER, MEDIA, AND CULTURE

141 SIX Cuba, 1959: Revolutionary Attraction and Journalism
Ximena Espeche

163 SEVEN Revolutionary Roses on the Cane Field: Staging Cuban Women in Socialist China, 1960–1965 *Siwei Wang*

FAMILY, CHILDHOOD, AND DAILY LIFE

187 EIGHT The Paradoxes of Paradise: Memories of Exile and Family Life in Revolutionary Cuba, 1972–1990 *Tanya Harmer*

212 NINE Between Two Empires: Youth, Identity, and Consumption in 1970s and 1980s Cuba *Alexis Baldacci*

234 TEN "We Were Like a Bomb": Child Refugees, Cuban Politics, and Argentine Revolutionary Organizations, 1970–2020 *Isabella Cosse*

256 ELEVEN Internationalizing the Revolutionary Family: Love and Politics in Cuba and Nicaragua, 1979–1990 *Emily Snyder*

279 Afterword *Ailynn Torres Santana*

287 List of Contributors

291 Index

FIGURES

20 1.1. Deolinda Rodrigues
24 1.2. *Heroínas de Angola* by Limbania Jiménez Rodríguez
27 1.3. *Tricontinental* magazine
29 1.4. The Kamy Squad and Limbania Jiménez Rodríguez
50 2.1. Cuban and Vietnamese diplomats
55 2.2. Nguyen Thi Binh in Havana
59 2.3. René Mederos poster, "As in Vietnam"
68 3.1. Angela Davis at exhibition in Havana
76 3.2. Alfredo Rostgaard poster, *Angela Davis*
80 3.3. Angela Davis in the Plaza de la Revolución
99 4.1. *Ink*
106 4.2. *Lampião da Esquina*
125 5.1. Echeverría Gaitán in Moscow
129 5.2. Irina circa 2008
167 7.1. Chinese documentary film *Cuba in Battle*
169 7.2. Catalog for photo exhibit displayed in Beijing
174 7.3. Production photo of *Cañaveral*
219 9.1. Cuban fashion at the World Festival of Youth and Students
223 9.2. A Cuban cartoon mocking foreign fashion
223 9.3. Demonstration during Mariel boatlift
235 10.1. The Santucho children

ACKNOWLEDGMENTS

This book is the culmination of a long-term endeavor. Some of the ideas developed here were first explored in the January 2020 issue of *Radical History Review*. We thank Heidi Tinsman and Melina Pappademos for the support and intellectual strength they gave that issue, the authors who contributed to the issue, and *Radical History Review* for giving us permission to reprint three of the essays from that issue in this book. A Tinker Fellowship at the Institute of Latin American Studies at Columbia University granted to Isabella in spring of 2022 facilitated crucial in-person conversations in the book's early stages.

Many colleagues, in both the United States and Latin America, have generously contributed to the project in ways large and small. Heidi Tinsman has been a long-term champion of this project. She provided crucial feedback on an early draft of the introduction and has offered multiple other forms of advice and support. The conference "Cuba y la izquierda latinoamericana: una historia de encuentros y desencuentros," hosted by the Universidad de la República in Montevideo in November 2022, was a valuable space to rehearse early arguments among like-minded scholars. We were also lucky to be able to present the introduction and an overview of the book in the workshop "La revolución cubana en el centro de las encrucijadas de la guerra fría," organized by the Universidad Nacional de San Martín in Buenos Aires in May 2024. We thank all the participants of the workshop for their insightful comments, especially Vera Carnovale, Marcelo Casals, Ximena Espeche, Marina Franco, Valeria Manzano, Martin Ribadero, and Daniela Slipak.

We are grateful for the University of Florida Press's interest in this book, and we feel especially lucky to have Stephanye Hunter as our editor. Her support and enthusiasm have contributed enormously to this project from the beginning. We are grateful to series editors Lillian Guerra, Devyn Spence Benson, April Mayes, and Solsiree del Moral for supporting our project. We also thank Lillian and the two other peer reviewers, Jessie Horst and Rachel Hynson, for their commitment and generosity. Their feedback has improved the book immeasurably.

Our respective institutions (Pace University, the Universidad Nacional de San Martín, and the Consejo Nacional de Investigaciones Científicas y Técnicas) helped us develop this project with intellectual stimulation and various other forms of support. We are grateful for a grant from Pace University's Westchester Faculty Council Scholarly Research Committee, which covered the costs of indexing and proofreading.

Finally, we would like to thank our authors for accepting our invitation to embark on this intellectual adventure, which we began in the midst of a pandemic. Bringing it to fruition has required numerous exchanges, dialogues, and revisions. Collective work is not always easy, but in our case, it has been greatly enriching.

INTRODUCTION

The Island and the World

Rethinking the Cuban Revolution Through Transnational and Sociocultural Histories

MICHELLE CHASE AND ISABELLA COSSE

It can be hard to remember the power and attraction that Cuba once exerted. Since the 1990s, the island has witnessed widespread economic hardship and global isolation, gradually seeming to symbolize socialism's failures rather than its promises. But from the 1959 triumph of the revolution until the fall of the Socialist Bloc, Cuba was a central reference for the Left throughout the world. The Cuban Revolution catalyzed the conviction that a historical change was possible and even imminent. It served as a central symbol and inspiration for the "new" Left that emerged in its wake. Cuba's attraction was global, visible in the adoption of Che Guevara's famous beret by the youths who revolted across Europe in 1968. Its symbolism was perhaps especially crucial for Latin America and among younger generations, but also for newly postcolonial and decolonizing nations in Asia and Africa.

This book revisits that significance, especially in the overlapping visions of leftist movements, progressivism, and revolutionary movements, by interrogating Cuba's global impact and how it reshaped the Left from the 1959 revolution to the end of the Cold War. It does so by studying the period through actors not always recognized as key players, such as women, rank-and-file militants, youth, and children. It also sheds new light on these processes through the lenses of gender, sexuality, family, and daily life, thereby connecting the profound transformations that occurred in these realms in the second half of the twentieth century with the global conflicts introduced by the Cold War and the Cuban Revolution's triumph.

The book also looks in the other direction, asking how global forces, actors, and trends impacted the Cuban Revolution, such as transnational models of consumption, feminist and gay rights movements, and national liberation projects from elsewhere in the Global South. Like the famous inverted map of Uruguayan artist Torres García, we rethink established perspectives by putting Cuba in the center and looking outward from the island, resulting in new perspectives on the transnational dynamics and flows of the period. As a result, this volume offers an alternative to hegemonic perspectives on this historical era—for example, centering Cuba and the Global South highlights the irony of referring to the Cold War as "cold," as these regions lived through cruel wars, dictatorships, and political violence.

The Cuban Revolution and the New Left explores Cuba's transnational encounters and political strategies and how they changed over time. The book attends to the beginning of the revolution, the year "zero," a short period when many futures seemed possible, but which closed after the 1962 missile crisis permanently realigned Cuba, placing it in firm alliance with the Soviet Union and under an embargo from the United States that persists to this day. Cuban revolutionaries had sought transnational allies even before coming to power, but transnational strategies became more important after 1962, both to subvert the isolation imposed by the United States and to avoid being subsumed by the Soviet alliance. The first few years of the revolution have been studied extensively, as have the rest of the decade of the 1960s, when Cuba became a global hub for leaders, militants, and intellectuals from varied leftist movements and organizations, all of whom came to the island to forge links, seek support, and build continental and global strategies partly modeled on Cuba's example. The Third World—as it was then known to contemporaries—seemed to be at the vanguard of these changes, the place where new futures were forged.[1] And Cuba took on an active role in supporting revolutionary movements in Latin America, a way of "exporting" the revolution. The 1960s were thus the heyday of the global Left's romance with Cuba.

The first major cracks in that relationship began in the late 1960s, first with Fidel Castro's 1968 endorsement of the Soviet invasion of Czechoslovakia, then culminating with the Padilla Affair of 1971, when the arrest and exaggerated "confession" of poet Heberto Padilla opened Cuba to the first widespread allegations of authoritarianism and repression for global intellectuals and artists who had previously supported Cuba without reservation.[2] The same year, the National Congress on Culture and Education signaled a more systematic and institutionalized intolerance of homosexuality. The following half decade was a period of censorship and intolerance in the arts now referred to as the Quinquenio Gris (Gray Years) and was accompanied by a more critical relationship with the global Left. Cuba's tighter relationship with the Soviet Union in this period—what Lillian Guerra has called the "red years"—also tarnished earlier hopes that the revolution would chart its own path, avoiding the pitfalls of Eastern European socialism.[3]

This book moves from that period of early power and influence in the 1960s to the revolution's gradually diminishing attraction for the global Left in the 1970s. Still, Cuba did not cease to be a referent for all groups on the Left at the same time. As Portugal's African colonies became independent after 1974, Cuba extended its political and military influence significantly in those regions. In the same period, Cuba resumed diplomatic relations with much of Latin America. As military dictatorships spread across the Southern Cone, some exiles negotiated new lives in Cuba, sometimes causing tensions or contradictions, for example, as Cuba maintained relations with both the Argentine dictatorship and Argentine revolutionary groups. At the same time, the spread of conflicts across Central America and the 1979 Nicaragua Revolution opened new fronts in the global Cold War and renewed hopes in revolutionary triumph. And in general, the belief in an egalitarian utopia that had improved conditions for the poorest continued to mute or limit criticism of authoritarianism on the Left.

We also need to recognize that political developments within Cuba were never entirely linear: periods of intolerance alternated with periods of relative openness or with the clearer articulation of rights, such as in the 1975 Family Code, which garnered significant attention from feminists abroad without tempering state repression of homosexuality. Similarly, while Cuban leaders continued to denounce consumption as a capitalist vice, they also tried to create competing socialist versions of fashion.[4] And later, remittances from relatives abroad—long considered enemies of the state—became crucial to sustaining daily life and prompted a softening of official discourse toward them. Thus, this book studies those different moments and encounters, both in Cuban and global history, analyzing Cuba's external projection while also recognizing the tensions inherent in those encounters with different actors of the global Left as well as within Cuba. That is to say, the Cuban Revolution and its reception by the global Left should not be viewed simply as an internally disciplinary and authoritarian state that nevertheless and perhaps paradoxically served to inspire and renovate a Left beyond the island's borders. Rather, political inspiration and renovation coexisted with political rigidity and repression, both within and beyond Cuba. This book examines the intersection of these forces, inside and outside of Cuba, and how they shaped and reinforced one another, even as they remained in constant tension.

Methodology and Historiography

Attention to Cuba's transnational influences and alliances is not new. Even for contemporaries, these global connections had clear importance and were part of the struggle to define the meaning of the revolution abroad. With the rise of transnational studies in the academy, scholarly interest in these processes has increased. Existing studies of the revolution's transnational influences and connections usually examine the island's relationship with the United States, the USSR, and its own exile population.[5] More recent scholarship has begun to explore revolutionary Cuba's relationship with the Global South.[6] But most of that existing scholarship relies on traditional political and diplomatic historical methods. Here we revisit these questions from a new angle: a sociocultural history of the political based on gender, sexuality, family, and daily life. As Michael Bustamante and Jennifer Lambe have recently noted, "Our knowledge of the social, cultural, and political history of revolutionary Cuba remains fragmented and, in many places, underdeveloped."[7] Our anthology responds to this challenge and, in so doing, draws on multiple methodological influences.

Our approach takes inspiration from the cultural history of the Cold War pioneered by Elaine Tyler May in her 1988 book *Homeward Bound: American Families in the Cold War Era*. Her book opens with the "kitchen debates" between Nixon and Khrushchev centered on daily life, rather than armed conflict or political economy, as an approach to understanding the Cold War. To understand foreign policy May analyzes assumptions about gender differences, including masculine power sustained by sexual potency and household authority, and a female sexuality that had to be contained and domesticated, which May argued was part of national security. Despite the originality of May's approach, it was never widely taken up in transnational studies of Latin American history.[8]

Following these foundational concepts, this book understands gender as a decisive category for political strategy and political praxis. We also consider the cultural imaginaries that sustained these political strategies, not only within Cuba but also among the varied actors involved in the wider struggles sparked by the revolution across the global Left. The book observes these cultural elaborations through the concrete experiences of the people who were involved in the historical process. Moreover, the book pays attention to the dimensions of family and daily life that amplify the political character of social reproduction, and which are crucial to understanding the political dynamics of the Cold War on a transnational scale. These combined categories of analysis shift the focus of attention from high-level political leaders, usually male, to newer actors, such as children, adolescents, and rank-and-file militants.

This book also draws on historiographical innovations that emerged in the Southern Cone in the 1990s and early 2000s, motivated by the need to fully understand the tragedy and experience of the mass human rights violations and state terrorism of the military dictatorships in ways that had not been captured by political science or sociological studies. Initially, this interest was expressed in the study of memory but later shifted toward understanding the historical events themselves, not only as refracted through memory.[9] These trends, loosely referred to as *historia reciente,* have also raised crucial questions about understanding revolutionary subjectivities from a gendered perspective, which we draw on here. A slightly distinct but overlapping body of scholarship connects the concerns of *historia reciente* with sociocultural studies of the sixties and seventies, and in the process explores new themes, actors, and questions to understand the political and to renew both our understanding of those years in Latin America and the field of *historia reciente.*[10] Our book connects the approaches and themes raised within *historia reciente* and the study of the "long sixties" with newer historiography on the Cold War, which focuses on transnational forces and the Global South, for example, by exploring the construction of revolutionary subjectivities as people, ideas, and practices crossed borders in the Americas and beyond.[11]

Focusing on transnational flows within and beyond Cuba necessarily incorporates perspectives from historiography on Cuba. On the one hand, we build on the existing historiography that has focused on Cuba's relations with the superpowers and with revolutionary states and movements in the Global South. This scholarship, including pioneering studies of Cuban support for African decolonization movements by historians like Piero Gleijeses and Christine Hatzky, has upended traditional assumptions about the global power dynamics of the Cold War by exposing Cuba's autonomy and proactivity on the global stage. On the other hand, we also engage with recent studies of revolutionary Cuba such as those by Anita Casavantes Bradford and Rachel Hynson that insist on the political importance of gender, childhood, and family to the revolution and in diaspora, especially in the 1960s, combining these themes with the transnational scope adopted by Gleijeses and Hatzky.[12] In addition, we also extend our study beyond the 1960s into the less-studied periods of the 1970s and beyond, when new themes and demands—such as homosexual rights, feminism, and youth consumption—put additional strains on Cuba's transnational relations.

The ambitious frame sketched out here is possible because the contributors themselves come from varied disciplinary traditions and geographical locations, which reflect these different scholarly approaches. Weaving together these interconnected historiographies is an intentional component of this anthology, as a way of responding to existing hierarchies and inequalities in the construction of knowledge.[13] With this interdisciplinary methodological approach, the volume aspires to make several contributions to the existing historiography and periodization of the Cuban Revolution.

First, this collection greatly expands our understanding of Cuban internationalism, which has thus far been studied primarily through Cuba's political impact on the New Left and support for guerrilla movements,[14] Cuba's evolving relations with foreign intellectuals and writers,[15] or a cultural project that placed Havana at the heart of an imagined "Tricontinental" alliance.[16] Such methods center actors such as, on the one hand, states, political leaders, and revolutionary movements, and on the other hand, artists and cultural workers. This existing historiography has led to watershed insights about how Cuba supported African liberation, pressed the Soviets on the question of national liberation, negotiated alliances with other underdeveloped states of the Global South, and generally inserted itself as a major protagonist in the global Cold War, alongside far larger powers like the United States and the Soviet Union. These findings have, in turn, reshaped how we understand the power dynamics of the global Cold War.

But by embracing newer methods rooted in studies of race, gender, emotion, or affect, we find that in the 1960s, Cuba's impact was never limited to questions of strategy or models of socialism. Its example was always also embedded in understandings of gender, sexuality, and intimacy, even before the rise of feminist and LGBTQ+ movements.[17] Indeed, essays in this volume show how transnational solidarity campaigns and interactions implicated the most fundamental aspects of human experience, including racial and gender identification, sexuality, family formation, and daily life. For example, Tanya Harmer and Rafael Cesar each show how militants from the Southern Cone and Angola, respectively, found the Cuban state's gender and racial policies to be less transformative than they had imagined. Harmer's study of militants from Chile and Uruguay who sought refuge in Cuba in the 1970s finds that they experienced life on the island as liberating but also restrictive, requiring daily negotiation over sexuality, reproduction, or childcare. Cesar's study of Cuban-Angolan relations finds significant disconnects between Cuba's endorsement of a discourse of "racelessness," upheld by some leftist Angolan leaders, against the demands for Black liberation expressed by other Angolan militants. Similarly, Emily Snyder's study of Cuban-Nicaraguan relations after the 1979 Sandinista revolution shows that Cuban internationalists themselves chafed against the limited state definitions of revolutionary "family" and bureaucratic state efforts to discourage binational relationships. All three authors explore the way historical actors contested those state imaginaries, in response pioneering their own ideas and practices of racial solidarity, gender equality, or family.

Other essays here use gender to provide new insights into the heyday of transnational solidarity in the 1960s and early 1970s. Authors Sarah Seidman, Siwei Wang, and Michelle Chase each explore the way transnational solidarity campaigns were shaped by ideas of gender and, conversely, how ideas about women's liberation and the gendered character of revolution were developed in a transnational exchange of ideas across the Global South. Seidman explores how Cuba's celebration of Angela Davis in the 1970s was informed by ideas of race and gender. Wang shows how Chinese theater directors, actors, and the general public responded to the visions of gender expressed in a Cuban play that was performed throughout China in the early 1960s. Chase unearths relations of solidarity between Cuba and Vietnam to argue that the Vietnam War helped Cuba hone its own understanding of women's roles in national liberation. In his essay on Cuban-Angolan relations, discussed above, Cesar too offers a view of the potential conflict around intersections of race and gender generated by these transnational encounters. These essays all show how transnational politics were shaped by more "grassroots" actors, not just national-level political leaders. They also ask new questions about the domestic uses or impacts of internationalist projects. For example, several essays here suggest that as the Cuban population increasingly felt fatigued or disillusioned by the mid- to late 1960s, external examples of sacrifice and heroism were seen as sources of renovation and inspiration.

Second, the transnational sociocultural historical approach sketched out in this book also gives us more insight into the famous development of Cuba's "New Man," sexuality, and masculinity. Recent contributions within Cuban history have stressed the disciplinary nature of these new imaginings, showing how they went hand in hand with repressive state practices to police nonconforming identities and practices of gender and sexuality, which the revolutionary leadership conceived of as challenging to revolutionary masculinity, or to discourage nonhetero/nonnuclear families by enshrining marriage and the nuclear family and/or criminalizing prostitution, especially in the 1960s.[18] These interventions have importantly reminded us that the so-called age of the Tricontinental, the apex of internationalist solidarity, coincided with Cuba's most repressive state policies toward gender nonconformity.[19]

But by looking transnationally, taking a longer period, and decentering the Cuban state in favor of other actors, the essays here by Felipe Caro and Robert Franco also uncover more porous and flexible ideas of Cuba's "New Man" as it traveled around the region. Caro shows how homosexual liberation movement activists around Latin America debated and contested Cuba's sexual policies. Franco explores the individual biography of one Mexican trans and disability activist who was inspired by and reshaped—indeed, we might argue re-radicalized—Che's image. Both authors thus explore the way the Cuban state's limited ideas concerning masculinity and sexuality could be reforged, contested, and reimagined transnationally by more grassroots actors, especially in the 1970s and 1980s, as the global Left developed more critical forms of engagement with Cuba.

Third, the book valorizes the arenas of daily life, the family, and childhood as central historical questions in and of themselves, not merely as a spin-off of studies of gender and sexuality, although the essays use gender as a key category of analysis. Sensitive to the different dimensions of intimacy that each of these approaches can convey, several chapters offer new insights into how revolutionary politics shaped personal and collective experience and vice versa. This angle also contributes to a history of emotion, conceived of as the connection between feelings, ideology, and politics. Isabella Cosse, Alexis Baldacci, Harmer, and Snyder each show how Cold War conflicts were entangled with families, children, and youth, both at the level of lived everyday experience, and as symbolically important metaphors for the revolutionary project. For example, Cosse shows the centrality of children to Cuba's internationalist discourse, arguing that the Cuban state focused on the children of Argentine militants to assuage tensions over its continued diplomatic relations with the Argentine dictatorship after 1976. In the process, Cosse and others also uncover the tensions and fissures that gradually emerged within the Latin American Left—not only along the more familiar lines of geopolitical alliances and strategies for taking power but concerning social relationships and daily life. Baldacci explores the way Cuban youths and the state negotiated questions of fashion and consumption in the context of contrasting models emanating from the Socialist Bloc and the US-based exile community. Far from inconsequential or superficial topics, Baldacci finds that style and consumer culture were central to definitions of revolutionary values, youth identity, and relations between individuals and the collectivity.

Fourth, this book contributes to understanding the attraction the Cuban Revolution exerted around the Global South in the early "revolutionary moment," when the future of the revolution was still wide open, and how that changed over time. In the early 1960s, observers around the world read the revolution against their own countries' revolutionary experiences and negotiated their expectations for Cuba through various forms of cultural expression. As Ximena Espeche shows, some Latin American journalists debated the future of the Cuban Revolution based on their own revolutionary histories and in the context of mid-century debates on the media and mass politics. Wang shows how Chinese publics thrilled to the new example of another Third World revolution but were also, based on their own recent revolutionary experience, highly sensitive and even demanding in terms of the gendered expressions of revolution that they expected in cultural projects.

Regarding periodization, this book attempts to look beyond the mythic, formative period of the revolution in the 1960s to begin studying the subsequent stages of revolutionary stagnation, institutionalization, and ascendant critique after 1971. While existing historiography has tended to emphasize the global Left's gradual disenchantment with Cuba, especially after 1971, this volume finds that Cuba continued to be a powerful referent and indeed a physical refuge for the Latin American Left throughout the decade. The global New Left was changing as feminist and homosexual movements consolidated, and as the rise of dictatorships in the Southern Cone sent a wave of activists into exile, including in Cuba. Thus, to the extent that the Latin American Left of the 1970s was simultaneously more demanding, more vulnerable, and more sensitive to questions of gender and sexuality, Cuba's relations with the Left became more complex. Franco's essay suggests that these dissonances were not always expressed through confrontation and denunciation but were also assuaged through reimagination and creative engagement. Caro's essay on gay rights activism suggests that although many homosexual groups were critical of Cuba, it remained a touchstone for their understandings of revolution and liberation. And essays by Snyder, Harmer, Baldacci, and Cosse also show that these negotiations and reimaginings took place within the island too, not just outside it.

Geographically, this book illuminates a series of connections that build on transnational historiographical bases, moving away from studies of nation-states, without ignoring the specificity of each national context. This book also tries to go beyond a single region's engagements with the Cuban Revolution. As the essays here observe, Cuba's influence was truly global, partly because the advent of the Cuban Revolution coincided with African decolonization and the rise of the Third World project and preceded the Sino-Soviet split. Chapters by Cesar, Wang, and Chase capture the early links between the Cuban Revolution and other national liberation movements and socialist revolutions of the Global South. Moving beyond the Americas to include studies of Cuban relations with Africa and Asia suggests that race and gender were important areas of engagement. In some instances, Cuban ideas of liberation emerged in productive conversation with other global movements, such as in Vietnam; in other examples, we see that these areas could be sources of contestation and conflict, as in Angola.

At the same time, the Cuban Revolution's impact in Latin America remained especially strong. Yet there were significant differences in how the Cuban Revolution's impact was felt across the region. Throughout the 1960s, Cuba served as a huge source of inspiration and an important nexus for connections between global revolutionary leaders. But by the mid-1970s, Southern Cone exiles—not always leaders, but often more grassroots militants—needed more direct forms of solidarity from Havana, such as refuge, asylum, and material aid. Harmer and Cosse each explore the nuances of those new relationships. Meanwhile the triumph of the Sandinista Revolution in 1979 opened new forms of collaboration between Cuba and Nicaragua, as Snyder shows. And the rise of demands for homosexual liberation and new forms of gendered identity throughout Latin America in the 1970s and 1980s led to debate and more critical forms of engagement, as Franco and Caro show.

Finally, although less prominently, these studies help illuminate later periods, such as the 1980s and the collapse of European socialism in the 1990s. By raising issues around consumption, LGBTQ+ mobilizations, and other internal tensions, the book illuminates crucial dynamics for understanding the challenges and weaknesses of the revolution. These challenges and tensions were always undoubtedly exacerbated by external pressures. Yet beyond the undeniable effects of the US embargo, the revolution's internal sociocultural tensions, which included daily life, experiences of gender and generation, family, and sexuality, also help explain the ultimate impossibility of creating a more democratic form of socialism, an economy based on solidarity, "new" men and women, and a new revolutionary sense of collectivity. The defeat of these values took place simultaneously within Cuba and elsewhere in the world. This book attempts to understand those advances and retreats, its contradictions and conflicts, which were shaped by national and international forces, and to provide a new window onto the Cuban Revolution's global rise and its gradual defeat.

Notes

1. We use the term Global South, inspired by other recent histories that explore transnational encounters across the postcolonial world during the Cold War, although we also recognize the potentially problematic homogenizing effects of the term, and its implication that the "Third World Left" can be analyzed separately from the "Left" in a global sense. On the historical emergence of the concept as a challenge to neoliberalism, see Vijay Prashad, *The Poorer Nations: A Possible History of the Global South* (Verso, 2014).

2. Claudia Gilman has documented the break in the "intellectual family" in *Entre la pluma y el fusil. Debates y dilemas del escritor revolucionario en América Latina* (Siglo XXI, 2003). For an exploration of how US intellectuals often uncritically reproduced Cuban government narratives about the revolution in the 1960s, see Lillian Guerra, *Patriots and Traitors in Revolutionary Cuba, 1961-1981* (University of Pittsburgh Press, 2023). On the early articulation of criticism from European leftist social scientists, see Paloma Duong, "Other Socialist Travels: René Dumont and Cuban Exceptionalism," *Cuban Studies* 53 (2024): 206–27.

3. Guerra, *Patriots and Traitors*, esp. 253–302. For an overview of historiography on the revolution, see Martín Ribadero, "La Revolución cubana: un balance historiográfico,"

Boletín del Instituto de Historia Argentina y Americana Dr. Emilio Ravignani 51 (2019): 204–34.

4. María A. Cabrera Arús, "The Material Promise of Socialist Modernity: Fashion and Domestic Space in the 1970s," in *The Revolution from Within: Cuba, 1959-1980*, ed. Michael J. Bustamante and Jennifer Lambe (Duke University Press, 2019), 189–217.

5. There is a vast literature on US-Cuban relations, often by political scientists. For historical interpretations, see multiple works by Louis A. Pérez, including *Cuba in the American Imagination: Metaphor and the Imperial Ethos* (University of North Carolina Press, 2008). For work on Cuban-Soviet relations, see Jorge Domínguez, *To Make a World Safe for Revolution: Cuba's Foreign Policy* (Harvard University Press, 1989); James G. Blight and Philip Brenner, *Sad and Luminous Days: Cuba's Struggle with the Superpowers After the Missile Crisis* (Rowman & Littlefield, 2007); Jacqueline Loss, *Dreaming in Russian: The Cuban Soviet Imaginary* (Austin: University of Texas Press, 2013); and Anne E. Gorsuch, "Cuba, My Love: The Romance of Revolutionary Cuba in the Soviet Sixties," *American Historical Review*, April 2015, 497–526. Histories of the Cuban exile community's relationship with the island include María de los Angeles Torres, *In the Land of Mirrors: Cuban Exile Politics in the United States* (University of Michigan Press, 2014) and Silvia Pedraza, *Political Disaffection in Cuba's Revolution and Exodus* (Cambridge University Press, 2007).

6. See, for example, Piero Gleijeses, *Conflicting Missions: Havana, Washington, and Africa, 1959-1976* (University of North Carolina Press, 2002); Christine Hatzky, *Cubans in Angola: South-South Cooperation and Transfer of Knowledge* (University of Wisconsin Press, 2015); and several essays in Joseph Parrott and Mark Atwood Lawrence, eds., *The Tricontinental Revolution: Third World Radicalism and the Cold War* (Cambridge University Press, 2022).

7. Bustamante and Lambe, *Revolution from Within*, 3–4.

8. Pioneering early publications that did adopt aspects of May's approach include Margaret Power, *Right-Wing Women in Chile: Feminine Power and the Struggle Against Allende* (Pennsylvania State University Press, 2002) and (without directly referencing May) Judith Filc, *Entre el parentesco y la política: Familia y dictadura, 1976-1983* (Editorial Biblios, 1997). The connection between gender and politics has also been incorporated in the *historia reciente* of the Southern Cone especially through the workshops "Historia, género y política en los 70." See, for example, Andrea Andújar, Débora D'Antonio, Nora Domíguez, Karin Grammático, Fernanda Gil Lozano, Valeria Pita, María Inés Rodriguez, and Alejandra Vasallo, eds., *Historia, género y política en los 70* (FFYL-UBA-Feminaria, 2005); Andrea Andújar, ed., *De minifaldas, militancias y revoluciones. Exploraciones sobre los 70 en la Argentina* (Ediciones Luxemburg, 2009).

9. *Historia reciente* was initially focused on phenomena linked to repression and politics. See Marina Franco and Daniel Lvovich, "Historia Reciente: apuntes sobre un campo de investigación en expansión," *Boletín del Instituto de Historia Argentina y Americana Dr. Emilio Ravignani* 49 (2017): 47. On the challenges posed by "recent" history, see Marina Franco and Florencia Levín, eds., *Historia reciente. Perspectivas y desafíos para un campo en construcción* (Paidós, 2007). A general up-to-date treatment can be found in Eugenia

Allier, *En la cresta de la ola. Debates y definiciones en torno al tiempo presente* (IIS–Bonilla Editores, 2020). For an overview, see the important collection published by the Red de Historia Reciente, Libros de la buena memoria, https://libros.fahce.unlp.edu.ar/index.php/libros/catalog/series/lbm. The journals *Contemporánea* (Universidad de la República) and *Tempo & Argumento* (Universidad Estadual de Santa Catarina) offer good examples of the importance of the field of *historia reciente* in the region. Scholars on memory were often early to adopt attention to gender, sexuality, and family. A classic study related to memory is Elizabeth Jelin, *Los trabajos de la memoria* (Siglo XXI, 2002). The publication of several books under her direction with the support of the Ford Foundation (e.g., Ludmila Catela Da Silva and Elizabeth Jelin, eds., *Los archivos de la represión. Documentos, memoria y verdad* [Madrid: Siglo XXI, 2002]) expressed how hegemonic studies of memory became within the field. Uruguayan scholars were pioneers in memory studies and the historic turn in studies of the dictatorships. See, for example, Gerardo Caetano and José Rilla, *El Uruguay de la dictadura (1973-1985)* (Banda Oriental, 1989); Isabella Cosse and Vania Markarian, *El año de la Orientalidad: identidad, memoria e historia en una dictadura* (Trilce, 1996). About the gender and feminist studies in the *pasado reciente*, see n. 8. On the relationship between *historia reciente* and Cold War history, see Aldo Marchesi, "Escribiendo la Guerra Fría Latinoamericana: entre el Sur 'local' y el Norte Global," *Estudos Historicos* 60, no. 30 (2017), https://doi.org/10.1590/S2178-14942017000100010; Vanni Pettinà, *La Guerra Fría latinoamericana y sus historiografías* (AHILA, 2024).

10. Eric Zolov, *Refried Elvis: The Rise of the Mexican Counterculture* (University of California Press, 1999); Heidi Tinsman, *Partners in Conflict: The Politics of Gender, Sexuality, and Labor in the Chilean Agrarian Reform, 1950-1973* (Duke University Press, 2002); Isabella Cosse, *Pareja, sexualidad y familia* (Siglo XXI, 2010); Isabella Cosse, *Mafalda: A Social and Political History of Latin America's Global Comic* (Duke University Press, 2019); Valeria Manzano, *The Age of Youth in Argentina: Culture, Politics, and Sexuality from Perón to Videla* (University of North Carolina Press, 2014); Karina Felitti, *La revolución de la píldora. Sexualidad y política en los sesenta* (Edhasa, 2012); Alfonso Salgado, "A Small Revolution: Family, Sex, and the Communist Youth of Chile During the Allende Years (1970–1973)," *Twentieth Century Communism: A Journal of International History* 8 (2015): 62–88; Vania Markarian, *Uruguay, 1968: Student Activism from Global Counterculture to Molotov Cocktails* (University of California Press, 2016); Marian E. Schlotterbeck, *Beyond the Vanguard: Everyday Revolutionaries in Allende's Chile* (University of California Press, 2018); Pablo Ben and Joaquín Insausti, "Dictatorial Rule and Sexual Politics in Argentina: The Case of the Frente de Liberación Homosexual, 1967–1976," *Hispanic American Historical Review* 97, no. 2 (2017): 297–325. On regional differences in Latin American historiography regarding histories of the New Left and global sixties, see Eric Zolov, "Marking the Contours of the Mexican 'New Left' in the 1960s: Mexico and the Southern Cone in Comparative Perspective," *Mexican Studies/Estudios Mexicanos* 39, no. 2 (2023): 185–214.

11. To some extent this approach to politics was anticipated in the pioneering 2008 publication *In from the Cold*, which focused on grassroots and everyday conflicts, and included dynamics such as gender and generation, as crucial to understanding the con-

frontations and the political praxis of the period. Like May's work, this approach was not widely emulated. Gilbert M. Joseph and Daniela Spenser, eds., *In from the Cold: Latin America's New Encounter with the Cold War* (Duke University Press, 2008). Also see the pioneering approach in Sandhya Shukla and Heidi Tinsman, eds., *Across the Americas, Imagining Our Americas: Toward a Transnational Frame* (Duke University Press, 2007), 1–33.

12. Anita Casavantes Bradford, *The Revolution Is for the Children: The Politics of Childhood in Havana and Miami, 1959-1962* (University of North Carolina Press, 2014).

13. Marcelo Casals, "Which Borders Have Not Yet Been Crossed? A *Supplement* to Gilbert Joseph's Historiographical Balance of the Latin American Cold War," *Cold War History* 20, no. 3 (2020): 367–72. Also see Vanni Pettinà, *La Guerra Fría latinoamericana*.

14. Van Gosse, *Where the Boys Are: Cuba, Cold War America and the Making of a New Left* (Verso, 1993); Aldo Marchesi, *Latin America's Radical Left: Rebellion and Cold War in the Global 1960s* (Cambridge University Press, 2018); Tanya Harmer, *Beatriz Allende: A Revolutionary Life in Cold War Latin America* (University of North Carolina Press, 2020); Jonathan Brown, *Cuba's Revolutionary World* (Harvard University Press, 2017); Markarian, *Uruguay, 1968*. Also see Renata Keller, *Mexico's Cold War: Cuba, the United States, and the Legacy of the Mexican Revolution* (Cambridge University Press, 2015).

15. Martín Ribadero and Grethel Doménech Hernández, "Dossier: Visiones, entusiasmos y disidencias de la Revolución Cubana en la escena intelectual latinoamericana de los años sesenta," *Cuban Studies* 52 (2022): 257–390; Gilman, *Entre la pluma;* Rafael Rojas, *Fighting Over Fidel: The New York Intellectuals and the Cuban Revolution* (Princeton University Press, 2015); Rafael Rojas, *La Polis Literaria: El boom, la Revolución y otras polémicas de la Guerra Fría* (Editorial Taurus, 2018).

16. Ann Garland Mahler, *From the Tricontinental to the Global South: Race, Radicalism, and Transnational Solidarity* (Duke University Press, 2018); Parrott and Lawrence, *Tricontinental Revolution;* Jessica Stites Mor, *South-South Solidarity and the Latin American Left* (University of Wisconsin Press, 2022).

17. We build on Gosse's pioneering work, and on recent studies of "Tricontinental" culture, which include the gendered and especially racialized dimensions of Cuban internationalism, especially by the late 1960s and early 1970s.

18. See Lillian Guerra, "Gender Policing, Homosexuality and the New Patriarchy of the Cuban Revolution, 1965–70," *Social History* 35 (2010): 268–89; Rachel Hynson, *Laboring for the State: Women, Family, and Work in Revolutionary Cuba, 1959-1971* (Cambridge University Press, 2019); Abel Sierra Madero, *El cuerpo nunca olvida: trabajo forzado, hombre nuevo y memoria en Cuba (1959-1980)* (Rialta Ediciones, 2022).

19. Tanya Harmer and Alberto Martín Álvarez refer to the period this way in their introduction to their coedited volume, *Toward a Global History of Latin America's Revolutionary Left* (University of Florida Press, 2021).

REVOLUTIONARY WOMEN

ONE

"The Voice of the Skin"

Racial Politics in Cuban-Angolan Cooperation, 1965–1967

RAFAEL CESAR

This chapter focuses on the early contacts between the Federation of Cuban Women (Federación de Mujeres Cubanas, FMC) and the Organization of the Angolan Woman (Organização da Mulher Angolana, OMA) during the Angolan War of Independence (1961–74) to explore the existence of a "politics of race-lessness" within the context of Cuban-Angolan cooperation (secretly as early as 1965, officially from 1975 to 1991). I focus specifically on the meeting of Limbania Jiménez Rodríguez, a white Cuban official and vice president of the FMC, with Deolinda Rodrigues, a black Angolan revolutionary and cofounder of the OMA, in Congo-Brazzaville in December 1966.[1] Limbania and Deolinda met when a contingent of Cubans went to Congo-Brazzaville to train the anti-colonial Popular Movement for the Liberation of Angola (Movimento Popular de Libertação de Angola, MPLA), then operating in exile in Congo-Brazzaville, for a military mission. Deolinda was a member of the MPLA.

I will compare Limbania's short memoir about the meeting, published in 1985 as a tribute to Deolinda and other women who were killed during the aforementioned military mission, with Deolinda's diaries published posthumously in 2003, which cover her period in Congo-Brazzaville. As I show in this chapter, Limbania Jiménez Rodríguez depicts Deolinda Rodrigues as a revolutionary who rejected race consciousness, supported white and mixed-race revolutionaries in the movement, and championed a colorblind independence movement and future postcolonial Angola—in line with the Cuban and the MPLA's discourse. In 2003, however, Deolinda's brother published her diaries, bringing to light a Deolinda harshly critical of and often against the presence and privileges of whites and mestizos in the independence movement, espousing an ideology akin to Black nationalism, and expressing the desire for an exclusively Black-ruled Angola. In spite of Deolinda's radicalism, her diary increasingly grows silent about racial matters in the revolutionary movement, peaking precisely during the period when Cubans, including Limbania, arrive at the MPLA military base in Congo-Brazzaville.

Much has been written about the Cuban "politics of racelessness," which characterized the revolution and the nation as colorblind, rejecting any expressions of race consciousness and imposing silence around the topic of racism, affecting particularly Black revolutionaries.[2] A good deal has also been written, but mostly in an uncritical and normalizing fashion, about a similar politics (with similar consequences) adopted in Angola by the MPLA, one of the main revolutionary movements and later government, during the war of independence and the 1975–2002 civil war period.[3] Little, however, has been written, and with limited scope or details, about the role of Cuba in supporting such a politics in Angola.[4]

But how can we "grasp" this history of forging a politics of racelessness, notoriously difficult due to the restricted access to archives, the immateriality of race relations, and the taboo nature of the topic in Cuba and, as I will show, also in Angola? And why focus on women to unearth a subject shaped by a male-dominated history?

Post-1959 Cuba's historiography is famously limited due to the closed archives of the revolution.[5] To a lesser but still high degree, the same can be said about Angola and its highly politicized process of national memorialization due to the concurrent narratives of rival nationalist movements and the lack, loss, or classification of documents due to the liberation and civil wars.[6] Things become more complicated when it comes to race relations—by definition, a phenomenon of social-symbolic construction, less possible to identify as the cause of social issues such as inequality in a context of formal equality, in comparison to class differences, which are material and measurable by nature. Much of what is related to "race," racism, racial politics, happens, in sum, in the margins of official history.

Curiously, in spite of, or perhaps precisely because of it being a male-made, male-focused, and male-authored history, focusing on men seems to lead mostly to the redundancy of official discourses of equality that do not reflect the social and political dynamics around race relations. Perhaps because women's history more often than not also happens on the margins, it is a place where we can also find the undeclared, unassumed aspects of mainstream history. It is perhaps also where race issues acquire even stronger expressions through the intersection with gender that, in the case of Black women, doubles the marks and effects of oppression. The contrast from women's perspective and their position in the making and writing of history, in turn, proves productive to revealing what the official discourse seems to disguise.

As I argue, the contrast between Limbania's misrepresentation of Deolinda's ideas and Deolinda's original words and thoughts in her diary point, on the one hand, to a constant background Cuban support for a politics of racelessness championed by a predominantly white and mixed-race Angolan revolutionary elite of the MPLA, at odds with the expectations of the majority Black militants, like Deolinda herself. On the other hand, the history of these two women—one Black, one white—never before read together (and Deolinda's mostly read through a limited colorblind lens)[7] shows the importance of thinking about gender in the Cuban revolutionary context—in this case, an international context—also through race.

This chapter starts with a brief biography of Deolinda Rodrigues along with a contextualization of the rise of Angolan nationalism and the first contact with Cubans, and the death of Deolinda. I focus on the aspects of Deolinda's trajectory that the MPLA has highlighted to create the public narrative of Deolinda in Angola. The following section then discusses Limbania's memoir, which contributed to this public face of a colorblind Deolinda, along with a short contextualization of Angolan and Cuban racial politics in the 1960s. I finally proceed to examining Deolinda's diaries and discussing the implications of her actual thoughts on race and revolution for the broader context of Cuban-Angolan cooperation.

Deolinda Rodrigues, the Martyr

Deolinda Rodrigues became an Angolan heroine identified with MPLA history for both her role in building the movement and her tragic history, which turned her into a martyr and the symbol of the woman who sacrificed her life in the name of Angolan independence following the MPLA's ideals, an image that represented her taking to the limit her alignment with the party.

Born in 1939 in Catete, a rural zone fifty miles from Luanda, Deolinda Rodrigues was the daughter of primary schoolteachers.[8] Her father also being a Protestant pastor, Deolinda was raised in an American Methodist mission, and unlike the vast majority of Black Angolans who were unable to access Western-style education under Portuguese colonial rule, she would learn to read and write Portuguese, English, and French, in addition to the Kimbundu she heard at home and in her region.

During Deolinda's childhood, nationalism in Angola flourished. As early as

FIGURE 1.1. A portrait of Deolinda Rodrigues from the early 1960s. Unknown photographer. Courtesy of Associação Tchiweka de Documentação (Luanda, Angola), Lúcio Lara Archive.

the 1940s, a series of cultural manifestations, particularly in literature and music, started to develop through the organization of parties, poetry recitals, and political meetings in established associations and popular clubs, mainly in Luanda, Angola's capital. Simultaneously, nationalist cultural and political movements would emerge in Portugal among Angolan university students. Luanda, a zone of Mbundu ethnicity, also had the second-largest white settler community in Africa, after only South Africa (peaking at approximately 350,000 people in the 1970s), due to a Portuguese settlement policy established in the 1930s. Angolan students in Lisbon, in turn, were predominantly white and mixed-race, also as a consequence of Portugal's segregationist settlement and education policies.

The MPLA emerged in that context between the late 1950s and early 1960s on the Luanda-Lisbon axis, idealized by the nationalist poet and intellectual Viriato da Cruz, a mixed-race man. Later, the leadership of the movement was transferred to Agostinho Neto, a Black man of Mbundu ethnicity—and Deolinda's cousin—who became Angola's first president. Although led by a Black man, the MPLA comprised a high number of white and mixed-race individuals, whose predominance was particularly noticeable in the higher echelons of the movement due to the educational levels and qualifications of white and mixed-race individuals, unattainable for the majority of Black Angolans under Portuguese colonial policies.

Also in the 1950s, the north of the country, neighboring the two Congos, saw the emergence of the liberation movement that would later become the National Front for the Liberation of Angola (Frente Nacional de Libertação de Angola, FNLA), led by Holden Roberto.[9] Unlike the MPLA, the FNLA's social base stemmed from the Bakongo population, predominantly Black and rural. One FNLA member, Jonas Savimbi, would later found the Union for the Total Independence of Angola (União Nacional para a Independência Total de Angola, UNITA) in 1966, established in the central highlands and the south, in the region of the Ovimbundu ethnicity, also a majority Black party. Both the FNLA and the UNITA opposed the MPLA due to its Marxist ideology and high presence of non-Black individuals, frequently labeling the MPLA a party of whites and mulattos that did not represent Angola's Black majority.

Living in Luanda amid the nationalist agitations, in 1956, a seventeen-year-old Deolinda joined a group of nationalists who would later be part of the MPLA like herself. The elders of the group resisted accepting her in the incipient liberation movement because Deolinda was a woman, deemed unreliable in the patriarchal Angolan political context of the 1950s. However, Deolinda's knowledge of typing and English were uncommon and useful, and the men decided to accept her. In the following months, Deolinda would type documents and serve as a translator, contacting foreign help to build the liberation movement.

In 1961, as the decolonization wave swept sub-Saharan Africa, Portugal lagged behind the "winds of history" and refused to release its colonies. Simultaneously, Angolan workers revolted against the harsh conditions of the Portuguese regime of forced labor for Black Angolans. That year, a group attacked the prison of Luanda to liberate political prisoners—an attack claimed by the MPLA—and in the north of the country, rural workers slaughtered approximately five hundred white settlers and several Black workers—an attack claimed by the FNLA. Portugal sent troops to Angola and the Angolan war of independence broke out.

At the time, Deolinda was in the United States, where she studied nursing at a Methodist institute in Michigan. Deolinda decided to abandon her studies to join the war efforts in Congo-Léopoldville,[10] where the MPLA had a military base close to the border with Angola. As the war progressed, the FNLA, also based in Congo-Léopoldville, became the MPLA's major rival during the struggle for independence, controlling the northern border of Angola. The shifting political scenario in Congo-Léopoldville after the assassination of Prime Minister Patrice Lumumba and new president Joseph Mobutu's support of the FNLA forced the MPLA and Deolinda to leave. In the neighboring Congo-Brazzaville, a revolution in the opposite direction in 1963 would overthrow an anti-communist president and bring to power the left-leaning Alphonse Massamba-Débat, who invited the MPLA to transfer its base to the country.[11] There, Deolinda would later meet Limbania.

During those politically troubled years in the Congos, Deolinda had become responsible for the Angolan Voluntary Refugee Assistance Corps, an institution of support for Angolan refugees in Congo-Léopoldville, and then became the MPLA's secretary of social assistance. She also cofounded the Organization of the Angolan Woman (OMA) in 1962. In that capacity, she and other colleagues contacted the Federation of Cuban Women (FMC). Through this and other connections, Deolinda spent the following years working with the MPLA in the two Congos and also traveled to the Soviet Union, Bulgaria, and China for meetings with other women's organizations and to participate in courses of political formation.

In the meantime, Cubans turned to Africa as it became an important theater of the Cold War. In 1965, Che Guevara secretly traveled to the eastern part of Congo-Léopoldville to train the first guerrillas to start what he envisioned as the spread of socialist revolutions in Africa. The Cuban mission led by Guevara managed to infiltrate approximately 120 Cuban guerrilla fighters in the country,[12] most of them Black men, dark-skinned enough to mingle with the local population unnoticed, a strategic move to initiate these operations. The choice of Black men also had an eye toward developing a larger international politics of solidarity: the presence of Black Cubans, Guevara and Fidel Castro believed, could help forge a cultural and political identification with the local Congolese population and gather their support, a critical aspect for the success of the mission. Since its inception, therefore, the Cuban missions in Africa have been concerned with exploring a global racial politics to reach their revolutionary goals.

But in practice, Che's ideas of revolution, based on "universalist" assumptions of class struggle and historical teleology, clashed with the ideas held by most local militants who, while understanding the broader dimension of the colonial phenomenon, frequently considered their main enemies to be their neighboring rival ethnic groups, divided by borders invisible to Guevara. The mission failed in a few months, and a disappointed Guevara would write in his diary, "There can be no advance unless it leads toward the destruction of the tribal concept." The movement could only succeed, he continued, "by educating the people in the revolutionary struggle, passing through the different stages of history at breakneck speed.... From the current primitivism, which in some cases is close to primitive communism, to slavery or to feudalism, it is necessary to move to *the most advanced concepts.*"[13]

Before his failed mission in the eastern part of Congo-Léopoldville, however, Guevara met with MPLA leader Agostinho Neto at the movement's base in Brazzaville as part of a series of visits to revolutionary movements in Africa. Guevara had a good impression of the MPLA and agreed to Neto's request for Cuban instructors to train MPLA members for the liberation struggle against Portugal.[14]

In May 1966, Cuban troops started to train a group of MPLA militants—the "Cienfuegos Squad"—to infiltrate Angola by land and open a new war front. The mission was a success, managing to reach Angola and join a military base in the woods, and Cubans and Angolans decided to form the "Kamy Squad" for a similar mission. Deolinda and four other women from the OMA—Engrácia dos Santos, Irene Cohen, Lucrécia Paim, and Teresa Afonso—joined the squad, receiving military and political training from Cubans in December 1966, departing in January 1967.

After two months of marching in the woods, however, the group became lost. Part of the group, including an injured and ill Deolinda, received orders to march back to the MPLA base. After another week marching back, on March 2, 1967, Deolinda and her comrades were captured by the rival FNLA after crossing territory controlled by the movement. The MPLA launched an international campaign accusing the FNLA of their capture and demanding the release of the group, unsuccessfully. During this period, the women were tortured and raped. At some point in 1968, Deolinda, Engrácia, Irene, Lucrécia, and Teresa were executed, dismembered, and buried at an undisclosed place, unknown to this day. Since Angolan independence in 1975, the MPLA has established March 2 as Angolan Women's Day, in their honor.

Deolinda Rodrigues, Heroine of Angola

From the time of her death onward, Deolinda became an Angolan heroine and a symbol of the revolutionary woman. In that spirit, as vice president of the FMC (who would keep constant contact with the OMA), Cuban internationalist fighter and author Limbania Jiménez published a book, *Heroínas de Angola* (1985), in tribute to Deolinda and her fallen female comrades. As an official, Limbania worked for the Cuban army's educational and political program for low-ranking officers and went to Congo-Brazzaville in such a capacity to keep training the soldiers in the internationalist mission.[15] As Limbania explains, as she arrived in Congo-Brazzaville in 1966, she became "deeply moved by the fact that five women were part of this guerrilla column, which had such an extraordinary mission before it, and . . . sensed that these fighters would occupy a prominent place in the history of Angola."[16] She then met and interviewed the five Angolan guerrilla woman ("las cinco muchachas," she writes) on two occasions.

Limbania would later write that her concern in publishing the book was "to reconstruct the history of their legendary march and compile the brief and intense biographies of the courageous female guerrillas" and "pay a modest tribute to Deolinda and her *compañeras*."[17] Following this idea, *Heroínas de Angola* is a

FIGURE 1.2. The cover of *Heroínas de Angola* (1985), published by Limbania Jiménez Rodríguez.

short book of approximately eighty pages containing brief biographies of the five guerrilla women, a recounting of their march with a map, and a series of pictures of them, "the only graphic record that exists of this group of heroines," as Limbania recalls.[18] The largest section of the book is devoted to Deolinda's history and work in the liberation movement.

As part of her declared work of spreading the history of these women in the revolution, likely also part of a broader concern with promoting the role of women in general in global revolutions,[19] Limbania opens the book with a short section that gives her readers an idea of these women's context and their different profiles. Engrácia, Lucrécia, and Teresa, of peasant origins, had difficulty speaking about their harsh experiences as colonial subjects in Angola, while Deolinda and Irene "possessed the loquacity" typical of urban women. She quotes the women on their views about Angola—the contrast between the rich natural resources and poverty, the colonial violence—and quotes Deolinda and her *compañeras* enumerating the common duties of women in the liberation movement: washing clothes, cooking, transporting food and medicine, taking care of the sick and refugees, teaching at the party's schools, serving as links between clandestine cells and the city, and recruiting people, especially women, to join the revolution.[20]

Limbania does not comment about the household and care labor given exclusively to woman, a double shift in the liberation movement—certainly not revolutionary in terms of gender—likely because of the impossibility or unwillingness to negatively expose the MPLA that the Cuban government and she herself supported. But in what seems to be a veiled critical perspective, she moves on to mention the Angolan female militants' strong interest when learning about the role of Cuban women in the revolution: "They were very pleased to learn of the incorporation of Cuban women into the tasks of the country's armed defense and that some of us held officer positions in the Revolutionary Armed Forces,"[21] Limbania writes, implying that she and the interviewees had similar expectations regarding the place of women in the Angolan revolution.

Strikingly, after this start and the introductory remarks about her concern with telling the history of guerrilla women, which together apparently pointed toward a broader discussion of gender and/or women and revolution, the author does not return to the topic of women's roles or situations in the book. By the end of the next paragraph, closing the short introduction, she introduces Deolinda, who features in the following and largest section of the book. Her initial description of Deolinda, then, gives the tone of the remainder of her biography, focused on Deolinda's commitment to the revolution—"an energetic and decisive woman who strongly defended her political ideas . . . [and was] very sensitive to injustices."[22] As gender is put aside in Limbania's discourse, race relations gain a prominent space in her description of Deolinda's ideology.

Limbania reconstructs the Angolan context through Deolinda's voice. "Deolinda was very knowledgeable about Angola," she begins. "She spoke to us about the economic roots of slavery in her country; about the necessary unity among the revolutionary forces; about *the division and damage caused by regionalism, tribalism, racism.*"[23] The main obstacle for liberation, Limbania explains, was the presence of the rival movement FNLA. Drawing on Deolinda's reported words about divisionism, racism, and tribalism, Limbania then reinforces the message describing the FNLA as an "organization *created on a tribal, regional, and racist basis,*" which had recently changed its name, which originally alluded to the north of Angola, to "hide its tribalist character."[24]

These two passages, as others we will discuss below, are striking for the presence of the word "racism" unaccompanied by any contextualization. To understand the specificity of the word, it is important to take into consideration the context in which Limbania first wrote and then published her book.

Race relations would increasingly deteriorate inside the MPLA a few years before Guevara's passage through the Congos. In 1962, the above-mentioned mixed-race poet and revolutionary Viriato da Cruz, founder of the MPLA, noticed the difficulty the MPLA had in recruiting Black Angolans due to its non-Black leadership. Cruz stepped down as executive secretary of the party and proposed that all whites and *mestiços* gave up their high-ranking positions to Black militants to gain the confidence of the population. In contrast, Agostinho Neto, a Black man recently elected the party's president, considered it strategic to have the support of well-prepared, well-educated white and *mestiço* nationalists, who in addition had international contacts. Neto considered Cruz's act a form of "racism." Joining forces with white and *mestiço* members, Neto expelled Viriato da Cruz from the MPLA and later executed two Black militants, Matias Miguéis and José Miguel, who had sided with Cruz.[25] After that, race relations became a constant background tension for the MPLA, reemerging in several moments of crisis, from internal, Black-led party revolts against the white/*mestiço* party elite, such as in 1977—an event known as Factionalism that resulted in the execution of an indeterminate number in the tens of thousands of people—to the accusations from the FNLA and UNITA of being a party that did not represent the Black majority. The conflict over whether "racism" should only describe the colonial-derived exploitation of the majority Black population or should also be extended to criticism of the fact that the MPLA leadership was disproportionately white and *mestiço* would continue to haunt the movement, as we shall see.

The Cuban Revolution, in turn, had faced a similar situation around the same time, when Black revolutionaries demanded actions against racial discrimination and to address the legacies of slavery that impacted Black Cubans. After initially supporting the cause by desegregating public spaces such as parks and beaches, as well as private businesses, among other measures, Castro soon moved, also in 1962, to claim that the revolution had solved racial inequality through class equality. Around that time, the revolution launched a backlash against race consciousness, considering it divisive and anti-revolutionary, closing Afro-Cuban associations, publications, and presses. It later extended its actions, criminalizing or stigmatizing Afro-Cuban cultural practices such as Santería. From the mid-1960s to the early 1970s, Black revolutionaries who expressed views on Black autonomy would be arrested, sent to forced labor camps, ostracized, or made to go into exile.[26]

On November 5, 1975, a few days before Angolan independence, Cuban forces launched "Operación Carlota"—named after an African woman who led a slave rebellion in the region of Matanzas on November 5, 1843—joining the MPLA to help it defeat the FNLA and encroaching South African troops. As they did so, Cuban leaders engaged in a double racial discourse targeting the international community: on the one hand, Fidel Castro declared Cuba an "Afro-Latin" nation, fashioning the support of Angola as repaying a historical debt to the land from where many Black Cubans' ancestors had come; on the other hand, along with the MPLA, it labeled FNLA's and UNITA's ideologies as racist, due to their anti-

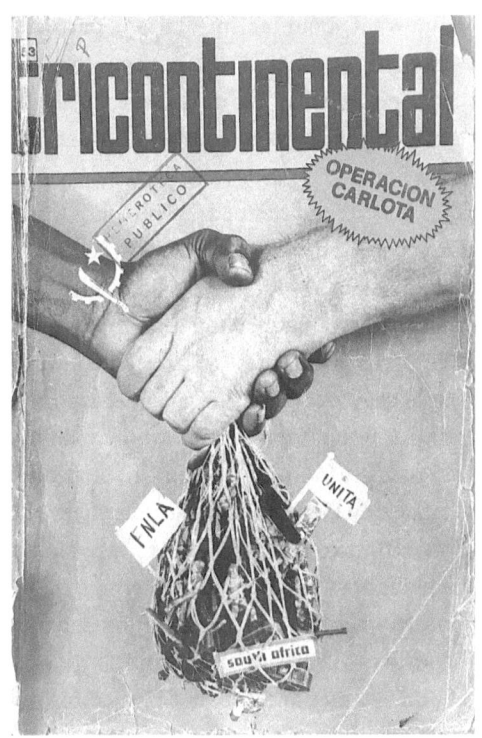

FIGURE 1.3. The cover of a *Tricontinental* magazine issue (1977) about Cuba's Operation Carlota in Angola illustrates the politics of racelessness. The two shaking hands represent the Cuban-Angolan socialist cross-racial, color-blind alliance fighting together against imperialist forces. In opposition, the nativist, Black-centered rhetoric of UNITA and FNLA is equated to the racism of South Africa's apartheid.

whiteness and ethnic attachments. These conflicting ideas about race and racism would be echoed in the relationship between Deolinda and Limbania.

As Limbania recounts, she would keep the notes from the interviews with Deolinda and her *compañeras* for ten years, until her return to Angola in 1976 as part of the first official mission right after independence. That year, aware of the five Angolan women's fate, Limbania looked for the few survivors of the Kamy Squad to collect testimonies about the march, Deolinda, and her fallen *compañeras*. Limbania's book would then be published another nine years later, in 1985. This means Limbania's research, writing, and publishing process covers three different high-stakes moments of Angolan history: the liberation struggle, in 1966; the moment immediately after independence, in 1976; and the simultaneous civil war chiefly against UNITA and the "global cold war" against South Africa in the 1980s, when the book was published. Although in 1966 the terms "tribalism" and "regionalism" would not be completely clear to her readers, in the 1980s, in contrast, tribalism and regionalism were recurring themes in accounts from the African fronts for readers who at this point had been following Cuba's missions on the continent for more than a decade.

But what about racism? Racism, particularly in the African context, was fundamentally associated with racism of white settlers against Black natives. In the 1980s, in particular, Cuba was entering the highest point of the war against South Africa on the Angolan southern border. In the Cuban press, the word "racism" was a constant presence, and one associated with apartheid. In the previous years, Castro had claimed Cuba's solidarity based on its shared African roots and characterized the cooperation with Angola as an anti-racist mission. With racism being associated with the colonizer side, what is racism about in Limbania's book? Is it racism against Blacks inside the movement? But how could that be the case in an African revolutionary movement whose goal is to liberate Black oppressed people in Africa? Or is it racism against whites? Are these two kinds of racism the same thing? Or is racism another name for tribalism and regionalism? Could Deolinda's readers in Cuba understand the configurations of racism in Angola? What about Limbania's other potential readers in the Spanish-speaking world? In this context, the choice not to explain the meaning of racism is striking from the point of view of the text's intention of providing the reader with the Angolan context—a lack of contextualization and dilution of meaning that inevitably take the form of silence about the topic.

And yet, race and racism are the most recurrent topic in Limbania's profile of Deolinda. Through the voices of Deolinda and her *compañeras,* Limbania continuously characterizes the unexplained racial context of Angola. As Limbania writes twenty years after her contact with the guerrilla women, she "preferred not to retouch the notes I wrote that same day of the meeting," incorporating "those notes that were biographical in nature," and "the rest, I transcribe below, the way they answered my questions."[27] Through this expedient, Limbania suggests authenticity through the unfiltered voices of the guerrilla women, while simultaneously characterizing them as possessing a refined revolutionary consciousness that rejected racial politics in terms that coincided with Limbania's own assessment of that context.

She writes, for example, that Irene Cohen, one of the *compañeras,* started her political life in 1960 when "she became involved in the activities of the Angolan Natives Group, which brought together Angolan intellectuals *without distinction of race,*"[28] where she would recite poems of Agostinho Neto and other MPLA members. Describing Deolinda's years in Congo-Léopoldville as a coming-of-age experience, Limbania writes, "There, Deolinda was able to *understand* more deeply *the tribalist, racial, counterrevolutionary background* of the organization headed by Holden Roberto (UPA [FNLA]) and noted with satisfaction how the MPLA's patient and firm work was gaining followers, *how necessary was the work of clarification and recruitment among the popular masses.*"[29] Limbania characterizes

FIGURE 1.4. The heroines of the Kamy Squad with Limbania Jiménez Rodríguez. *From left to right*: Teresa Afonso, Lucrécia Paim, Irene Cohen, Limbania Jiménez Rodríguez, Josefa Gualdino (who fell ill and could not join the mission), Engrácia dos Santos, and Deolinda Rodrigues. Unknown photographer. Courtesy of Associação Tchiweka de Documentação (Luanda, Angola), Limbania Jiménez Rodríguez Collection / Lúcio Lara Archive.

Deolinda's stance as a "maturation" for it being aligned with the MPLA's (non-) racial politics, and such politics as the parameter that measured her general level of revolutionary consciousness.

As already mentioned, Limbania does not provide details in her use of the terms "racism" and "racial background." These, in spite of their centrality to Limbania's text—and reportedly among Deolinda's main concerns—are never specified, contextualized, or exemplified to provide Deolinda's context to the reader. And although Limbania does not provide any explanation for Angola's racial political background, she leaves to Deolinda's voice the suggestion of racism being her— Deolinda's? Limbania's?—main racial concern in that context. In the most significant passage of Deolinda's biography where she has her political voice reproduced, Limbania transcribes a letter Deolinda wrote to a friend about the situation of the MPLA and the FNLA in Congo-Léopoldville. Limbania returns to the matter of unity and division and writes, "Deolinda worked actively to strengthen relations with students and leaders of other tendencies, who at that time had not yet shown themselves in their true role as agents of imperialism, because she knew the damage caused by the division among the nationalist forces. . . . In the following

[Deolinda's] words, we can appreciate her ideas in this regard," and she quotes Deolinda from a letter she had access to:

> I am attentive to the arrival of Mario [de Andrade, one of MPLA's leaders] and Holden [Roberto, FNLA's leader] to contact them both. The students allied to the UPA [FNLA] are undergoing positive transformations, although *they are very conservative regarding the* mestizaje *of the MPLA; a racial antagonism is being created, which also brings with it its burden of prejudice.*[30]

Limbania's history of Deolinda is clear in depicting an Angolan heroine aligned with the MPLA's ideals and a view characterized by the rejection of race consciousness. Particularly in the passage above, Deolinda gains a higher revolutionary status for her nonconformity to the rejection to "the *mestizaje* of the MPLA," here referring to the multiracial configuration of the party—a *mestizo* configuration meaning the presence of whites, *mestiços,* and Blacks. Race politics, according to Limbania's depiction, is central to Deolinda's value as a revolutionary and, along with her devotion to the MPLA, what made Deolinda a heroine of Angola.

Although Deolinda had stood out as a militant for her multiple roles, many of her external activities for the MPLA were restricted to meeting with other women—spaces and situations often marginalized from the hard politics and the main decisions about the liberation process. As such, in a male-dominated party in a deeply sexist context—a double sexism rooted simultaneously in the modern-colonial and the local-traditional patriarchy—Deolinda never deserved from her party the honor of a work or book about her. It took a revolutionary Cuban woman to give Deolinda a prominent place in Angolan history. Limbania's book is to this day the only one devoted to Deolinda. Along with a series of institutional material occasionally published by the OMA and the MPLA that retells Deolinda's militant history, Limbania's book completes the public profile of Deolinda. As a Third World revolutionary woman, Limbania Jiménez took the responsibility of recording the history; and in history, the profile takes its place as that of another Third World revolutionary woman, whose main characteristic in her biography is her political commitment to fighting beyond racial divisions, particularly against the discrimination of whites and *mestiços.* Her thoughts and actions along those lines, then, helped turn Deolinda into an exemplary militant and, together with her tragic history, a heroine of Angola.

Deolinda Rodrigues, in Her Own Words: Racial Violence, Trauma, and Black Internationalism

But *who was* Deolinda? As a typist, translator, writer of official letters and reports, host of the MPLA's radio show, founder of the OMA, martyr, and heroine, Deolinda's voice was constantly *mixed* in the official discourses. However, in 2003, one year after the end of the civil war and the definitive solidification of power by the MPLA, with Deolinda's image long crystalized as the revolutionary model, Roberto de Almeida, Deolinda's younger brother, revealed he had in his possession his sister's diaries and a collection of letters, which he then published as books. Ranging from September 9, 1956, the day she was accepted in the liberation movement, to March 1, 1967, the day before she was captured by FNLA forces during her attempt to return to Congo-Brazzaville, Deolinda's diary for the first time revealed her voice.

The diary, particularly in the first years until 1962, is constantly interrupted by periods of several months, and the entries become more frequent as Deolinda arrives in Congo-Brazzaville and grows progressively more involved with the movement and the problems she witnesses and fights against, particularly regarding race relations. As I seek to show in the following sections, Deolinda struggles with frequent censoring of her strong and public opinions regarding race relations in the movement, resorting to her diary to safely elaborate on the racial politics of the movement, in a process of public silencing of her voice. However, as her racial consciousness and racial tensions in the movement rise, the silence also reaches her diary, a process that happens concomitantly and increasingly with the Cuban presence in Congo-Brazzaville, culminating with Limbania's arrival. The silence and later dissonance between Deolinda's voices—in Limbania's book, on the one hand, and in her diary, on the other—in turn, raise pressing questions about the process of forging the politics of racelessness in Angola, particularly through the transnational alliance established with Cuba at the time.

The first five entries of Deolinda's diary—or what was published of it, or what was retrieved by her brother—reveal from the very beginning the two main challenges that Deolinda would face in both the movement and society: being Black and being a woman—and being radical about the intersection of these two vectors of oppression. In her first entry, she registers her apprehension with being accepted in the liberation movement at age seventeen as "the elders are reluctant because I'm a woman." Upon her acceptance, the following entries in her diary start to show an increasing use of racially charged language, calling white persons always by the pejorative terms "ngueta," "kangundos," and "bezugos," generally meaning an "ignorant white" person (the first two Kimbundu words).

In 1958, Deolinda registers in her diary two traumatic situations related to racial violence where such language is the release valve in her writings. On April 17, Deolinda witnesses a white man "wildly beating" a Black worker. Deolinda and a *quitandeira*—a female street vendor—who was at the scene screamed to call for people's attention and help. Deolinda felt demoralized as a Black Angolan person seeing the impossibility of reaction from the Black man being beaten and Black passers-by who were watching the scene: "What struck me was the paralysis of the Black man who was being whipped and the others," she registers in her diary. "He [the Black man] was stronger than the *ngueta*, but he only groaned. Damn!" The effects from witnessing this scene are emotionally profound, likely traumatic for Deolinda: "This situation makes me think of suicide! What a life!" A couple of months later, her younger brother Roberto is beaten by a white man—a stranger—for not taking off his hat to salute him on the street. "The fucking *ngueta* hit the little boy," she writes, and says that her father could only complain to "another *ngueta*." "What are we here in Luanda? Everything but human beings. And until when will this shitty life last?"[31] she writes in another note. Deolinda was then nineteen years old.

Other passages also reveal the formation of a revolutionary consciousness through her socioracial experiences in Angola and the Civil Rights era in the United States, radically different from what she would reportedly tell Limbania. For example, while studying in Brazil briefly in 1959, Deolinda corresponded with Dr. Martin Luther King Jr., detailing Angola's liberation struggle and seeking advice on fighting for independence. Their correspondence took a religious tone: reflecting her Methodist upbringing, she asked whether lying to protect her comrades' names under interrogation would be a sin. Dr. King replied that she was under no obligation to do so, and sent her his book *Stride Toward Freedom* to guide her reflection on the issue. In the same exchange, she inquired about trading her stamp collection for a subscription to *Ebony* magazine. While in Congo-Léopoldville, Deolinda's reading of James Baldwin fueled a reflection on race and gender in her colonial context. Recalling interactions she had with Canadian United Nations peacekeepers on a mission in Congo at the time, she wrote in her diary: "I just finished reading *Another Country* by James Baldwin. Now I understand . . . the bestial gazes of the Canadians," she notes, drawing a parallel between her experiences and Baldwin's own exploration of racism, gender, and power in interracial relationships in the US in his novel published just two years before. "To white men, I, like all Black women, am just a prostitute, chasing after white men. To white women, all Black men die for their light skin," she concluded. While Deolinda's automatic association of prostitution with exploitation reflected prevailing, unchallenged views about sex work at the time, it also underscored the continuous reduction of the Black female body to a commodity in different contexts.[32] While in the United States, Deolinda also contacted Black women's associations, such as the National Council of Negro Women and the National Association of Colored Women's Clubs, among others.[33]

Those international experiences, readings, and exchanges progressively forged her view of the Angolan liberation struggle as part of Black internationalism and a global struggle against racial oppression. "In a sense, the struggle is not so much between the West and the East," she writes from the United States to a friend, "but between Blacks and whites; that is why our support comes from the Afro-Asian bloc and we have nothing to do with the puppets of the UN, nor with other white people, whether they are from one bloc or the other."[34] The rise of such consciousness, combined with her deeply critical view of colonialism in Angola, would in turn shape her relationship with the liberation movement, particularly concerning the racial distribution of power. Deolinda would grow critical of what she saw as an overrepresentation of white and *mestiço* militants in the movement's leadership as well as the refusal of these same non-Black militants and leaders to debate race relations in the MPLA—which Deolinda and many of her Black comrades ultimately interpreted as an expression of internal colonialism in the movement.

By late 1964, and increasingly throughout mid-1965 until early 1966, Deolinda began to challenge the situation described above. Her November 1, 1964, diary entry registers an exchange she overheard in which Eduardo, a *mestiço* militant whom she saw as privileged, claimed in a conversation with a group of comrades that "the revolution started in the cities (intellectuals) and from there it spread to the people"—in other words, suggesting that the *mestiço* Angolan urban intellectual elite deserved credit for beginning the liberation struggle. Another comrade (likely Black) retorted, "What are you saying? The people who suffer are the ones who stand up. This kind of thing makes me want to leave [the movement] and never come back."[35] Here, her diary testifies to the disputes about the political primacy of the movement, a cause of concrete power struggles, where well-educated white and *mestiço* militants were positioned as the political and military leaders of the revolution, and most Black militants as pawns.

Deolinda's reflection about this debate, and her own rejection of Eduardo's claim, then, spark her questioning of what racism is, a reflection that continued in her diary. "Africans," she writes using a capital A for "Africans" that is not used in Portuguese, "never consider mulattos as representatives of the Angolan people because of their privileged past," concluding by saying that only those who blind themselves from reality "do not accept this truth or consider it racism."[36]

Deolinda's words about the "mulattos" foreshadowed the rising racial tensions in the movement. Between early March and late May 1965, Deolinda registers in her diary a series of conflicts between the Black and *mestiço* militants. It is not clear what exactly caused such a divergence, but Deolinda sides with the Black militants. This situation becomes a central political question of the movement at the time, with meetings summoned to discuss the differences between the groups, leading Deolinda to record a series of reflections and form a strong opinion regarding race and racism in the revolutionary Angolan context.

In March 1965, her diary entries for four days in a row contain short entries about a growing dispute around the topic of racism. On the one hand, Deolinda transcribes the speech of two *mestiço* women accusing her and other Black comrades of racism: "You guys have to stop this racism. You talk about Portuguese colonialism just to hurt me."[37] On the other hand, Deolinda continues her reflection about the notion of racism in her historical and revolutionary context. After attending a meeting to discuss the "mulatto question," as she called it, she privately expressed frustration with what she viewed as *mestiço* defensiveness and exaggerated sense of victimization, reflecting,

> The crux of the matter is the existing socioeconomic gap, which brings about all the revolt and humiliation. . . . *Let those who also call themselves nationalists, and are here with us, understand this too, and not limit themselves to a very relative sacrifice. This is my racism.* I swear to all the mulattos and Portuguese women directly or indirectly involved in the MPLA that I will fight with ever greater force against everything that does not contribute to the well-being of the most exploited Angolan masses.[38]

It is important to note that Deolinda was not "anti-white" or "anti-*mestiço*" in principle. Throughout her diary, Deolinda often acknowledges the importance of having whites and *mestiços* as allies. Beyond any "utilitarian" perspective about their presence in the movement, she also considers that race issues were bound—although not reduced to—class differences, as she hints in the passage above mentioning the "socioeconomic gap," and were a central issue to be addressed. In other passages in her diary, Deolinda also acknowledges that Black individuals can be the enemies (and should "be eliminated, if necessary") and that her ultimate goal is "a decent, dignified, and abundant life for all whites and Blacks who share this goal."[39]

However, Deolinda frames race relations historically, and the idea that largely predominates in her diary is that it was necessary to first create a real situation of equality before relations became harmonious between Black Angolans, the lower layer of the colonial society, and whites and *mestiços*, who predominantly occupied the upper spaces of the Angolan social pyramid. She would "not accept an immediate leveling," in her words, among these racial groups in the movement or a colorblind approach to the distribution of power due to her witnessing, inside the movement, what she considered to be the reproduction of the colonial structure the movement was fighting against, with privileges—of labor, provisions, safety, comfort, and power—given to white and *mestiço* militants. Deolinda does not provide any signs of changing this perception; to the contrary, she shows signs of radicalization, which was still true in her last days, when she was interviewed by Limbania Jiménez Rodríguez.

Against Universalism

The perception of this repeating colonial structure of racial hierarchy inside the anti-colonial movement—the special treatment enjoyed by white and *mestiço* militants because that was, in Deolinda's words, "customary in the land"—in turn, leads Deolinda to deepen her reflection about the accusations of racism she suffered. Deolinda notices, in the constant confrontations with her non-Black comrades, the rhetorical use of authoritative arguments based on European leftist intellectual traditions. Deolinda seems to reject those as incapable of translating the specific local and historical challenges of the Angolan liberation struggle and the colonial background of her time-space.

In one of her most brutal passages, Deolinda questions the usefulness of such theories for Black militants by asking: "Who is easier to influence? The intellectual who reads a lot or the illiterate who doesn't read the theories to influence the negro?"[40] It is relevant to note that Deolinda was not anti-intellectual, as the passage above could suggest. An avid reader and engaged in teaching literacy classes in the movement, Deolinda sought, however, different intellectual traditions to support the understanding of that political process, as her readings and quotes of James Baldwin and Martin Luther King Jr. evince—in that case, seeking an international Black radical tradition as opposed to leftist European thought. Contrary to Limbania's depiction, Deolinda rejected generalized approaches of the racial phenomenon and questioned in her diary variations of "universal" theories. Although Deolinda would not fully articulate her understanding or a conceptualization of racism, she reflects on her own reality and her perception of the impossibility to fit it into universal theories, to then refine her questionings of what racism was in that context.

> Nor do I believe that the rich, whether they be Portuguese, American, or Angolan desire the well-being of the poor. . . . *Let the mulattos and "universalist" Blacks of the MPLA call this racism.* But whether married to a Black

woman or not, for me the Portuguese are Portuguese, white is white, rich is rich, and to a certain extent they have nothing in common with me as far as targets are concerned. . . . Good relations without violence or hate, only when we are on equal footing. Not before that.[41]

Deolinda distrusts and rejects universalist approaches to race, politics, revolution, and humanity more broadly, which she identifies with the European experience and mentality. Specifically, Deolinda rejected the consequence of labeling as "racism"—what today is called "reverse racism"—any policy that sought historical racial reparations. Worried about concrete and immediate emancipation and power for Angolans, Deolinda evokes the history of colonization as a basis to conclude that Black leadership and freedom would not be possible under Eurocentric political models and thought, which she criticizes.

> These "advanced, international" theories they bring up to save their skin are no longer convincing to us. When they find themselves lost, there is nothing they won't employ to distract Blacks and take advantage of our stupidity. Isn't that what the Portuguese navigators and conquerors did to our ancestors? Isn't that what the so-called mulatto and Portuguese "democrats and progressives" want to use to fool us?[42]

"Advanced and international theories" echoed Guevara's call for the militancy to learn the "most advanced concepts" in order to achieve unity between the different ethnic origins in Congo-Léopoldville. In the Angolan case, the advanced theories were applied to Black-white race relations, and to reject the Black militants' denunciation of a racially marked imbalance of power in the movement—a form of Eurocentrism that enabled, in her vision, the privileged treatment of non-Black militants. In another entry, Deolinda criticized the movement's maximum leader, Agostinho Neto, on similar grounds: "Neto is very influenced by so-called 'advanced and comprehensive theories' and whatnot. He's not politically or morally [a] virgin."[43] Deolinda had a comprehensive understanding of race relations in the revolutionary context, which, unlike the rationalized and abstract universalist/humanist approach of most white and *mestiço* Angolans—as well as Cuban official ideology—combined the multiple layers of social and affective life, individual interests, and the colonial structure.

Deolinda's rejection of "advanced theories" is directly related to her opposite view of racism in relation to Limbania's view—and the view Limbania attributed to Deolinda. A notion of racism that equated in the anti-colonial struggle both anti-white and anti-Black racism, without considering the sociohistorical structures of

Angola and the colonization, was possible for Limbania, who, as a white woman at a high-ranking position in the army and the Cuban Communist Party, could claim to be a universal human, a product of the universal revolution, and speak on behalf of other people and the revolution itself. For Deolinda, a Black woman in the struggle—not an abstract universal human, but a historically situated colonial subject—this approach was both politically and affectively impossible.

In September 1965, Deolinda wrote her last entry on racial issues in the movement. Deolinda vented about a militant—a mixed-race man—who had been temporarily suspended due to indiscipline and yet continued to have access to private conversations and meetings with the other, also light-skinned, leaders. "Is it normal for the leaders to remain connected to those who have been suspended?" she asked in an apparent mix of discomfort and outrage. At this point, however, Deolinda was growing increasingly silent about the topic of race, both publicly and in her own diary, questioning her ability to express her views about the situation. "There are certain aspects of the struggle that I shouldn't mention at this stage.... It's best to mention my doubts here in the Diary to avoid any problems." And as if bringing her reflections about race in her diary to a close, Deolinda's last words about the preferential treatment light-skinned leaders gave each other then seemed to encapsulate the dynamics and the relation between race, politics, and the power to speak: "Perhaps the 'voice' of the skin," she wrote with a pinch of irony, "is stronger in them than their political principles."[44]

Between September 1965 and July 1966, Deolinda still recorded some notes: the scarcity of goods, hunger in the barracks, the militants' low morale and increasing regionalist disputes (she uses the term "tribalism" in one such note), selfishness, lack of collaboration between women in the literacy class, a physical fight between the two wives of a polygamous man, excitement with military training—"Yesterday we started to learn how to handle the PM 44 [submachine gun]. A delight!"[45]— comments on her menses, and her feeling of familiarity listening to Ray Charles's "I Can't Stop Loving You." There are no further mentions of race issues.

Deolinda would only return to her diary in January 1967 to narrate the march that led to her death. Per Deolinda's own annotations, Cubans were already present in the MPLA base during 1965. Her sudden total silence in the diary, in July 1966, coincided exactly with the arrival of extra Cuban personnel and the military and political training they gave to MPLA militants for the Cienfuegos Squad, which preceded Deolinda's squad. In December 1966, Deolinda would receive military and political training for the Kamy Squad and be interviewed by Limbania Jiménez Rodríguez, a member of the intelligence team and political educator herself, before the final journey. In a context in which Cubans likely already knew about the racial tensions in the Angolan revolutionary movement—and could easily identify with their own recent experiences of Black dissent—how could that have conditioned the encounter between Deolinda and Limbania?

Although we can mostly speculate, this does not close the topic but, on the contrary, brings up new pressing questions regarding the role of Cubans in supporting or shaping the revolutionary (and later postcolonial) Angola's racial discourse. After all, while Deolinda's silence is in part related to the MPLA's leadership politics of racelessness, it is in the conversation with Limbania that Deolinda reportedly not simply silences but above all changes her position.

Why, after a lifelong commitment to restoring Black people's political autonomy, shaped by a radical Black consciousness and a constant and coherent understanding of race as a historical and political category, would Deolinda have suddenly become silent about race and experienced a conversion to a politics of racelessness that, in the way it was conceived in her context, disempowered Black Angolans? Why would this have happened a few months after she had reached the peak of her elaboration on race relations as shown in her diaries? Why would Deolinda have changed precisely when the Cubans arrived in the MPLA base? Considering the unlikelihood of such a radical change, what, then, explains the change in her voice? What does it mean in this context? Could Limbania have edited Deolinda's voice in her interviews? Could Deolinda have edited her own voice as she was being interviewed by Limbania? Did Deolinda postpone her desire to speak about racism to Cubans, just as she had done with her white and *mestiço* Angolan comrades? What does it tell us about the Cuban role in this process? How does it help us characterize this role—for example, as a direct or an indirect role?

After Deolinda: History-Writing and Racial Politics in Angolan-Cuban Cooperation

More traces of this history were found in the process of publishing Deolinda's diary, pointing to a Cuban role not only in making that history—of hegemonizing the racelessness discourse—but also in writing the history of an Angolan liberation marked by a supposedly hegemonic discourse of racelessness.

Roberto de Almeida, Deolinda's brother, seems to have felt his sister's urgency to speak. But why did he not publish her diary in 1975, in the wake of Angolan independence, when the MPLA inaugurated a massive national book-publishing program, through which now canonical Angolan writers such as Pepetela, Luandino Vieira, and many others could voice their histories of the anti-colonial struggle and utopias for the new nation and a politics of racelessness that is present in their works? Roberto de Almeida's preface to Deolinda's diary, dated from 1975, indicates his intention to publish the diary at that time.

Deolinda's harsh words about some of her MPLA comrades and her dissonant racial ideology certainly contributed to this silencing. But in the general context, the shaping of Deolinda's image and voice seems to go beyond Angolan borders. A few months after Roberto de Almeida wrote the preface, Cubans launched Operación Carlota, inaugurating a mass Angolan-Cuban military campaign against South Africa, the FNLA, and UNITA. In 1976, Limbania Rodríguez arrived in Angola for a second time for an official mission between the FMC and OMA, and she started to collect the information for her book about the Angolan heroine. In this environment, at the height of the Angolan-Cuban cooperation, what information might Limbania have received from her local informants? If Deolinda herself edited her voice when speaking about the Angolan problems with a Cuban official when Cubans did not yet have such a strong presence in Angola, what might have been the situation of other people talking to Limbania in 1976, when the Cuban presence was strong?

Limbania talked to Roberto de Almeida at that time, and apparently, Roberto de Almeida did not transmit to Limbania Deolinda's Black nationalist ideology. Why not? Or, if he did, could Limbania have decided to exclude or change it in her memoir? The delay in publishing Deolinda's diary meant that, before her direct voice became available, it was Limbania's words about Deolinda—the image of her condoned by her organization—that echoed the Cuban-MPLA racial ideology, showing its strength and role in shaping the Angolan political elite's similar racial politics. More than the impact Limbania's memoir may have had itself, it provides some debris of this likely broader history of a transnational process, South-South cooperation in which Cuba supported the forging, legitimization, and establishment of a politics of racelessness in Angola—and how, by what means, and in which circumstances it happened.

After the outbreak of the civil war in 1975, Cubans became the predominant international actor sustaining the MPLA's fight and national project. They also supported a political imaginary of racelessness. Deolinda Rodrigues's case, then, shows that the Cuban role is characterized in two different but intersectional domains: making the history that hegemonized the Angolan discourse of racelessness, on the one hand, and simultaneously writing the history that confirms this discourse of racelessness.

This powerful Cuban voice in the international context of both war, at the time, and the circulation of political discourses, later—much more powerful than the Angolan voice itself—in turn expands the Cuban role, from making this history to also writing this history. By comparing Limbania's book with Deolinda's diary, we see a discursive operation that publicly identifies racelessness with a "true" revolutionary consciousness—a condition for Deolinda and her peers to become "Heroines of Angola"—recording racelessness as a hegemonic ideology, either among militants in general or exploring that idea through the image of key figures in Angolan nationalism, such as Deolinda Rodrigues, even though this was contrary to her beliefs. In this process, Deolinda's voice starts as a Black radical voice; it silences itself in the context of the MPLA internal conflicts backed by Cubans; and finally, it changes into the opposite political stance—for a politics of racelessness—in a Cuban publication that recorded her voice in history.

Deolinda went on her final mission in the first months of 1967, and her plans to speak her truth about race relations in the movement after independence (after postponing it for years) could not be fulfilled. Given the continuation of the MPLA's history of suppressing race relations with continuous, strategic, and effective support from the Cuban mission, it is likely that she would have never been able to speak her truth in the following years, and that the publication of her diaries in the 2000s, were she alive, would have been an untimely and censored initiative. Deolinda's tragic death, ironically, finally allowed her to speak her truth and her voice to be heard. Through her written, postponed legacy, Deolinda could speak and reveal the racial tensions inside the anti-colonial movement and the suppression of Black emancipatory racial politics in an anti-colonial context.

While the tensions around different racial politics in the MPLA are a well-known chapter of its history—with many details of how they were administered still obscure—Deolinda's voice also illuminates the transnational conditions that sustained the Angolan political elite's racial discourse against the collective voice of a great part of its own (Black) people. By contrasting her diary, where we can hear her critical voice about race relations and racism in the movement, with Limbania's memoir, which alters Deolinda's voice according to the Cuban official discourse in confluence with the MPLA's official discourse on race, Deolinda provides the debris that helps reconstitute the history of how that Angolan political elite of the time relied on the transnational relation with Cuba to impose the politics of racelessness in the liberation struggle. A history that took place in the margins of the official male-made and male-authored history, whose complexities we can grasp from an alternative history that a Black woman was in the process of making—and written as much through her potent voice as through her deafening silence.

Acknowledgments

The author would like to thank Michelle Chase for her invaluable help with editing this chapter.

Notes

1. Currently the Republic of the Congo. Throughout this chapter, I will identify the Republic of the Congo and the Democratic Republic of the Congo by the customary use of "Congo" followed by the respective capital.

2. See Carlos Moore, *Castro, the Blacks, and Africa*, Afro-American Culture and Society (Center for Afro-American Studies, University of California, 1988); Alejandro de la Fuente, *A Nation for All: Race, Inequality, and Politics in Twentieth-Century Cuba* (University of North Carolina Press, 2001); Mark Q. Sawyer, *Racial Politics in Post-Revolutionary Cuba* (Cambridge University Press, 2006); Devyn Spence Benson, *Antiracism in Cuba: The Unfinished Revolution* (University of North Carolina Press, 2016); and Anne Garland Mahler, *From the Tricontinental to the Global South: Race, Radicalism, and Transnational Solidarity* (Duke University Press, 2018), among others.

3. See John A. Marcum, *The Angolan Revolution*, vol. 2, *Exile Politics and Guerrilla Warfare (1962–1976)* (MIT Press, 1978); Douglas L. Wheeler and René Pélissier, *Angola* (Praeger, 1971); Patrick Chabal, *A History of Postcolonial Lusophone Africa* (C. Hurst, 2002); and Jean-Michel Mabeko-Tali, *Guerrilhas e lutas sociais: o MPLA perante si próprio (1960–1977): ensaio de história política* (Mercado de Letras, 2018), among others. Mabeko-Tali is the exception: a critical analysis that considers how the politics of racelessness reflected and supported the worldview and interests of white and mixed-race Angolan revolutionaries.

4. Jorge I. Domínguez, "Cuban Foreign Policy," *Foreign Affairs* 57, no. 1 (1978): 83–108, https://doi.org/10.2307/20040054; Henley Adams, "Race and the Cuban Revolution: The Impact of Cuba's Intervention in Angola," in *Race, Ethnicity, and the Cold War: A Global Perspective*, ed. Philip Muehlenbeck (Vanderbilt University Press, 2012), 200–226; Magdalena López, "Challenging a South Red Atlantic: A Post-Liberationist Critique of the Caribbean Hispanic," in *New Perspective on Hispanic Caribbean Studies*, ed. Magdalena López and María Teresa Vera-Rojas (Palgrave Macmillan, 2020), 47–66.

5. Michael J. Bustamante and Jennifer L. Lambe, eds., *The Revolution from Within: Cuba, 1959–1980* (Duke University Press, 2019).

6. Christine Messiant, "Em Angola, até o passado é imprevisível: A experiência de uma investigação sobre o nacionaliso angolano e, em paticular, o MPLA: fontes, críticas, necessidades actuais de investigação," in *Actas do II Seminário Internacional sobre a História de Angola: construindo o passado angolano: as fontes e a sua interpretação: Luanda, 4 a 9 de Agosto de 1997*, ed. Jill Dias and Rosa Cruz e Silva (Comissão Nacional para as Comemorações dos Descobrimentos Portugueses, 2000), 803–59; Mabeko-Tali, *Guerrilhas e lutas sociais*.

7. Margarida Paredes, *Combater duas vezes: mulheres na luta armada em Angola* (Verso da História, 2015); Margarida Paredes, "Deolinda Rodrigues, da Família Metodista à Família MPLA, o Papel da Cultura na Política," *Cadernos de Estudos Africanos* 20 (2010): 11–26, https://doi.org/10.4000/cea.135; Larissa Souza, "Militância, escrita e vida: a poesia de Deolinda Rodrigues," *Cadernos Pagu* 51 (December 6, 2017), https://www

.scielo.br/j/cpa/a/wnx56bs93NLRQkV4SRBfsHj/?lang=pt; Patrício Batsîkama, "Poder no Feminino. Caso da Deolinda Rodrigues 'Langidila,'" *África[s]—Revista do Programa de Pós-Graduação em Estudos Africanos e Representações da África* 7, no. 13 (2020), https://revistas.uneb.br/index.php/africas/article/view/9403; Noemi Alfieri, "Deolinda Rodrigues: entre a escrita da história e a escrita biográfica. Recepção de uma guerrilheira e intelectual angolana," *Abriu: estudos de textualidade do Brasil, Galicia e Portugal* 10 (2021): 39–57.

8. Throughout this chapter, I will refer to Deolinda Rodrigues and Limbania Jiménez Rodríguez by their first names to avoid confusion between their similar last names. The short biography I present here is based on Deolinda Rodrigues, *Diário de um exilio sem regresso*, 1st ed. (Luanda: Editorial Nzila, 2003); Deolinda Rodrigues, *Cartas de Langidila e outros documentos*, 1st ed. (Luanda: Editorial Nzila, 2004); Limbania Jiménez Rodríguez, *Heroínas de Angola*, Ediciones políticas (Ed. de Ciencias Sociales, 1985); Paredes, *Combater duas vezes*.

9. In its early years this movement used the name Union of the North Angolan Peoples (UPNA) and then Union of Angolan Peoples (UPA). I am using FNLA as this is the current name and the one used during most of Deolinda's history covered in this chapter.

10. Currently the Democratic Republic of the Congo (formerly Zaire) or Congo-Kinshasa since the renaming of the capital Léopoldville to Kinshasa in 1966.

11. Piero Gleijeses, *Conflicting Missions: Havana, Washington, and Africa, 1959-1976* (University of North Carolina Press, 2003).

12. Gleijeses, *Conflicting Missions*, 109; Edward George, *The Cuban Intervention in Angola, 1965-1991: From Che Guevara to Cuito Cuanavale* (Routledge, 2012).

13. Ernesto Che Guevara, *Pasajes de la guerra revolucionaria: Congo* (Editorial de Ciencias Sociales, 2013), 273 (my emphasis).

14. Gleijeses, *Conflicting Missions*, 81–84.

15. Limbania Jiménez Rodríguez, interview by Paulo Lara and Associação Tchiweka de Documentação, March 16, 2010, Fundo ATD, Associação Tchiweka de Documentação, https://www.tchiweka.org/audiovisuais/9001001001.

16. Jiménez, *Heroínas de Angola*, 4. All translations from Limbania, Deolinda, and others are mine.

17. Jiménez, *Heroínas de Angola*, 5.

18. Jiménez, *Heroínas de Angola*, 4.

19. See Michelle Chase, "The Heroic Example of the Vietnamese Woman: Gender and Solidarity in Cuba's Age of the Tricontinental," in this volume.

20. Jiménez, *Heroínas de Angola*, 9–10.

21. Jiménez, *Heroínas de Angola*, 10.

22. Jiménez, *Heroínas de Angola*, 16.

23. Jiménez, *Heroínas de Angola*, 10 (my emphasis).

24. Jiménez, *Heroínas de Angola*, 21 (my emphasis).

25. Marcelo Bittencourt, *Estamos juntos!: o MPLA e a luta anticolonial (1961-1974)*, vol. 1 of 2 vols. (Kilombelombe, 2008); Mabeko-Tali, *Guerrilhas e lutas sociais*.

26. Moore, *Castro, the Blacks, and Africa*; Fuente, *A Nation for All*; Sawyer, *Racial Politics*; Benson, *Antiracism in Cuba*; Lillian Guerra, *Visions of Power in Cuba: Revolution, Redemption, and Resistance, 1959-1971* (University of North Carolina Press, 2012); Lillian Guerra, "*Poder Negro* in Revolutionary Cuba: Black Consciousness, Communism, and the Challenge of Solidarity," *Hispanic American Historical Review* 99, no. 4 (2019): 681–718, https://doi.org/10.1215/00182168-7787175.

27. Jiménez, *Heroínas de Angola*, 8.
28. Jiménez, *Heroínas de Angola*, 34 (my emphasis).
29. Jiménez, *Heroínas de Angola*, 27 (my emphasis).
30. Jiménez, *Heroínas de Angola*, 22–23 (my emphasis).
31. Rodrigues, *Diário*, 30–32.
32. Rodrigues, *Diário*, 52.
33. Rodrigues, *Cartas de Langidila*, 92.
34. Rodrigues, *Cartas de Langidila*, 90.
35. Rodrigues, *Diário*, 76.
36. Rodrigues, *Diário*, 77.
37. Rodrigues, *Diário*, 96.
38. Rodrigues, *Diário*, 97 (my emphasis).
39. Rodrigues, *Diário*, 99.
40. Rodrigues, *Diário*, 55.
41. Rodrigues, *Diário*, 51 (my emphasis)
42. Rodrigues, *Diário*, 98.
43. Rodrigues, *Diário*, 99.
44. Rodrigues, *Diário*, 132.
45. Rodrigues, *Diário*, 161.

TWO

The Heroic Example of the Vietnamese Woman

Gender and Solidarity in Cuba's Age of the Tricontinental

MICHELLE CHASE

In January 1966, during the Tricontinental Conference held in Havana, the president of the Federation of Cuban Women (FMC), Vilma Espín, met two women delegates from Vietnam. The meeting must have had a strong impact on her. In subsequent months she praised Vietnamese women as a model "not just for us but for all peoples" and promised that Cuban women would follow their heroic example.[1] That summer, she publicly gifted the pistol she herself had used in the Sierra Maestra to Nguyen Thi Dinh, vice commander of the armed forces of South Vietnam's National Liberation Front and president of the Women's Union for the Liberation of South Vietnam. A few years later, Espín led an FMC delegation to Vietnam, providing a colorful account of her trip on Cuban television when she returned. Espín's praise came at the apex of Cuban expressions of solidarity for Vietnam in the wake of the Tricontinental; it was one of many references to the "heroic Vietnamese woman" made by Cuban leaders, artists, and journalists from the mid-1960s to the early 1970s. Indeed, similarly glorified images of Vietnamese women swept the world in this period, although the meanings attributed to the images differed.[2] This chapter examines the way the revolutionary Vietnamese woman was held up as a model for Cuba's own New Woman, and in some ways even for Cuba's New Man.

The symbol of the revolutionary Vietnamese woman was not a simple reflection of events within Vietnam, nor was it a Cuban construction that developed in isolation. It was the result of the deliberate transmission of such imagery by actors within Vietnam and Cuba.[3] Indeed, the fact that Espín's enthusiasm for the Vietnamese cause was at least partly sparked by meeting several Vietnamese delegates to the 1966 Tricontinental Conference in person suggests that Cuban understanding of the "heroic" Vietnamese was forged through concrete interpersonal encounters. This chapter pieces together the transnational networks of solidarity and diplomacy that enabled such encounters and traces the way messages regarding women's wartime roles and emancipation within revolutionary struggle traveled along these circuits from Vietnam to Cuba.

Cuban women were prominent in these solidarity efforts. Melba Hernández, one of the earliest members of the revolutionary movement known as the 26th of July, played a particularly crucial role as founding president of the Cuban Committee of Solidarity with South Vietnam (Comité Cubano de Solidaridad con Vietnam del Sur), a group that organized innumerable delegations and acts of solidarity throughout the 1960s. Vilma Espín, founding president of the FMC, helped raise awareness about Vietnam among Cuban women and insisted on increased solidarity with Vietnam at congresses of women from the Socialist Bloc. The prominent Afro-Cuban writer Marta Rojas formed part of a new generation of international women journalists that covered the Vietnam War and was the first female Latin American war correspondent to travel south of the seventeenth parallel, the boundary that separated North from South Vietnam. Cuba did not have the equivalent of the many independent feminist and maternalist groups that mobilized around Vietnam in the Global North. Yet in Cuba, too, women leaders used the Vietnam War to advance their own interpretations of women's revolutionary roles.

The symbol of the revolutionary Vietnamese woman resonated in Cuba because it encapsulated key conflicts of the period. First, the symbol legitimized and reinforced Cuban ideas of women's emancipation within national liberation and revolutionary movements. It did so at a time when competing ideas of women's liberation emphasizing feminist autonomy and individual equality were emanating from the second-wave feminism of the Global North. The circulation of images of Vietnamese women at war coincided with—and served as a catalyst for—the escalation of transnational struggles over how to define legitimate forms of feminism as the second-wave feminism of the Global North grew.[4] The symbol of the "heroic" Vietnamese woman validated Cuban understandings of women's liberation as part of a broader anti-capitalist and revolutionary struggle at this crucial juncture.

Second, the symbol of the revolutionary Vietnamese woman embodied the militant approach to global anti-imperialist struggle that Cuba's famous 1966 Tricontinental Congress helped codify. Recent scholarship has begun to view

The Heroic Example of the Vietnamese Woman 45

"Tricontinentalism" as a distinct period and worldview within the longer history of anti-imperialism, which sought to unite Marxism with anti-imperialism and emphasize similarities between the national liberation struggles in Latin America, Africa, and Asia.[5] It called for a radical remaking of global power dynamics and served as an implicit rejoinder to Soviet accommodation and moderation in the mid-1960s. The visual and discursive emphasis placed on Vietnamese women's willingness to use arms shored up Cuba's dogmatic insistence on armed struggle as the preferred path to revolution and national liberation in this period by showing that the "whole people" of Vietnam were willing to engage in guerrilla warfare.[6]

Finally, Cuban depictions of the revolutionary Vietnamese woman reflected the island's growing preoccupation with the urgency of increasing production and the consequent need for the entire populace to contribute to agricultural labor. In the late 1960s, Cuban leaders emphasized increasing sugar production in an ultimately fruitless effort to develop the island's economy and avoid complete economic dependency on the Soviet Union. Women were increasingly called on to join the workforce, including through voluntary (unremunerated) agricultural labor, and both men and women were mobilized en masse for the so-called Ten Million Ton sugar harvest of 1969–70.[7] This context explains why Cuban solidarity efforts often emphasized Vietnamese women's willingness to work. The "heroic" Vietnamese woman was presented in the Cuban media as a positive, aspirational model that linked these various realms of struggle—national liberation movements, women's emancipation, and the "battle" for production.

The images of revolutionary Vietnamese women that circulated in the Cuban media thus illuminate the often-overlooked gendered aspects of Tricontinentalism, for they connected the Cold War conflict over women's emancipation with support for national liberation movements. They also expand on our understanding of internationalist solidarity by showing how it was used domestically with an aspirational, even disciplinary, function in enjoining Cubans to labor. Finally, these images show us how ideas about women's mobilization and liberation emerged in lateral transnational conversations. Existing scholarship often suggests that these reflected domestic dynamics emerging from the 1959 revolution or from Cuba's earlier first-wave feminism, or perhaps in dialogue with the Eastern Bloc.[8] But ideas about women's emancipation also developed within the context of South-South interactions, including across the socialist South.[9]

The Mutual Expressions of Cuban-Vietnamese Solidarity

Through the early 1960s, mutual acts of diplomatic recognition and solidarity brought Cuba and Vietnam closer together. As several historians have shown, the National Liberation Front (NLF) of South Vietnam, which formed in 1960 to oppose the US-supported anti-communist regime of Ngô Đình Diệm, became extremely adept at cultivating international support through its diplomacy.[10] Through trips and press conferences abroad and by hosting visitors to Vietnam, the NLF successfully garnered international support for some of its demands and disseminated its own narrative about US aggression. NLF diplomats learned to craft their messages to appeal to specific constituencies. For example, in the West they sought to influence not only formal policymakers but also more grassroots diplomats and social movements, especially the anti-war and feminist movements of the United States, Europe, and Canada.[11] Within the Soviet Union and China, the NLF also waged specific diplomatic campaigns, such as requesting additional matériel and claiming to adhere to each socialist power's particular revolutionary doctrine. Finally, the NLF also reached out to the Non-Aligned Movement (NAM), such as in a campaign advocating for postwar neutrality for South Vietnam in the early 1960s.[12]

But how did Cuba fit into Vietnamese foreign policy? Judging from the visits of high-profile leaders from the socialist Democratic Republic of Vietnam (DRV) and the NLF to the island, both the DRV and NLF valued their relations with Cuba. This likely reflected Cuba's unique position as the only Latin American country in the Socialist Bloc and its willingness to press the Soviet leadership for more support for Third World insurgencies. Cuba may have also seemed like a valuable springboard for influencing the NAM—in which Cuba increasingly sought a leadership role—and other countries of the Global South. Finally, Cuba enjoyed unsurpassed prestige and influence within the Latin American Left, helping shape the Left's interactions with the world. As Tanya Harmer and Alberto Martín Álvarez note, left-wing Latin American groups "often discovered the world beyond the Americas via Cuba. Through its interactions with countries and peoples in Africa and Asia, especially, Cuba made the Third World relevant, intelligible, and relatable for Latin American audiences."[13]

Havana's role as a revolutionary hub in the 1960s contributed to this influence. The many international congresses held there created forums for the articulation of commonalities across the Global South, including between Vietnam and Latin America. For example, in 1964, taking advantage of the many international delegations that attended Cuba's annual 26th of July celebrations, local solidarity groups hosted an event to show international visitors a film about Vietnam provided by the NLF.[14] At the Tricontinental Congress of January 1966 and the Latin American Student Congress of July 1966, delegates from the Venezuelan guerrilla group Armed Forces of National Liberation (Fuerzas Armadas de Liberación Nacional) and South Vietnam's NLF publicly exchanged flags, weapons, and war trophies.[15] The fact that the DRV and NLF both had formal diplomatic representation in Havana also helped establish connections. For example, members of the Guatemalan guerrilla group Rebel Armed Forces (Fuerzas Armadas Revolucionarias) met with the NLF's permanent mission in Havana in 1966.[16] For Vietnamese diplomats, Cuba opened a gateway to the Americas.

Existing scholarship has tended to ignore Cuban initiatives toward Vietnam, perhaps because compared to its previous efforts in Algeria, Congo, and Latin America, and to its subsequent involvement in Angola or Ethiopia, Cuban support for Vietnam was much less extensive and less oriented toward military aid or training. During the Vietnam War, Cuba sent medical teams and food, including ten thousand tons of sugar in 1965.[17] Cuba also sent some construction workers, some of whom worked on the Ho Chi Minh trail.[18] After 1968 it also provided Vietnam with aid in health services, agriculture, construction, fishing, sugar, industry, education, sports, and research, mostly conducted through small groups of Cuban internationalists.[19] Cuba sent no troops, matériel, or military advisers, although Fidel Castro made his willingness to send volunteers loud and clear at the Tricontinental Congress in January 1966, famously stating that Cuba was willing to support Vietnam not just with sugar but also with "our blood."[20] He subsequently reiterated Cuba's willingness to send military aid, stating later that year, "There is not one single combat unit in our armed forces that is not prepared to go to Vietnam."[21] Still, Cuban-Vietnamese relations can primarily be characterized as cultural diplomacy.

Symbolically, Cuba's political support for Vietnam was significant. Events in Vietnam helped Cuban leaders develop a "Tricontinentalist" vision of anti-imperialist solidarity and shared struggle. In a December 1963 speech, Che Guevara argued that Vietnam served as a "laboratory" for US imperialism for a future assault on Latin America. He also rehearsed ideas that would be more famously iterated in his message to the Tricontinental, arguing for a commonality of struggle in "America, Asia, and Africa, the three oppressed continents."[22] Che argued for a global consciousness, as individual besieged nations recognized their common predicament and the strength that might be derived from common struggle. By 1966, assertions that Cuba and Vietnam were involved in shared or parallel struggles against US imperialism were common. Unlike the racial logic that was used to justify later expressions of Cuban solidarity with Angola, solidarity with Vietnam was based on the shared determination of two small, underdeveloped countries to stand up to US imperialism. As Fidel Castro said in 1967, it was "natural" and "logical" "that a country like ours, threatened by similar dangers [of imperialism], would feel toward Vietnam the deepest solidarity."[23]

Diplomatically, Cuba was a pioneer in supporting Vietnam in several ways.

In 1962 Cuba became the first country in the world to host a permanent diplomatic mission of the NLF, awarding it the status of a foreign embassy.[24] In 1965 it was the first to recognize the Provisional Revolutionary Government (PRG) of South Vietnam. In 1969 Cuba became the first and only country to appoint an ambassador to the "liberated" zones of South Vietnam.[25] Four years later, Fidel Castro famously toured the NLF-held areas of Quang Tri Province despite ongoing bombing from US forces. He was the first and only foreign leader to undertake such a trip.[26]

Within the Socialist Bloc, Cuba took the lead in urging more solidarity and support. The Cuban government gave unqualified verbal support to the government of North Vietnam and to the National Liberation Front, in contrast to the Soviet Union's initially more cautious response.[27] Cuba's rhetorically more aggressive and militant stance on Vietnam was consistent with Cuba's attempt to forge an independent foreign policy in the mid-1960s, diverging from the Soviet Union's emphasis on peaceful coexistence by supporting armed revolutionary movements in Latin America and Africa until the late 1960s, when economic crises on the island forced Castro to reiterate Cuba's public support for the USSR. With conditions in Vietnam escalating as Cuban-USSR relations reached a nadir, Cuban leaders saw Vietnam as a litmus test for Soviet commitments to defend national liberation movements in the Global South from imperialist aggression.[28]

Vietnam's geopolitical importance in this period helps explain why the Cuban government funded solidarity efforts geared toward the Cuban populace. The most important institutional vehicle for these efforts was the Cuban Committee of Solidarity with South Vietnam (hereafter referred to as the Comité), founded in fall of 1963.[29]

According to the Comité's official history, it was founded with a number of mass organizations and unions duly represented.[30] But in practice, the Comité was driven by the energy of Melba Hernández, who was appointed as its founding president. As one of the earliest members of the 26th of July Movement, Hernández must have enjoyed respect and powerful contacts.[31] But like other women leaders of the 26th of July, she had been passed over for ministerial positions. It is not entirely clear why she was chosen to lead the Comité, but the fact that she was one of the few revolutionary insiders to have visited Vietnam worked in her favor.[32] As founding president of the Comité, she became an active public figure within Cuba over the next ten years. By traveling to Vietnam and hosting visiting Vietnamese diplomats, Hernández eventually became a trusted emissary for the NLF and developed excellent relations with the DRV and NLF diplomats stationed in Havana. After the fall of Saigon in 1975, Hernández was appointed Cuban ambassador to reunified Vietnam.

FIGURE 2.1. A group of Cuban and Vietnamese diplomats including (*from left to right*) Raúl Valdés Vivó, Cuban ambassador to the "liberated zones" of South Vietnam; NLF representative Ly Van Sau; Comité Cubano de Solidaridad con Viet Nam del Sur president Melba Hernández; and NLF leader Tran Buu Kiem. Unknown photographer. Published in *Por Viet Nam: A 10 Años de la Constitución del Comité Cubano de Solidaridad con Viet Nam del Sur, Hoy con Viet Nam, Cambodia y Laos* (Instituto Cubano del Libro, 1974).

Led by Hernández, the Comité served as Cuba's principal conduit for the NLF's messaging, translating NLF points into solidarity campaigns designed to raise the Cuban public's consciousness of the Vietnam War. The Comité's many activities within Cuba included holding special acts on important anniversaries; launching voluntary work campaigns dedicated to Vietnam; renaming neighborhood centers, daycares, and even towns after Vietnamese figures or places; and leading specific campaigns in support of exemplary individuals, such as martyred NLF activist Van Troi. Indeed, the Comité provided the organizational infrastructure for nearly all the public events related to Vietnam for the next decade. Hernández also organized delegations of Cuban intellectuals, journalists, and doctors to Vietnam. These delegations resulted in the formation of an influential cohort of Cuban experts on Vietnam, who then disseminated their experiences to national and international audiences.[33] Thus solidarity initiatives provided the institutional frameworks and experienced spokespeople that transmitted ideas about the role of women in the Vietnamese struggle to Cuban and foreign publics.

The Revolutionary Woman as Global Icon

Most historiography on the images of militant women produced by socialist states and by revolutionary, anti-fascist, and national liberation movements has debated the extent to which such depictions challenge versus reinscribe traditional ideals of femininity or sexuality. Some have argued that images of militiawomen empowered women but only by desexualizing or masculinizing them in the model of their male counterparts.[34] Others argue that militant images of women were predominantly intended to mobilize men,[35] or that a focus on militaristic activity "pushed aside more diverse considerations of what a feminist socialist ideology of gender might look like."[36] Yet other scholars have argued that militant depictions of women could be liberating in the sense of offering gender without sexualization, decoupling womanhood from essentialized understandings of femininity and sexuality, and effectively creating new socialist models of gender and female beauty.[37] While socialist states clearly instrumentalized militant images of women, to mobilize them for national demands in either labor or defense, some historians have argued that militant depictions of women nevertheless had radical potential and could be embraced by women to legitimize their own activism.[38] Scholars also recognize that these iconographic images of revolutionary women were not nationally bounded; they traveled within the socialist camp and were exported by socialist states to build international support.[39]

The transnational circulation of iconic imagery of militant revolutionary women predated the Cold War.[40] But from the mid-1960s to the early 1970s—the apex of "Tricontinentalism"—the global circulation of such images peaked. As Juliane Noth has argued, images of militiawomen "became emblems of international solidarity" by the mid-1960s, circulating among socialist countries and revolutionary movements.[41] The period also led to the closer identification of such imagery with decolonization, the spread of socialism to the Global South, and Black radical movements, eclipsing their earlier association with European anti-fascist, revolutionary, and partisan movements. The Cuban Revolution of 1959 and the organization of popular militias over the next few years led to a barrage of photographs of armed Cuban women, which were circulated throughout the early 1960s by both the Cuban government and foreign photographers working with commercial media outlets. In China in the same period, the deepening conflict with the Soviets, the Great Leap Forward, and the expansion of defensive militias all contributed to the rise and spread of images of revolutionary women, meant to establish China's greater militancy and socialist commitment as compared to the Soviet Union.[42]

Perhaps no other conflict was more closely associated with images of revolutionary women than the Vietnam War. This was no accident: it reflected the proactive and intentional messaging of Vietnamese organizations. The emancipation of women was a central pillar of the NLF's platform. As scholar Thy Phu argues, communists "martialed the symbol of revolutionary Vietnamese women to link two causes, women's emancipation and national liberation."[43] North Vietnamese mass organizations also directly addressed women's importance to the struggle during the war years. The Vietnam Women's Union of North Vietnam delineated women's "three responsibilities" in the war: relieving men at work so they could go to the front; encouraging others to enlist; and engaging in combat themselves. The Young Pioneers and the Vietnamese People's Army, as well as press outfits such as the Vietnam News Agency, all disseminated various images of revolutionary women, ranging from glamorous young women with guns to militant mothers to humble peasants.

These images were disseminated locally to explain the cause and recruit other Vietnamese to the war effort. They were also, very intentionally, disseminated beyond Vietnam in order to elicit sympathy from multiple publics. We know that imagery of revolutionary Vietnamese women had a strong impact in the Global North, especially among anti-war and feminist groups.[44] But there has been much less research on how such images informed the Socialist Bloc or the Global South.[45] The Cuban case provides us with an unusual example of how the icon of the revolutionary Vietnamese woman was interpreted in another socialist state of the Global South.[46]

Women's Liberation and National Liberation in Vietnam and Cuba

The earliest example of extensive Cuban media attention to women in the Vietnamese struggle emerged out of the very first delegation that the Comité organized. This was the pioneering trip taken by Cuban journalists Marta Rojas and Raúl Valdés Vivó, who spent six weeks embedded with the NLF in fall 1965, touring the "liberated" territories of South Vietnam.[47] This trip was foundational in many ways. It was the first major collaboration of the NLF and the Comité. Rojas and Valdés Vivó were likely the first Latin American war correspondents to travel south of the seventeenth parallel, and their trip resulted in the most detailed reporting on the Vietnamese war regions that the Cuban press had yet published.[48] The trip would be a life-changing event for both journalists, who subsequently became something like informal ambassadors on behalf of the NLF in Cuba. In 1969, Valdés Vivó was named ambassador to the NLF-held areas of the south. He was later sent as a Cuban envoy to war-torn Laos and Ethiopia. Rojas traveled to Vietnam a dozen more times and covered the fall of Saigon in 1975.

Because the NLF designed the journalists' itinerary, the 1965 trip provides us with insight into the NLF's agenda in its outreach to foreign journalists.[49] Notably, the NLF clearly wanted to reflect women's contributions to the war effort and to convey the fact that women were in positions of political leadership. For example, the NLF ensured that the journalists enjoyed access to high-profile women leaders and heard many stories both of women's bravery and activism and of enemy forces' abuse of women. Consequently, Rojas and Valdés Vivó's resulting reportage—serialized in Cuba's preeminent daily newspaper *Granma* in late 1965—paid significant attention to women as political actors, including as political activists and leaders, not just as victims. The journalists profiled various women, including Nguyen Thi Dinh, a founder and military commander of the NLF,[50] and Phan Thi Quyen, the widow of martyred student leader Nguyen Van Troi and a political activist in her own right.[51] The mere depiction of women's militancy in wartime was not an argument about women's emancipation or gender equality per se, although it did inevitably reference ideas about women's political participation and revolutionary female subjectivity. But Cuban attention to the conflict in Vietnam soon resulted in more specific discussions of women's liberation and how it was linked to national liberation struggles.

In December 1966, Marta Rojas published a four-part series in *Granma* called "Sisters in Arms," focused on women in the Vietnam War. It was given prominent placement on the paper's editorial page. The series seems to have been commissioned by the FMC and may have reflected the growing interest FMC leaders began to take in Vietnam in 1966.[52] The "Sisters in Arms" series provided the Cuban media's first extensive and explicit analysis of Vietnamese women's liberation and how this issue was conceived of by Vietnamese women's organizations.[53] The series summarized the "five duties" for women as delineated by the Women's Union for the Liberation of South Vietnam: fight against the enemy, join agricultural duties, attend to the sick and wounded, care for and educate children, and keep revolutionary morale high. The series also conveyed the main conclusions of the congress of Vietnamese women held in South Vietnam in 1965, which discussed women's liberation in relation to the anti-imperialist struggle.

Furthermore, the "Sisters in Arms" series framed women's liberation in a way that unequivocally validated Cuban leaders' own understanding of this process. Notably, the series echoed language commonly used by Fidel Castro and Vilma Espín to describe women in Cuba, signaling to readers the similarity of the two struggles. For example, the series described Vietnamese women as "doubly heroic" and proclaimed that the women's movement was "part of the national liberation movement and the class movement. Only by liberating South Vietnam, giving land to campesinos, and ending unemployment can we liberate women."[54] The NLF recognized the decisive importance of women's incorporation into politics, armed revolution, and productive labor, Rojas argued, while the Vietnamese woman "is conscious that fighting for power for the whole people is the only way to fully conquer equal rights and that the inevitable path to gain that power is through the armed struggle. . . . And once power is conquered, the way to enforce that equality . . . is by incorporation into productive labor and education."[55]

The series also argued that participation in the national liberation struggle was, in and of itself, a liberating process for women. As Rojas glossed one of the "lessons" of the 1965 congress, the women's movement in South Vietnam was a revolutionary movement that changed women's lives "in the very process of struggle and through the very process of struggle," which pushed women into new roles as they joined the war effort.[56] Prior to the war of liberation, "the Vietnamese woman was a servant and even a slave to the man," Rojas argued. "It has been through revolutionary struggle and political education that they have passed to the front row [*primer plano*] of the revolutionary movement."[57]

The Cuban media reinforced these ideas by publishing interviews and other texts from women leaders of the NLF. For example, a long article by South Vietnamese military leader Nguyen Thi Dinh published in *Granma* in 1969 provided further arguments about how women's military participation in the South Vietnamese liberation struggle and women's emancipation were linked, arguing that "the South Vietnamese woman knows how to tightly tie her burning patriotism, her yearning for the liberation of the country, and her desire to liberate herself."[58] Interviewed by *Prensa Latina* several years later, she argued that Vietnamese women "are very conscious that only in a socialist regime, in which the worker is free of oppression and exploitation, will they be fully emancipated."[59]

The Cuban view of the Vietnam War as having propelled women's activism, militancy, and leadership was also reinforced by female NLF leaders during their visits to Cuba. These visits—like the itinerary organized for Rojas and Valdés Vivó—reflected the decision on the part of the NLF and DRV to publicize women's leadership and involvement in the war. In sharp contrast to the difficulties Vietnamese women faced when seeking permission to visit Western countries, in Cuba the women were given celebratory treatment, full state honors, and ample publicity.[60]

There were several high-profile visits of NLF women leaders to Cuba in this period, including the 1972 state visit of NLF foreign minister Nguyen Thi Binh ("Madame" Binh) and the 1974 and 1978 visits of the NLF commander Nguyen Thi Dinh, who was accompanied by a small delegation of militiawomen.[61] The

FIGURE 2.2. NLF foreign minister Nguyen Thi Binh poses with Cuban leaders including Osvaldo Dorticós and Fidel Castro during her 1972 visit to Havana. Unknown photographer. Published in *Por Viet Nam: A 10 Años de la Constitución del Comité Cubano de Solidaridad con Viet Nam del Sur, Hoy con Viet Nam, Cambodia y Laos* (Instituto Cubano del Libro, 1974).

DRV also sent young women militias to Cuba on delegations, such as Dang Thi Thanh, a twenty-three-year-old anti-aerial gunner described as having shot down "half a dozen" US planes,[62] who formed part of the North Vietnamese delegation to the 1966 Tricontinental conference, and Ngo Thi Tuyen, a young militiawoman famed for carrying twice her own weight in ammunition to aid the defense of the Thanh Hoa Bridge, who visited Cuba later that year.[63]

Cuban media coverage of these visits often stressed the women's continued femininity, maternalism, or physical attractiveness alongside their military or political accomplishments. In some ways, this served to temper or domesticate female military prowess by combining it with references to maternalism and female sacrifice. Vietnamese women leaders were also savvy in their conscious embodiment of multiple images of femininity. For example, during her July 1974 state visit to Cuba, NLF vice commander Nguyen Thi Dinh met several Cuban military commanders and oversaw a military parade in her honor. Dressed in a

The Heroic Example of the Vietnamese Woman 55

military suit with insignia pinned to her chest, she was given the Orden Playa Girón, a medal awarded to distinguished foreigners. The following day, still decorated with various medals and insignia but now wearing a traditional white dress and checkered scarf, she visited the FMC headquarters and the "Viet Nam Heróico" daycare, a visit that strategically allowed her to project a softer and more feminine image.

What these publications and encounters suggest is that, unlike the differing conceptualizations of women's liberation often found between Vietnamese groups and feminist groups of the Global North, Vietnamese and Cuban understandings of women's liberation closely aligned. Like the NLF and VWU (Vietnam Women's Union), the Cuban Comité de Solidaridad and the FMC argued that the Vietnamese conflict showed that women's liberation and national liberation were mutually constitutive. The Cuban media's glorification of Vietnamese women echoed the qualities of sacrifice, militancy, maternalism, and anti-imperialist dedication regularly praised in Vietnamese media. And like their Vietnamese counterparts, but unlike in the Global North, the Cuban media offered patently militant images of women as participants in, and even leaders of, armed combat, so long as it did not hamper a woman's femininity.

The view of women's liberation as a constituent part of national liberation had been expressed in Cuba since the early 1960s as the revolution increasingly addressed the "woman question," but it gained importance later in the decade as second-wave feminism in the Global North began to offer competing understandings of women's emancipation. Fidel Castro had famously praised the small women's battalion within the Rebel Army during the Cuban Revolutionary War (1956–58).[64] He subsequently referred to this as one justification for women's inclusion in the revolution, implying that women had won the right to inclusion with their contribution to guerrilla warfare. But other male leaders were ambivalent or even hostile toward women's participation in armed struggle.[65] After the revolution's triumph, women who had fought in the Sierra Maestra were often reassigned to civilian duties, and the mandatory military service established in 1963 applied only to men.[66] While women did join civilian militias, their participation in them may not have been widespread until the formation of the new Territorial Troop Militia in the 1980s.

Given Cuba's own cautious and gradual embrace of women's participation in insurrectionary warfare, the celebration of Vietnamese women may have helped popularize and solidify ideals of women as combatants, serving as a bridge between Cuba's contested ideas of women's revolutionary roles in the early 1960s and the more resolutely militant images of women revolutionaries that Cuban visual culture helped codify and spread domestically in publications like *Mujeres*, and internationally through posters from the Organization of Solidarity with the Peoples of Africa, Asia, and Latin America (Organización de Solidaridad de los Pueblos de Africa, Asia, y América Latina, OSPAAAL) and publications such as the *Tricontinental Bulletin,* in the late 1960s and 1970s.[67] Although we lack access to documentation of internal debates within Cuban organizations, we can speculate that the powerful imagery of women in Vietnam was embraced by FMC leaders who wished to emphasize women's importance as revolutionary actors within Cuba.

The "Battle" of Production

The Cuban Comité and other mid-level leaders frequently celebrated what they viewed as the Vietnamese capacity for labor. This was perhaps a peculiarly Cuban interpretation of the revolutionary Vietnamese woman, but one that made sense given the Cuban government's ongoing attempts to battle absenteeism. The escalation of the Vietnam War in the mid- to late 1960s coincided with Cuba's feverish attempts to develop the economy in a last-ditch effort to resist total economic dependency on the Soviets. The unrealistic ten-million-ton target for the 1970 sugar harvest, along with rising rates of absenteeism in the workforce, resulted in an enormous campaign to rally the population for agricultural labor in the late 1960s.[68] Demand for labor turned government attention toward the "reserve pool" of labor represented by women who were not in the formal workforce. As a result, one of the FMC's primary activities in the late 1960s was to mobilize women across the country to perform voluntary agricultural labor.[69] As Vilma Espín warned at an FMC plenary in December 1970, "We can't leave underdevelopment [behind] until all the women fit to work are doing so."[70] Indeed, some male leaders angrily blamed the ultimate failure of the 1970 harvest on idle women and housewives.[71] For Cuban leaders, then, women and their labor formed a linchpin of the island's desperately needed economic takeoff.

For this reason, evidence of Vietnamese women's commitment to labor had special resonance in Cuba in this period. A nearly constant emphasis on labor, especially agricultural labor, as the current stage of Cuba's anti-imperialist struggle was the prism through which the Vietnamese example was filtered in the 1960s, both by the FMC and the Comité. FMC leaders Yolanda Ferrer and Vilma Espín, as well as other FMC delegates who traveled to the DRV in 1969 and 1970, all commented extensively on how impressed they were by Vietnamese women's incorporation into production. After her 1969 trip, Ferrer praised women's roles in production and defense, writing that there was not "one single task" that Vietnamese women did not participate in.[72] After her 1970 trip, Espín described extensively on television how she had seen women taking over factory work previously done by men.[73] And in her speech at the World Congress of Women in Helsinki in 1969, Espín explicitly connected these themes—Vietnam's anti-imperialist struggle, Cuba's corresponding "battle" of production, and women's "heroism":

> The Viet Nam Solidarity movement is ever-present in the minds of our people. Without abandoning . . . our preparedness to defend ourselves against enemy aggression[, w]e are at present waging the main battle in production. We . . . consider the struggle of the Vietnamese people, exemplified by that of the heroines of Viet Nam, as our own. Our farm labor brigades bear their names, and in homage to them, we . . . pursue [production targets].[74]

Vietnamese groups also stressed women's simultaneous participation in combat and in productive labor. For example, this was a core message of the VWU, which included among its "three duties" the demand that women should carry on production and fight when necessary. And the VWU's magazine *Women of Viet Nam* often featured photos of women working with rifles temporarily at rest nearby. But in addition to showcasing women in work or defense, the NLF also seemed to emphasize leisure, at least approved forms of leisure, such as popular theater or music, in the midst of warfare and work, perhaps as evidence of the indominable spirit of those in the war zones. For example, during their 1965 tour, Rojas and Valdés Vivó were repeatedly exposed to examples of music, orchestras, theater, and cultural publications.[75] Yet Cuban media more often focused on the importance of maintaining productive labor in the face of hardship.[76] Thus the issue of labor provides an example of where Cuban messaging built on, yet slightly diverged from, the messaging of the NLF and VWU.

The emphasis on the inspirational Vietnamese capacity for labor was clearly articulated in the campaign the Comité launched in 1969, "As in Vietnam," which included events throughout the year to commemorate the tenth anniversary of the NLF's founding, but which also coincided with preparations for Cuba's Ten Million Ton Harvest. The slogan enjoined Cubans to emulate their ostensibly harder-working and more politically committed Vietnamese counterparts. When, in spring of 1969, Melba Hernández proclaimed that Che's "New Man" could be found in Vietnam, she implied that Cubans would need to follow Vietnam's example in order to achieve the levels of determination and sacrifice that the impending Ten Million Ton sugar harvest would require.[77]

For the "As in Vietnam" campaign, the Comité produced a series of posters—hung up by the hundreds around the country and reproduced in the media—that explicitly paired images of Vietnamese warriors with Cuban agricultural laborers. As the Comité explained, "Solidarity activities with Vietnam served, as always, to

FIGURE 2.3. A 1970 poster by René Mederos urges Cuban workers to emulate their Vietnamese counterparts. The caption reads, "As in Vietnam: tenacity, organization, discipline, daily heroism in work." The poster was printed by the Comité Cubano de Solidaridad con Viet Nam del Sur. Courtesy Lincoln Cushing / Docs Populi archive.

stimulate productive tasks among Cuban workers."⁷⁸ The Comité had designed emulation campaigns before. But unlike those earlier campaigns, with their vague references to sacrifice, the 1969–70 campaign posed the duty of Cubans in agriculture much more explicitly.

One of the posters from the "As in Vietnam" campaign, created by legendary printmaker René Mederos, captures the way Vietnamese women could serve as models even for Cuban men. The poster features a man, portrayed in black and white on the bottom half of the poster, cutting cane with a machete. The upper half of the poster shows a Vietnamese woman depicted in color, also engaged in agricultural labor, but with a rifle prominently strapped to her back. The figures are connected in a way that suggests the Cuban man is picturing the Vietnamese woman as he works, so that the image simultaneously suggests two parallel anti-imperialist struggles as well as the socialist concept of emulation. It is an interesting example for its subversion of gender expectations, as only the woman is armed for combat, and for implying that even Cuban men should emulate Vietnamese women. Scholarship on the New Man has stressed more aggressive, typically masculine qualities, such as waging guerrilla warfare, but the concept could also emphasize internationalist commitments and, at least in this case, striving to emulate the exceptionally "heroic" women of Vietnam.

The linking of solidarity with Vietnam and agricultural labor in this period reminds us that internationalist commitment was not limited to the Cubans who traveled abroad to offer military, medical, or educational support—it could also be demonstrated by dedication to national production, inspired by the example of Vietnam. It also reminds us how much the state's emphasis on forging productive citizens with proper revolutionary consciousness in this period was bound up with ideals of internationalist dedication, spurred by examples from other national liberation movements and revolutionary states.[79]

Conclusions

The symbol of the revolutionary Vietnamese woman spread around the globe in the late 1960s. Cuba, too, embraced and disseminated the symbol, using it to stress that women's emancipation could be achieved partly through their participation in national liberation movements. If Cuban discourse in the early 1960s could be more tentative and ambivalent regarding women's militancy, these ideas were fortified by Cuban understandings of the struggle in Vietnam. Vietnam, a small impoverished postcolonial country engaged in direct conflict with US forces, provided inspiring examples of women's anti-imperialist dedication. The Vietnam War helped consolidate Cuba's emerging understanding of women's liberation, particularly the necessity of women's participation in revolutionary guerrilla warfare and the fact that national liberation and women's liberation would be mutually constitutive. In many ways, these Cuban ideas reflected domestic reinterpretations of NLF and DRV messaging, but slightly repurposed for a Cuban context. Cuban messaging put strong emphasis on the Vietnamese woman as aspirational partly because of her dedication to labor, offering analogies that situated Cuba's own current anti-imperialist struggle as primarily a battle for production.

Cuba's engagement with Vietnam helps us understand the way Cuban leaders like Vilma Espín conceptualized women's emancipation in this period. While in Cuba they often emphasized women joining the paid labor force and acquiring political consciousness, they also argued for the necessity of women's active participation in national liberation struggles globally.[80] And they insisted that women's emancipation would require profound structural changes and true national autonomy. In 1975, at the International Women's Year Conference in Mexico City, Espín gave a blistering speech that highlighted the necessary intertwining of national liberation and women's liberation. She contrasted the oppression of women in capitalist countries and the colonial world with the advances of women in the Socialist Bloc. She praised Vietnam as the culmination of the postwar wave of decolonization: "The triumph of the people is inevitable when one fights ardently to conquer it. Vietnam has demonstrated this. In all those struggles, women have been present."[81] For Espín, national liberation was, ipso facto, women's emancipation. That conference and other events helped draw Cold War battle lines between the feminisms of the Global North, which stressed legal equality and sexual autonomy, and those of the Global South, which stressed the intertwined nature of gender and class inequality. As this essay has argued, these consequential ideas were developed transnationally, especially in encounters between Cuba and Vietnam.

Acknowledgments

The author would like to thank Isabella Cosse and Lorraine Bayard de Volo for their comments on previous drafts.

Notes

1. "El ejemplo de las mujeres vietnamitas en su lucha por la liberación, contra el imperialismo yankqui, es único en la historia, no solo constituye un ejemplo para nosotros, sino para todos los pueblos." As cited in Marta Rojas, "Destaca Vilma Espín ejemplo de las mujeres vietnamitas," *Granma*, January 22, 1966, 6. The Vietnamese women delegates were Dang Thi Thanh (for the DRV) and Le Thi Cad (for the NLF).

2. On the embrace of revolutionary Vietnamese women by feminist, maternalist, Black radical, and New Left groups, especially in the United States and Canada, see Judy Wu, *Radicals on the Road: Internationalism, Orientalism, and Feminism During the Vietnam Era* (Cornell University Press, 2013).

3. See Thy Phu, *Warring Visions: Photography and Vietnam* (Duke University Press, 2022), for an in-depth discussion of how the figure of the revolutionary woman was debated within Vietnam (both north and south), and intentionally disseminated internationally. Phu argues that we should see the revolutionary Vietnamese woman as not just an image but a symbol or icon, laden with meaning, that "conjure[d] a collective, a sense of solidarity" (89).

4. Jocelyn Olcott, *International Women's Year: The Greatest Consciousness-Raising Event in History* (Oxford University Press, 2017); Kristin Ghodsee, *Second World, Second Sex: Socialist Women's Activism and Global Solidarity During the Cold War* (Duke University Press, 2019).

5. Anne Garland Mahler, *From the Tricontinental to the Global South: Race, Radicalism, and Transnational Solidarity* (Duke University Press, 2018); R. Joseph Parrot and Mark Atwood Lawrence, *The Tricontinental Revolution: Third World Radicalism and the Cold*

War (Cambridge University Press, 2022); Jessica Stites Mor, *South-South Solidarity and the Latin American Left* (University of Wisconsin Press, 2022).

6. On the Vietnam War as a "war of the people," see Miguel Ribas, "Ni la bomba atomica salvará a Estados Unidos en Viet Nam," *Granma*, June 10, 1967, 6. On Cuba's dogmatic insistence on armed revolution in this period, see Aldo Marchesi, *Latin America's Radical Left: Rebellion and Cold War in the Global 1960s* (Cambridge University Press, 2019).

7. See Lillian Guerra, *Patriots and Traitors in Revolutionary Cuba, 1961–1981* (University of Pittsburgh Press, 2023), 181–82, on the importance the state placed on voluntary manual labor, especially agricultural labor, for forging correct revolutionary consciousness among Cuban citizens, including women.

8. Julie Shayne, *The Revolution Question: Feminisms in El Salvador, Chile, and Cuba* (Rutgers University Press, 2004); Teresa Díaz Canals, *Palabras que definen: Cuba y el feminismo nuestroamericano* (CLACSO, 2015).

9. I have addressed the way Cuban women sought inspiration from national liberation movements and socialist states in Asia in "Hands Off Korea: Women's Internationalist Solidarity and Peace Activism in Early Cold War Cuba," *Journal of Women's History* 32, no. 3 (2020): 64–88, and "Picturing Solidarity: Photography and Cuban Internationalism During the Vietnam War," *Trans Asia Photography* 13, no. 1 (2023).

10. See especially Robert Brigham, *Guerrilla Diplomacy: The NLF's Foreign Relations and the Viet Nam War* (Cornell University Press, 1999).

11. Wu, *Radicals on the Road*; Phu, *Warring Visions*.

12. Brigham, *Guerrilla Diplomacy*.

13. Tanya Harmer and Alberto Martín Álvarez, "Introduction: Globalizing Latin America's Revolutionary Left: Historiography, Approaches, and Context," in *Toward a Global History of Latin America's Revolutionary Left* (University of Florida Press, 2021), 2.

14. *Por Viet Nam: A 10 Años de la Constitución del Comité Cubano de Solidaridad con Viet Nam del Sur, Hoy con Viet Nam, Cambodia y Laos* (Instituto Cubano del Libro, 1974), 27.

15. Photo caption, *Granma*, August 6, 1966, 1.

16. "Ningún revolucionario debe quedarse a la expectativa de lo que ocurre en Viet Nam, dicen las FAR guatemaltecas al FNL," *Granma*, July 21, 1966, 6.

17. Jorge Domínguez, *To Make a World Safe for Revolution: Cuba's Foreign Policy* (Harvard University Press, 1989), 127.

18. Raúl Valdés Vivó, *El gran secreto: Cubanos en el camino Ho Chi Minh* (Editora Política, 1990).

19. Domínguez, *To Make a World Safe*, 174.

20. Speech printed as "Cualquier movimiento revolucionario podra contar con Cuba," *Granma*, January 3, 1966, 1, 4–6.

21. "Dedicamos este 26 de julio al heróico pueblo de Viet Nam," *Granma*, July 27, 1966, 1.

22. *Por Viet Nam*, 23, 21. Antoni Kapcia argues that Che may have convinced other Cuban leaders of Vietnam's importance. See his "Revolutionary Soulmates? Cuba's Slow

Discovery of Vietnam," in *Protest in the Vietnam War Era*, ed. Alexander Sedlmaier (Palgrave Macmillan, 2022).

23. "Año del Viet Nam Heroico," *Mujeres*, February 1967, 3.

24. "Entrevista con Hoang Bich Son, jefe de la Misión del FLN en Cuba," *Granma*, December 19, 1965, 5.

25. Domínguez, *To Make a World Safe*, 127.

26. Sergio Alejandro Gómez, "Fidel Taught Us to Love Vietnam," *Granma*, April 6, 2018, http://en.granma.cu/cuba/2018-04-06/fidel-taught-us-to-love-vietnam; Daina Caballero Trujillo, "Fidel and Cuba in the Heart of Vietnam," *Granma*, October 2, 2018, http://en.granma.cu/mundo/2018-10-02/fidel-and-cuba-in-the-heart-of-vietnam06/2/2021.

27. Domínguez, *To Make a World Safe*, 70.

28. Piero Gleijeses, *Conflicting Missions: Havana, Washington, and Africa, 1959-1976* (University of North Carolina Press, 2002), 96.

29. *Por Viet Nam*, 9.

30. *Por Viet Nam*, 10.

31. See Lorraine Bayard de Volo, *Women and the Cuban Insurrection: How Gender Shaped Castro's Victory* (Cambridge University Press, 2018), 97–99, for an analysis of the way gender, race, and class expectations shaped perceptions of the women leaders of the 26th of July Movement.

32. *Por Viet Nam*, 10. As Siwei Wang notes in this volume, she also visited China in the early 1960s.

33. For example, some of the Cuban experts who had traveled to Vietnam in delegations sponsored by the Comité testified in the Russell Tribunal sessions on Vietnam.

34. Tina Mai Chen, "Gendered Globality as a Cold War Framework: International Dimensions of Chinese Female Bodies in the 1960s," *positions: asia critique* 28, no. 3 (2020): 603-30; Tina Mai Chen, "Socialism, Aestheticized Bodies, and International Circuits of Gender: Soviet Female Film Stars in the People's Republic of China, 1949-1969," *Journal of the Canadian Historical Association* 18, no. 2 (2007): 53-80; Juliane Noth, "Militiawomen, Red Guards, and Images of Female Militancy in Maoist China," *Twentieth-Century China* 46, no. 2 (2021): 153-80.

35. Mary Nash, "Women in War: Milicianas and Armed Combat in Revolutionary Spain, 1936-1939," *International History Review* 15, no. 2 (1993): 269-82; also see Lillian Guerra, *Visions of Power in Cuba: Revolution, Redemption, and Resistance, 1959-1971* (University of North Carolina Press, 2012), 240-42.

36. Chen, "Socialism," 71.

37. Anna Krylova, *Soviet Women in Combat* (Cambridge University Press, 2011); Suzy Kim, "From Violated Girl to Revolutionary Woman: The Politics of Sexual Difference from China to North Korea," *positions: asia critique* 28, no. 3 (2020): 631-57.

38. Kim, "From Violated Girl"; Wang Zheng, *Finding Women in the State: A Socialist Feminist Revolution in the People's Republic of China, 1949-1964* (University of California Press, 2017).

39. Chen, "Gendered Globality"; Chen, "Socialism"; Kim, "From Violated Girl."

40. Nash, "Women in War"; Krylova, *Soviet Women in Combat*.

41. Noth, "Militiawomen," 163.

42. Siwei Wang, in this volume, shows how Cuban-Chinese dialogues around proper revolutionary gender expressions dovetailed in the 1962 Chinese production of the Cuban play *Cane Field*.

43. Phu, *Warring Visions*, 26.

44. Phu, *Warring Visions*, 86, 90; Wu, *Radicals on the Road*.

45. For recent explorations of how this image circulated in the Global South, see Thy Phu, Evyn Lê Espiritu Gandhi, and Donya Ziaee, "Icon of Solidarity: The Revolutionary Vietnamese Woman in Vietnam, Palestine, and Iran," in *Cold War Camera*, ed. Thy Phu, Erina Duganne, and Andrea Noble (Duke University Press, 2023). For a recent study of Socialist Bloc women's activism in Vietnam, see Francisca de Haan, "The Vietnam Activities of the Women's International Democratic Federation (WIDF)," in Sedlmaier, *Protest in the Vietnam War Era*, 51–82.

46. I have addressed the role of photography in consolidating Cuba-Vietnam solidarity in Chase, "Picturing Solidarity."

47. Marta Rojas, "Con armas de fuego y razón," *Granma*, December 31, 1965.

48. Róger Calero, "Feria del libro de La Habana destaca la solidaridad entre Cuba y Vietnam," *El Militante*, March 2, 2020, https://themilitant.com/2020/02/22/feria-del-libro-de-la-habana-destaca-la-solidaridad-entre-cuba-y-vietnam/.

49. On the NLF's organization of the itinerary, see Marta Rojas, "Phong: Viento de rebeldía," *Granma*, November 30, 1965, 6. Indeed, many of the same messages transmitted to Rojas and Valdés Vivó were later reiterated by subsequent Cuban journalists, such as about the safety of children in war zones, the support of intellectuals, the continuation of cultural life within the liberated zones, and the danger inflicted by US attacks—suggesting that the NLF sought to convey a cohesive set of messages.

50. Raúl Valdés Vivó, "El glorioso apellido de innumerables hermanos," *Granma*, December 15, 1965, 5.

51. Marta Rojas, "Espaldarazo al 'poder,'" *Granma*, December 22, 1965, 4.

52. In January of that year, the Tricontinental Congress brought Vietnamese women delegates into direct contact with the FMC leadership, perhaps for the first time. One month later, the FMC's second-in-command, Dora Carcaño, joined a ten-day delegation to Vietnam, led by the Soviet-sponsored Women's International Democratic Federation (WIDF). The same month, Espín announced that International Women's Day in March 1966 would be dedicated to the women of Vietnam. I thank Francisca de Haan for sending me the WIDF pamphlet that was published after the 1966 visit, *Vietnam: Une délégation de la Fédération Démocratique Internationale des Femmes*, which reprints Carcaño's statement. For a study of the WIDF's involvement in Vietnam, see de Haan, "Vietnam Activities of the WIDF."

53. In late 1965 Prensa Latina's Hanoi correspondent published an interview with Li Thi Xuan, vice president of the Vietnamese Women's Union, that also discussed the "three re-

sponsibilities." Jesús Martí Díaz, "Madre, productora y combatiente: la mujer vietnamita," *Granma*, November 13, 1965, 2.

54. Marta Rojas, "Hermanas de Armas (IV y final): Doblemente Heroicas," *Granma*, December 22, 1966, 2.

55. Marta Rojas, "Hermanas de Armas (III): Vietnam como ejemplo," *Granma*, December 21, 1966, 2.

56. Rojas, "Hermanas de Armas (IV y final)."

57. Marta Rojas, "Hermanas de Armas: La mujer en el primer plano de la lucha en Viet Nam (I)," *Granma*, December 17, 1966, 2.

58. Nguyen Thi Dinh, "El papel y la capacidad de la mujer sudvietnamita dentro del movimiento de guerra de guerrillas, en la etapa de ofensivas generales y levantamientos simultáneos," *Granma*, March 10, 1969, 7.

59. Roberto Díaz, "Luchamos por la independencia, la paz, y el futuro feliz de la familia," *Mujeres*, April 1976, 68–69.

60. Wu, *Radicals on the Road*.

61. Magalí García, "Llego a nuestro país la heroína sudvietnamita Nguyen Thi Dinh," *Granma*, July 19, 1974, 2.

62. Mario G. Del Cueto et al., "En Cuba: Diario de una conferencia," *Bohemia*, January 7, 1966, 58–73.

63. Marta Rojas, *Escenas de Viet Nam* (Instituto Cubano del Libro, 1971), 77.

64. Bayard de Volo, *Women and the Cuban Insurrection*, 210–12. For a history of the woman's battalion, see Teté Puebla, *Marianas en Combate: Tete Puebla y el pelotón femenino Mariana Grajales en la guerra revolucionaria cubana, 1956-58* (Pathfinder Press, 2003).

65. De Volo discusses reluctance within the Rebel Army to accept women as combatants. See *Women and the Cuban Insurrection*, 212–16.

66. For example, in 1959 Teté Puebla was named head of an army unit dedicated to helping the family of war victims; beginning in 1964 she oversaw schools for war orphans and ran a Social Security program for the army in Oriente. Puebla, *Marianas*, 59–61.

67. Stites Mor, *South-South Solidarity*; Lani Hanna, "Tricontinental's International Solidarity: Emotion in OSPAAAL as Tactic to Catalyze Support of Revolution," *Radical History Review* 136 (2020): 169–84; Alberto García Molinero, *La imagen trincontinental: La feminidad, el Che Guevara, y el imperialismo a través del arte grafico de la OSPAAAL* (Ariadna, 2022).

68. We still await social histories of the massive 1970 harvest, but Rachel Hynson gives some insight into the long work hours and other sacrifices it required. See her *Laboring for the State: Women, Family, and Work in Revolutionary Cuba, 1959-1971* (Cambridge University Press, 2020).

69. For example, the FMC mobilized thousands of women to work in agriculture to celebrate International Women's Day in 1968 and 1969, and other symbolic dates. Guerra, *Visions of Power*, 241.

70. "No podemos salir del subdesarrollo mientras todas las mujeres aptas para trabajar no lo estén haciendo," *Granma*, December 11, 1970, 3.

71. Michelle Chase, *Revolution within the Revolution: Women and Gender Politics in Cuba, 1952–1962* (University of North Carolina Press, 2015), 169.

72. Yolanda Ferrer, "Mujeres del Viet Nam Heroico," *Mujeres*, October 1967, 56–58.

73. "Cuando se habla de Viet Nam, está presente en todo momento Ho Chi Minh," *Granma*, May 28, 1970, 4.

74. "Cuba: Vilma Espín de Castro," *Women of the Whole World* 4 (1969), 6.

75. See "En Vietnam todo el pueblo pelea con todas las armas," *Granma*, November 21, 1965, 6.

76. René Mederos's brilliant set of silk screens, based on his 1969 trip, is one exception, including depictions of the cultural events that the NLF tried to highlight.

77. "'En Viet Nam existe ese hombre nuevo de que habló el Che,' dijo Melba Hernandez," *Granma*, May 5, 1969, 3.

78. *Por Viet Nam*, 126–27.

79. On state projects to mold revolutionary citizens and mentalities in the 1960s and 1970s, see Guerra, *Patriots and Traitors*.

80. See Rafael Cesar's contribution in this volume on the way this imaginary was projected in Angola.

81. Espín, "Sólo cambios profundos en las estructuras económicas y sociales ponen fin a las desigualdades para alanzar la liberación de la mujer," *Granma*, June 26, 1975.

THREE

Angela Davis in Cuba as Symbol and Subject, 1960–1970s

SARAH J. SEIDMAN

There is a photograph in Angela Y. Davis's recently deposited archive that speaks volumes about her time in Cuba.[1] The candid snapshot shows Davis flanked by Fidel Castro on one side and government official Telma Bornot, who coordinated Davis's visit to the island in 1972, on the other. Davis's fellow visitors and comrades Franklin and Kendra Alexander stand nearby with several women. Almost everyone is turned toward Davis, who is in turn looking at a wall of posters bearing her image and name.[2]

The image of Davis peering at representations of herself is one of countless photographs of the activist-scholar taken in Cuba after she was targeted by the US government in 1970, was defended by leftist activists worldwide as a global symbol of repression and resistance, and initiated a tour of socialist countries who had mobilized for her release. As this photograph exemplifies, more than the many other African American activists who encountered the Cuban Revolution in the 1960s and 1970s through visits or exile, Davis was exalted in Cuba through both her iconic image and her physical self.

In this chapter, I explore how gender facilitated encounters between Angela Y. Davis and the Cuban Revolution during those decades. Davis has written that her identity as a "black woman Communist" precipitated US government actions against her.[3] This identity in turn strengthened Davis's relationship with Cuba, whose socialist state, large Black population, and purported egalitarianism toward women drew the scholar and activist several times beginning in 1969. I argue that Davis's gender, operating in tandem with her socialism, Blackness, and membership in the American Communist Party (CPUSA), provided a stage that

FIGURE 3.1. Angela Davis, *fourth from right*, with Telma Bornot, *fourth from left*, Fidel Castro, *third from right*, Franklin and Kenda Alexander, *second and third from left*, and others at an exhibition in Havana featuring posters about Davis. Unknown photographer, 1972. Angela Davis Papers, Schlesinger Library, Harvard Radcliffe Institute.

did not exist for the range of prominent, noncommunist, Black male activists and intellectuals who allied with the Cuban Revolution in the 1960s and 1970s. The institutional scaffolding created by the Cuban Communist Party (Partido Comunista de Cuba, PCC) and particularly the Federation of Cuban Women (Federación de Mujeres Cubanas, FMC) gave Davis officially sanctioned and highly visible platforms from which to speak and be seen. The visibility the Cuban state provided helped solidify Davis as a symbol of US repression, and her freedom as a victory for international solidarity.

Davis was part of a broader network of African American activists who encountered the Cuban Revolution in the 1960s and 1970s.[4] Delegations from the Student Nonviolent Coordinating Committee (SNCC), the *Black Scholar* journal, and the Black Panther Party visited the island; Robert F. Williams, Eldridge Cleaver, and Huey P. Newton all lived there in political exile, while Stokely Carmichael enjoyed a standing offer to take refuge there. Assata Shakur, and others, stayed. Many of these figures grew disillusioned with Cuba along racial lines; others lodged critiques but remained supportive of the revolutionary project. A large body of work on racism in Cuba has woven African American visitors' and exiles' experiences into arguments showing how pronouncements of racial equality in Cuba remained disconnected from ongoing racism and in fact facilitated repression of Black nationalism of Black citizens and visitors alike.[5] While some have explored gender and sexuality in these studies, fewer scholars have examined African American women's experiences with the revolution in the 1960s and 1970s.[6] Davis was the only famous woman in the Black liberation movement who sought solidarity or refuge in Cuba during those decades—and no one else was treated the way she was.[7] Limited access to Cuban archives has led to a reliance on African Americans' own writings and Cuban print publications as sources, here complemented by archival materials from both Cuba and the United States held in US archives. The problem of archives and the marginalization of Afro-Cuban accounts has contributed to a piecemeal historiography on African American and Cuban connections, none of which has thoroughly engaged with Angela Davis's encounters with Cuba. In addition to her reception on the island, this chapter centers Davis's own experiences there in the late 1960s and 1970s and the meaning she made of Cuban solidarity.

Davis has had a singular presence on the US Left and in Cuba among both government entities and everyday people. In addition to being an African American woman and a onetime member of the CPUSA, Davis is an accomplished professional academic and public intellectual who spent sixteen months in jail after being accused and ultimately acquitted of murder. She is a historic figure who continues to have impact, yet she is wary of her idolization and private about her personal life. Davis's attributes—her education, cosmopolitanism, and appearance—attracted widespread interracial interest.[8] Her combined anti-imperialism, anti-racism, and Marxist orientation appealed particularly to Cuban leaders as well as everyday Cubans. Taking an intersectional approach to understanding how Davis's identity and ideology were expressed in Cuba and interpreted by the Cuban state—and focusing on the role of gender within this mix—teaches us about not only Davis's unique positionality but also the complexities of transnational solidarity and the Cuban revolutionary project.

BECOMING ANGELA DAVIS

Davis's upbringing laid the foundation for her activism: her dedication to racial justice, her membership in the CPUSA, and her advocacy of gender equality. Born to a politically engaged middle-class family in 1944 in Birmingham, Alabama, family friends included Black CPUSA members James Jackson and Esther Cooper Jackson and the family of Carole Robertson, who was killed in the 1964 bombing of the Sixteenth Street Baptist Church. Intent on leaving the segregation and racial terrorism that gave the city the nickname "Bombingham," Davis finished high school at the progressive Elisabeth Irwin School in New York City, where she lived with a family in Brooklyn and participated in the city's Marxist youth culture.[9]

The Cuban Revolution played an important role in Davis's burgeoning internationalism. In 1962 Davis traveled abroad for the first time to Helsinki, Finland, for the Eighth World Festival for Youth and Students, founded as a postwar anti-fascist international friendship organization that brought youth from around the world to countries in the Soviet sphere. In Helsinki it was the Cubans, wearing pins of doves with machine guns and moving their delegation's conga line from the stage into the audience and then the street, that struck Davis as the festival's "most impressive event."[10] Davis later furthered her understanding of colonialism while studying abroad in Paris as a college student at Brandeis University and pursued graduate studies with Frankfurt School theorist Theodor Adorno in Germany. She attended the Dialectics of Liberation Conference in London in 1967, where she heard Stokely Carmichael speak about the Third World before he flew to Havana for the Organization of Latin American Solidarity (Organización Latinoamericana de Solidaridad, OLAS) conference. These travels and interactions helped Davis form a global philosophy of liberation. "The new places, the new experiences I had expected to discover through travel turned out to be the same old places," she wrote in the early 1970s, "the same old experiences with a common message of struggle."[11] These formative experiences shaped decades of Davis's public life, from a transnational approach to scholarship to activism regarding Palestinian liberation and ongoing solidarity with Cuba.

In addition to her internationalism and interest in socialism, gender drove Davis to find a political community that would ultimately lead her to Cuba. A longing to participate in the Black liberation movement brought Davis back to the United States, where she resumed graduate studies with Herbert Marcuse at the University of California, San Diego, and became active on campus and in Los Angeles. Davis grew frustrated with the gender politics of groups like the largely autonomous West Coast branch of SNCC, critiquing their resistance to Marxism and internal dissent. Men she encountered tended to "confuse their political activity with an assertion of their maleness."[12] In search of an intellectual and political collective, she joined the CPUSA in the summer of 1968. In particular, the party's new Che-Lumumba Club, affiliated with the Southern California chapter, beckoned. An all-Black collective started by Charlene Mitchell and Franklin and

Kendra Alexander the previous year, the club taught Marxist ideology and engaged with college students, workers, and community members in Los Angeles. The club reflected the political flexibility of the California Communist Party under the leadership of women such as Mitchell and Dorothy Healy, in contrast to a more centralized, doctrinaire, and male-led party in New York.[13] As Black power gained ascendance and the CPUSA struggled to remain relevant, Mitchell, the Alexanders, and above all Davis offered ties between the Old Left and the New. These ties would prove crucial to connecting with the Cuban Revolution.

In the summer of 1969, Davis embarked on a transformative visit to Cuba. Traveling with a CPUSA delegation for the annual July 26 Cuban independence celebration, the group traversed the island and worked in coffee and sugarcane fields as part of the *gran zafra* (great harvest) campaign to cut ten million tons of sugarcane for the 1970 season as an economic and symbolic victory for the revolution. Davis participated in official activities common to visiting delegations and spent time with Cuban residents of a small town on the eastern end of the island where they lived and worked.[14] We "began to feel as if we had taken root in this small village in Oriente," she recalled. Despite not speaking Spanish, or perhaps because of this, she felt particularly accepted by Cuban children. Davis called the trip "a great climax in my life. Politically I felt infinitely more mature."[15] The energy of the Cuban Revolution—first encountered as a conga line through the Helsinki streets—and its defiance of the United States had a profound effect. "The Cubans' limitless revolutionary enthusiasm" left "a permanent mark" on Davis's existence.[16]

Davis's 1969 visit came at an important moment for Cuba's relationship to the world. As the revolution completed a decade in power, some allies shifted. As the government increased censorship and embarked on a period of cultural repression that came to be called the Quinquenio Gris (Gray Years) by 1971, it lost previous supporters in the global arena, particularly European intellectuals. Yet the same period witnessed the rise of new forms of solidarity: 1969 inaugurated the Venceremos Brigade, interracial delegations of Americans who traveled to Cuba to work on the *gran zafra* and tour the island. Although the harvests failed, the brigades and the model they established with the Cuban state continued for decades. Davis recounted Castro himself explaining the Cuban state's shift from "emphasizing armed struggle to mobilizing mass movements" and hosting delegations rather than exalting individuals.[17]

The late 1960s also reflected a new strategy regarding the Cuban leadership's search for African American allies. As the revolution's most experimental phase ended, its visible solidarity with individuals in the Black liberation movement came to a close. But African Americans continued to look to Cuba's shores, and Cuban leaders embraced organized delegations and a quieter hosting of subsequent exiles as part of the turn toward institutionalizing the revolution.[18] In an extraordinary statement Davis delivered privately to fellow CPUSA members after her visit in 1972, Davis claimed that Castro had told her that the government was increasingly interested in working with African American communists after previous encounters with Black activists had soured. Naming Robert F. Williams, Stokely Carmichael, and Eldridge Cleaver, Davis recalled Castro saying that when these figures "turned on Cuba and criticized the Cuban Revolution, criticized socialism," the Cuban state "felt that they had been in error by establishing such strong relationships with them at that time."[19] The Cuban government never spoke out publicly about these interactions, making this admission, as reported by Davis, quite unusual. Yet the summer of 1969 encapsulated this shift: as Cuban leadership sent the controversial Black Power Movement figure Eldridge Cleaver off of the island on a plane bound for Algeria, it welcomed the Venceremos Brigade, Davis's delegation, and a separate delegation by Black CPUSA leader Henry Winston.

Like many other Black visitors, Davis paid close attention to the racial politics of the revolution and its convergence with socialism. As one of three people of color on her delegation, she recounted the trio discussing it "incessantly." Davis lauded the revolutionary state for opposing segregation in Cuba upon its seizing of power in 1959—which occurred through laws such as land redistribution and free health care, and an antidiscrimination campaign announced by Castro.[20] Moreover, she emphasized the revolution's gains toward "the destruction of the material base of racism." Davis wrote of seeing Black Cubans in the workforce in "factories, schools, hospitals and wherever else we went." Davis never declared racist practices in Cuba over, and her repeated comments about Cubans of all skin tones interacting suggests an overemphasis on everyday contact over the racial repression that persisted from white government leadership. But she wrote that she was "immensely impressed" by Cuba's efforts to eradicate racism, and convinced that "only under socialism could this fight against racism have been so successfully executed."[21]

Davis wrote less about women after her 1969 visit, but she recognized the roles Cuban women played in the revolution and the challenges they faced. On the one hand, she was impressed with the militancy of Cuban women, writing admiringly to incarcerated activist and close friend George Jackson after her first trip to the island of "women patrolling the streets with rifles on their backs—defending the revolution." On the other hand, she alluded to sexism in Cuba, describing "young *compañeras* educating their husbands and lovers—demythologizing *machismo*."[22]

While many white women who traveled to Cuba with the Venceremos Brigade struggled with feelings of alienation from Cuban women and perceived of their gender roles in society as objectifying, Davis, along with members of the Third World Women's Alliance who also traveled with the Venceremos Brigade, wrote about Cuban women more from a vantage point of kinship than distance.[23] As the 1970s progressed, Davis increasingly viewed gender as a crucial variable for the Cuban revolutionary project.

Davis's first trip to Cuba coincided with her catapult into the public sphere. Around the time of her visit in the summer of 1969, a student and FBI informant writing for the University of California, Los Angeles (UCLA) newspaper mentioned the Communist Party membership of a newly hired philosophy professor. The *San Francisco Examiner* picked up the article, named Davis, and published her home address and information related to a recent legal gun purchase.[24] The UCLA regents sought to terminate Davis immediately in response. She successfully appealed amid ongoing threats, but her teaching contract was not renewed. A year later, in August 1970, the state of California implicated Davis in the deaths of a judge, district attorney, and jurors taken hostage during courtroom proceedings against one of the three "Soledad Brothers" accused of killing a guard at a central California prison.[25] Davis was far from the courthouse that day, but authorities charged her with conspiracy, kidnapping, and murder. Proclaiming her innocence and questioning her ability to receive a fair trial, Davis went underground for two months before her apprehension in New York in October 1970.[26] She spent sixteen months in jail in New York and California and endured a highly publicized seven-month trial that at one point sought the death penalty. Ultimately, she was acquitted of all charges.

Davis's connection with Cuba hardened ideological sentiment and US government action against her. While the press did not report on her visit to the island during the summer of 1969, a lengthy article published in the *Los Angeles Times* when Davis was underground suggested a connection between her visit and her alleged role in the subsequent events in Marin County. Claiming "the pattern is clear," conservative columnist Georgie Anne Geyer and foreign correspondent Keyes Beech characterized Castro's Cuba as a "revolutionary factory for the processing and refining of American radicals for export back to the United States."[27] The media also repeatedly suggested that Davis had fled there, particularly when her sister Fania Davis was identified on a Canadian boat bound for the island with the Venceremos Brigade in the summer of 1970.[28] Fania was still in Cuba when Davis was captured.[29] While Davis wrote that she had considered and then rejected the idea of fleeing abroad and specifically to Cuba, her connection there nevertheless helped cast her as a subversive enemy of the United States.

Icon of Repression

During the course of her imprisonment and trial, Davis became a contested symbol of persecution. The Black liberation movement expressed widespread support for and identification with Davis. James Baldwin wrote to her in prison, "We must fight for your life as though it were our own—which it is," while the *Black Scholar* echoed in an editorial, "Her struggle is our struggle, and her victory shall be our victory."[30] Groups such as the Third World Women's Alliance and Harlem Black Women to Free Angela Davis rallied around Davis during her imprisonment and trial. White women such as Gloria Steinem also participated in the Free Angela Davis campaign, but Davis's case became a wedge issue in the burgeoning US women's movement. Stories of Betty Friedan asking the Third World Women's Alliance to put down signs supporting Davis at the 1970 Women's Strike for Equality March in New York spread far and wide. Third World Women's Alliance founder Frances Beale's experience of being told that "Angela Davis has nothing to do with women's liberation," and her response that Davis had "everything to do with the kind of liberation we're talking about," reflected the conflicts of the US women's movement.[31]

Under the leadership of Fania Davis and fellow CPUSA member Franklin Alexander, the National United Committee to Free Angela Davis (NUCFAD) sustained a highly organized campaign that framed Davis's fight as part of a larger struggle of incarcerated and oppressed people in the United States and beyond.[32] A range of global solidarity groups—less divided by US debates—called for Davis's freedom, and women often mobilized for her through the Women's International Democratic Federation.[33] Davis received particular support from Germany and France, where she had lived.[34] John Abt, a CPUSA member on Davis's legal team, found that, like Black communities in the United States, internationally "people everywhere not only identify with her but see her freedom struggle as indissolubly linked with their own aspirations." Fania Davis emphasized, "It's up to the entire world to save her."[35] Angela Davis acknowledged the effects of her support around the world. The movement abroad "exerted serious pressure on the government," she affirmed in her autobiography, and "stimulated the further growth of the mass movement at home."[36]

Cuba played an integral role in the global campaign to free Davis. As it had done with other global solidarity campaigns, the Cuban state apparatus mobilized various sectors around her liberation. A government-led multiagency committee formed devoted to her release. Advocates ranging from schoolchildren to government leaders spoke out in her defense. Two songs, "Por Ángela," by the prominent Cuban songwriter Tania Castellanos, and "Canción para Ángela Davis," written by Pablo Milanés on a record by Milanés and Silvio Rodriguez (Cuba's two largest names in *nueva trova*), reflected her prevalence in popular culture and reached Davis in jail. Moreover, Cuba helped cement the image of Davis as a global signifier for US repression: the Organization of Solidarity with the Peoples of Africa, Asia, and Latin America (Organización de Solidaridad de los Pueblos de Africa, Asia, y América Latina, OSPAAAL) declared that the charges against her were "against the entire black movement," while the magazine *Romances* echoed that Davis symbolized the African American freedom struggle and the fight against US imperialism.[37] The Cuban press provided extensive, continuous coverage with images, while the state's seasoned propaganda arm created a range of graphics—including perhaps the best-known poster of Davis worldwide. Artist Elizabeth Catlett wrote in a letter to the scholar Bettina Aptheker, a longtime friend and defense lawyer to Davis, that "her picture is seen in remote places" on the island, and that no one "had not heard of her struggle."[38]

Cuban women's initiatives spearheaded by the Federation of Cuban Women formed to proclaim her innocence and free her from prison. A petition for Davis was a central component of the March 8, 1971, International Women's Day Conference in Havana. Catlett, the African American artist based in Mexico City who attended the conference, characterized the petition as a unifying gesture for disparate women, "one way of joining together in a common cause."[39] In June of that year the Federation of Cuban Women convened a meeting to form the Comité de Solidaridad con Angela Davis, or Solidarity Committee with Angela Davis, devoted to her release.[40] The woman chosen to lead the committee of representatives from a range of Cuban groups had long-standing ties to revolutionary leadership: Telma Bornot, of the Ministry of Armed Forces, had participated in Castro's 26th of July Movement and the founding of the FMC in Oriente Province. The committee denounced the incarceration of Davis to the international community and sought to channel existing solidarity in Cuba.[41] FMC publications *Mujeres* and *Romances* published a stream of coverage of Davis's imprisonment and trial.[42]

Two black-and-white images from the United States and Cuba in 1970 illustrate how Davis became not just a symbol of repression but also a visual icon. The first, a reprint of a somber photograph of her wearing round sunglasses, a dashiki, and her signature halo Afro, appeared alongside another photograph on the "Wanted" flyer for Davis issued that August by the FBI. The second image, a poster drawn by Cuban artist Alfredo Rostgaard folded and shipped internationally as part of the *Tricontinental* magazine created by OSPAAAL, also depicted Davis with round sunglasses and an Afro.[43] Yet Rostgaard's poster, perhaps created in response to the FBI flyer, depicted Davis with two sets of arms, one in handcuffs and the other raised above her head breaking her chains. A halo of light encircled these

FIGURE 3.2. Alfredo Rostgaard, *Angela Davis,* OSPAAAL, 1970. Courtesy Lincoln Cushing / Docs Populi archive.

second arms, exaggerating her Afro and invoking religious icons. Both images, created respectively by US and Cuban state-sanctioned organizations and widely circulated nationally and internationally, helped craft Davis as an icon. If the FBI flyer intended to facilitate her capture and imprisonment, Rostgaard's image sought to set Davis free.

Rostgaard's poster of a statuesque Davis invokes a statue in Cuba that embodies liberation. In the city of Matanzas, a well-known statue of "Cuba Libre" in the form of a woman stands on a step in front of Cuban independence leader José Martí, who rises behind her on a higher pedestal. Unlike the staid Martí, Cuba Libre raises her arms and jubilantly breaks her chains. The statue was erected in the early years of the Cuban Republic, after Spain and then the United States departed Cuba in the aftermath of the Spanish-American War. Rostgaard's image, created while she was in jail, equates Davis with the iconic Cuba Libre and suggests that Davis, like Cuba, can gain freedom from US domination.[44]

The most renowned depiction of Davis emerged from Cuba. Unlike Rostgaard's 1970 poster, which came from the more freewheeling Havana-based international solidarity organization OSPAAAL, Felix Beltrán's 1971 *Libertad Para Angela Davis*

76 Sarah J. Seidman

(Freedom for Angela Davis) came from the Cuban Communist Party. As head of the party's propaganda department, Beltrán was supplied with photographs of Davis and tasked with creating a poster. He likely used a photograph that appeared on flyers from the New York Committee to Free Angela Davis, rendering Davis's profile in stark outline with red skin and black hair against a deep blue background.[45] Beltrán intended the red and blue to invoke the American flag, while the rounded edges of her features reflected his approach to a pop art aesthetic. Beltrán created other unused prototypes of Davis, as well as a second poster for International Children's Day that juxtaposed an image of Davis as a child published in *Newsweek* with the caption "Since she was a girl she suffered discrimination."[46] But it was the blue, black, and red poster, originally printed in a small run in the thousands, that was reproduced beyond Cuba and ended up in poster collections around the world. Variations of the image appeared on magazine covers, postcards, and billboards in Havana.[47] Beltrán's image became the most important image of Davis worldwide.

The proliferation of Davis's image in Cuban iconography far surpassed the visual presence of other African American radicals. While Cuban artists created several posters to express solidarity with the Black liberation movement and groups such as the Black Panther Party, the only other individual represented was George Jackson, in a 1971 poster by Raphael Morante, after he was killed in prison. SNCC leader Stokely Carmichael's 1967 visit elicited a tremendous media presence in the *Tricontinental* magazine and bulletin—referred to by Carmichael as a "bible in revolutionary circles"—but no posters.[48] Robert F. Williams's exile preceded the revolution's graphic apex, but his presence in Cuban discourse emerged through pronouncements or cultural forms such as "Radio Free Dixie," created by Williams himself. Huey Newton, who was added to a preexisting OSPAAAL image made into a postcard after he was jailed in 1968, never appeared on a poster and received no Cuban press coverage during his exile on the island in the mid-1970s.[49]

A postcard-writing campaign using Beltrán's image shows how Cubans further crafted a global iconography of liberation for Davis driven by the state. Several countries sent mail to Davis in jail. France shipped postcards featuring a black-and-white photograph of a rose and the words "Angela Davis" on the front, with cursive prose printed on the back that left room for a personalized signature. East German children created their own unique cards. Cuban postcards featured a pink-and-black version of Beltrán's image of Davis, with the words "Libertad para Angela Davis y sus hermanos de lucha," or "freedom for Angela Davis and her brothers in struggle," on the front, and signatures or messages written or typed on the back. Some were simply signed by individuals or neighborhood Committees for the Defense of the Revolution (Comités de Defensa de la Revolución, CDR), which, as local arms of the Cuban Communist Party, were tasked with organizing this mandatory postcard-writing campaign.[50] Some personal messages, however, suggest how individuals considered Davis. Cecilia Silveira Cabrera explained that she used the familiar *tú* form of "you" because "we consider you a sister," while art school student Angelina D. Garcia invited Davis to Cuba upon her release so that they could "get to know [her] personally."[51] Among the global campaigns for Davis, Cuba's stands out for its unified visual iconography as well as a consistent ideology that foregrounded gender.

Davis's gender was also intrinsic to her representation in Cuban culture. Images rendered her as regal, strong, determined, and feminine. A 1972 article in *Cuba* magazine cited Cuban posters of Davis as contributing to an artistic tradition of portraying women as integral to the Cuban Revolution.[52] Cuban press coverage of Davis took a specific interest in her appearance. One maudlin article in *Granma* described her physique admiringly and at length. The author emphasized her tall and elegant stature, her light-skinned "bronze" coloring, and, most of all, her "large" naturally styled hair, described as cascading over her temples and partially covering her long neck.[53] The FMC-run *Romances* ran an article on Davis alongside a rare fashion spread of Black Cuban model and performer Mayda Limonta.[54] The cover juxtaposed the two faces, Davis drawn in outline, Limonta with processed hair styled in a way that referenced but did not fully promote the Afro.

While Davis's hair and fashion also elicited scrutiny in the United States, appearance in Cuba was more closely regulated by the state. Davis has critiqued the way history depoliticized her struggle to render her "remembered as a hairdo," yet in Cuba, just as in the United States, the Afro attracted political as well as aesthetic interest.[55] Americans in Cuba in the late 1960s recounted receiving or witnessing hostility toward the style's adherents.[56] Both countercultural long hair and overt symbols of Blackness were discouraged on the island; the Afro falls squarely into both subversive categories.[57] Davis's revolutionary credentials and Cuban institutional affiliations with women's groups and communists, however, blunted criticism of her hairstyle. Some have suggested that she made the style more acceptable.

Davis worried about becoming a symbol, yet she acknowledged the power of her own image in determining her fate.[58] "The circulation of various photographic images of me," she later wrote, "played a major role in both the mobilization of public opinion against me and the development of the campaign that was ultimately responsible for my acquittal."[59] Upon her release, the Cuban Committee to Free Angela Davis admitted, "With [good] reason we feel like participants in this great triumph." The group reiterated its invitation to Davis to visit Cuba, given the "extraordinary admiration of our people."[60]

Davis, Gender, and Cuba

Davis's status in Cuban visual culture as a heroic and symbolic figure rose further when she accepted the Cuban state's invitation for a return visit following her acquittal in the fall of 1972. Davis and fellow Black CPUSA members Kendra and Franklin Alexander traveled to the Soviet Union, the German Democratic Republic, Bulgaria, Czechoslovakia, Cuba, and finally Chile, six countries with socialist governments that had played large roles in the campaign to secure her freedom. The trip was intended as an expression of thanks but also a chance to pledge international solidarity in person, witness "socialism in the concrete," and further campaigns at home.[61] Arriving at José Martí International Airport at two in the morning, the three friends and comrades encountered a throng of supporters that would continue to mob them throughout their nine-day visit. Tellingly, the itinerary from the Central Committee of the Cuban Communist Party shows that the first two meetings occurred with the PCC and the FMC. The delegation then traversed the island by plane, meeting with political and cultural leaders as well as everyday Cubans. During a trip to Cuba's Isle of Youth, young student inhabitants clutching flowers "offered their young hearts to the beloved visitor" by flocking to Davis, prompting her to abandon her official motorcade and lead a parade in the torrential rain.[62]

The Cuban state showered Davis with honors, including, in a solemn ceremony with President Osvaldo Dorticós and Fidel Castro, the Orden Playa Girón (Order of the Bay of Pigs)—the highest decoration bestowed by the Cuban government.[63]

Davis reciprocated the show of enthusiasm and support. Speaking to a crowd estimated at three-quarters of a million people in Havana's Plaza de la Revolución during events commemorating the twelfth anniversary of the Cuban CDRs, Davis described the reception upon her arrival in Cuba as the warmest and most enthusiastic of any place she had traveled.[64] On the dais with Castro she described the Cuban Revolution as the "greatest inspiration" for the struggle for socialism and against racism and imperialism in the United States, and referred to Cuba as her "true home."[65] Speaking at the University of Havana upon receiving an honorary doctorate in political science, Davis spoke of unity, "the real possibility of achieving unity in our struggle."[66] Davis did not speak to and was likely not privy to details about internal dissent and repression in Cuba—including at the University of Havana—but instead focused on her reception on the island and the

FIGURE 3.3. Angela Davis in the Plaza de la Revolución with Osvaldo Dorticós, *left,* Fidel Castro, *right,* and others, 1972. From the photo collection held at the Tamiment Library, New York University, by permission of the Communist Party USA.

example of the revolution to others.[67] She acknowledged the support of Cubans "whether three years old or sixty" and upon her departure thanked the Cuban people for receiving her with "such fervor."[68]

Davis's gender offered a particularly effective platform in Cuba from which to be seen. The FMC, the state-supported national women's organization active in Davis's solidarity campaign, hosted her delegation. The FMC provided an institutional structure for Davis unavailable to African American men in Cuba, as there was no male equivalent to the group and organizations based on race had been dissolved and banned in the early years of the revolution. The apparatus of gender provided a stage for Davis to engage with Cuban audiences approved by the highest echelons of government.[69] Gender also shaped her valorization in the Cuban press. Davis's mobilization against the American criminal justice system, and her involvement in anti-racist, anti-imperialist, and anti-capitalist struggles qualified her as a feminized warrior in the existing framework of Cuban revolutionary culture.

Davis's vaunted reception in Cuba occurred in the context of long-standing veneration for the figure of the revolutionary woman warrior in Cuban society. The Cuban trope of militant heroines traces back to the nineteenth century, where *mambisas,* women fighters for Cuban independence, risked their lives and those of their family members to obtain freedom from Spain.[70] The *mambisas* enshrined as symbols in Cuban popular culture and nationalist discourse exuded bravery without sacrificing femininity. Their roles as mothers and sisters were emphasized, suggesting a willingness to risk their bodies, as well as their children and family, for a nationalist cause. Black and white Cuban women had served as such symbols: Afro-Cuban Mariana Grajales Cuello reportedly sent ten of her eleven sons into battle against Spain, including Cuban independence leader Antonio Maceo, and was immortalized as the mother of Cuban independence.[71]

Nearly one hundred years later, women played important roles in the formation of the Cuban Revolution. A small group of women, including Celia Sánchez and Haydée Santamaría, joined Castro's group of rebels in the Sierra Maestra and were immortalized as fighters alongside the *barbudos,* or bearded rebels.[72] Women comprised an estimated 10 to 20 percent of urban underground networks in the late 1950s, where they strategized and relayed messages, provided safe houses, and transported materials with minimal visibility. Cuban women purposefully engaged the trope of maternalism in their fight against Batista, emphasizing their status as mothers, daughters, and wives of martyrs and insurgents. Women also mobilized upon the revolution's victory, creating "Women's Revolutionary Brigades" and women's sections of the 26th of July Movement, which provided a presence at rallies, organized other women at the grassroots level, and generated support for government initiatives.[73]

The Federation of Cuban Women arose from the dismantling of these earlier groups. While other organizations based on race, religion, or other markers of identity were prohibited after 1960, the state continued to view women as an interest group to be mobilized for the revolution. Founded that year on the directive of Fidel Castro, the FMC was led for nearly five decades by Vilma Espín, who fought with the 26th of July Movement against Batista and married Raúl Castro. With nearly two million members and fourteen thousand employees in the mid-1970s, the organization played a major role in Cuban society. It provided job programs, educational opportunities, childcare, and women's health initiatives that sought to improve the conditions of women's lives.[74] It also followed a hierarchical structure and served to harness Cuban women to the mostly male-led Cuban revolutionary project.[75] Like the grassroots groups that preceded them, and women's organizations in other socialist states, the FMC emphasized capitalism's exploitative practices against women over gender discrimination by men. It explicitly rejected a feminist approach to gender equality and left little room for dissent. Espín claimed, "We have never had a feminist movement."[76] She also asserted, "We hate the feminist movement in the United States," calling women who mobilized against men "absurd" and anything but revolutionary.[77] The FMC provided little space for public disagreement on this topic before the mid-1970s. But recent scholarship has shown that Cuban women were not monolithic by examining Black Cuban women in the cultural sphere, including documentary filmmaker Sara Gómez, who highlighted challenges for women under the revolution in her largely obscured body of work.[78] The FMC did provide spaces for women to come together, as well as opportunities for interactions with women such as Davis, Catlett, and others from around the world at conferences and events. Yet overall, the FMC precluded the possibility of an openly grassroots women's activism.

The FMC, a women's organization in a state apparatus without many women leaders, was the logical host for the highest-profile woman from the United States to visit Cuba since the revolution. Davis's own ambivalence about the US women's liberation movement made the question of feminism moot. Moreover, the FMC's position as an arm of the socialist state shaped by the Old Left made it a fitting choice to coordinate visiting members of the CPUSA. Women were prominent members of the prerevolutionary communist organization, the Partido Socialista Popular (Popular Socialist Party, or PSP), where they had articulated a platform of gender equality, and after the revolution they reemerged to occupy prominent positions within the FMC. Because the PSP had not initially opposed Batista or supported Castro, 26th of July members reacted to PSP involvement in the FMC and across the Castro government by 1960 with skepticism or sometimes disdain.[79] But the Old Left roots of many FMC members, and their familiarity with organizing and centralized hierarchy, provided a fitting institutional base for Davis at the intersection of gender and communism—one uniquely accepted by the Cuban state.

Gender also continued to shape her representation in public discourse. Depicted as both feminine and a fighter, coverage of Davis differed from that of male visitors. An extensive spread in *Granma,* "Entre la Arcilla y la Obra," or "Between Clay and Work," epitomizes this dual charge.[80] The article featured two photographs of Davis at a daycare center, one with children standing in neat lines holding placards of her visage, and the second showing her reaching into a crib and smiling at an infant. A third, in contrast, showed Davis in a hard hat speaking to a large crowd of workers and students in the new Alamar housing complex. Journalist Felix Pita Astudillo, who often covered American visitors to the island, compared Davis's engagement with children, the clay that could be shaped to lead Cuba's revolutionary future, with the hardness of Cuban workers—pillars of Cuba's ongoing struggle. In addition to dwelling on Davis's interactions with children, Astudillo depicted the visit of "our Angela" as "indescribable" and "emotional," words not used to describe African American men visiting or living in Cuba.

Davis elaborated on her 1972 visit to Cuba at a CPUSA meeting upon her return. Like she did in 1969, Davis lauded Cuba's fight against racism, reporting, "We were extremely impressed by the way in which racism is being dealt with on a continual basis in Cuba."[81] But in the same meeting, an official, private gathering for party comrades that was recorded, Davis acknowledged that "there were substantial problems in the area of women." Davis and Kendra Alexander noted the absence of women in leadership positions in government and the Cuban Communist Party. She also emphasized a "deeply ingrained male supremacist" attitude on the island, and, relative to the Soviet Union and other countries they visited in 1972, a lack of awareness or intent about combating this supremacy. Davis recounted to ensuing laughter several discussions where their delegation raised the issue and found enthusiastic allies in Cuban women, along with polite men who "thanked us for the criticisms and suggestions." Despite the humor she employed, Cuban gender relations troubled Davis.

Davis returned to Cuba in 1974 at a moment of reexamination of the roles of Cuban women. She came to attend the second congress of the FMC, which included nearly two thousand members and delegates from fifty-five international women's organizations.[82] Attendees broke into commissions on the topics of Cuban housewives, working outside of the home, rural women, families, children living under socialism, and international solidarity. The conference anticipated the upcoming International Year of the Woman in 1975 and the UN Decade for Women from 1975 to 1985. Other Latin American women's organizations had a strong influence on Cuban women at these gatherings, expanding the possibilities for new conversations about feminism and gender equality.[83] The FMC congress also occurred amid a series of significant domestic events heralding changes for women in Cuba, above all the February 1975 passage of the Family Code, modeled on East Germany, which mandated equal housework and childcare responsibilities for Cuban husbands and wives. Although the Family Code did not usher in gender equality, its passage and the congress heralded a more active role by the Cuban state and the FMC regarding women's rights.

While the FMC congress suggested the possibility of change, Davis's presence confirmed her steadfast, special position in Cuban revolutionary culture. It also signaled her increased attention to gender on the island. In her speech at the congress, Davis reiterated her support for the Cuban Revolution and her belief that socialism lent itself to women's rights, declaring, "The example of Cuba has confirmed that there cannot be true emancipation for women without a socialist revolution," just as there couldn't be "socialist revolution without the participation and emancipation of the woman."[84] Conference leaders bestowed on her the prestigious Ana Betancourt Award, named for a Cuban independence fighter against Spain, and designated Davis as a conference president of honor. Five years after her first visit to Cuba, she continued to be seen as a militant yet feminine ally—an enduring symbol of anti-imperialism, anti-capitalism, anti-racism, and women's rights.[85]

Conclusions

Angela Davis became more than a heroic woman in Cuba; she became a visually iconic revolutionary ideal. During her time on the island Davis emphasized her role not as an individual but as part of a larger struggle and a symbol of what fruit grassroots movements could reap. When traveling with Communist Party delegations in 1969 and 1972, she accepted Cuban accolades in the name of the CPUSA and claimed to speak not as an individual but in the name of "the other America."[86] The Cuban press echoed this designation by describing Davis's reception in familial and collective terms, where Cubans "received their sister in struggle as the most pure revolutionary ideal, as the representative of the other United States."[87] Like NUCFAD, she saw her role as a representative, not a cult of personality. This inescapably gendered position helped make Davis a lasting name—and face.

Did Cubans get to know Davis "personally," as Cuban student Angelina D. Garcia requested on her postcard?[88] Some young Cubans forged a connection with Davis through the campaign for her freedom and her subsequent presence in Cuban culture. One photograph from Davis's own collection shows a racially diverse group of girls ecstatically clapping and reaching out to her during a visit to their school.[89] Davis wrote in a press release back in the United States that "perhaps even more impressive" than the massive rallies during her international tour were "the spontaneous reactions of young and old alike."[90] Yet her 1972 visit was orchestrated under high-level auspices of the state, and Cubans recall Davis's visit as occurring in an official capacity. Davis's multipronged identity and ideological affiliations provided her with accepted structures of credibility, security, and visibility on the island not often afforded to other Black liberation activists, who had no corresponding organization to bolster their goals for the US or international movements, nor to shape their reception in Cuba. The Cuban Revolution's embrace of Davis continued its pattern of solidarity with African American activists, but Davis's gender combined with her race and communist affiliation made her an accepted individual and a beloved icon.

Davis never openly criticized Cuba. The Cuban state extended refuge to African American activists for a range of reasons, including a shared opposition to US policies, Cold War pragmatism, and overlapping anti-imperialist, anti-racist, and anti-capitalist ideologies. Yet, given the resources the Cuban government expended on Black radicals on the island and the low tolerance for criticism of the revolution of any kind, Cuban leadership became wary of extending support and refuge to those who levied critiques. Undoubtedly Davis felt grateful to the revolutionary state and the Cuban people for supporting the campaign for her freedom, and for welcoming her repeatedly to the island. Her global philosophy of liberation may have prioritized US aggression toward Cuba over the revolution's shortcomings or steered her toward support for the radical vision of the Cuban struggle even if it had not come to pass. Further, her continued adherence to socialism precluded a denunciation of the Cuban Revolution along those grounds. But if socialism helped ensure Davis's relationship with Cuba, gender elevated it.

Furthermore, Davis's encounters with Cuba must be considered within the revolution's broader global politics. In the aftermath of the failed *gran zafra* sugarcane harvest that Davis witnessed in the summer of 1969, the revolutionary state turned increasingly to the Soviet Union for economic support and the apparatus of communism to structure Cuban society. These turns had ideological impact. Davis's communist affiliation made her attractive for Castro, and in Davis's notes from her trip she both acknowledged their arrival's "coinciding with the tightening of relations between Cuba and World Socialist communities" and jotted down the desire, either by the CPUSA, Castro, or both, for the CPUSA to "assert more leadership" of the motley Venceremos Brigade. She reflected a larger shift from the more experimental era that characterized the Cuban Revolution's first decade to the greater institutionalization of the 1970s—a transitional figure who was embraced as an individual but represented a centralized organization. Davis may have been different than those who came before her, but she also proved to be the last of the exalted icons from the United States.

Davis eventually dropped her CPUSA affiliation, although she remained an advocate of socialism. In the decades following her initial visit to Cuba, she wrote increasingly about women. Her seminal work *Women, Race, and Class* examined the racism and class divisions between US women from slavery into the twentieth century, while *Women, Culture, and Politics* incorporated women around the world.[91] In the short introduction to the 1988 edition of her autobiography, Davis wrote more about the women's liberation movement than in the first edition, expressing regret that she "was not able to also apply a measuring stick which manifested a more complex understanding of the dialectics of the personal and the political."[92] Studies of women's liberation have changed precipitously since 1988. Yet thinking through Davis's encounter with the Cuban Revolution in the 1960s and 1970s also benefits from a dialectic: one that positions Davis's political symbolism alongside her multifaceted personhood.

Notes

1. Sarah Seidman, "Angela Davis in Cuba as Symbol and Subject," in *Radical History Review* no. 136, pp. 11–35. Copyright 2020, MARHO: The Radical Historians' Organization, Inc. All rights reserved. Republished by permission of the copyright holder, and the Publisher. www.dukeupress.edu.

2. Box 578, folder PO 64, Papers of Angela Y. Davis, Schlesinger Library, Radcliff Institute, Harvard University.

3. Joe Walker, "Angela Davis," undated pamphlet, *Muhammed Speaks*, section 2, box 2, folder 18, Communist Party of the United States of America Records (old processing system), Tamiment Library and Robert F. Wagner Labor Archives, New York University (hereafter CPUSA Records).

4. For more on this broader topic, see Ruth Reitan, *The Rise and Decline of an Alliance: Cuba and African American Leaders in the 1960s* (Michigan State University Press, 1999); Anne Garland Mahler, *From the Tricontinental to the Global South: Race, Radicalism, and Transnational Solidarity* (Duke University Press, 2018); and Sarah Seidman, "Venceremos Means We Shall Overcome: The African American Freedom Struggle and the Cuban Revolution, 1959–1979" (PhD diss., Brown University, 2013).

5. Carlos Moore, *Castro, the Blacks, and Africa* (University of California Press, 1988); Alejandro de la Fuente, *A Nation for All: Race, Inequality, and Politics in Twentieth-Century Cuba* (University of North Carolina Press, 2001); Mark Q. Sawyer, *Racial Politics in Post-Revolutionary Cuba* (Cambridge University Press, 2006); Devyn Spence Benson, *Antiracism in Cuba: The Unfinished Revolution* (University of North Carolina Press, 2016); Lillian Guerra, "*Poder Negro* in Revolutionary Cuba: Black Consciousness, Communism, and the Challenge of Solidarity," *Hispanic American Historical Review* 99, no. 4 (2019): 681–718.

6. Ian Lekus, "Queer Harvests: Homosexuality, the U.S. New Left, and the Venceremos Brigades to Cuba," in *Imagining Our Americas: Toward a Transnational Frame*, ed. Sandhya Shukla and Heidi Tinsman (Duke University Press, 2007), 249–81; Karen W. Tice, "The Politics of US Feminist Internationalism and Cuba: Solidarities and Fractures on the Venceremos Brigades, 1969–1989," *Feminist Encounters: A Journal of Critical Studies in Culture and Politics* 2, no. 1 (2018): 1–15.

7. For more on later exiles Assata Shakur and Nehanda Abiodun, see Teishan Latner, *Cuban Revolution in America: Havana and the Making of a United States Left, 1968–1992* (University of North Carolina Press, 2018).

8. Dayo F. Gore and Bettina Aptheker, "Free Angela Davis and All Political Prisoners! A Transnational Campaign for Liberation," in *Women and Social Movements in the United States, 1600–2000* (Alexander Street, 2014).

9. Kum-Kum Bhavnani and Angela Davis, "Complexity, Activism, Optimism: An Interview with Angela Y. Davis," *Feminist Review* 31 (1989): 66.

10. Angela Davis, *Angela Davis—An Autobiography* (International Publishers, 1988 [1974]), 123.

11. Davis, *Angela Davis*, 122, 125.

12. Davis, *Angela Davis*, 161.

13. Beth Slutsky, *Gendering Radicalism: Women and Communism in Twentieth-Century California* (University of Nebraska Press, 2015), 154.

14. Davis, *Angela Davis*, 209.

15. Davis, *Angela Davis*, 216.

16. Davis, *Angela Davis*, 203, 216.

17. "National Committee Meeting. Reports on Angela Davis Delegation to Cuba, Chile, USSR, GDR, etc.," October 17, 1972, box 62, disc 1-2, CD 93, Communist Party of the United States of America Audio Collection, Tamiment Library and Robert F. Wagner Labor Archives, New York University.

18. Carmelo Mesa-Lago, *Cuba in the 1970s: Pragmatism and Institutionalization* (University of New Mexico Press, 1978).

19. "National Committee Meeting." See also Robert F. Williams to Fidel Castro, The Black Power Movement Part 2: The Papers of Robert F. Williams, August 28, 1966, 25, reel 2 (microfilm); Eldridge Cleaver, *Soul on Fire* (Word Books, 1978), 108; Stokely Carmichael and Ekwueme Michael Thelwell, *Ready for Revolution: The Life and Struggles of Stokely Carmichael (Kwame Ture)* (Scribner, 2003), 633-34.

20. Benson, *Antiracism in Cuba*, 6.

21. Davis, *Angela Davis*, 210.

22. Davis, *Angela Davis*, 371.

23. Tice, "Politics of US Feminist Internationalism and Cuba," 5-8.

24. William Tulio, "FBI Student Spy in CPUSA Answers Criticism," *UCLA Daily Bruin*, July 1, 1969; Ed Montgomery, "Maoist Prof Poses Problem for Regents," *San Francisco Examiner*, July 9, 1969.

25. Davis, *Angela Davis*, 6.

26. Linda Charlton, "F.B.I. Seizes Angela Davis in Motel Here," *New York Times*, October 14, 1970.

27. Georgie Anne Geyer and Keyes Beech, "Parade of Radicals to Havana: U.S. Bombers' Tactics Linked to Cuba Visits," *Los Angeles Times*, October 13, 1970.

28. "Alabama Press Search for Angela Davis," *Los Angeles Times*, August 18, 1970; "Says Angela's Sister Aboard Ship to Cuba," *Chicago Defender*, August 26, 1970.

29. Sarah Van Gelder, "The Radical Work of Healing: Fania and Angela Davis on a New Kind of Civil Rights Activism," *YES!*, February 18, 2016.

30. James Baldwin, "An Open Letter to My Sister, Miss Angela Davis," *New York Review of Books*, January 21, 1971; "Angela Davis: Black Soldier," *Black Scholar* 2, no. 3 (1970): 1.

31. Kimberly Springer, *Living for the Revolution: Black Feminist Organizations, 1969-1980* (Duke University Press, 2005), 89.

32. "One Million People Sponsor Freedom for Angela Davis," box 4, folder 15, Angela Davis Legal Defense Collection, Schomburg Center for Research in Black Culture, New York Public Library.

33. Charlene Mitchell, *The Fight to Free Angela Davis: Its Importance for the Working Class* (New Outlook, 1972), 4-5. See also All India Students Congress, "Youth Accuses

Imperialism," and United Coalition for Angela Davis Day, "End Racism and Repression," section 2, box 2, folder 18, CPUSA Records; "Luckacs' Statement," box 4, folder 15, Angela Davis Legal Defense Collection.

34. Alice Kaplan, *Dreaming in French: The Paris Years of Jacqueline Bouvier Kennedy, Susan Sontag, and Angela Davis* (University of Chicago Press, 2012), 210–14.

35. Gore and Aptheker, "Free Angela Davis."

36. Davis, *Angela Davis*, 398.

37. "OSPAAAL Supports the Afro-American People," *Black Panther*, November 28, 1970; M. S., "Angela Davis: Esta mujer, alegre y profunda," *Romances*, September 1972, 14–15.

38. Catlett to Aptheker, 12 March 1971, in Gore and Aptheker, "Free Angela Davis."

39. Catlett to Aptheker, 12 March 1971, in Gore and Aptheker, "Free Angela Davis."

40. "Mensaje de la FMC al Comité de Solidaridad con Angela Davis," *Granma*, December 9, 1970.

41. "Constituyen Comité por la Libertad de Angela Davis," *Granma*, June 17, 1971.

42. "Declaración del Comité por la Libertad de Angela Davis," *Mujeres*, July 1971, 12; Mireya Casteñada, "¿Por qué Angela?," *Romances*, March 1971, 70–71.

43. Carmichael and Thelwell, *Ready for Revolution*, 697.

44. Thanks to Lillian Guerra for suggesting the connection between the poster and the statue.

45. The photograph was taken by F. Joseph Crawford at a September 9, 1969, press conference. See Ben Marks, "Trailing Angela Davis, from FBI Flyers to 'Radical Chic' Art," *Collectors Weekly*, July 3, 2013.

46. Marks, "Trailing Angela Davis."

47. See "Declaración del Comité," *Mujeres*, and postcards to Angela Davis, box 138, folder 19, CPUSA Records. While this chapter focuses on the 1970s, it is worth noting that this image was reappropriated by Cuban artist Liliam Dooley in the 2021 graphic *Libertad Para Luis Manuel*. Dooley superimposes imprisoned Cuban artist and activist Luis Manuel Otero Alcántara over Davis's profile, demanding his release from jail as Cubans had demanded for Davis. See Ernesto Menéndez-Conde, "Los Carteles de la OSPAAAL y el Efecto de Halo," in *Armed by Design: Posters and Publications of Cuba's Organization of Solidarity of the Peoples of Africa, Asia, and Latin America (OSPAAAL)*, eds. Lani Hanna, Jen Hoyer, Josh MacPhee, Sarah Seidman, and Vero Ordaz (Common Notions Press, 2025), 255–257.

48. "No Tenemos Otra Alternativa que Tomar las Armas," *Granma*, August 3, 1967; "Entrevista Radio Habana Cuba a Stokely Carmichael," *Granma*, August 5, 1967.

49. *Black Panther*, September 14, 1968, 3.

50. Guerra, "*Poder Negro* in Revolutionary Cuba," 708.

51. Garcia to Davis, box 138, folder 19, CPUSA Records.

52. Adelaida De Juan, "Cuba: La Mujer Pintada," *Cuba*, March 1972, 15–21.

53. Feliz Pita Astudillo, "No Podría Haber Sido de Otro Modo, Angela: Un inenarrable fenómeno de masas," *Granma*, October 8, 1972. See also Tanisha C. Ford, *Liberated Threads: Black Women, Style, and the Global Politics of Soul* (University of North Carolina

Press, 2015); Maxine Leeds Craig, *Ain't I a Beauty Queen? Black Women, Beauty, and the Politics of Race* (Oxford University Press, 2002).

54. Casteñada, "¿Por Qué Angela?," 70–71; Yara, "Imagen y colorido de Mayda," *Romances*, March 1971, 24–25.

55. Angela Y. Davis, "Afro Images: Politics, Fashion, and Nostalgia," *Critical Inquiry* 21, no. 1 (1994): 37–45, quotation on 37; Robin D. G. Kelley, "Nap Time: Historicizing the Afro," *Fashion Theory* 1, no. 4 (1997): 339–51, esp. 339.

56. Margaret Randall, *To Change the World: My Years in Cuba* (Rutgers University Press, 2009), 55–56.

57. Kelley, "Nap Time," 339–52; Kobena Mercer, *Welcome to the Jungle: New Positions in Black Cultural Studies* (Routledge, 1994), 97–128.

58. Davis, *Angela Davis*, xv–xvi.

59. Davis, "Afro Images," 39.

60. "Declarada Inocente Angela Davis," *Granma*, June 5, 1972; "Reiteran Invitación a Angela Davis," *Granma*, June 8, 1972.

61. "Reason for trip," box 86, folder 6, Papers of Angela Davis.

62. "Desbordamiento popular en la Isla de la Juventud," *Granma*, October 4, 1972; Felix Pita Astudillo, "Angela Davis en la Isla de Juventud," *Granma*, October 4, 1972.

63. Felix Pita Astudillo, "Recibe Angela Davis la orden 'Playa Giron,' la más alta condecoración instituida por el Gobierno Revolucionario de Cuba," *Granma*, October 5, 1972.

64. Juana Carrasco, "Ofrece Angela Davis conferencia de prensa," *Granma*, September 27, 1972.

65. Printed in *Granma* as "verdadero patria," October 8, 1972.

66. Angela Davis, "Speech Given at Havana University on October 4, 1972," page 5, box 86, folder 6, Papers of Angela Davis.

67. For example, the closing of the journal *Pensamiento Crítico* led by the Department of Philosophy at the University of Havana. See Guerra, "*Poder Negro* in Revolutionary Cuba," 710–11.

68. Felix Pita Astudillo, "No Podría Haber Sido de Otro Modo, Angela," *Granma*, October 3, 1972; Felix Pita Astudillo, "Mensaje de Angela Davis al Pueblo de Cuba minutos antes de partir rumbo a Chile," *Granma*, October 6, 1972.

69. "Recibió Vilma Espín a Angela Davis en la Federación de Mujeres Cubanas y le entrego el carnet que la acredita como miembro de la organización," *Granma*, September 28, 1972.

70. K. Lynn Stoner, "Militant Heroines and the Consecration of the Patriarchal State: The Glorification of Loyalty, Combat, and National Suicide in the Making of Cuban National Identity," *Cuban Studies* 34 (2003): 71–96.

71. Stoner, "Militant Heroines," 72, 74–75.

72. Michelle Chase, "Women's Organizations and the Politics of Gender in Cuba's Urban Insurrection (1952–1958)," *Bulletin of Latin American Research* 29, no. 4 (2010): 440–58; Lorraine Bayard de Volo, *Women and the Cuban Insurrection: How Gender Shaped Castro's Victory* (Cambridge University Press, 2018).

73. Michelle Chase, *Revolution within the Revolution: Women and Gender Politics in Cuba, 1952–1962* (University of North Carolina Press, 2015), 77, 97, 85–86, 117.

74. Chase, *Revolution within the Revolution*, 6, 39, 61.

75. Lois M. Smith and Alfred Padula, *Sex and Revolution: Women in Socialist Cuba* (Oxford University Press, 1996), 32, 45, 50.

76. Maxine Molyneux, "State, Gender, and Institutional Change: The Federación de Mujeres Cubanas," in *Hidden Histories of Gender and the State in Latin America*, ed. Elizabeth Dore and Maxine Molyneux (Duke University Press, 2000), 298.

77. Molyneux, "State, Gender, and Institutional Change," 299. See also Tice, "Politics of US Feminist Internationalism and Cuba," 9.

78. Devyn Spence Benson, "Sara Gómez: *Afrocubana* (Afro-Cuban Women's) Activism After 1961," *Cuban Studies* 46 (2018): 134–58.

79. Chase, *Revolution within the Revolution*, 108, 122–25.

80. Astudillo, "Un día inolvidable con nuestra Angela."

81. "National Committee Meeting."

82. Bhavnani and Davis, "Complexity, Activism, Optimism," 76–77; Juana Carrasco, "'Voy a tartar de poner en alto el legado de la orden 'Ana Betancourt' y lo que ello significa y el legado de la mujer cubana y lo que ello significa,'" *Granma*, December 3, 1974.

83. Molyneux, "State, Gender, and Institutional Change," 298.

84. Carrasco, "Ofrece Angela Davis conferencia de prensa"; Marta Rojas, "Intervienen delegaciones de otros países; jefes de organizaciones políticas y ministros del Gobierno Revolucionario en el II Congreso de la Federación de Mujeres Cubanas," *Granma*, November 27, 1974.

85. Juana Carrasco, "Llegó a Cuba la dirigente Comunista Angela Davis, invitada para el II Congreso," *Granma*, November 26, 1974; Mirta Rodríguez Calderón, "Presidieron Fidel y Dorticós la Sesion Inaugural del II Congreso de la FMC," *Granma*, November 26, 1974.

86. Davis, "Discurso Pronunciado por la Compañera Angela Davis," *Granma*, October 8, 1972.

87. Astudillo, "Un día inolvidable con nuestra Angela."

88. Garcia to Davis, box 138, folder 19, CPUSA Records.

89. Box 578, folder PO 64, Papers of Angela Y. Davis.

90. "Statement by Angela Davis on her Recent Tour of Socialist Countries," page 2, box 86, folder 6, Papers of Angela Y. Davis.

91. Davis, *Women, Race, and Class*; Davis, *Women, Culture, and Politics*. See also Salem, "On Transnational Feminist Solidarity."

92. Davis, *Angela Davis*, viii.

SEXUALITY

FOUR

The Orphans of the Sierra Maestra

Cuba and the Homosexual Movements in Latin America, 1960–1990

FELIPE CARO ROMERO

Today, queer rights are an important part of leftist or liberal politics and have become a polarizing issue, pitting progressives against the political Right. However, history shows us a very different landscape. Leftist projects have not always embraced gay and lesbian movements, and when they did, controversies, questions, and debates often arose. Although there has been some scholarly interest in the interplay of progressive and queer politics, there is still much to understand about this complicated relationship.[1]

This chapter explores the responses of Latin American homosexual organizations to the Cuban Revolution, perhaps the most controversial event in the complicated history of leftist and gay, lesbian, and transexual movements in Latin America. Since the mid-1960s, the Cuban Revolution's treatment of homosexuals has not only garnered harsh criticism from skeptics but also divided supporters of the revolution. As we will see, some supporters have been very critical of the Cuban government's repression of homosexuals, and others have diminished or excused it. However, a point of view that has been largely ignored in the discussion has been the positions of the gays and lesbians who organized in Latin America during the 1970s and early 1980s. In the aftermath of Stonewall, gay liberation organizations emerged not only in the United States and Europe but also in Argentina, Mexico, Colombia, Brazil, Venezuela, and Peru. They were inspired, connected, and empowered by a network of radical queer intellectuals, actions, and ideas that traveled along the continent through magazines, personal connections, and political campaigns.[2] These organizations had different and contradictory positions on the Cuban Revolution due to Cuba's repression of homosexuals and gender nonconforming people in general. However, I argue that the Cuban Revolution remained a key reference point for Latin American homosexual organizations, despite the many criticisms of the revolution's treatment of people who deviated from the norms of gender and sexual orientation. Recovering these debates and controversies, this chapter offers new insight into these complex relationships from the 1960s to the late 1980s.[3]

To understand these debates, I will delve into the magazines and newspapers of the homosexual organizations that were at the core of the groups' strategies and theoretical development of ideas regarding sexuality, revolution, and politics in general. Groups used these publications to pose questions, discuss current and past issues, and offer solutions. Specifically, I will center my analysis on the following Spanish- and Portuguese-language magazines: *SOMOS* from Argentina; *El Otro, Ventana Gay,* and *De Ambiente* from Colombia; and *Lampião da Esquina* from Brazil. I will also address discussions in periodicals from the United States, Mexico, and, more briefly, Chile and Peru. Exploring this history of contradictions between leftist and queer politics through the lens of the Cuban Revolution reminds us that homosexual organizations were not passive spectators; they had agency, and they also demonstrated a strong heterogeneity in their thoughts and actions.[4]

While some argued that it was impossible to support both gay rights and the Cuban Revolution, others opined that it was necessary to overlook the revolution's mistakes to advance the goals of the Left. This chapter raises the issue of what it means to seek an emancipatory revolution and explores the local debates inside and across leftist organizations around the meaning of solidarity, justice, and revolution and how this complex network of ideas was tailored through the hopes and fears of activists linking different Latin American experiences, both among themselves and with the Global North.

Cuban State Homophobia and the First International Reactions

Sexual battles have long been an important arena for the global Left. However, the first half of the twentieth century showed us how a revolutionary government can quickly turn into a homophobic state. Cases like those of Germany during the Weimar Republic and the Second World War or of revolutionary and later Stalinist Russia are prime examples of an intellectual transmutation that goes from liberation to repression. Following this "Sexual Thermidor," which saw a conservative turn in understandings of gender and sexuality in the 1930s in both Germany and Russia, the Third International (an international workers' organization) became the vanguard of sexual conservatism in orthodox Marxism.[5] All parties and organizations that gravitated around the Soviet Union accepted the idea of homosexuality as a vicious degeneration of a decadent bourgeoisie. In fact, Cold War ideology in the United States also conceived of homosexuality as sickness and immorality. It was not until the world protests of 1968, the explosion of new political demands and movements related to personal life, and the organization of homosexuals that some left-wing parties started to reevaluate their positions on the legitimacy of homosexuality.

In Cuba, the support of the USSR after 1961 shaped the ideological foundations of the revolution and made Cuba a stronghold of communism in Latin America and the Western Hemisphere.[6] In 1961, just after the US-sponsored Bay of Pigs invasion, Fidel Castro declared the Cuban Revolution to be socialist; six months later he declared himself a Marxist.[7] The new government viewed homosexuality as a capitalist by-product, born out of the degeneration of the corrupt presence of prostitution and vice brought on by the United States during the dictatorship.[8] In 1965, the first Military Units to Aid Production (Unidades Militares de Ayuda a la Producción, UMAP) were established.[9] These camps were used by the Cuban government as forced labor facilities for unruly and nonconformist groups. Homosexuality, viewed as a weakness born of the degeneration of capitalism and therefore not suited for "new men," was to be cured in those camps through "hard work."[10] The exact number of people who were sent to those camps is unknown, as the Cuban government has discouraged historical research on the subject.[11] Recent scholarship, like that of Abel Sierra Madero, has shown the active role of the state in the erasure of this history and the selective amnesia instituted by the government.[12]

Even at the time, the UMAPs were highly controversial in leftist circles.[13] Many public figures on the Left outside Cuba pushed for the abolition of them, and homosexual activists and intellectuals campaigned for their dismantlement. Among the many campaigns against the UMAPs, two episodes are of note. One was the denunciation made by the openly homosexual beat poet Allen Ginsberg during his visit to Cuba in 1965 as a jury member for Casa de Las Americas, Cuba's famous cultural institute and publishing house.[14] During his trip, Ginsberg questioned both government officials and young homosexuals on the streets of Havana about the treatment of gays on the island. According to Ginsberg, he was unceremoniously expelled from the island due to this relentless questioning, his suggestion that Raúl Castro was a homosexual, and his assertion that Che Guevara was attractive.[15] Upon his return to the United States, Ginsberg denounced the homophobia of the revolutionary government. The other relevant reaction against the UMAPs was the public demonstration arranged in New York City by the Mattachine Society on Easter Sunday in front of the United Nations building in 1965. The Mattachine Society was a homophile organization that had been active since 1950 that wanted the recognition of homosexuals as first-class citizens in the United States. Although its tactics were deemed insufficient or even complacent by younger generations, the Mattachine Society continued its activism for more than twenty years.[16] The fact that they protested the UMAPs in 1965 is an indicator that as early as the mid-sixties, homosexual groups abroad were aware of the mistreatment of the gay and lesbian communities on the island and were ready to act in their defense.

Although the UMAPs closed in 1968, the repression of homosexuals did not stop. Although there was no official government statement regarding homosexuality at the time, a hostile ambiance had been created by various statements made by the revolutionary leadership in addition to the existence of the UMAPs.[17] In 1971, this discrimination was institutionalized at the First National Congress of Culture and Education. The congress's resolutions unequivocally denounced homosexuality as a social problem, condemning the "social pathological character of homosexual deviations" and resolving that "all manifestations of homosexual deviations are to be firmly rejected and prevented from spreading." The statement added, "It was resolved that it is not to be tolerated for notorious homosexuals to have influence in the formation of our youth based on their 'artistic merits.'"[18] Delegates represented homosexuality as a disease and as a threat, especially to youth.[19] Similarly, as a way of eliminating or containing homosexuality, the state established a new penal code in 1979. While the new code removed the criminalization of "private forms" of same-sex practice in effect since 1938, it also reinforced some legal penalties against public expressions of homosexuality, such as up to months of imprisonment and a fine for those who "made public ostentation of their homosexual condition" or who undertook "homosexual acts in public places or private ones [that can be] seen by others."[20] This penal code, a revision of the penalization established in the Cuban Social Defense Code of 1938, remained active until 1988.

Cuban State Homophobia and the Responses of Homosexual Liberation Groups in the United States and Europe

The Stonewall riots birthed an ensemble of ideas and operations in interaction with cross-continental countercultural movements, global protest, and the anti-colonial struggles in Africa and Asia. In the beginning the gay liberation wave spread across the United States after the riots. The first anniversary of Stonewall (in 1970) mobilized a great number of organizations and more than two thousand people; the following year, gay liberation organizations appeared in England, Canada, and Australia, and later in France, Germany, and Italy. These organizations were marked by their heterogeneity. However, liberation and emancipation related to sexuality, along with all other forms of oppression, were at the core of these organizations' ideas and claims. Thus, gay liberation had close ties with unorthodox leftist organizations like anti-racist and Third World solidarity groups, but also anarchist, Trotskyist, and, most notably, feminist groups.

The Anglo-speaking gay liberation movement quickly recognized the paradox of supporting the Cuban Revolution as a Third World revolution against US imperialism while the Cuban government concurrently persecuted homosexuals. And due to the closeness of most of the groups to various types of leftist organizations, Cuba's treatment of homosexuals became something that required explanation, denunciation, or both. The US Venceremos Brigades and Cuba's First National Congress of Culture and Education (1971) both had an impact on deliberations on the subject.

The Venceremos Brigades were a project organized beginning in 1969 by the US student activist organization Students for a Democratic Society in which (mostly white) US students traveled to Cuba to help harvest sugarcane.[21] These brigades provided an opportunity for radical US youth to engage in active solidarity, but they also allowed participants to scrutinize the minutia of revolutionary daily life while also—according to some gay radicals—serving as propaganda for the revolution. Many members of gay liberation groups joined the first and second brigades in November 1969 and February 1970. What they saw and experienced in Cuba left the movement divided in two, a rupture that would continue to develop throughout the 1970s and 1980s. Moreover, these two positions established a baseline for understandings of Cuba that Latin American homosexual liberation groups subsequently supported, contested, or debated.

In one position, more lenient gays praised Cuba's literacy campaign and redistribution of wealth. These revolutionary accomplishments were seen as mitigating factors that justified or at least assuaged the mistreatment of homosexuals. According to this position, such mistreatment had to be seen as part of a whole.[22] Of the UMAPs, it was said that they were quickly closed and thus should not be used as an excuse to discount the many successes of the revolution. Finally, some of those who defended Cuba argued that Cuban homophobia was a "Hispanic" problem, a cultural inheritance from a colonial past that was reinforced by US imperialism. Of course, by imbuing certain cultural dispositions with notions of naturalization, these advocates made an assessment that we can now appreciate as verging on racism.[23]

The second position was critical of Cuban state homophobia and called out the incoherence of supporting a revolution but condoning homophobia. Those who advocated this position were preoccupied with the precedent that the Cuban Revolution was setting for future revolutions, a precedent that didn't include homosexuality. As an article in the US periodical *Come Out* argued, "The fight of the Cuban and other Third World people against the imperialism of the United States and its lackeys cannot be won by maintaining the attitudes of cultural and sexo-economic systems which support and are nurtured by sexism, male individualism, capitalism, and imperialism."[24]

Castro's own statements seemed to confirm that fear. In an interview published in 1969, two years before, the revolutionary leader had announced: "We would never come to believe that a homosexual could embody the conditions and requirements of conduct that would enable us to consider him a true Revolutionary, a true Communist militant. A deviation of that nature clashes with the concept we have of what a militant Communist must be."[25] Statements such as these were troublesome for international homosexual organizations because of the implications they would have for the politicization of homosexuality, as many less radical or even conservative gay organizations were using this homophobia as an excuse to advance anti-leftist ideas. As one homophile outlet in California wrote, to differentiate themselves from supporters of Cuba: "The morality of these people [the Cuban leadership] does not correspond to the prestige of the Revolution."[26] Some gay radicals feared that Marxism and homosexuality would be seen as incompatible; they felt the need to fight Cuban homophobia but did not want to renounce the possibility of a true revolution.[27] The future of the revolution, the radical left-wing homosexuals thought, could not remain in heterosexual hands.[28]

The declaration of Cuba's First Congress of Culture and Education in 1971 helped bolster this perspective. As previously described, congress delegates produced a document calling homosexuality pathological and banning gays from representing the revolution abroad or influencing youth (for example, as teachers). An overwhelming wave of rejection for the document was felt in all the gay liberation organizations, including across the Atlantic. The London-based magazine *Ink* dedicated the front page of its 1971 issue to the subject of Cuban homophobia by altering the famous Korda photo of Che, adding red lipstick and blue eye shadow. And despite the insistence of some gay defenders that it was important to contextualize homosexual persecution as part of a bigger picture, the critical perspective dominated most of the 1970s in the Anglo-speaking world, especially thanks to the writings of journalist and gay rights activist Allen Young. He had

FIGURE 4.1. The cover of the English publication *Ink* satirizes the Cuban Revolution's stance on homosexuality. Available at https://commons.wikimedia.org/wiki/File:Ink_glf_cover.jpg.

participated in one of the Venceremos Brigades and published some accounts of his trip. Most famously, Young interviewed Ginsberg and published abstracts of their conversation in several queer magazines. His documentation of Cuba's institutionalized homophobia mapped out a critical stance that gained adherents among many gay rights defenders in the United States.

Sexual and Political Revolutions in Argentina and Mexico

Like their North American and European counterparts, the homosexual liberation movements in Latin America had strong intellectual and personal links with the regional Left, but in Latin America, the Cuban Revolution had a stronger impact and therefore opened more intense debates. Argentina's Nuestro Mundo (1968), which later turned into the Front for Homosexual Liberation (Frente de Liberación Homosexual) in Argentina (1971), was one of the first homosexual movements in Latin America. It was shortly followed by the Frente de Liberación Homosexual in Mexico (1971).[29] All these organizations came from a leftist background, as some of their founders were former members of communist parties. The organizations undertook similar activities, including workshops about sexuality, self-care meet-

The Orphans of the Sierra Maestra 99

ings for acceptance, and public demonstrations. And in each case, they were largely unrivaled domestically, as they were the only homosexual organizations in their respective countries, with only a few small predecessors to their own groups.[30] Therefore, the idea of creating alliances with other sectors became fundamental, and thus, solidarity became a central part of the organizations' political projects.

The Argentinean Frente was born amid a tumultuous time between dictatorships and fleeting democratic experiments. The leaders of the Frente emerged from labor organizations, intellectual circles, and leftist organizations. The organization tried to establish an alliance with radical political organizations with the goal of joint political and sexual liberation. But it failed. In fact, during protests, leftist followers of Juan Domingo Perón chanted slogans reinforcing stereotypes about homosexuality while also distancing themselves from homosexual groups to "clean" their own image, as they had themselves been accused of homosexuality by the Peronist Right. They chanted slogans like, "We're not fags, we're not junkies, we're FAR and Montonero soldiers" (referencing armed leftist groups).[31] As both leftists and proponents of homosexual rights, Cuba was a complex issue for members of the Frente de Liberación Homosexual. At first, members rejected the island's institutionalized homophobia, denouncing the First National Congress of Culture and Education and saying Cuba's retrograde sexual politics were "akin to that of puritanism and of fascists, McCarthyists and inquisitors," juxtaposing Cuba's attitude with the more progressive politics of the Soviet Union under Lenin.[32] However, the death of the historic leader Perón as a representative of social justice and the weight of isolation in the political arena convinced the Frente of the necessity of allyship; thus, many members decided to compromise their positions on the Cuban government, out of fear of being left alone and without domestic support. Such was the conclusion of one *SOMOS* article that called for the communion of all the oppressed; although it recognized widespread homophobia, it argued for a union of the movement with "the people."[33]

Argentina's Frente de Liberación Homosexual engaged with debates on homosexuality and revolution taking place within the global Left. In 1973, some Frente activists translated and published a speech given by Huey Newton, one of the founders of the US Black Panther Party (BPP), in their bulletin *Homosexuales*. The Newton speech argued that homosexuals should be regarded as the most oppressed people in the world and that the Black liberation movement should join forces with the gay liberation movement.[34] The idea of homosexuality as a potentially revolutionary condition soon developed in Latin America and was widely accepted by some of the homosexual movements of the region. Sometime later, in 1974, *SOMOS* published a response by Allen Young to a BPP member's criticism of Young's denouncement of Cuba.[35]

This Young response, which addressed the problem of covering up systemic violence of one group in the name of the liberation of another, illustrated the division among the activists who couldn't compromise with homophobia in the name of the revolution but nevertheless understood the necessity of union. Young rejected the BPP member's idea of self-sacrifice for the revolution, since homosexuals weren't volunteers; he also denounced the false reading of homosexuality as a capitalist vice. Young further argued that it was important not to be silent in the face of injustice and that it was precisely because the Cuban government did not allow criticism that international campaigns such as the one he was undertaking had value, as it was a form of solidarity with people who could not denounce their own mistreatment. By translating and printing only the more critical side of a New Left US debate, the Frente de Liberación Homosexual gave priority to one side of the discussion while also introducing the possibility of another perspective. Unfortunately, the debate about solidarity could not go further, as the 1976 coup and resulting dictatorship abruptly ended the Frente de Liberación Homosexual. The group's last issue of *SOMOS* called for the Left to overcome petty differences and form an all-encompassing anti-fascist union.[36]

During the 1970s the Cuban Revolution became a formative issue in spurring the coordination of existing gay and lesbian organizations in Mexico (unlike in Argentina) and in developing ties with the domestic Left, despite divergences among gay and lesbian activists in terms of how to interpret or respond to the treatment of homosexuals in Cuba. As mentioned above, the Frente de Liberación Homosexual de México was short-lived, but out of its disintegration in 1973, various groups emerged: Homosexual Front of Revolutionary Action (Frente Homosexual de Acción Revolucionaria), which was mostly male; Grupo Lambda, a mixed group with strong lesbian leadership; and Oikabeth, a lesbian organization. From the time of their formation, these groups had divergent or ambiguous positions on the Cuban Revolution that were largely determined by the backgrounds of their activists. For example, Grupo Lambda, which was heavily influenced by the Trotskyism of the Revolutionary Workers Party (Partido Revolucionario de los Trabajadores, PRT), denounced the homophobia not only of Cuba but of all the socialist states, including the USSR and China, arguing that these states generated "persecution and repression against lesbians and homosexuals whom they deem 'social scum' or a product of the 'decadence of capitalism.'"[37] The specific mention of lesbianism, which was not particularly visible in Cuban public discourse, reflected the prominence of lesbian activists in Mexico, a somewhat unusual profile within Latin American homosexual liberation groups.

Surprisingly, despite their various political differences, it was the Cuban Revolution that made all these Mexican homosexual groups join forces. On July

26, 1978, the Frente Homosexual de Acción Revolucionaria sent a contingent of thirty homosexuals to an enormous demonstration in commemoration of the twentieth anniversary of the Cuban Revolution.[38] The rally took place in Mexico City and mobilized some twenty-five thousand people. Most of the other groups at the demonstration, including student and worker movements in Mexico City, warmly welcomed the Frente Homosexual de Acción Revolucionaria's participation in the demonstration and in local political life. For example, as one pamphlet stated enthusiastically after the march, "We were joined by [No podían faltar] the *compañero* electricians, students, as well as the new organization El Frente de Homosexuales de Acción Revolucionaria!"[39] As a result of this warm welcome from the Left, other lesbian and homosexual groups, including Oikabeth and Grupo Lambda, decided to seek similar engagement with other leftist groups. Thus, just hours after the 1978 demonstration, the very same day, the first general union of lesbian and homosexuals was formed to coordinate greater activities. Two of these events were the tenth anniversary demonstration of the Tlatelolco Massacre in October of the same year, where the lesbian and homosexual contingent was welcomed with applause,[40] and Latin America's first Pride parade in 1979.[41]

In 1980, as Mexican homosexual liberation organizations were still struggling to frame their views on revolutionary Cuba, a new episode—the Cuban Mariel boatlift—deepened the division between the Left and the homosexual liberation movements. It also added a new voice to the global public debate: that of Cuban homosexuals themselves. In April 1980, after a group of Cubans forced their way into the Peruvian embassy in Havana to seek asylum, the revolutionary government announced that anyone who wanted to leave Cuba could do so. This led to a massive migration of Cubans to the United States that came to be known as the Mariel boatlift. Among the wave of Cubans that left for exile were many homosexuals, including famous writer Reinaldo Arenas. Arenas was an acclaimed novelist (albeit predominantly known outside Cuba) who had grown disenchanted with the revolution due to its institutionalized anti-homosexual politics. His denunciations of the treatment of homosexuals and his publication of novels abroad without official permission had landed him in prison in Cuba; after his 1976 release, he spent his last few years on the island living in secrecy and fear.[42] Because of this persecution, Arenas became a symbol of anti-Cuban politics, but also of the mistreatment of homosexuals by the Left.

The *marielitos*, as the refugees who arrived in the United States on the 1980 boatlift were called, became a particularly contentious subject both inside and outside the global gay liberation movement and deepened the debates on whether homosexuals should support the Cuban Revolution or not. *Marielitos*' testimonies became the subject of the widely debated documentary film *Improper Conduct*, directed by Néstor Almendros and Orlando Jiménez and released in 1984. In this film, various *marielitos,* including Arenas, explained the many abuses homosexuals had been subjected to by revolutionary authorities. *Improper Conduct* spurred a clearer division between supporters and critics of the Castro government. On the one hand, pro-Cuban intellectuals denounced the film as misleading and exaggerated, noting that the UMAPs had a brief lifespan. One pair of US scholars, who never had their texts translated to Spanish, went as far as claiming that prerevolutionary Cuba had not had a consolidated gay community and that the *marielitos* and their intellectual endeavors (as they sought to find a magazine) were the foundation of a new Cuban Right. On the other hand, *marielitos,* led by Arenas, and other US intellectuals, including Young, continued to denounce the homophobia of the revolution, now linking it to a broader criticism of Castro's growing authoritarianism. For Arenas, his fight against Cuban socialism from exile became a central struggle for the rest of his life. He took his own life in 1990, several years after contracting HIV. In his last letter he blamed his misfortunes on Fidel Castro, writing, "The sufferings of exile, the pain of being banished from my country, the loneliness, and the diseases contracted in exile, would probably never have happened if I had been able to enjoy freedom in my country."[43] His and others' voices added the weight and authenticity of personal experiences of repression on the island to the critical perspectives developing transnationally.

In Mexico, the debate sparked by the *marielitos* did not result in huge pronouncements from the various homosexual organizations, as they were preparing for the second Pride march in 1980 and did not want to contest an issue as celebrated by the social movement scene and the Left as the Cuban Revolution. The organizations resolved to condemn Cuban repression against homosexuals but also defend the revolution against the imperialist aggression of the United States. The second Pride parade, the biggest of those first years, counted between five and seven thousand attendees and had the support of the Workers Revolutionary Party, the Mexican Communist Party, and the Workers Socialist Party (POS), all pro-Cuban organizations.[44] Thus, while Mexican homosexual liberation activist groups did not ignore or countenance evidence of state repression against homosexuals in Cuba, they balanced the moral imperative of critique against the strategic importance of developing allies on the domestic Left.

Colombia and Brazil: From Mariel to the AIDS Crisis

In Colombia and Brazil, homosexual organizations started to emerge in the late 1970s and early 1980s, slightly later than in Argentina and Mexico. For this second wave of Latin American homosexual liberation organizations, the Mariel boatlift had a strong impact on the way they reacted to and engaged with the Cuban Revolution. Although local organizations embraced diverse positions, criticism of Cuba's treatment of homosexuals was now more prominent. However, the late 1980s also signaled the escalation of the AIDS crisis, which forced many gay activists to focus on personal survival.

In Colombia, the Homosexual Liberation Movement of Colombia (Movimiento de Liberación Homosexual de Colombia, MLHC) was the organization that most discussed Cuba's homophobia.[45] Heavily influenced by one of its founders, León Zuleta, a philosophy student and former member of the Colombian Youth Communist Organization, the MLHC had maintained a strongly Marxist approach to its analysis of sexuality in its first few years.[46] In 1978, they even dedicated a page in one of their magazines to the Day of the Heroic *Guerrillero,* a commemoration of the death of revolutionary Ernesto "Che" Guevara.[47] However, after the Mariel exodus and the coming of a second generation of activists into the MLHC, they adopted a critical approach to the Cuban Revolution. On the *marielitos* issue, the Movimiento distinctly denounced Cuba's homophobia by describing the treatment of local homosexuals as "akin to the way that German homosexuals were treated during the Nazi regime or Russian homosexuals during the Stalinist regime." Yet they defended themselves from accusations of being reactionaries by joining their claims with the testimony of Nicaraguan revolutionary poet Ernesto Cardenal, who had traveled to Cuba and denounced the violent treatment of homosexuals on the island in 1970.[48]

The other topic discussed in Colombia's homosexual organizations was the implementation of Cuba's new Socialist Penal Code of 1979, which retained legal penalties against public manifestations of homosexuality. This mirrored the discussion they were having in Colombia at the same time, during the redaction of a new penal code in the country. The MLHC thought that this was the perfect opportunity to end Cuba's criminalization of homosexuality, which had been legal in Colombia since 1890. For Colombian activists, both countries' penal codes, the new Cuban and the old Colombian, represented antiquated ways of understanding sexuality: the former as a continuation of a puritanical Stalinist tradition and the latter as a Catholic moralist one.[49]

In Brazil, much like in Mexico, the closeness of the homosexual movements with the mainstream Left shaped their approaches to Cuba. Discussions of supporting the local Left had already generated a clear division among the homosexual liberation groups in the country. In 1980, during the first National Homosexual Congress in São Paulo, a schism occurred based on whether the many activists and groups gathered should join the Labor Day demonstration in support of an ongoing metalworkers' strike. One group decided to support the workers and went out to the demonstration as openly homosexual workers, while another group—citing the mistreatment of homosexuals by the Latin American Left, especially in Cuba—decided to go on a trip to the local zoo instead.[50] This example illustrates how homosexual movements in Brazil remained divided on whether to ally themselves with leftist comrades or remain steadfast in their rejection of leftist movements that remained pro-Cuba.

The Brazilian positions echoed debates taking place transnationally. An autonomist faction believed that homosexual activists should not partner with the Left. They argued that such a relationship was contradictory and asserted, inadvertently echoing Castro, that a gay person could never be a revolutionary.[51] Other activists offered a more nuanced critique of Cuba from a more progressive autonomous perspective. These positions were expressed in a translated interview with Italian film director Pier Paolo Pasolini, published by the gay liberation magazine *Lampião da Esquina*. Pasolini, an open leftist and Catholic Marxist, criticized the Soviet and Cuban arguments for anti-homosexual policies as "defending the people" (meaning the nation) because for him it sounded very similar to Adolf Hitler's call decades before for the defense of the Aryan race.[52] Pasolini concluded that no matter how much time had passed since the horrors of World War II, for homosexuals, discrimination had never ended, and was exemplified by Cuba. These arguments reinforced the perception in a part of the homosexual movements that the Left had nothing good to offer, thus deepening the division between some queer activists and the Brazilian Left.

Taking a different stance, a left-wing or revolutionary group within the Brazilian movement firmly believed in the possibility of a simultaneous sexual and social revolution, but it nevertheless maintained a strong stance regarding the treatment of homosexuals by the Cuban Revolution. These notions are encompassed in a special issue (1981) of *Lampião da Esquina* dedicated to discussing the problem in Cuba. In this issue, the editors dubbed the homosexuals of Cuba "the orphans of the Sierra Maestra." Because the editors were interested in the possibility of a truly emancipatory revolution, they accused the Cuban government of being Stalinist, as it hadn't permitted any serious criticism of the revolution, including but not limited to the mistreatment of homosexuals. The persecution of prominent homosexual figures, the editors argued, especially in the arts and humanities, was akin to that of the Spanish Inquisition. In addition to reiterating the denunciations of Arenas, this wing of the Brazilian movement also recognized an event that no other Latin American group mentioned: the Night of the Three Ps. This night, October 11, 1961, consisted of a series of raids that took place in Havana and had the objective of cleansing the city of undesirables: prostitutes, pimps, and pederasts (which referred to the widespread idea of homosexuals as corrupters

FIGURE 4.2. A 1981 issue of *Lampião da Esquina* dedicated to the issue of homosexuality in Cuba referred to gay Cubans as "the orphans of the Sierra Maestra." Courtesy of Centro de Documentaçao Prof. Dr. Luiz Mott (CEDOC LGBTI+), available at https://cedoc.grupodignidade.org.br/colecoes/.

of youth). Among the detained was the famous writer Virgilio Piñera, who was quickly released but who suffered ostracism after the incident due to his open homosexuality. Most of the arguments made in this journal issue came from an interesting article titled "Cuba: des anos de caca das bichas" (Cuba: the years of queer hunting). It was a Portuguese translation of an unpublished article from the Argentinean magazine *SOMOS*, but due to the dissolution of the organization in 1976, the article had remained unpublished until that moment.[53]

The delayed publication in Portuguese of an Argentinean article not only shows the connection between the ideas of various homosexual liberation groups in Latin America but also the continuation of a discussion about Cuba that had started in Argentina. After criticizing Cuba, the text ended with a list of the revolution's educational accomplishments, including an account of how many Cubans had learned to read and write and enrolled in universities.

The Armed Left After the Cuban Revolution

The refusal to recognize the mistreatment of homosexuals by the Cuban Revolution was not only a problem for the diaspora, the international Left, and homosexual political groups; it soon became a matter of dispute wherever guerrilla groups emerged in emulation of what happened in 1959. Twenty years later, just a year prior to the Mariel boatlift, the Sandinista National Liberation Front (FSLN) overthrew the Somoza family in Nicaragua. The Sandinistas were strongly influenced by the Cuban example but also sought to avoid some of Cuba's mistakes. While the Sandinistas made no official statement, rumors circulated among the international Left that the Sandinistas were said to have had a very progressive stance on homosexuality. The ambivalence of the leadership regarding this subject made the FSLN an object of support and speculation for homosexual movements. As early as 1978, gay organizations in the United States voiced their support for the Nicaraguan Revolution and against US imperialism, hoping for a different outcome from that in Cuba. In 1979, an organization called Gays for the Nicaraguan Revolution was founded in San Francisco; with it, other US groups like Gay Latino Alliance started to support the new Nicaraguan government that was seeming to correct the errors of the past.[54]

In reality, the Sandinistas had a contradictory position on homosexual rights. It was understood that some gays and lesbians had participated in the armed struggle. Once in power, the Sandinistas at least tolerated, but did not actively support, the political organizing of homosexuals, earning the Sandinistas the admiration of not only US-based organizations but also Latin American groups, and seeming to offer a marked contrast with the Cuban Revolution.[55]

This support culminated when Rita Arauz, an openly lesbian Sandinista member of the San Francisco Gay Latino Alliance (who had returned to live in Nicaragua in 1984), decided to run for president of the International Lesbian and Gay Association in the late 1980s. At the same time, she participated in the creation of the first Nicaraguan gay and lesbian organizations, which, with the support of lesbian icon and then Health Minister Comandante Dora María Téllez, started to work on the health crisis sparked by the AIDS pandemic.[56] The Sandinistas' public tolerance of queerness, however, hid the homophobic side of the revolution, for harassment, detentions, and censorship of meetings of the new movement began quickly and quietly.[57]

Justified by the leadership as protection against the US-backed contra insurrection, these crackdowns on the emerging Nicaraguan gay, lesbian, and transgender movement led to its weakening. Eventually, the movement was so debilitated that it was unable to organize to defend its interests under the new, post-Sandinista government of 1990, and it had to suffer the humiliation of the Nicaragua National Assembly's broadening of the anti-sodomy law.[58]

Far more violent were the actions of other guerrillas in South America who used homosexuality as a scapegoat to further their own agendas. One radicalized faction of Revolutionary Armed Forces of Colombia—People's Army (Fuerzas Armadas Revolucionarias de Colombia—Ejército del Pueblo, FARC-EP) in Colombia called the Ricardo Franco Front (Frente Ricardo Franco, FRF) realized a massive purge known as the Tacueyó Massacre in 1984, when the group executed 164 guerrilla fighters within their own movement. When another guerrilla group, the 19th of April Movement (Movimiento 19 de Abril, M-19), expressed concern about the violence, the FRF responded that the M-19 "should instead worry about solving grave problems like the homosexualism that plagues a big portion of its own leadership."[59] With their statement, the FRF implied that their rationale for the massacre was to purge itself from the threat posed by homosexuals. In Peru, on May 31, 1989, the Túpac Amaru Revolutionary Movement (Movimiento Revolucionario Túpac Amaru) murdered eight people after a raid on a gay bar in the city of Tarapoto. This was part of their "social cleansing" policy, and it is now known as the Night of the Gardenias, after the name of the bar.[60] This was not an isolated incident for the Túpac Amaru Revolutionary Movement, as this armed group persecuted sexual and gender nonconforming individuals systematically.[61] All these examples show the violent response that the armed Left had toward homosexuality. Yet it is also important to note that homophobia was not a monopoly of the armed Left.[62] The first ever recorded demonstration of queer people in the streets of Latin America was a 1973 protest against the democratic socialist government of Salvador Allende in Chile due to the increased police brutality that targeted homosexuals and trans people during his administration.[63] This was but a prime example of the homophobia that some groups faced when looking for support in fellow revolutionaries or reformists in Latin America.

The continuous disenchantment that many queer organizations and intellectuals felt over the homophobia of the Left is best exemplified by Pedro Lemebel, a Chilean artist and former member of the Chilean Communist Party. He wrote in his 1986 poem "Manifiesto (Hablo por mi diferencia)":

> I am not Pasolini asking for explanations
> I am not Ginsberg expelled from Cuba
> I am not a faggot dressed as a poet
> I don't need a costume
> Here is my face . . .
> I am not gonna change for Marxism
> which rejected me so many times
> I don't need to change
> I am more subversive than you . . .[64]

Echoes of the Revolution

Things only started to change for queer people in Cuba at the end of the twentieth century, after the loss of Soviet aid forced Cuban leaders to forge more international alliances, at a time when many countries perceived gay rights as indicative of modern values. In 1988, the penal code was changed, eliminating the criminalization of the "public ostentation" of a homosexual "condition." In 1989 the National Center for Sexual Education (Centro Nacional de Educación Sexual, CENESEX) was founded. Although CENESEX had no legal authority, it pushed for the public discussion of more positive LGBTQ+ (lesbian, gay, bisexual, trans, queer, and beyond the heteronormative spectrum) policies. The report of a visit by a representative of the International Lesbian, Gay, Bisexual, Trans, and Intersex Association (ILGA) in 2003 concluded that although by that time there was no official repression of sexual dissent, people were still too afraid to organize. CENESEX, under the leadership of Mariela Castro (daughter of Raúl Castro and Vilma Espín), made some progress regarding the treatment of trans people and HIV research, but its authoritarian nature has not eluded criticism.[65]

In 2010, the Mexican newspaper *La Jornada* published a two-part interview with Fidel Castro. It was conducted by journalist Lira Saade, who at one point in the conversation claimed that it was the persecution of homosexuals that drove many leftists away from unconditionally supporting the Cuban Revolution. To this Fidel responded: "Yes, those were moments of great injustice, great injustice! Whoever did it. If we did, then we . . . I'm trying to delimit my responsibility in all of this because, of course, personally I don't have those type of prejudices."[66] To the question of who was directly responsible for the homosexual persecution, Fidel answered, "If anyone is responsible, that is me." And after being pressured for a more detailed explanation on the issue, Fidel said that due to the counterrevolutionary actions instigated by the United States, the issue of the arms race (referring to the October missile crisis), and his many assassination attempts, he never had a second thought on the issue: "In the end, nevertheless, if one must take responsibility then I take mine. I'm not going to blame others."[67] The interview ended, however, with Saade reminding readers that Cuba was a different country now, framing the founding of CENESEX as the definitive overcoming of that ugly past, showing the editorial line of the newspaper, which was both left wing and supportive of Cuba. Still, this interview made news around the globe because it was the first time Fidel blamed himself for the mistreatments of homosexuals during the early years of the revolution.[68] Fidel's published apology was convincing for many contemporary leftists, who (like some homosexual movements of decades before) found it discomfiting to think of the Cuban Revolution as perpetuating harm against gays, lesbians, and trans people.

But just as an authoritarian Cuba government of the 1960s could not afford to allow a movement as "controversial" as the LGBTQ+ one to flourish, neither does the government of today allow queer people to organize outside of the auspices of CENESEX. As if to prove this point, even after the death of Fidel, censorship was afoot in the island. In Cuba there are no Pride parades. This means that, unlike all other Latin American countries, Cubans don't publicly commemorate the Stonewall riots of 1969. However, since 2008 Cubans have commemorated the international day against homophobia with a *conga* every 16th of May, sponsored by CENESEX, as part of the growing acceptance of LGBTQ+ issues by the government and as an opportunity for organizations to come out in public. In 2019, CENESEX decided to cancel the yearly Conga Against Homophobia and Transphobia due to "new tensions in the international and regional context." This action prompted a massive, organized response from members of the LGBTQ+ community and their allies that challenged state control by celebrating the event without government permission.[69]

The demonstration ended in violence when riot police attacked the people on the street. Seemingly in contrast with this episode, in 2022 a new family code was approved by referendum (with 66.87 percent approval), opening the way for equal marriage and adoption for homosexuals. This campaign, not surprisingly, was backed by Mariela Castro, proving that although queerness now has a place in Cuban society, its time and place are still being controlled by the government.

Conclusion

The global Left has not always supported LGBTQ+ movements, nor have those movements always considered themselves part of the Left. As we have seen, inside homosexual movements, there have been a multitude of notions, readings, opinions, and ideas that have often clashed. To consider both the Left and the homosexual movement as atemporal monoliths that have remained the same, homogenous and coherent, is a disservice not only to their history but also to the general history of political thought, where discussions and dissent are a fundamental part of the process. What has been presented here is only a small part of the complex relationship between the Left and the homosexual movement in Latin America. Cuba, as we have seen, was a catalyst for the exploration of what it meant to truly pursue a revolution. Latin American homosexual movements used the Cuban example to understand their own realities and asked whether it was possible to have a truly integral revolution, one that ensured both socioeconomic justice and sexual freedom. Some groups, for example, in Mexico, tried to excuse the behavior of the Cuban Revolution by appealing to its importance in Third World countries; they expected the Cuban revolutionary leadership's perspective to change over time and thus drew parallels with their own context and their relationship with their local Left. But many other organizations, such as in Colombia or Brazil, were critical of the revolution, calling it an example of what not to do while hoping for a truly democratic revolution and suffering from their disenchantment with their own failed relationships with the Left.

Communication across this network of homosexual activists and organizations also demonstrates that the movement was fairly connected not only with the Global North but within the region. The flow of articles, interviews, and declarations reveals the stream of ideas across borders and the blossoming of a queer intellectual tradition in Latin America. Recognition of that queer intellectual tradition, in its many variations, can only be achieved through careful and nuanced considerations of issues like those presented here.

In the conclusion to his seminal work on Cuba homosexuality, Ian Lumsden declared that what happened on the isle was an imperfect revolution for an imperfect world. Despite his critical view, this statement illustrates one side of the debate: that we should overlook the "mistakes" of the revolution in the face of its many successes. Indeed, the various groups of Latin America's homosexual movements desperately needed an example of emancipation; when faced with the contradictions of Cuba, they struggled to make sense of the state-sanctioned homophobia of what activists in the Global North called a "Third World revolution." What has been presented here shows that in looking for a truly emancipatory revolution, many homosexual organizations tried to explain a failure that is still yet to be understood. The revolutionary Cuban government's early and persistent unwillingness to include gays, lesbians, and trans people in the revolutionary agenda should now give way to accountability. Contemporary leadership should allow and encourage deep and thorough research on the many abuses the revolution committed toward homosexuals during the first thirty years. Only with this openness to atone and learn can we really start to reflect on the repercussions of what was done, without myths and ideologically based prejudices. And in doing so, we can finally take a step toward that dream that the orphans of the Sierra Maestra relinquished many years ago: a complete revolution.

Notes

1. Raphael de la Dehesa, *Queering the Public Sphere in Mexico and Brazil: Sexual Rights Movements in Emerging Democracies* (Duke University Press, 2010); James N. Green,

"'Who Is the Macho Who Wants to Kill Me?' Male Homosexuality, Revolutionary Masculinity, and the Brazilian Armed Struggle of the 1960s and 1970," *Hispanic American Historical Review* 92, no. 3 (2012): 437–69; Felipe Caro and Patricio Simonetto, "Sexualidades radicales: los Movimientos de Liberación Homosexual en América Latina (1967–1989)," *Izquierdas* 46 (2019): 65–85; Pablo Ben and Santiago Insausti, "Dictatorial Rule and Sexual Politics in Argentina: The Case of the Frente de Liberación Homosexual, 1967–1976," *Hispanic American Historical Review* 97, no. 2 (2017): 295–325; Luis Rivera-Vélez and Morgane Reina, "Introduction. Les droits LGBTQIA+ en Amérique latine: une reconnaissance sous tension," *Cahiers des Amériques Latines* 98 (2021): 19–42.

2. I reject the very racist/neocolonial idea that gay liberation spread from the United States and Europe to the rest of the world. Much has already been written on how in Latin America, homosexual liberation was created and developed by interacting with movements and ideas worldwide. See Caro and Simonetto, "Sexualidades radicales."

3. Few texts have been centered around this issue. The main precedent is volume 136 of *Radical History Review* (2020) edited by Isabella Cosse and Michelle Chase.

4. In this chapter I will use the word "homosexual" as it was the preferred and common word used during the studied period, but the reader must take into account that this word may refer to other sexual or gender identities or experiences today known differently.

5. For an overview, see Gert Hekma, Harry Oosterhuis, and James Steakley, "Leftist Sexual Politics and Homosexuality," *Journal of Homosexuality* 29, nos. 2–3 (2010): 1–40; Daniel Healey, "The Russian Revolution and the Decriminalization of Homosexuality," *Revolutionary Russia* 6, no. 1 (2008): 26–54.

6. Evilin Ling, "Un estudio sobre el porqué del cambio al comunismo en la revolución cubana" (PhD diss., Lunds Universitet, 2011), https://lup.lub.lu.se/luur/download?func=downloadFile&recordOId=2335406&fileOId=2335410.

7. Fidel Castro, "Discurso pronunciado por Fidel Castro Ruz, presidente de la República de Cuba, en la concentración celebrada en la Plaza de la Revolución 'José Martí,'" December 22, 1961, http://www.cuba.cu/gobierno/discursos/1961/esp/f221261e.html.

8. Lillian Guerra, "Gender Policing, Homosexuality and the New Patriarchy of the Cuban Revolution, 1965–70," *Social History* 35, no. 3 (2010): 281.

9. Roberto Garcés Marrero, "Los primeros años de la Revolución cubana y las Unidades Militares de Ayuda a la Producción (UMAP)," *Historia Crítica* 71 (2019): 104.

10. Garcés, "Los primeros años," 100. Although homosexuals were sent to UMAPs, some scholars have argued that they were a minority and that the camps were full of heterosexuals. See Ian Lumsden, *Machos, Maricones, and Gays: Cuba and Homosexuality* (Temple University Press, 1996), 66.

11. According to Lillian Guerra, between thirty and forty thousand persons passed through the UMAPs. Moreover, seventy-two people died due to extreme conditions, and 180 committed suicide. There was no explanation about why those people were in the camps. See Guerra, "Gender Policing," 268. These numbers are still highly disputed and

are part of broader debates over the history of the first years of the revolution. See, for example, Abel Sierra Madero, *El cuerpo nunca olvida: Trabajo forzado, hombre nuevo y memoria en Cuba (1959-1980)* (Rialta Editores, 2022), chap. 5.

12. Sierra Madero, *El cuerpo nunca olvida,* 228.

13. Garcés, "Los primeros años," 109.

14. Allen Ginsberg, interview by Allen Young (1972), in Allen Young, *Gays Under the Cuban Revolution* (Grey Fox Press, 1981).

15. Young, *Gays Under the Cuban Revolution,* 20.

16. John D'Emilio, *Sexual Politics, Sexual Communities: The Making of a Homosexual Minority in the United States, 1940-1970* (University of Chicago Press, 1992).

17. Several articles condemned homosexuality, for example, the intervention of Samuel Feijoo in the newspaper *El Mundo.* See Garcés, "Los primeros años," 98-100.

18. Originally published in *Casa de las Americas* 65-66 (1971): 4-19.

19. Rafael Ocasio, "Gays and the Cuban Revolution: The Case of Reinaldo Arenas," *Latin American Perspectives* 29, no. 2 (2002): 86-87.

20. Secretaría de Justicia, *Código Penal: Ley No. 21 de 15 de febrero de 1979* (Ministerio de Justicia, 1980).

21. Ian Keith Lekus, "Queer Harvests: Homosexuality, the U.S. New Left, and the Venceremos Brigades to Cuba," *Radical History Review* 89 (2004): 57-91.

22. Ellen Bedoz, Bernard Lewis, and Allan Warshawsky, "Dialogue," *Come Out* 1, no. 3 (1970): 13.

23. "Homosexuals in Cuba: An Exchange from Gay Liberation," *Gay Liberator* 1, no. 4 (1970): 5.

24. "The Cuban Government Has Come Out with an Open Expression of Official Homosexual Oppression," *Come Out* 2, no. 7 (1971): 4.

25. Lee Lockwood, *Castro's Cuba, Cuba's Fidel* (Vintage Books, 1969), 107.

26. "Oppression in Cuba—1971," *Vector* 7, no. 8 (1971): 46.

27. Craig Alfred Hanson, "Marxism? Freedom?" *Gay Liberator* 31 (1973): 19.

28. Pierce Wayne, "Gays in Cuba—A Detroit Socialist Responds," *Gay Liberator* 5 (1970): 5.

29. See Patricio Simonetto, *Entre la injuria y la revolución. El Frente de Liberación Homosexual, Argentina, 1967-1976* (Universidad Nacional de Quilmes, 2017); Ben and Insausti, "Dictatorial Rule."

30. Such as the group SOMOS in Argentina, which was active before the Stonewall riots. See Simonetto, *Entre la injuria y la revolución.*

31. Ben and Insausti, "Dictatorial Rule"; Isabella Cosse, "Infidelities: Morality, Revolution, and Sexuality in Left Wing Guerrilla Organizations in 1960s and 1970s Argentina," *Journal of the History of Sexuality* 23, no. 3 (2014): 436-37.

32. Rodolfo Rivas, "La situación de los Homosexuales en Cuba," *SOMOS* 2 (1974): 8.

33. "Comunicado del FLH de la Argentina sobre la Muerte de J. D. Perón," *SOMOS* 4 (1975): 4-5.

34. See Ben and Insausti, "Dictatorial Rule," 310.

35. Allen Young, "Más de Cuba. Algunas razones por las que no nos callaremos," *SOMOS* 5 (1971): 6–10.

36. Simonetto, *Entre la injuria y la revolución*, 54.

37. "¿Qué es Lambda?" in Norma Mogrovejo, *Un Amor que se atrevió a decir su nombre. La lucha de las lesbianas y su relación con los movimientos homosexual y feminista en América Latina* (P y V Editores, 2000), 101.

38. Mogrovejo, *Un Amor que se atrevió*, 94.

39. "Manifestación 26 de julio," *Unión. Órgano Informativo del Sindicato de Trabajadores de la Universidad Nacional Autónoma de México* 11 (1978): 1.

40. As recounted by an eyewitness account. See Carlos Monsiváis, "Envío a Nancy Cárdenas, activista ejemplar," *Debate Feminista* 10 (1994): 263.

41. Mogrovejo, *Un Amor que se atrevió*, 122.

42. Cited in Ocasio, "Gays and the Cuban Revolution," 94.

43. Ocasio, "Gays and the Cuban Revolution," 86–94.

44. Mogrovejo, *Un Amor que se atrevió*, 126.

45. The MLHC was a national organization that encompassed different groups in various cities of the country from 1978 until 1989. They published three different magazines and managed to organize the first Pride demonstration of the country in 1983. For more information on the subject, see Felipe Caro Romero, "Más allá de Stonewall: el Movimiento de Liberación Homosexual de Colombia y las redes de activismo internacional, 1976–1989," *Historia Crítica* 75 (2020): 93–114.

46. For his whole life Zuleta considered himself an unorthodox Marxist but a Marxist, nonetheless.

47. "8 de octubre día del guerrillero heroico," *El Otro* 4 (1978): 4.

48. "Refugiados Cubanos," *Ventana Gay* 1 (1980): 8.

49. Felipe Caro, "Más que un acto público de cariño. Activismo frente a la despenalización de los actos homosexuales en Colombia," *Americanía* 12 (2023): 203–30; "Del Código Cubano," *Ventana Gay* 6 (1981): 25.

50. James Green, "The Emergence of the Brazilian Gay Liberation Movement," *Latin American Perspectives* 21, no. 1 (1994): 48.

51. Pedro Rocha Nogueira, "Gays, Alvos de Tiros para Revolucionarios Heteros," *Journal Gay International* 4 (1980): 20.

52. Pier Paolo Pasolini, "Desbloqueando o tabu," *Lampiao* 2, no. 24 (1980): 6.

53. "Cuba: dez anos de caca ás bichas," *Lampiao* 3, no. 33 (1981): 10.

54. Emily Hobson, "'Si Nicaragua Venció': Lesbian and Gay Solidarity with the Revolution," *Journal of Transnational American Studies* 4, no. 2 (2012): 6–8.

55. "Solidaridad Gay," *De Ambiente* 14 (1989): 14–15.

56. Hobson, "Si Nicaragua Venció," 15.

57. About this subtle and even hidden homophobia two texts are fundamental. One is the re-edition of a series of interviews originally published in 1981 that, after the loss of the revolution, was revisited and broadened: Margaret Randall, *Sandino's Daughters Revis-*

ited: *Feminism in Nicaragua* (Rutgers University Press, 1995). See a more recent discussion of LGBTIQ+ history in Karen Kampwirth, *LGBTQ Politics in Nicaragua: Revolution, Dictatorship, and Social Movements* (University of Arizona Press, 2022).

58. Mogrovejo, *Un Amor que se atrevió*, 338.

59. Letter published December 21, 1985. See Dario Villamizar, *Las guerrillas en Colombia: Una historia desde los orígenes hasta los confines* (Penguin Random House, 2017), 513.

60. Comisión de la Verdad y Reconciliación, *Informe Final de la Comisión de la Verdad y Reconciliación* (CVR, 2003): 432–33.

61. Antonio López Díaz, "Los indeseables de Tarapoto," *El País*, April 4, 2016, https://elpais.com/elpais/2016/04/01/planeta_futuro/1459513097_580273.html.

62. Only one insurgent group of the region has openly embraced the utopia of a sexual and social revolution: the Mexican Ejercito Zapatista de Liberación Nacional (Zapatista Army of National Liberation). In a speech about the identity of Subcomandante Marcos, he himself declared: "Marcos is a gay in San Francisco." See "Comunicado de prensa del Subcomandante Marcos. 28 May 1994," *Bibliotecas Virtuales de México*, https://palabra.ezln.org.mx/comunicados/1994/1994_05_28.htm.

63. Pabli Yasser Balcazar, "Enyegüecidas: La primera protesta pública del disenso sexual en Chile," *Moléculas Malucas*, December 23, 2021, https://www.moleculasmalucas.com/post/enyeguecidas.

64. Pedro Lemebel, "Manifiesto (Hablo por mi diferencia)," *Revista Anales* 7, no. 2 (2011) [1986]: 218–21. Translated by the author.

65. Sexual Orientation and Gender Identity Research, *Cuba: Country Report for Use in Refugee Claims Based on Persecution Relating to Sexual Orientation and Gender Identity*, International Human Rights Program, University of Toronto, October 30, 2009, 13, https://ihrp.law.utoronto.ca/utfl_file/count/documents/SOGI/Cuba_SOGI_2009.pdf. While CENESEX has certainly altered the discourse surrounding homosexuality in Cuba and made LGBTQ issues a legitimate area of study, it has done little to change the country's culture of homophobia.

66. Carmen Lira Saade, "Entrevista con Fidel Castro (II Parte): 'El mundo del futuro tiene que ser común para todos,'" *Cubadebate*, August 31, 2010, http://www.cubadebate.cu/especiales/2010/08/31/entrevista-de-la-jornada-con-fidel-castro-segunda-parte/.

67. It has been disputed whether Fidel was himself homophobic or had any prejudices. Lumsden argues that there is no indication that the revolutionary leader had such feelings toward homosexuality. As proof of this, he cites his friendship with openly recognized homosexual Alfredo Guevara. See *Machos, Maricones, and Gays*, 64. However, I find such a definitive statement problematic not only because of the public policies that the revolutionary government enacted but also because interpretations of feelings like those made by Lumsden don't take into account the fact that people not only can contradict themselves but also, and more often than not, can change their minds about any topic whatsoever. So rather than ask whether Castro was homophobic, we could ask how he reacted in different moments in time to the subject of homosexuality.

68. "Fidel Castro admitió su responsabilidad en persecución de homosexuales," BBC

News Mundo, August 31, 2010, https://www.bbc.com/mundo/america_latina/2010/08/100831_cuba_castro_homosexuales_entrevista_pea.

69. "Cancelación de desfile gay organizado por Mariela Castro molesta a comunidad LGBTI," Radio Televisión Martí, July 5, 2019, https://www.radiotelevisionmarti.com/a/ministerio-de-salud-cancela-desfile-gay-organizado-por-mariela-castro/238561.html.

FIVE

Transgressing Che

Irina Layevska Echeverría Gaitán, Disability Politics, and Transgendering the New Man in Mexico, 1964–2001

ROBERT FRANCO

Clutching a cigarette in her hand, the disability rights and transgender activist Irina Layevska Echeverría Gaitán stares off screen at the interviewer as the smoke collects around her.[1] The camera is rolling, but the shot remains frozen on her face, framed by a shelf full of books and a mop of black hair. Even in the grainy footage, her thick eyebrows are clearly furrowed as she collects her thoughts. "Che spoke of the creation of the New Man," she utters, "and the New Man does not yet exist. There are men who are new, but there is no New Man."[2]

Born in 1964 to communist parents who were later arrested during the 1968 student protests, Echeverría Gaitán was a child of the Mexican student and leftist movements that emerged in the wake of the Cuban Revolution. In her infancy, she began showing signs of muscle and nerve degeneration in her arms and legs, which would eventually be diagnosed as Charcot-Marie-Tooth disease and would worsen as she aged. Her disability, however, did not stop her from participating in various leftist parties and organizations in Mexico and abroad. Bearing a striking resemblance to Ernesto "Che" Guevara, Echeverría Gaitán modeled herself after Che's "New Man" in her youth. At age thirty-six she began transitioning to a woman, adding a new layer of radicalism to her militancy.

In this article, I use the life of Echeverría Gaitán, pieced together from interviews, her 2008 *testimonio* (testimonial text) titled *Carta a mi padre* (Letter to my father), and a 2011 documentary about her life, *Morir de pie* (Die standing), as a lens to examine the circulation and appropriation of the discursive New Man and the figure of Che Guevara in Mexico. For many traditional leftists, these models of revolutionary masculinity did not align with gay men, women, trans folk, or those with disabilities. However, I argue that Echeverría Gaitán used the futurist, universal, and self-developmental aspects of the New Man to reject exclusionary leftist politics. Upholding the New Man as an aspirational yet abstract goal enabled Echeverría Gaitán to formulate a radically transgressive subject position and provided a discourse with which to construct a militant identity that was inclusive and oppositional to the masculinist and ableist revolution.

In his 1965 essay "El socialismo y el hombre en Cuba" (Socialism and Man in Cuba), Che Guevara outlined the utopian citizens known as the New Man and Woman. "To build communism it is necessary," he writes, "simultaneous with the new material foundations, to build the new man and woman."[3] Highlighting the ways capitalism constructed a consciousness of individualism and the myth of the self-made man, Guevara argued that these new men and women needed to have values such as moral perfection, community centeredness, and the willingness to sacrifice private interests for collective transformation. In the initial phases of revolution, these characteristics of selflessness and moral strength were embodied in the vanguard—soldiers like Fidel Castro who set aside commitments to family for their comrades and country. However, Guevara envisioned that self-development and education through physical work and integration into cadres would enable the birth of an entire society of new men and women, making these subjects always both aspirational and in the process of becoming.[4]

As it spread throughout Latin America, the New Man became a figure of contestation, particularly in the generational divides of the Left over armed struggle, sexual liberation, and feminism.[5] Popular and literary iterations of the New Man made him a patriarchal and masculinist figure, rejecting "sexual deviants" such as homosexuals and sex workers as counterrevolutionary.[6] Women, while less clearly incorporated into the revolution's construction of the utopian citizen, were able to use the figure of the New Woman to vocalize their revolutionary valor, echoing similar ableist discourses of physical capability as those of the New Man.[7] Echeverría Gaitán's disability and gender affirmation, on the other hand, put into question prevailing ideas of who could embody the New Man and New Woman. Despite the normative connotations of physical perfection and gendered order applied to these figures, I demonstrate how marginalized subjects could still use them to create meaning in their own lives.

Designated male at birth, Echeverría Gaitán constructed herself using the rubric of the New Man early in her life, even modeling her appearance after Che Guevara. While this gender performance had as much to do with concerns for safety as admiration for Che, her appropriation of the New Man allowed her to lay claim to a revolutionary identity while distancing herself from the disablism and sexism of her contemporaries. Later, Echeverría Gaitán drew on the New Man's ideals of self-construction to embrace her feminine identity as a New Woman.

Echeverría Gaitán's transformation from New Man to New Woman invites us to consider a number of epistemological tensions. As scholars of *testimonio* literature have discussed, writing a "life story" involves selective uses of memory in the construction of historical narratives about the self and subaltern truth. Similarly, Echeverría Gaitán's testimony is an act of retroactive reconstruction that interprets past experiences and events as a journey of recognizing how she has always understood herself.[8] And given that I draw from materials recorded before and after the date she indicates she began changing her gender expression, her narrative elucidates how testimonies are shaped by the particular historical moments during which they are recounted. Whether it is her proclaiming her desire to be the New Man amid the crises on the Left during the 1990s, or her framing of herself as a New Woman after the politicization of Mexico's transgender movement two decades later, her testimony is a striking example of how the subjective act of reconstructing a life story changes over time. Despite its remarkability, Echeverría Gaitán's life has been overlooked in the history of leftist struggle. A new wave of biographical work and studies of leftist private life, however, urges us to more seriously consider stories like hers, for they reveal how the creation of new subjectivities often entails challenging, usually for the better, the dominant moral paradigms of revolutionary movements.[9]

Transgressing Temporality

Echeverría Gaitán's life story gives us an exceptional account of revolutionary action in the years after the Cuban Revolution. But it is not without its limits. She cannot always disclose full names of individuals or exact dates of events, either due to the shortcomings of memory, the need to protect fellow militants, deteriorated relationships, or all three. Furthermore, since narrating her life is a political act, it is under the constant process of revision depending on historical context.[10] Interviews from the 1990s, for example, show Echeverría Gaitán confessing her desire to be a New Man while expressing hope for a socialist futurity after the dissolution of the Soviet Union. In contrast, narrating her *testimonio* in 2008 served as an outlet for her frustrations with the disablism and transphobia she was encountering in Mexico City. Updated interviews with me in 2018, meanwhile, occurred after significant legal gains in her gender affirmation, which were crucial to her understanding of self. With the opportunity to reassess her life trajectory, she now asserts that she has always been striving to be a New Woman.

Scholars have theorized how the bodily alienation and forced gender assignments that often mark the adolescence of sexual and gender minorities generate such heterogeneous experiences of time and identity.[11] In the case of Echeverría Gaitán, although she was read and treated as a disabled man for many years, she narrates her experiences entirely in the feminine. She is and always has been Irina, an experience of trans temporality that insists on the continuity of self between her early childhood and the moment she met her namesake (the nurse who cared for her in Moscow).[12] Never shifting gender pronouns or mentioning a dead name from childhood, she occupies a queer sense of time that Jack Halberstam defines as "the perverse turn away from the narrative coherence of adolescence."[13]

Echeverría Gaitán's experiences are also intersectional. Her *testimonio*, titled *Carta a mi padre*, opens with her earliest and most tangible memory—the stinging sensation of an operation—highlighting how the corporeal alienation wrought by disability can precede the bodily difference of being transgender.[14] Littered throughout her writings and interviews are multidimensional experiences of disablism coupled with violent rejections of her displays of femininity, informing and constituting one another.[15] Nevertheless, the autonomy she asserted in fashioning herself using her overlapping identities changed what disabled, transgendered, and New Man (and later, New Woman) could mean. In doing so, she offers a way of discussing identity that does not rely on essentialist notions of disability or the floating signifier of transgender.[16]

Despite the heterogeneous temporalities and intersectional experiences that punctuate her life story, one is nevertheless struck by the way Echeverría Gaitán attempts to give it order. Although she is resistant to a temporal shift in pronouns that would give her narrative a male past and female present, she does recognize her process of affirmation in terms of a fixed beginning and end. She, for example, does not identify as a trans woman (*transexual* or *trans*), arguing that trans is not a permanent designation of a person but rather a temporary term that describes the process of gender affirmation.[17] This understanding of trans time is indicative of what Alba Pons Rabasa has shown to be a result of the adoption of the medical model of transgender in Mexico during the late 1990s and early 2000s in which "the discursive shift from transgender as a political identification and political strategy to the medical categorization . . . has converted transgender into a phase through which the subject passes in his or her 'process of transition.'"[18] Echeverría Gaitán's comments in *Carta a mi padre* reveal her engagement with these discursive shifts in order to give her life a sequential order: "Transsexuality was only a process. What am I? A woman. Who am I? Irina. Who was I? Irina. I was hidden, repressed, scared, but I was there. All I needed was a process to be born, and here I am."[19] Using a language of birth, she situates her eventual arrival as the culmination of a process of gaining the language and knowledge necessary to articulate her identity. But even in this chronological timeline, slippages in temporality remain as she also expresses herself as always having existed.

Although the asynchronism of her gender identity—that is, her identification as Irina even as she was inscribed in the historical record and the memories of her contemporaries as a different gender—resists a division of before and after, Echeverría Gaitán organizes her life around a temporal regime of transition and futurity. Rather than characterize this as a case of transnormative narration in which trans histories conform to the linear conventions of a transition story, scholars must take into account the political ideologies that also govern temporalities.[20] I maintain that Echeverría Gaitán's narrative of transition is due to her commitments to the futurist project of socialism and the revolutionary subjectivity espoused in Che Guevara's utopian citizen. Based on developmental discourses, this subjectivity can be achieved by developing one's militancy, which leads to a transcendental moment of rebirth into revolutionary consciousness that frees one from a painful personal history.[21] The logic of a future-oriented self-construction and erasure of past trauma figures heavily in the testimony of Echeverría Gaitán. In addition to her own dead name, she never mentions her parents' names, likely due to her deteriorated relationship with them.[22]

Overall, in ways similar to how trans histories have been coded to fit an ideological project of distinguishing a chaotic past from a stable future, the New Man and New Woman give coherence to Echeverría Gaitán's life.[23] This emphasis on the potentiality of futurity pushes us to expand the trans historicist imperative of searching for accounts of gender variability in the past ("trans before trans") by also asking who is "trans after trans"—a project especially crucial in a region such as Latin America that is consistently presented as existing in a time "before" or outside of sexual modernity.[24]

Admiring the New Man

Irina Layevska Echeverría Gaitán was born on October 12, 1964, between two of the most profound events to mark the late twentieth century: the Cuban Revolution of 1959 and the 1968 Tlatelolco Massacre. The former made Cuba a major exporter of revolutionary ideas and culture to the Global South, particularly after the publication of Che Guevara's "Socialism and Man in Cuba."[25] For a younger generation of activists and leftists in Mexico disillusioned by the USSR, Cuba provided a new way of envisioning social change at a time when the promises of redistribution from the Mexican Revolution (1910–20) were coming to a halt. The latter, meanwhile, was a generational clash of political discontent regarding the democratic legacy of the Mexican Revolution and the government's failure to fulfill its promises to reduce widespread inequality. Tlatelolco left an indelible mark on Mexican society, shattering the tenuous façade of political stability under the Institutional Revolutionary Party (PRI).[26]

Echeverría Gaitán's birth, as fate would have it, was also a product of the Cuban Revolution—her parents met while at a march in support of the revolution in July 1963. Her mother, Yolanda Gaitán, was a militant of the Mexican Communist Party (PCM) and worked for the party from 1962 to 1968, while her father, Rodolfo Echeverría, rose through the party's ranks. In October 1968, when Echeverría Gaitán was about to celebrate her fourth birthday, her father returned from a trip to Moscow and was arrested in the crackdown following the student massacre. While he had managed to escape the bloodshed at Tlatelolco, he was rounded up with other student activists and sent to the dreaded Lecumberri prison where he would spend the next three years incarcerated.[27] With Rodolfo's arrest, Echeverría Gaitán's mother took over the household while also serving as head of the Comité de Familiares de Presos Políticos (Committee of the Relatives of Political Prisoners).[28]

As the child of communist militants, Echeverría Gaitán's upbringing was influenced by the gender, sexual, and family politics of the PCM. In the years after its founding in 1919, the PCM positioned itself as the moral alternative to the Mexican government and the Catholic Church. It did so by emphasizing militant decency in its publications and making labor and policy demands based on the nuclear family such as restrictive protections for women's work and a male-centered family wage.[29] Propaganda in the newspaper *El Machete* (1924–38) mocked homosexuals and sex workers, with some of the most virulent homophobia and heterosexism coming from prominent members such as Diego Rivera.[30] The PCM's approach to women's issues was no more progressive. Strict gender divides and *machista* (sexist) attitudes were rampant despite the indispensable work of women within the party.[31] Overall, the PCM in these early decades reflected the homophobic and sexist attitudes that were widespread in Mexican society before the Cuban Revolution.

Growing up in a communist family during the Cold War was a formative experience for Echeverría Gaitán and her two sisters. Despite stigmatization from neighbors, her parents remained fiercely loyal to communist ideals, which they imparted to their children. "I was educated," explains Echeverría Gaitán, "with a morality that we in those days called revolutionary morality."[32] Her mother also championed revolutionary ideas in the home, teaching her children about contraception and sexually transmitted diseases. However, Echeverría Gaitán discloses, "homosexuality was very badly viewed. My mother had friends who were gay and lesbian, but she could not stand the possibility of her children being that way."[33] Although Mexico's 1968 generation challenged sexual taboos and incorporated some levels of tolerance in their friendships, the PCM remained hostile to many of these new trends.[34]

Upon the arrest of her father in 1968, Echeverría Gaitán's weekends were spent visiting the infamous Lecumberri prison. By then she was around four years old and had begun showing signs of her illness. She needed to walk with orthopedic shoes, which caused onlookers to stare and guards to mock her during visits. As her muscle issues progressed, her family turned a blind eye and refused to discuss the matter. Echeverría Gaitán recalls that her mother would say: "Nothing is wrong, everything is normal, we are a normal family." In her *testimonio*, Echeverría Gaitán dismisses this emphasis on normalcy, a disablist discourse constructed to erase difference in favor of a universal ideal, by characterizing it as her mother's "fantasy."[35]

Despite her mother's disablism, Echeverría Gaitán remained fairly close with her, whereas her relationship with her father was characterized by conflict. Though she initially admired him for his arrest as a revolutionary, their relationship deteriorated upon his release in 1972. Echeverría Gaitán claims that her father was abusive, humiliating her and attacking her physically. He demanded she act as an *hombrecito* (tough man), perhaps reflecting the anxieties around the emasculation of disabled youth who are urged to "fight it like a man."[36] Echeverría Gaitán states that while she was aware of her desire to be a woman throughout her life, it was these early clashes with her father that stirred her desire to explore her femininity in order to express her emotions.[37]

In July 1972, Echeverría Gaitán's father took her to Romania for a leg operation after her family petitioned the USSR for medical support. Soon after their arrival, she remembers him abandoning her at the hospital to travel around Europe to conduct party affairs. For Echeverría Gaitán, this was yet another example of her father's abuse and absence. However, as she slowly pushed him away, she found solace in the figure of Che Guevara, whose condition of asthma gave Echeverría Gaitán a sense of kinship with the revolutionary.[38]

> Che for me was more than an emblematic person. Che became my image of an ideal father. My biological father, we had a very conflictive relationship.... My mother, in her bedroom, had a very large portrait of Che. It was not the typical image. He did not have a beret and had short hair, with a

trimmed beard. I dreamed that he was my dad and I talked to him. I always said "Papa" to him. But it was not only the image. Che was a man who had a very strong physical disability. His asthma prevented him from doing many things. In the most agitated or most complicated moments of the armed struggle in which he participated, asthma beat him, but it never defeated him. He never complained. And so I wanted to be like him.[39]

Che Guevara served as substitute father figure for Echeverría Gaitán—one who did not abuse her and shared her physical difficulties. By keeping a portrait of Che in their home, her mother initiated the process of her daughter's self-construction in his image.

Aiming for Che

In 1979, Echeverría Gaitán was sent to Moscow's Central Clinical Hospital. Known as the "Kremlin Hospital," it offered the highest quality medical care in the Soviet Union and catered to highly ranked party officials and esteemed "foreign comrades" such as Diego Rivera.[40] Since the right to free health care was extended to foreigners, Echeverría Gaitán was able to stay for over a year and was joined by other foreign guests getting medical attention.[41] Manuel Marulanda Vélez, cofounder of the Revolutionary Armed Forces of Colombia—People's Army (FARC), tutored her in leftist theory; Daniel Ortega, one of the leaders of the Sandinista National Liberation Front in Nicaragua (FSLN), shared her medical wing; and Palestine Liberation Organization (PLO) chairman Yasser Arafat allegedly attempted to marry her mother. In Moscow she would also meet Irina, a nurse whose attentive care impacted Echeverría Gaitán so much that she adopted her name.[42]

Away from most of her family and more mature than during her time in Romania, Echeverría Gaitán felt a sense of freedom to begin exploring her gender and sexuality in Moscow. About a year into her stay, she began dating a boy from Iraq. When he would refer to her as his boyfriend, she remembers that she would correct him and demand to be called his girlfriend. After their first sexual encounter, she notes that he finally began believing that she was a woman, stating it was because she made love like one. She writes, "I felt so realized and complete. . . . He was the first to accept me as a woman." The time and space away from her family, while freeing, was also temporary. Returning to Mexico in 1981 "forced me to hide all emotion."[43]

In 1981, Echeverría Gaitán began using a wheelchair, a shift in mobility that further conflated her body with her disability.[44] As a result, she began radicalizing her militancy. Around 1984, frustrated with the messages of caution imposed on

FIGURE 5.1. Echeverría Gaitán in Red Square in Moscow, wearing a beret and beginning to use a wheelchair.

her, she went to Nicaragua to aid in a literacy campaign. While there, she affirms that she took up arms and other duties such as training injured and disabled guerrillas to use weaponry. She also asserts that the Contras overran her rural camp and almost killed her, but she managed to escape by flinging herself off her wheelchair and crawling away: "Without realizing it, I crossed the border with Costa Rica and came upon their encampment. I fired my gun and hit a few. The Sandinista National Liberation Front decorated me." Whether or not Echeverría Gaitán truly did accomplish this extraordinary feat matters less than her narration of the event, which articulates her desire to occupy the role of the sacrificial New Man. In fact, when asked why she went to Nicaragua, she stated she felt like if she was going to die, she wanted a romantic death like Che Guevara's.[45]

While Echeverría Gaitán was recovering in Moscow and fighting in Nicaragua, the terrain of sexual politics was rapidly changing as a visible and vocal gay and lesbian movement emerged in Mexico by the end of the 1970s.[46] The demands for greater rights and respect from gay men and lesbians were initially met with visceral homophobia from militants of the PCM, even as the movement endorsed a socialist agenda. During a solidarity march for the Cuban Revolution held on July 26, 1978, gay men and lesbians connected their liberation to the goals of the revolution by chanting "Socialism without Sexism" and "Revolution in the Factory and the Sheets." They were met with jeers from members of the Communist Party, who refused to march alongside them and yelled "Faggots."[47] By 1980, however, the conversation around sexual politics began to shift as the sexual rights movement's leaders made contact with PCM officials. As a result, during its Nineteenth Congress in 1981, the party officially endorsed feminism and freedom of sexual orientation as part of its defense of individual privacy, although this moderate tolerance would wax and wane over time.[48]

The Communist Party's long-standing opposition to sexual liberation stands in stark contrast to the policies of the Workers' Revolutionary Party (PRT), a Mexican Trotskyist opposition party that emerged in 1977 and was affiliated with the Fourth International. Although it also supported the Cuban Revolution, the PRT did not follow the homophobic line of Castro. It even had an organized collective of lesbian and gay militants known as the Homosexual Work Commission. Following the example of the United Secretariat of the Fourth International, in 1979 the PRT adopted a resolution calling for the abolition of women's oppression and an end to the discrimination of sexual minorities.[49]

For many members of the sexual rights movement, the Cuban Revolution was initially prominent in their political imaginary during these years of activism. As Braulio Peralta, a militant of the Mexican gay and lesbian movement, noted, "In 68 we all adored Fidel Castro, we did not criticize Stalin, we believed that the Socialist Bloc represented hope . . . with a future for everyone, including homosexuals. Now we know all too well that this was not true."[50] While Peralta constructs a memory of disappointment and failure after the Cuban Revolution, others like Arturo Vázquez Barrón reconcile the hopes of revolution with the homophobia that followed 1959. In his words, "Our fight was for what we called socialism without sexism . . . to purge socialism of the remnants of homophobia."[51]

The opposing attitudes of Peralta and Vázquez demonstrate Cuba's contested image and the divergent ways its revolutionary ideals of liberation and autonomy could be interpreted. For some, the homophobia of the Cuban experience after 1961 served as a cautionary tale regarding the continued repression of sexual minorities under socialism. For others, the liberatory promises of Cuba could be salvaged: they believed socialism without sexism could be achieved by defending the emancipatory aspects of the Cuban Revolution while reforming the homophobia of leftists. This plasticity of the image of Cuba and belief in its redemption would serve Echeverría Gaitán in the years to come.

Breaking with her communist upbringing, Echeverría Gaitán joined the PRT in 1988. She claims this was due to her disagreement with former PCM leaders to ally with moderate sectors of the PRI in the 1988 presidential elections, but it is also likely that the PRT's tolerance toward sexual minorities appealed to her. "In the PRT there was respect and camaraderie regarding diverse gender and sexual minorities," she recalls, "which was not the case in the PCM."[52] By 1993, Echeverría Gaitán had risen through the ranks of the PRT to become part of its Central Committee. Although her fellow militants frequently expressed disdain or pity toward her, they also recognized her tenacity and ability to organize.[53]

Throughout this period, Echeverría Gaitán remained a fierce advocate of the revolutionary promises of socialism and the Cuban Revolution. With the onset of the "Special Period" of economic crisis after the 1991 dissolution of the Soviet Union, Echeverría Gaitán worked as part of the PRT to organize the Committee of Solidarity "¡Va por Cuba!" which brought crucial supplies to the island. Between 1991 and 1994, during some of the island's worst shortages, the group sent three boatloads of diesel oil to Cuba. During her third mission to the island in 1994, Echeverría Gaitán married Nélida Reyes Guzmán, another PRT militant and Cuba sympathizer. Their marriage was a socialist partnership, with equality between them and a mutual dedication to defending the revolution.

The Special Period in Cuba and the fall of the Berlin Wall in 1989 gave Echeverría Gaitán cause for reflection in the face of the downward trajectory of revolutionary movements that marked the decade. In an undated interview from the 1990s, Echeverría Gaitán expressed her disappointment in the collapse of the Socialist Bloc but a continued hope in the futurist project of the New Man. Claiming that her entire life had been dedicated to the formation of herself into a New Man and recalling the speech by Castro on the need to educate future generations to be like Che, she stated: "What do I hope for? Well, I do not expect something utopian. I just hope the people wake up. . . . Che talked about the New Man, and the new man does not yet exist. There are new men, but there is no New Man. There will be one, two, three."[54] Echeverría Gaitán's meditations on the New Man speak to her desire for a plurality of possibilities in the future of revolutionary militancy. Noting the lack of a true utopian subject in her lifetime, Echeverría Gaitán emphasized the potential for diversity in the New Man to come—perhaps hinting at gender variability but certainly asserting her hopes for a revolutionary figure that did not carry the sexism and ableism of her contemporaries. Yet the realities of the late 1990s in the terrain of leftist politics, and in her personal life, also meant projecting these hopes onto an indeterminate future.

During these years of armed struggle and leftist activity in Mexico and abroad, the aims of living up to the New Man, combined with her resemblance to Che, made Echeverría Gaitán's militancy distinct. She writes how the discovery of her resemblance to him in the 1980s dramatically changed her understanding of self:

I needed an anchor to hold onto, and I found it when I was lent a beret at school and one of my friends commented: "Hey, you look a lot like Che Guevara." You cannot imagine what that was like for me; it was like a glass of cold water in the desert. I finally had an identity. I had never liked the one I had from childhood, but with this discovery I could have a personality to hold onto without being suffocated.[55]

With a beret and beard in the style of Che, Echeverría Gaitán constructed herself as a revolutionary in his image. In addition to imitating his appearance, she adopted her own interpretation of the moral and ethical code of the New Man. Her performance, however, clashed with the machismo of her fellow militants, who were surprised to learn that she cooked and washed dishes. They would also become enraged when their girlfriends and wives would come to Echeverría Gaitán to vent their frustrations about their relationships.[56]

Echeverría Gaitán changed the appearance of the traditional revolutionary figure to include her disability. She also formed an alternative identity, one that cloaked her transgender subjectivity. This performance of Che and the New Man, however, was not the crystallization of masculinity or a "reidealization of hyperbolic heterosexual gender norms."[57] Rather, her version was a redefining of what the New Man could be, for it did not carry the machismo of previous iterations. In fact, she claims it enabled her to test the boundaries of her femininity and embody a revolutionary womanhood. She writes, for example, that she grew out her hair under the auspices of being a rebel. But in reality, it was one of the few opportunities she had to express her womanhood.[58] Echeverría Gaitán recalls attempting to promote her femininity while also embodying these iconic signs of rebellion and masculinity. By collapsing the gender binaries into one another in her memory of revolutionary activity, she is able to resolve the psychological conflict and temporal disjunction that she feels upon seeing past photos of herself ("I am seeing someone who I was but at the same time I did not want to be").[59]

Echeverría Gaitán's self-construction as Che lays bare the necessity that undergirds gender performances for survival. In her words: "What happens is that when you are living in a society where masculinity is so central and you have been taught that you have to be a man, well, I could not upset my family, much less my mother. And so it was better to appear as Che than as something else."[60] Intuiting the ways that her family's insistence on hypermasculinity coincided with the increasing demands of her disability as she shifted to a wheelchair, Echeverría Gaitán built a gender performance that appeased her social circle. Resembling Che, Echeverría Gaitán could stake a claim to the aspects of revolutionary masculinity that were open to her—such as clothing and facial hair—yet at the same

FIGURE 5.2. Irina circa 2008.

time allow her to manage her gender identity without incurring punishment during a hostile time in her life.[61]

Becoming Irina

Starting in 2000, Echeverría Gaitán began to lose her eyesight as muscular dystrophy affected her optic nerves. For aid in confronting this new crisis, she appealed to Cuba. After a number of exams with Cuban physicians, she was told she would eventually lose her eyesight. Upon her return to Mexico, she contemplated committing suicide but was stopped by her wife Nélida, who emphasized her need to mourn, give in to her emotions, and explore her femininity. It was then that Echeverría Gaitán began to seriously inquire what it meant for her to be a woman. Her first step was trying on a dress belonging to her wife, which she marks as the day she became the true Irina: August 24, 2001. She would begin hormone treatment and change her appearance soon after.

The years leading up to Echeverría Gaitán's gender affirmation witnessed the rapid expansion of the transgender movement in Mexico, with groups such as Eón Inteligencia Transgenérica (Aeon Transgender Alliance) emerging in Mexico City from the mid-1990s onward. The politicization of the transgender movement involved an alliance with sexologists and the deployment of medical discourses in order to make rights-based claims. Such discourses included establishing transgender as a transitory clinical category with the end goal being a subject's sense of concordance between sex and gender.[62] Echeverría Gaitán's narration of her affirmation, particularly the ways she frames it as a transition that ended on seeing herself as a woman, demonstrates the acquisition and strategic deployment of this knowledge. By framing her gender affirmation as a process, she is able to reconcile it with her political commitment to constant self-construction. The multiplication of her political commitments to her various identities thus reflects the gradual radicalization of her political consciousness. For this reason, she concludes her *testimonio* discussing both her battles to make Mexico City a more accessible space and the legal struggle to have her gender affirmation recognized in the civil registry (a right that was won in Mexico City in 2008). Framing her affirmation as complete also reasserts a vital sense of agency over her body. While Echeverría Gaitán attests to feelings of corporal failure due to her disability throughout her life, it was the chronological rubicon of puberty that presented a newer sensation of untimeliness and loss of her bodily autonomy.[63] As an adult, however, she was able to regain control over her gender expression, which represents a crucial turning point in her militancy. So while she was always Irina, she can also provide a date for when Irina appeared.

Echeverría Gaitán's changing relationship with her body and identity meant ending her resemblance to Che Guevara. As she recounts:

> I went to Cuba and when I arrived at the hotel, I looked at myself in the mirror. I removed my beard and mustache and went to Loma El Taburete, Che's last campsite before going to Bolivia. I climbed the hill in my wheelchair, three kilometers on pure dirt, I fell several times but I kept getting up until I arrived. And at the foot of a tree that was at the edge of the cabin, among the stars . . . I thanked him and said goodbye to that physical image.[64]

In *Exile and Pride*, Eli Clare explains that the daily struggle of disabled folk to navigate an inaccessible world is often framed as a metaphoric mountain.[65] For Echeverría Gaitán, this mountain was both symbolic and literal. During her journey to Loma El Taburete, Echeverría Gaitán resolved that her gender did not constitute a separate aspect of either her disability or her militancy. In fact, transitioning became the most radical expression of her revolutionary identity. Without the need for gender performance in the image of Che, Echeverría Gaitán contends she could focus more attention on playing her part in constructing a new world, even if "doing it as a woman is very complicated in a world dominated by a patriarchal culture where the Left is also contaminated by macho concepts and methods."[66]

Echeverría Gaitán's changing appearance did not mean a departure from Guevara's utopian citizen. Rather, in transitioning she could continue the process of expanding the image of the revolutionary figure. When asked about who could occupy the role of the New Man, Echeverría Gaitán reinterpreted the words of Che, replying:

> Che referred to the New Man as a concept of humanity, not as a gender, just as we refer to *Man* as the human species. But that *New Human Being* will not come alone; it is a process of formation that will give rise to ideological self-formation from the breaking of vices and attitudes of selfishness, to build a community for the benefit of all. That being the case, the concept is inclusive for gays, lesbians, trans folk, and all expressions of gender dissidence, regardless of their disability status.[67]

In this reformulation, the New Man becomes a concept for all of humanity, including sexual minorities and those with disabilities. By reflecting on the New Man after assuming the gender expression she had always felt, Echeverría Gaitán was able to reinterpret the language of Guevara to make the New Man a universal figure of any gender who combines the futurist goals of socialism with a desire for broad inclusion. This reinterpretation incorporates those who were excluded from the utopian visions of past generations and celebrates their differences as part of the revolution.

For an individual undergoing the process of gender affirmation, the gendering of this human being was crucial. Echeverría Gaitán does not identify as a gender-neutral New Human Being, but rather as a New Woman. By interviewing her in 2018, I provided Echeverría Gaitán with the opportunity to rework her past as she had always experienced it. When asked, for example, if she felt she was still part of the futurist and socialist vision of Che Guevara, Echeverría Gaitán responded, "I have dedicated my entire life to my ideological self-transformation to become the New Woman, for the construction of socialism, not the one that they wanted to impose with Stalin, but a real one."[68] While in past interviews Echeverría Gaitán had emphasized her self-construction as the New Man—possibly indirectly hinting at its gender variance—in this instance she was able to explicitly express her true desire to make herself a New Woman.

Historically, the figure of the New Woman was "constantly present" in revolutionary images but "did not play a central role in official discourse."[69] Echeverría Gaitán's reinterpretation of the New Woman makes her central to revolutionary discourse. She is, nevertheless, complementary to the New Man. Even while she elevates Che Guevara to a universal model, stating that he "remains a key piece of my existence to build myself as a New Woman," she retains the gender difference he delineated between New Man and Woman.[70] Echeverría Gaitán thus invites us to reconsider the contested desires for the mutability of gender in the process of transitioning, as her shift from one revolutionary model (the New Man) to another (the New Woman) is coded along a binary and given a conceptual framing as rebirth.

Affirming herself as a New Woman put Echeverría Gaitán in confrontation with her social circle. Most of her family disowned her upon hearing the news. Pondering the rejection from her family, specifically her father, she writes, "There's something I do not understand: you have gay friends, Dad, and you do not treat them like you treat me."[71] Although she still affiliates with the PRT, she also notes there were mixed responses to her transition. "The reaction was diverse," she states. "There were those who supported me and were allies in my rebirth. There were also those who got angry and stopped talking to me, others got scared, and others, well, they left and promised to return and never did."[72] She also claims she was expelled from the Zapatista Army of National Liberation for "gender betrayal."[73]

Not everyone reacted to Echeverría Gaitán's transition with visceral rejection. Some reexamined their revolutionary principles to find acceptance. One friend, referred to only as Luis in her *testimonio,* stands out because of his acceptance of Irina's gradual transformation.[74] Luis fulfilled Echeverría Gaitán's vision that the ideals of liberation and autonomy espoused in revolutionary discourse could be inclusive of transgender individuals. And despite some initial difficulties, her wife Nélida Reyes Guzmán also remained at her side. Reyes Guzmán states this was possible by "problematizing your own prejudices and then working on them.... What I discovered in my process with Irina is that love has no gender."[75] Their marriage enabled Reyes Guzmán to reconfigure her partnership to make room for Echeverría Gaitán's self-construction.

In the end, Echeverría Gaitán's clashes with family and fellow militants expose some of the central contradictions regarding sexual politics. First is the known existence and even friendships with sexual minorities but the violent public rejection of their rights. Second is the differentiation of transgender rights from gay and lesbian rights, with the latter seemingly being more acceptable. Her parents' and comrades' relationships with gay men and women were not free of sexism, and their rejection of her gender affirmation highlights how misogyny extends into transmisogyny.[76] Though her disability—likely read as outside of her control—did not preclude her from participating in revolutionary activities, entering womanhood was seen as a transgressive choice that did. Their negative reactions highlight a general anxiety around the role of the feminine body on the Left and foreshadowed the controversy that transgender inclusion continues to elicit among contemporary progressive movements.[77]

Conclusion

When he introduced the concept of the New Man and Woman in 1965, Che Guevara did not reckon with the masculinist and exclusionary politics of the period. He did, however, propose a futurist vision of development that required constant self-construction in order to achieve revolutionary consciousness. For a generation of feminist, sexual minority, and disabled revolutionaries born in the aftermath of the Cuban Revolution, these principles laid the foundation for expanding who could participate in constructing a new world.

Armed with a gun and a vision of Che, Irina Layevska Echeverría Gaitán was one of these revolutionaries. As a youth, Echeverría Gaitán was expected to occupy the role of the virile New Man envisioned by her parents. However, the social stigma and lack of accessible public spaces that constructed her disability, the cultural values that emasculated her body, and the conservative sexual politics that rejected her gender identity alienated her from the masculinist, able-bodied revolutionary subject embodied by men like her father.[78] She nevertheless drew on the models of Guevara, the New Man, and the New Woman at different moments in her life to make meaning of her gender identity and disability, all the while amending them to her militancy and refuting their sexist, ableist, and transphobic iterations.

Echeverría Gaitán documented her engagement with these ideals by writing her own *testimonio*, published as the Left was resurging in Latin America during the region's "Pink Tide" and Mexico's transgender movement was making landmark legal gains. Writing her own memories gave Echeverría Gaitán the opportunity to dispute the restrictive gender ideals of her family and, above all, the Left. While her contemporaries rejected the identitarian politics she championed, Echeverría Gaitán demonstrated how revolutionary praxis could be reconciled with the cultural turns that would mark the last decades of the twentieth century and whose unresolved legacies continue to haunt political activism today.

Notes

1. Robert Franco, "Transgressing Che: Irina Layevska Echeverría Gaitán, Disability Politics, and Transgendering the New Man in Mexico, 1964–2001," in *Radical History Review* no. 136, pp. 75–97. Copyright 2020, MARHO: The Radical Historians' Organization, Inc. All rights reserved. Republished by permission of the copyright holder, and the Publisher. www.dukeupress.edu.

2. Quotation from *Morir de pie*, directed by Jacaranda Correa (Mediam9, artfilms, FOPROCINE, Canal 22, 2011). Translations from Spanish are by the author. Thank you to

Irina Layevska Echeverría Gaitán for sharing her story. Jocelyn Olcott, Pete Sigal, Kevan Antonio Aguilar, and Farren Yero, in addition to the two anonymous reviewers, generously provided me with thoughtful feedback. I would also like to extend my gratitude to Michelle Chase, Isabella Cosse, Heidi Tinsman, and Melina Pappademos for their patience and guidance.

3. Ernesto Che Guevara, "Socialism and Man in Cuba," in *Che Guevara Reader*, ed. David Deutschmann (Ocean Books, 2003), 217.

4. Guevara, "Socialism and Man," 227.

5. Patrick Barr-Melej, *Psychedelic Chile: Youth, Counterculture, and Politics on the Road to Socialism and Dictatorship* (University of North Carolina Press, 2018), 158–61, 234; Roger N. Lancaster, *Life Is Hard: Machismo, Danger, and the Intimacy of Power in Nicaragua* (University of California Press, 1992), 40, 175; with some differences of interpretation, Vania Markarian, *Uruguay, 1968: Student Activism from Global Counterculture to Molotov Cocktails*, trans. Laura Pérez Carrara (University of California Press, 2017), 126–32.

6. Ian Lumsden, *Machos, Maricones, and Gays: Cuba and Homosexuality* (Temple University Press, 1996); Pedro Porbén, *La revolución deseada: prácticas culturales del hombre nuevo en Cuba* (Editorial Verbum, 2014), 25–26.

7. On these questions see Ileana Rodríguez, *Women, Guerrillas, and Love: Understanding War in Central America* (University of Minnesota Press, 1996), 46, 108–9; Rosario Montoya, *Gendered Scenarios of Revolution: Making New Men and New Women in Nicaragua, 1975-2000* (University of Arizona Press, 2012), 8; Ana Serra, *The "New Man" in Cuba: Culture and Identity in the Revolution* (University Press of Florida, 2007), 109. For more on women's roles in revolutionary movements, see Michelle Chase, *Revolution within the Revolution: Women and Gender Politics in Cuba, 1952-1962* (University of North Carolina Press, 2015); Karen Kampwirth, *Women and Guerrilla Movements: Nicaragua, El Salvador, Chiapas, Cuba* (Pennsylvania State University Press, 2002); Alejandra Oberti, *Las revolucionarias. Militancia, vida cotidiana y afectividad en los setenta* (Edhasa, 2015).

8. Daniel James, *Doña María's Story: Life History, Memory, and Political Identity* (Duke University Press, 2000), 123; Arturo Arias, ed., *The Rigoberta Menchú Controversy* (University of Minnesota Press, 2001); Jocelyn Olcott, "Cold War Conflicts and Cheap Cabaret: Sexual Politics at the 1975 International Women's Year Conference," *Gender and History* 22, no. 3 (2010): 733–54.

9. Isabella Cosse, "Infidelities: Morality, Revolution, and Sexuality in Left-Wing Guerrilla Organizations in 1960s and 1970s Argentina," *Journal of the History of Sexuality* 23, no. 3 (2014): 415–50; James Green, *Exile within Exiles: Herbert Daniel, Gay Brazilian Revolutionary* (Duke University Press, 2018); Gerardo Leibner, *Camaradas y compañeros. Una historia política y social de los comunistas del Uruguay* (Trilce, 2011); Jocelyn Olcott, "'A Plague of Salaried Marxists': Sexuality and Subsistence in the Revolutionary Imaginary of Concha Michel," *Journal of Contemporary History* 52, no. 4 (2017): 980–98; Alfonso Salgado, "'A Small Revolution': Family, Sex, and the Communist Youth of Chile During the Allende Years (1970-1973)," *Twentieth Century Communism* 8 (2015): 62–88; Marisa Silva Schultze, *Aquellos comunistas (1955–1973)* (Taurus, 2009); Mary Kay Vaughan, *Portrait of*

a Young Painter: Pepe Zúñiga and Mexico City's Rebel Generation (Duke University Press, 2015).

10. Judith Halberstam, *In a Queer Time and Place: Transgender Bodies, Subcultural Lives* (New York University Press, 2005), 77.

11. Carolyn Dinshaw, Lee Edelman, Roderick A. Ferguson, Carla Freccero, Elizabeth Freeman, Judith Halberstam, Annamarie Jagose, Christopher S. Nealon, and Tan Hoang Nguyen, "Theorizing Queer Temporalities: A Roundtable Discussion," *GLQ: A Journal of Lesbian and Gay Studies* 13, nos. 2–3 (2007): 177–95.

12. M. W. Bychowski, Howard Chiang, Jack Halberstam, Jacob Lau, Kathleen P. Long, Marcia Ochoa, C. Riley Snorton, Leah DeVun, and Zeb Tortorici, "'Trans*historicities': A Roundtable Discussion," *TSQ: Transgender Studies Quarterly* 5, no. 4 (2018): 662–64.

13. Quoted in Dinshaw et al., "Theorizing Queer Temporalities," 182.

14. Eli Clare, "Body Shame, Body Pride: Lessons from the Disability Rights Movement," in *The Transgender Studies Reader 2*, ed. Susan Stryker and Aren Z. Aizura (Routledge, 2013), 261–62.

15. Kimberlé Crenshaw, "Demarginalizing the Intersection of Race and Sex: A Black Feminist Critique of Antidiscrimination Doctrine, Feminist Theory, and Antiracist Politics," *University of Chicago Legal Forum* 139 (1989): 139–68.

16. Lennard J. Davis, *Bending over Backwards: Disability, Dismodernism, and Other Difficult Positions* (New York University Press, 2002), 12–14; Robert McRuer, "We Were Never Identified: Feminism, Queer Theory, and a Disabled World," *Radical History Review* 94 (2006): 148–54, 151.

17. While the use of transgender (*transgénero*) has been gaining ground in recent decades, breaking from the historic designation of *travesti*—subjects who adopt feminine expressions in dress and language but who are traditionally placed in the spectrum of homosexual desire—Echeverría Gaitán does not use this term. Vek Lewis, *Crossing Sex and Gender in Latin America* (Palgrave Macmillan, 2010), 6–7.

18. Alba Pons Rabasa, "From Representation to Corposubjectivation: The Configuration of Transgender in Mexico City," *TSQ: Transgender Studies Quarterly* 3, nos. 3–4 (2016): 388–411, quotation at 395.

19. Irina Layevska Echeverría Gaitán, *Carta a mi padre: Testimonio de una persona transexual con discapacidad* (CONAPRED, 2008), 81.

20. Bychowski et al., "'Trans*historicities,'" 664.

21. María Josefina Saldaña-Portillo, *The Revolutionary Imaginary in the Americas and the Age of Development* (Duke University Press, 2003), 66.

22. In order to obtain this information, I had to ask her and other acquaintances directly.

23. Fernanda Carvajal, "Image Politics and Disturbing Temporalities: On 'Sex Change' Operations in the Early Chilean Dictatorship," *TSQ: Transgender Studies Quarterly* 5, no. 4 (2018): 621–28.

24. Leah Devun and Zeb Tortortici, "Trans, Time, and History," *TSQ: Transgender Studies Quarterly* 5, no. 4 (2018): 518–39.

25. Yinghong Cheng, *Creating the "New Man": From Enlightenment Ideals to Socialist Realities* (University of Hawaiʻi Press, 2009).

26. Renata Keller, *Mexico's Cold War: Cuba, the United States, and the Legacy of the Mexican Revolution* (Cambridge University Press, 2015), 53–57; Louise Walker, *Waking from the Dream: Mexico's Middle Classes After 1968* (Stanford University Press, 2013), 93; José Luis Rivas Ontiveros, *La izquierda estudiantil en la UNAM: organizaciones, movilizaciones y liderazgos (1958-1972)* (Universidad Nacional Autónoma de México, Facultad de Estudios Superiores Aragón, 2007), 128–29; Jaime Pensado, *Rebel Mexico: Student Unrest and Authoritarian Political Culture During the Long Sixties* (Stanford University Press, 2013), 150–51; Eric Zolov, *Refried Elvis: The Rise of the Mexican Counterculture* (University of California Press, 1999), 107–15.

27. For more on the history of Lecumberri, see Sergio García Ramírez, *El final de Lecumberri: Reflexiones sobre la prisión* (Porrúa, 1977); Lessie Jo Frazier and Deborah Cohen, "Defining the Space of Mexico '68: Heroic Masculinity in the Prison and 'Women' in the Streets," *Hispanic American Historical Review* 83, no. 4 (2003): 617–60; Gladys McCormick, "The Last Door: Political Prisoners and the Use of Torture in Mexico's Dirty War," *The Americas* 74, no. 1 (2017): 57–81.

28. Irina Layevska Echeverría Gaitán, email interview with author, August 8–12, 2018.

29. John Lear, *Picturing the Proletariat: Artists and Labor in Revolutionary Mexico, 1908-1940* (Austin: University of Texas Press, 2016), 87–91, 109–10.

30. Daniel Balderston, "Poetry, Revolution, Homophobia: Polemics from the Mexican Revolution," in *Hispanisms and Homosexualities*, ed. Sylvia Molloy and Robert McKee Irwin (Duke University Press, 1998), 57.

31. Jocelyn Olcott, *Revolutionary Women in Postrevolutionary Mexico* (Duke University Press, 2005), 38.

32. *Morir de pie.*

33. Echeverría Gaitán, interview.

34. Barry Carr, *Marxism and Communism in Twentieth-Century Mexico* (University of Nebraska Press, 1992).

35. Echeverría Gaitán, *Carta a mi padre*, 19, 24; Lennard J. Davis, "Introduction," *The Disability Studies Reader* (Routledge, 2013), 1–14.

36. Daniel J. Wilson, "Fighting Polio Like a Man: Intersections of Masculinity, Disability, and Aging," in *Gendering Disability*, ed. Bonnie G. Smith and Beth Hutchison (Rutgers University Press, 2004), 121.

37. June Fernández, *10 ingobernables: Historias de transgresión y rebeldía* (Libros del K.O., 2016), 32.

38. Echeverría Gaitán, *Carta a mi padre*, 38.

39. *Morir de pie.*

40. William Richardson, "The Dilemmas of a Communist Artist: Diego Rivera in Moscow, 1927–1928," *Mexican Studies/Estudios Mexicanos* 3, no. 1 (1987): 49–69; Loren R. Graham, *Moscow Stories* (Indiana University Press, 2006), 243; Michael Voslensky, *Nomenklatura: The Soviet Ruling Class*, trans. Eric Mosbacher (Doubleday, 1984), 216–17.

41. Alexander Hazanov, "Porous Empire: Foreign Visitors and the Post-Stalin Soviet State" (PhD diss., University of Pennsylvania, 2016), 248–49; Briggitte Studer, *The Transnational World of the Cominternians*, trans. Dafydd Rees Roberts (Palgrave Macmillan, 2015), 71.

42. Fernández, *10 ingobernables*, 17. Yolanda Gaitán rejected the proposal, allegedly stating she was worth more than the oil he promised in return.

43. Echeverría Gaitán, *Carta a mi padre*, 42.

44. Tobin Siebers, "Disability, Pain, and the Politics of Minority Identity," in *Foundations of Disability Studies*, ed. Matthew Wappett and Katrina Arndt (Palgrave Macmillan, 2013), 17–28.

45. Fernández, *10 ingobernables*, 13 (quotation), 17–19.

46. Rodrigo Laguarda, *Ser gay en la ciudad de México: Lucha de representaciones y apropiación de una identidad, 1968-1982* (CIESAS, 2009), 57.

47. Juan Jacobo Hernández, *Entrevistas. Archivo Histórico del Movimiento Homosexual en México, 1978-1982* (ENAH–Colectivo Sol CONACYT, Publicaciones digitales UNAM, 2004), 14.

48. Carr, *Marxism and Communism*, 288–89.

49. Rafael de la Dehesa, *Queering the Public Sphere in Mexico and Brazil: Sexual Rights Movements in Emerging Democracies* (Duke University Press, 2010), 80–82, 89–90.

50. Braulio Peralta, *Entrevistas. Archivo Histórico del Movimiento Homosexual en México, 1978-1982* (ENAH–Colectivo Sol CONACYT, Publicaciones digitales UNAM, 2004), 23.

51. Arturo Vázquez Barrón, *Entrevistas. Archivo Histórico del Movimiento Homosexual en México, 1978-1982* (ENAH–Colectivo Sol CONACYT, Publicaciones digitales UNAM, 2004), 8.

52. Echeverría Gaitán, interview.

53. *Morir de pie*.

54. *Morir de pie*.

55. Echeverría Gaitán, *Carta a mi padre*, 40.

56. Fernández, *10 ingobernables*, 24–25.

57. Judith Butler, *Bodies That Matter: On the Discursive Limits of "Sex"* (Routledge, 1993), 125.

58. Echeverría Gaitán, *Carta a mi padre*, 40.

59. *Morir de pie*.

60. *Morir de pie*.

61. Halberstam, *In a Queer Time and Place*, 77.

62. Pons Rabasa, "From Representation to Corposubjectivation: The Configuration of Transgender in Mexico City," 395.

63. Echeverría Gaitán, *Carta a mi padre*, 39; Elizabeth Freeman, "Introduction," *GLQ: A Journal of Lesbian and Gay Studies* 13, nos. 2–3 (2007): 163.

64. *Morir de pie*.

65. Eli Clare, *Exile and Pride: Disability, Queerness, and Liberation* (Duke University Press, 2015), 1–2.

66. Echeverría Gaitán, interview.
67. Echeverría Gaitán, interview.
68. Echeverría Gaitán, interview.
69. Serra, *The "New Man" in Cuba*, 109.
70. Echeverría Gaitán, interview.
71. Echeverría Gaitán, *Carta a mi padre*, 63.
72. Echeverría Gaitán, interview.
73. Fernández, *10 ingobernables*, 21.
74. Echeverría Gaitán, *Carta a mi padre*, 77.
75. *Morir de pie*.
76. Julia Serano, "Skirt Chasers: Why the Media Depicts the Trans Revolution in Lipstick and Heels," in Stryker and Aizura, *Transgender Studies Reader 2*, 226–30.
77. Rodríguez, *Women, Guerrillas, and Love*, 32–35; Carol Riddell, "Divided Sisterhood: A Critical Review of Janice Raymond's The Transsexual Empire," in *The Transgender Studies Reader*, ed. Susan Stryker and Stephen Wittle (Routledge, 2006), 144–58; Stephen Whittle, "Where Did We Go Wrong? Feminism and Trans Theory—Two Teams on the Same Side?," in Stryker and Wittle, *Transgender Studies Reader*, 194–202.
78. Wilson, "Fighting Polio Like a Man," 121; Cynthia Barounis, "Cripping Heterosexuality, Queering Able-Bodiedness: *Murderball*, *Brokeback Mountain* and the Contested Masculine Body," in Davis, *Disability Studies Reader*, 381–88.

GENDER, MEDIA,
AND CULTURE

SIX

Cuba, 1959

Revolutionary Attraction and Journalism

XIMENA ESPECHE

Emma Pérez Téllez—Cuban journalist, poet, educator—compared Fidel Castro with a courtesan, and she did so by quoting the play *Gigi:* "Leave her alone, leave her alone. Can't you see she has her own methods . . . and they work?"[1] According to Pérez, just by changing the gender, one could say the same about Fidel Castro. With this device, Pérez warned all those trying to give the revolutionary leader advice to understand that he had his own methods, and they were working. It was mid-February 1959. The revolution had triumphed just a month and a half prior, and Castro had quickly left Havana to install himself in the Sierra Maestra, the place, he believed, that had lit the final flame of victory.[2] He thought his presence there was imperative, to show that he intended to honor his promises of improving the lives of Cubans.

Gigi had been written by Colette, a French author and cabaret artist; after its 1944 publication, it was adapted into a Broadway play in 1951, then a successful Hollywood film in 1958. It became world famous when it won the Oscars for Best Film and Best Director. For this reason, Pérez's audacity was extremely effective. With the image of Gigi, she conjured an alternative vision of the hypersexualized revolutionary leader, who supposedly embodied "true masculinity" as well as the image of the "unredeemed" messiah.[3] Pérez's alternative vision introduces a new angle, relevant for understanding the expectations and anxieties that the revolution mobilized. In particular, it sheds light on understudied questions about the different modes with which journalists referred to the impact of the revolution and its leaders on global and Cuban public opinion—that is, the effort to understand how Castro and the revolution gained support via a series of notions such as seduction, persuasion, manipulation, "brainwashing," the supposed ability to influence consciousness—concepts most recently associated with the circulation of news about the experiences of prisoners in war in Korea.[4]

In this chapter I argue that those associations were related to the universe of shared anxieties—of enormous relevance during the Cold War—regarding the centrality of emotions. In particular, these concepts played a role in the tension between coercion and consent in mass politics.[5] This approach allows us to better understand the intertwining of the personal, political, and professional dimensions of the impact of the revolution; it complicates our analysis of journalistic evaluations of action and political leadership.[6] The centrality of emotions was often gendered. Notions of intimacy and sexuality had ruled colonial imaginaries of the Caribbean for centuries. Now, in the midst of radical political change in 1959, these imaginaries fused with these emergent anxieties around media power to generate a current of writing centered on "revolutionary attraction." From this perspective, I analyze the writings of three prominent journalists in Cuba in 1959: the Spanish-Cuban Emma Pérez Téllez, the Bolivian René Zavaleta Mercado, and the North American Jules Dubois. My objective is to explore the underlying concerns about the power of the mass media in relation to political action, thus displacing the more common focus on the problem of freedom of expression. While a key concern in that period, the problem of freedom of expression cannot be fully understood without attending to the context of the era's profound anxieties regarding media power and its political usage.[7]

Revolutionary Attraction

In 1959, the manipulation of the masses and of public opinion was a long-term concern in intellectual and cultural fields. It was an important topic at the end of the nineteenth century, was reactivated in the 1930s and 1940s around Nazi-Fascist propaganda, and raised further concern during the Korean War (1950–53). During the Cold War, journalists across a broad ideological and political spectrum worried about the interference of the mass media and of charismatic political leaders in political and social life, something that could also affect journalists themselves. The conflict was conceived of as a "psychological war": a competition for global hearts and minds to support either capitalist or communist lifestyles.[8] The idea of manipulation produced anxiety that transcended politics per se. It was connected to a spiraling alarm over the impact of the media, amplified by the appearance of television.[9] To fully understand its meaning, it is key to pay attention to the evaluations of various journalists regarding the Cuban revolutionary capacity to attract support, modify or model behaviors, and manage collective emotions.

Already during their confrontation with Batista, the revolutionaries carefully constructed their public image. Among other actions, they invited foreign correspondents to visit the Sierra Maestra, generating news coverage of great impact. Throughout 1959, the revolution was subject to constant media scrutiny. Existing studies of media coverage of the revolution have been mostly dedicated to US journalists (and Latin American or European journalists, to a lesser degree), the work of journalists who participated in the new Cuban agency Prensa Latina, or in the construction of the revolution's public image.[10] Here, in contrast, I focus on three journalists from different political-ideological positions—two from Latin America and one from the United States—keeping in mind the particular temporality of that first decisive year of the revolution. All three, in their writings on Castro and the revolution, referenced revolutionary attraction. As a way to highlight rising anxieties over media power in the Cold War, I study how the journalists assumed that this revolution, understood in the framework of a particular informational battle within the Cold War, affected subjectivities.

At the same time, this approach brings to the forefront the problem of the temporality of the event. It seems to me fundamental to highlight the *before Cuba*. That is, it is common to note the enormously transformative potential of the revolution in its first moment, its condition as a watershed that opened a new epoch, the radicalization of the 1960s and 1970s.[11] But when focusing on 1959, it is important not to take subsequent events for granted. What happened in Cuba was not a pure novelty; it was one more link in a series of Latin American revolutions during the Cold War and had two close precedents that directly interpellated it: the revolutions of Guatemala and Bolivia.[12] Journalists as well as other contemporaries conceived it this way.

We begin with the writing of Emma Pérez Téllez—of Spanish origin but living in Cuba since she was a child—and the articles she published in *Bohemia*. Pérez, who has scarcely been studied, undertook a significant ideological journey from communism to militant anti-communism; she supported the revolution valuing it as humanistic and democratic, then later denounced it as totalitarian and communist. It is interesting to read her voice and trajectory in counterpoint with those of the two other journalists studied here. Zavaleta Mercado was a special envoy in Cuba for the La Paz daily *La Nación*. At the time, he was a young member of the Movimiento Nacionalista Revolucionario (MNR), the group that had led the non-Marxist revolution in Bolivia in 1952. He distanced himself from the revolution in the mid-1960s, in fact criticizing it from a position of critical Marxism. For his part, Dubois was an established anti-communist "Cold Warrior" who worked as

Latin America correspondent for the *Chicago Tribune*. He had closely followed events in Cuba since the attack on the Moncada barracks in 1953; he collaborated with *Bohemia* and would publish a book dedicated to Castro in 1959. He chaired the commission for Freedom of the Press at the Inter-American Press Association (IAPA), which brought together daily newspapers of the region, and served as an anti-communist weapon in the bipolar conflict. Dubois's writing and trajectory are well known. Pérez and Zavaleta Mercado have garnered far less expert attention.[13] All three acted, reflecting their local specificities, with different paradigms regarding journalism and the value of information. Zavaleta Mercado did so from the position of an officialist newspaper, although he did not give up his critical independence. Pérez considered it important to explain the particularities of the Cuban case in a bipolar world. Dubois was considered a "champion of freedom of expression," central to US debates of the period. In 1959, Pérez and Zavaleta Mercado saw as positive the attraction exercised by Castro and the revolution, which they considered an opening to a period of social, economic, and democratic progress in the region. On the other hand, Dubois argued that communist influence had deformed the revolution, which he had initially supported.

To understand these visions of revolutionary attraction, it is essential to consider the sexualized and feminized representations of the island, created especially by Americans, in the nineteenth and early twentieth centuries. These constructions imagined Cuba as a desirable woman, a younger sister, a territory of modern lust. Before and after the triumph, the revolutionaries presented themselves as establishing a new moral order against all the economic, social, and sexual exploitation associated with the defeated regime.[14]

The earliest coverage of the revolutionary movement stressed its novelty, seeming to break the binarism of the Cold War. Such coverage allowed the revolutionaries to bypass dictatorial censorship. And, as numerous studies reveal, even before the triumph the revolutionaries were able to use the media to shape their global public image to sustain national and international interest and support.[15] So the revolution opened a celebratory unanimity of the present as opposed to the past.[16] One day after the triumph, Fidel Castro stated: "Now is when the revolution begins."[17] This "now" should be understood as the affirmation that political actions in a decisive historical juncture defined the course of events. The media was central to these constructions.

The logics of news production and distribution contributed to these strategies based on the value given to novelty and scoops. Even before the victory, the "televised drama" of the revolution, with Castro as its main protagonist, was central to the public's strong attention and commitment.[18] The international press amplified and helped construct the guerrillas' heroic masculinity with Castro at the center of a "phallocratic brotherhood" linked to youth, rebels "with a cause."[19] These hypersexualized images were associated with the Latin/emotional character of the revolutionaries, in contrast to a supposedly rational political logic identified with the Anglo-Saxon.[20] Unlike these works, I argue that there were significant variations related to the reference and evaluation of Castro's hypersexualization and revolutionary sensuality. These variations were also connected to different evaluations of political action and leadership, including the concrete use that the revolutionaries themselves gave to the media, entangled with the rising anxieties around media power. For each of these three journalists, reporting was much more than a profession or a duty. Information helped clarify a hidden intention that eventually had to be revealed: who was seducing whom.

Persuasion as Revolutionary Pedagogy

In a special issue of *Bohemia* magazine dedicated to the revolutionary triumph, Emma Pérez argued that the novelty of the revolution was the original mark of a transhistoric Cuban quality because it connected with "our deepest tradition."[21] This was in reference to a key figure, part of the heroic genealogy of the revolution: José Martí, the teacher, poet, educator, journalist, and revolutionary who would mark Cuban political identity from the struggles for independence from Spain at the end of the nineteenth century onward.[22] Pérez, who taught pedagogy at the University of Havana, referred to Martí's children's literature. In other writings, Pérez also referred to Simón Bolívar, one of the most important leaders of the wars of independence; she used these historical references to define Castro's figure. During the first months of 1959, Castro, Martí, and Bolívar functioned in Pérez's writings as a triad characterized by the pedagogy of example, linked to the relationship between communication, teaching, and various ways in which the author referred to seduction and/or persuasion. Referring to Castro, for example, she argued, "He uses all the means of persuasion within his reach as a negation of violence."[23]

The few extant analyses of Pérez's work and trajectory are focused on her activity as a poet. Or they discuss her in relation to her husband, the writer Carlos Montenegro.[24] And, thus, they neglect an original figure in journalism whose contributions included the publication of the clandestine newspaper *Sierra Maestra*.[25] Later, her *Bohemia* articles on the revolution's media contributions can be seen as a pedagogical intervention because she combined the profession of informing with the formation of opinion, central in the framework of a revolution.

We must remember that *Bohemia,* founded in 1908, was one of the most significant publications in the country; it complemented its political analysis with articles on fashion or gossip. In 1959, it reached half a million subscribers.[26] Its pages had both criticized and endured Batista's censorship, and it celebrated the revolutionary triumph. It functioned as an organ of revolutionary pedagogy and contributed to the centrality given to Castro as the epitome of the struggle.[27] Throughout that first year, its pages included various anti-communist pro-revolutionary positions. Indeed, Pérez herself had been a member of the Communist Party until 1947, and thereafter a fervent anti-communist.

During 1959, Pérez celebrated the fact that "the Cuban Revolution—and this is Fidel Castro's constant teaching—represents the transcendence of capitalism and communism."[28] Initially she asserted that the revolution needed practical actions rather than emotional declamations, but this view coexisted with a pragmatic analysis around the necessary use of emotions in political action.[29] Let us examine this latter idea in detail. For example, in February 1959, in the article in which she compared Castro to the apprentice prostitute Gigi, with which this chapter begins, Pérez considered Castro's decision to leave Havana and go to the Sierra Maestra, along with engineers and architects, as virtuous: "Fidel Castro's words correspond to deeds." With one stroke, she legitimized her own activity as a journalist and the validity of the leader's actions.[30]

Later, in May, she claimed that Castro had captured the attention of the region's inhabitants on his trip through the Southern Cone. She covered part of the itinerary (São Paulo, Rio de Janeiro, and Brasilia) and testified that the response he provoked was not fanaticism.[31] For Pérez, Castro turned the peoples of Latin America into an "enormous seminar." The term "seminar," she recalled, "comes from sowing," and it was a "dialectical admiration."[32] In this analysis Castro represented mastery of the ultimate meaning of the revolution: he connected Martí's actions with the present.[33] In June, when Castro asserted that the revolution would form "men free in their mental powers [*fueros mentales*]," Pérez pronounced, "That is to educate."[34] In October, she assured readers that Castro's words in the opening ceremony of an event in Ciudad Libertad had shown him to be a "public teacher"; "he demonstrated the universality of his power of seduction, conquering applauses and kisses in his tender audience."[35]

These are all overlapping images that refer to Castro's *cursus honorum:* teaching, politics, and his training in a Jesuit school and as a lawyer. How did Pérez link this vision with the image of a prostitute? This figure had a long tradition in nineteenth-century French literature, a subgenre that the writer Colette had reinvented with a play, *Cheri,* and in 1944 with the publication of *Gigi.* Nearly sixteen years old, Gigi, raised by her mother and aunt, former courtesans, to satisfy the tastes of potential clients, initially refuses a contract with a family friend eighteen years older, Gaston Lachaille, who has seen her become a woman.

Finally, she agrees to the terms of the contract, a gesture that sparks Lachaille's love for the girl, and he asks for her hand in marriage. Although Gigi seems unaware of the true extent of her upbringing, she nevertheless knows a good deal about the family business and knows what she wants for herself in the future.[36] The Hollywood version of 1958 deepened the aseptic picaresque that Pérez took up in her comparison.

Pérez argues that there is a virtuous relationship of the "methods" used by the courtesan with teaching and secrecy. Thus she complicates a common definition that associates seduction with deceit, based on secret trickery, generally linked to the achievement of a sexual favor.[37] She proposes a reading of the pedagogue as a kind of seducer, a concept reinforced in her articles on Castro in the Southern Cone and at the school event. Pérez thus takes into account the associations that, from classical philosophy, compared communication with a love relationship, and linked teaching and learning as part of that communicational act.[38]

In addition, for Pérez, Castro had turned television "into the stage of a tireless teacher" and thus made every house a classroom.[39] Television was, then, a medium that the revolutionaries used, especially Castro; by then, moreover, Havana had one of the highest percentages of television sets per capita in the region.[40] In Pérez's view, Castro's qualities gained legitimacy by presupposing that there was transparency between words and deeds, between the images shown by the television cameras and reality.[41] In the context of the public discussion of whether or not the revolution was communist and concerns over communist influence, Pérez argued that, if Castro had lied, "the television cameras, those implacable scrutinizers that discover everything, would have exposed him in every Cuban house." Her argument rested on the figure of the leader and on the validity of a technical medium, television.[42] Similarly, Pérez characterized the Cuban people by saying, "There hasn't been a people more difficult to deceive in a long time!"[43]

The true meaning of the facts that Castro's teachings would show was completed with her reference to Bolívar, in an article published when the Cuban leader was about to visit the Bolivarian cradle of Venezuela, his first trip abroad after the revolutionary triumph.[44] Pérez read in Bolívar's correspondence that Bolívar claimed to "love" his comrades in arms. Thus, she argued, Bolivar used a "spontaneous seduction, mixed with deliberation," which constituted a "political weapon."[45] If she said this about Bolívar in March, in June she argued that Castro persuaded, and that persuasion was a negation of violence. According to her analysis of "Operation Truth" (the press campaign the revolutionaries launched around the trials and executions of those accused of violating human rights during the Batista dictatorship), the violence of those trials was unquestionable, but it had not been generated by the revolution. It was a remnant of dictatorial violence that the trials and executions would put an end to.[46] In addition, Pérez criticized the "super-powerful media" that found time to criticize violence now, but not during Batista's rule.[47]

For Pérez, then, Castro was not a manipulator, and publicity/propaganda in his hands thereby changed meaning. Like Gigi, like Bolívar, his actions were those of a seducer. According to some experts, manipulation is an abuse of power in which the victim cannot discern the true scope of the manipulator's intentions. In contrast, Pérez argued that Castro operated through persuasion. Persuasion is separated from manipulation by a blurry line, where the one who is being persuaded remains an active participant.[48] Pérez exceeds common sense with respect to the Weberian figure of the charismatic leader. She decouples seduction, understood as deception or associated with bad leadership, and brings it closer to the sense of persuasion. It values the masculine condition from a position that allows a certain mischievousness and does not conceive it under the weight of an overwhelming sexuality. Here there is no messiah or puritan hero of an ordered revolution.[49] According to Pérez, manipulation was exercised by the two opposing positions in the Cold War: consumer capitalism and totalizing communism.[50] Against this manipulation, revolutionary attraction based on humanism allowed a material and spiritual transformation of old constructions and practices: "The visits of great world celebrities are worth pure gold to make countries attractive today," she wrote.[51] Based on this, Pérez observed the figure of the leader in another sense: Castro himself and the revolution constituted for her a beneficial publicity. They challenged the bad publicity, the one that referred to Cuba as "the most crapulous country in the world." According to the author, when the world press applied the word "idealistic" to the revolution, and to Castro as its greatest symbol, Cubans "thank God for having been born."[52]

For Pérez, the picaresque involved the very decision of whom to invite, and what to report about the country and the revolution.[53] Her words showed the overlapping of fast and slow changes. For example, during the first months of 1959, the world of tourism experienced a sort of continuity that was only broken in 1961.[54] At that time, the new government and the tensions with the United States dissolved the "carnival atmosphere" that had characterized tourism in the country.[55] The revolutionary government deployed a battery of actions to eradicate prostitution, in which the image of the prostitute as a victim of exploitation under the Batista dictatorship was converted into that of a threat to the revolution.[56] One wonders if, in that different atmosphere, Pérez would have suggested the comparison between Castro and Gigi.

Among the causes of Pérez's distancing from the revolution and subsequent counterrevolutionary militancy, it is plausible that the fears she expressed very early on about the threat posed by a certain type of bureaucratic expression, in contrast to more open and unexpected political expressions and logics, played a role.[57] Or that, despite her earlier hopes to the contrary, she eventually considered persuasion and seduction to constitute manipulation in Castro's exercise of power after all.[58]

Pérez's articles continued to appear in *Bohemia* until August 1960. After that, her name could not be found there or in any other Cuban publication. That same year, she went into exile first in Mexico and then in the United States. From there, she worked to communicate the reasons for her disillusionment with the revolution, about which we need further research. Her memory and relevance on the island were practically erased.[59]

The Danger of Novelty

If for Pérez Castro was persuasive and seductive, Zavaleta Mercado argued that Castro "embodied in his figure all the characteristics of a legendary character." He explained to his fellow countrymen how the image of the revolutionaries in their olive-green uniforms was an "unusual" epic. As a result, "even the coldest Saxon objectivity passes from interest to passion."[60] In his notes as special envoy to cover Operation Truth, he argued that on the island there was a "truly tropical unanimity," "the unanimity of repudiation, the infatuation of the epic."[61] These images of the Latin as passionate were common in the Latin American as well as the US press. Zavaleta Mercado was aware that it was the construction of a public image, and like other Latin American colleagues, he valued that emotionality positively.[62]

Zavaleta Mercado's coverage of the Cuban Revolution was part of his larger analysis, in which the novelty of Cuba was shaped, problematically, by another revolutionary experience, particularly that of Bolivia, whose revolution was no longer a novelty.[63] In both revolutions he recognized the struggle against disinformation. On April 9, 1952, the Nationalist Revolutionary Movement took La Paz, capital of Bolivia, with the support of miners' unions, police forces, and workers' militias. It was the beginning of one of the most important revolutions of the twentieth century in Latin America. But, if the Cuban Revolution was at its zenith, Bolivia's was a "revolution in retreat": since 1956 Bolivia's economy had been in crisis, and by January 1959 it was economically dependent on a US aid package. This helped the moderate sector of the MNR gain greater weight in defining the path of the revolution, stopping more radical redistributive initiatives.[64] As others have noted, both revolutions had a defining impact on Zavaleta Mercado's later political and ideological positions and intellectual production.[65]

Zavaleta Mercado arrived in Cuba at the end of January 1959. At the time, he was working in Montevideo as an attaché of the Bolivian embassy and actively participated in Uruguay's cultural world. He was a special envoy of the influential Bolivian newspaper *La Nación,* founded by the MNR.[66] For Zavaleta Mercado, participating in a pro-government newspaper did not imply a renunciation of internal criticism.[67]

His articles reported on the Cuban situation, but also reflected on political dynamics and how these were linked to the role of information under capitalism. Zavaleta Mercado analyzed the revolution in Cuba through the prism of the Bolivian experience. Based on the latter, he believed that there were limits to the public's willingness to accept revolutionary transformation.[68] And the US government's anti-communist policies could therefore take advantage of the fact that inevitably revolutionary nationalism—in both countries—would not be equally appealing to all audiences.[69] Zavaleta Mercado also criticized the way economic and political interests shaped international mass media. For example, he questioned international press coverage of Operation Truth, "because the world's information is directed and fabricated."[70]

His articles function as an analysis of the construction of news, and the role played by novelty. He explained that regarding the revolution, "journalistically, the month of January absolutely corresponds to it. Obviously." The problem was that very obviousness: the image of Castro as a "legendary character" and the "intoxication" of the revolution as parts of an already well-known tropical epic. Therefore, critical attention had to be paid to these newsworthy scenes. Before, the global press and televised images had been attentive to what he synthesized as "the police and the long party of Batista's militarist mechanisms." Now that news space was occupied by the "spectacularism that Cuban tropicalism squanders in all aspects of the country's life."[71] The journalist recalled the relationship between the United States and the Batista government until 1958, which had also had its honeymoon. In the face of such information management, he welcomed Castro's words about the possible creation of a news agency, which would eventually become Prensa Latina.[72] An agency that could explain the value of this novelty outside the needs of those media that shared the interests of the market and the geopolitics led by the United States. One of Zavaleta Mercado's concerns in this regard was the Inter-American Press Association (IAPA), an organization he considered to represent the interests of powerful media companies, aligned with the United States. He wrote about it in a series of articles after his trip to Cuba, in which he denounced the structure of the media. Among other things, he identified Jules Dubois as a counterrevolutionary press operator.

Zavaleta Mercado's interventions, like those of Pérez Téllez, were part of a common universe of topics revisited again and again, in which the attraction exerted by the revolution and its main leader was a central concern. The experience of a revolution such as Bolivia's showed the need for caution. Among Zavaleta Mercado's concerns were the effects and effectiveness of revolutionary attraction once the promised transformations began to put pressure on diverse interests: how novelty, which the revolution needed and drew strength from, was also a danger—the danger of a revolution that did not know how to manage its charm.

The Threat of Communist Infiltration

Dubois had followed the revolutionary struggle closely.[73] We can say almost that he had done it and tried to show a kind of "intimacy," as we shall see. In 1959, he used *Bohemia* among other platforms to celebrate the triumph. In the first issue of *Bohemia* published after the revolutionaries came to power, the "Edition for Freedom," which included a series of special articles, he was syndicated together with the American journalist Herbert Matthews as "friends of Cuba." Both of them gave firsthand reports of Castro, fundamental for the revolution's communications strategy (Matthews's in 1957, Dubois's in January 1959).[74] Dubois maintained an almost weekly column under the title "American News" between February 1 and August 9, 1959, in which he was presented with the double virtue of being both a "fighter for a noble and just cause"—that is, freedom of the press and expression— and a "good journalist."[75] As a star reporter for the conservative *Chicago Tribune*, he covered "revolutions, dictatorships, and other upheavals." With that title, the *Tribune* announced a series of articles on Castro and the revolutionary triumph between February 8 and 16.[76] But he had already written about the revolution in its very beginning after and before the triumph, demonstrating his closeness with the facts and with its most important leaders, Fidel and Raúl Castro. Two scenes seemed to summarize the intimacy: when Dubois interviewed Fidel Castro on January 4, he described how "Castro sat on a desk with one foot on a chair. My left foot occupied the other part of the chair as we talked." And on January 6, in the interview with Raúl Castro, he demonstrated how he was always very near to the main subjects: "'How is Deborah,' I asked Raúl. I had first met her when she was one of the underground leaders in the city. 'She is here with me,' he replied and then added, 'You know she is going to marry me.'"[77]

In October 1959, the *Tribune* claimed that the revolutionary government's transformation into an authoritarian state had been carried out "swiftly." As the pace of events accelerated, the nuances of Dubois's position changed, in tune with the political conjuncture.[78] In his first article in *Bohemia* he justified Operation Truth.[79] In his last article, he ironically explained that Castro should ensure democratic elections and then afterward, yes, he could devote himself to his "favorite pastime and govern the country by television and radio."[80] *Bohemia* also changed its position on the correspondent as the relationship between Dubois and Castro broke down. In September it criticized the attacks on Dubois and continued to consider him a suitable representative of journalistic objectivity. But a month later, in October, it accused him of being the architect of a strategy to sow suspicions that the revolution was being co-opted by communism.[81] Castro too changed his opinion of Dubois. At the beginning of September, he defended Dubois, considering the accusations erroneous, but by the end of the same month, Castro himself launched accusations against Dubois on television.[82] In this period, Dubois's Latin American colleagues began to question him, considering him an agent of imperialism. They maintained that his job as correspondent was an alibi, and that his former jobs were proof of his true identity (intelligence officer, Pentagon official, and instructor at the Fort Leavenworth Intelligence School, where he had purportedly taught Carlos Castillo Armas, the military officer who had deposed Guatemalan President Jacobo Arbenz in 1954).[83]

Between support and censure of the revolution and Castro's leadership, Dubois also published two books in which he compiled his journalistic experience. In April 1959, *Fidel Castro: Rebel, Liberator or Dictator?* was published; it came out in Spanish that same year. A few months later he published *Freedom Is My Beat*, a sort of autobiography, in which he narrated his relationship with the defense of freedom of the press and information in his work as a journalist in Latin America. The first book reprinted articles from the *Tribune*, compiled documents, and showed the intimacy he had achieved with the Cuban leader.[84] The book revealed that intimacy, as well as the legitimacy it offered the correspondent as an expert on the region (expertise that had allowed him to criticize US foreign policy before 1959). After the revolutionary triumph, Dubois identified Castro in his first articles in the *Chicago Tribune*, in *Bohemia*, and in his book published in April as a legitimate "caudillo," "an artist of political intrigues," who had learned "something of psychological warfare," a "skilled manipulator" with a "dominant personality."[85]

His first criticism of the revolution and Castro had also appeared in April, directed at the government's project to create a news agency, which would later become Prensa Latina.[86] That same month, a memo from the US embassy in Havana, entitled "Growth of Communism in Cuba," considered possible actions that might be taken to curb that growth, including the communist capacity for infiltration in the revolutionary government and in various sectors of public life; it also recalled the danger of communist media manipulation.[87] This memo can be read as the reverse of the fears Dubois expressed regarding the revolutionary government forming its own news agency. For Dubois, Castro's interest in a Cuban news agency was explained by three factors. The first was Castro's "resentment" against the US agencies that had covered the Operation Truth trials and shootings. The second was the news agency's goal of reporting on Cuban events according to the wishes and strategies of the revolutionary leader. The last one was to give continuity to Peronism's efforts with the creation of Agencia Latina (where the first director of Prensa Latina, the Argentine Jorge R. Masetti, had worked).

Indeed, Agencia Latina (1949–54) had been the Peronist government's attempt to intervene in the media ecosystem of the region, particularly in Brazil, in its dispute with US news agencies.[88] Dubois was concerned about the growth of a propagandistic media management that he considered totalitarian, and which he understood as communist-Peronist. In May, in the *Tribune* and in *Bohemia*, he argued that in Cuba there was indeed "infiltration" (in the military, not in the civilian sphere) but not communist "domination."[89] According to an internal US State Department memo, Dubois was already worried in June about the possibility of communist infiltration in the Cuban army; above all, he feared that Castro's mistakes would impact his own reputation as a journalist.[90] In August he ironically asserted that the attack on the Moncada Barracks on July 26, 1953, was a "heroic defeat," and that the anniversary celebrations had been carried out "with all the skill of propaganda directors, who can give some lessons to the [advertising] specialists who occupy the Madison Avenue offices in New York." He hinted that it was a publicity stunt, tending to excite the fanaticism of the population. The advertising aspect here is superimposed on the propagandistic aspect: more than a gimmick to sell a product in the market, it is a gimmick to generate political support. Thus, his statement that "Castro's government of the people, by the people and for the people, by television, is the most effective political weapon of the present" could refer, at the same time, to two issues: first, to an objective analysis of the facts—Castro's use of television—and second, a criticism of that form of government, because he considered it a looming threat, related to anxieties related to the power of television.[91]

Dubois's criticism of Prensa Latina linked several of his obsessions, including the authoritarian character of Castro's leadership, which thus linked it to the leadership of Perón (Dubois had been a correspondent in Argentina during Perón's government)—that is to say, the Argentine military man whom he considered had come to power illegitimately, and who sustained a media policy based on the logic of centralization, internal control, and the geopolitical importance of disseminating Peronism outside the country's borders.[92] It was a first warning in a series of others Dubois made during those months (about communist advances in the army, for example). Once he had abandoned any positive analysis of the revolution, he transformed warnings into a teleology, that of communist infiltration, with himself as the one who had correctly predicted events. In April he argued that ever since the 1920s, communists in Latin America had planned to "infiltrate, control, and agitate in labor movements, student movements, the universities, the high schools, the arts, and letters, and in all mass media communications" as part of their "global master plan."[93] In November, the *Tribune* praised Dubois's analysis as someone who in Latin America had "rounded up the facts . . . and [h]ow they fit with communism's audacious drive to envelop the western hemisphere."[94]

On October 21, a plane departing from the United States flew over Havana, dropping anti-revolutionary propaganda and, according to Prensa Libre, bombs. In response, Ernesto Guevara—a key figure in the founding of Prensa Latina— declared: "We will not be [another] Guatemala, we are Cuba."[95] Prensa Latina was a powerful weapon in the revolutionary arsenal, as historian Renata Keller asserts. But it was something more: for the revolutionaries, and particularly for Guevara, it constituted a political and cultural attempt to break what he considered to be a repetition of the past, that is, the defeat of Latin American revolutions. It was a question of securing the present—in Castro's terms, the break represented by the revolution, based on the notion of the "now."[96] To avoid defeat, as had happened in Guatemala, it was essential to avoid the propaganda campaigns and diplomatic operations organized by the CIA that contributed to the coup d'état that toppled Guatemalan revolutionary leader Jacobo Arbenz.[97] For Dubois, on the other hand, it was necessary to prevent Cuba from becoming like Perón's Argentina.

In October, Dubois asserted that Castro "is either a captive of the Communists and their fellow travelers, or he is in total agreement with them." Castro was thus both a captive and, as he had been for Dubois, a captivating subject. Dubois further warned that he used "television, radio, and mass concentrations 'to educate and to orient' the people of Cuba in the most complete and methodical brainwashing operation ever undertaken in contemporary Latin American History."[98] The suspicions that he ironically wielded in August—likening the guerrillas to advertising executives—escalated further in October. With his change of heart, Dubois virulently attacked everything he had previously appreciated about the Cuban leader. He considered "brainwashing" in Cuba a reality. That idea was at the heart of Cold War anxieties. Castro's abilities as a "skilled manipulator," seen as justified as long as it favored Western values, had now become a dangerous brainwashing powerhouse against Western democracy.[99] In November, at a Rotary conference, Dubois claimed that Castro was like Hitler and that his "Anti-American Hate" campaign was even worse than Perón's.[100]

For Dubois, "brainwashing" functioned as a way to understand the character of infiltration, at least as far as Castro and the Cuban people were concerned: the quality of deception systematized by communism in a technique of behavioral control. At the same time, it allowed him to establish a distance that also softened his prior closeness to Castro. Detecting this infiltration was a way of exposing and legitimizing his own skill as a journalist, demonstrating to the public that he had not allowed himself to be influenced.

Conclusions

We have followed here the course of events in which the implications of what revolutionary attraction meant for three journalists led to a multiplicity of options that were operating at the *same time*. From the beginning, Pérez warned that the legitimacy of the revolution was in its humanism as a representation that overcame bipolar politics, and in the figure of a leader whose greatest attributes were those of a seducer who turned the abject into decorum. Dubois conditioned his support on how he analyzed revolutionary decisions: co-opted or not by communist influence. Zavaleta Mercado warned, as an envoy from one revolution to another, about the dangers of information management, that the revolutionaries did not understand in its full scope the problem of being a novelty.

As we have seen, Pérez and Zavaleta Mercado shared an awareness of the value of information, the importance of the weight of propaganda and publicity—sometimes using the terms interchangeably—and of their dangers. According to Zavaleta Mercado, moreover, novelty and scoop were a benefit and a detriment to the revolution.

The objective of informing and defining the scope of this novelty, present and future, and the political direction that the revolution would assume, was in tension with the attempts to keep a distance or justify revolutionary influence. At stake was an old fear of the value of emotions in the analysis of social protest, related to the manipulation of the population, and the population's degree of passivity before the charismatic tricks of a leader.[101] For this reason they distinguished Castro's quality from that of the mere manipulator, the demagogue. Revolutionary attraction seemed to be pristine and also effective, the strategy of a shared emotion. According to Pérez, Castro turned seduction into a political weapon—like Gigi, like Bolívar—and a tool for teaching the values of the revolution—like Martí. In that sense, he "civilized violence," not from a messianic perspective but from a measured picaresque. But this perception, as we saw as a result of Dubois, shifts according to the political definitions of the revolution. Dubois's attraction to Castro thus changes meaning. A "positive" leader, who manages to communicate with the masses and be the medium of a transcendent objective (democracy, freedom), for Dubois becomes a negative leader, a manipulator, an expression of the abuse of power and brainwashing—and thus the revolution reopened fears sparked during the Korean War about the "programming" of subjects who would work against democracy.

At stake in all three authors were debates about revolutionary attraction: the analysis of the value of information, its true scope, how facts and words affected the behavior of subjects, including journalists—in short, the way in which the revolution developed an attractive power that changed its meaning as they perceived the closure of the "now."

Acknowledgments

I am very grateful for the readings and comments from Matías Farías, Martina Garategaray, Silvina Merenson, and especially the editors of this volume, Michelle Chase and Isabella Cosse.

Notes

1. "Déjala, déjala. ¿No ves que tiene sus propios métodos... y le dan resultado?" Emma Pérez, "Fidel Castro tiene sus propios métodos... y le dan resultado," *Bohemia*, February 15, 1959, 30–32. Pérez chose to use the Spanish translation of the French play done by Victoria Ocampo from the English version translated and adapted by Anita Loos. See *Gigi*, adapted by Anita Loos, translated by Victoria Ocampo (Sur, 1955).

2. Julia Sweig, *Inside the Cuban Revolution: Fidel Castro and the Urban Underground* (Harvard University Press, 2002).

3. Van Gosse, "'We Are All Highly Adventurous': Fidel Castro and the Romance of the White Guerrilla, 1957–1958," in *Cold War Constructions: The Political Culture of United States Imperialism, 1945–1966*, ed. Christian G. Appy (University of Massachusetts Press, 2000), 238–56; Lillian Guerra, *Heroes, Martyrs and Political Messiahs in Revolutionary Cuba, 1946–1958* (Yale University Press, 2018), and "Searching for the Messiah: Staging Revolution in the Sierra Maestra, 1956–1959," in *The Revolution from Within: Cuba, 1959–1980*, ed. Michael J. Bustamante and Jennifer L. Lambe (Duke University Press, 2019), 67–94.

4. See, among others, Andreas Killen and Stefan Andriopoulos, eds., "Editor's Introduction: On Brainwashing: Mind Control, Media, and Warfare," *Grey Room* 45 (2011): 7–17; Daniel Pick, *Brainwashed: A New History of Thought Control* (Profile Books, 2022).

5. Christopher Simpson, *Science of Coercion: Communication Research and Psychological Warfare, 1949–1962* (Oxford University Press, 1994).

6. Isabella Cosse, "Masculindades, clase social y lucha política (Argentina, 1970)," *Revista Mexicana de Sociología* 4, no. 18 (2019): 825–54.

7. Other perspectives related to US discussions about free press and free speech can

be found in Sam Lebovic, *Free Speech and Unfree News: The Paradox of Press Freedom in America* (Harvard University Press, 2016). About the relations between information, objectiveness, and ideology in the United States and the USSR, see Benno Nietzel, "Propaganda, Psychological Warfare and Communication Research in the USA and the Soviet Union During the Cold War," *History of the Human Sciences* 29, nos. 4–5 (2016): 59–76.

8. Ellen Herman, *The Romance of American Psychology: Political Culture in the Age of Experts* (University of California Press, 1995).

9. Yeidi M. Rivero, *Broadcasting Modernity: Cuban Commercial Television, 1950–1960* (Duke University Press, 2015); Jennifer Lambe, "The Medium Is the Message: The Screen Life of the Cuban Revolution, 1959–1962," *Past and Present* 246, no. 1 (2020): 227–67.

10. Guerra, *Heroes*; Guerra, "Searching for the Messiah"; Patricia Calvo González, *¡Hay un barbudo en mi portada!!!: la etapa insurreccional cubana a través de los medios de comunicación y propaganda 1952–1958* (Iberoamericana, 2021); Hernán Vaca Narvaja, *Masetti. El periodista de la revolución* (Sudamericana, 2017); Martín Ribadero y Gretel Domenech Hernández, "Presentación del Dossier: Visiones, entusiasmos y disidencias de la Revolución cubana en la escena intelectual latinoamericana de los años sesenta," *Cuban Studies* 52 (2023): 257–64.

11. Claudia Gilman, *La pluma y el fusil. Debates y dilemas del escritor revolucionario en América Latina* (Siglo XXI, 2003).

12. On the temporality of the event, see William H. Sewell Jr., "Historical Events as Transformations of Structures: Inventing the Revolution of the Bastille," in *Logics of History: Social Theory and Social Transformation* (University of Chicago Press, 2005), 225–70. For a different interpretation, see Rafael Rojas, *El árbol de las revoluciones. Ideas y poder en América Latina* (Turner, 2021).

13. On Dubois, see, for example, Enrique Camacho Navarro, "Fidel Castro en la perspectiva estadounidense. El primer año de la revolución," in *Desde el Sur. Visiones de Estados Unidos y Canadá desde América Latina a principios del siglo XXI,* vol. 2, ed. Paz Márquez-Padilla, Germán Pérez Fernández del Castillo, and Remedios Gómez Arnau (UNAM, 2003), 45–63. On Pérez, see Rafael Rojas, "La desaparición de Emma," *Rialta*, https://www.librosdelcrepusculo.com.mx/2012/06/la-desaparicion-de-emma-perez.html?m=1. Zavaleta Mercado has been studied—see, for example, Luis Tapia, "Historias e interpretaciones del 52," in *La producción de conocimiento local: historia y política en la obra de René Zavaleta Mercado* (Muela del Diablo Editores, 2002), 130–44—but not his work on the Cuban Revolution.

14. See, among others, Louis Pérez Jr., *Cuba in the American Imagination: Metaphor and the Imperial Ethos* (University of North Carolina Press, 2010), 235.

15. Guerra, "Searching for the Messiah," 71.

16. Louis A. Pérez Jr., *Cuba: Between Reform and Revolution* (Oxford University Press, 2006), 238.

17. "Difundióse una entrevista con Fidel Castro," *La Prensa*, January 13, 1959.

18. Lambe, "The Medium Is the Message," 255.

19. Diana Sorensen, *A Turbulent Decade Remembered: Scenes from the Latin American*

Sixties (Stanford University Press, 2007), 17; Michelle Chase, *Revolution within the Revolution: Women and Gender Politics in Cuba, 1952-1962* (University of North Carolina Press, 2015); Abel Sierra Madero, *Fidel Castro, El Comandante Playboy: Sex, Revolution and Cold War* (Hypermedia, 2019).

20. Ximena Espeche, "Between Emotion and Calculation: Press Coverage of Operation Truth (1959)," trans. Laura Pérez Carrara, *Radical History Review,* January 2020, 129–41.

21. Emma Pérez, "Nuestro vino de plátano, y si sale agrio, es nuestro vino," *Bohemia,* February 1, 1959, 24–26, 152–53, 25, 54.

22. Lillian Guerra, *The Myth of José Martí: Conflicting Nationalisms in Early Twentieth-Century Cuba* (University of North Carolina Press, 2006); Sorensen, *A Turbulent Decade Remembered,* 17.

23. Emma Pérez, "De Usted también diremos algo," *Bohemia,* June 28, 1959, 46–121, quotation on 46.

24. Rojas, "La desaparición de Emma."

25. Emma Pérez, "El 'territorio libre de los Pinos' no puede vestirse de limpio," *Bohemia,* July 12, 1959, 46–48, 123–25.

26. Guerra, "Searching for the Messiah," 67.

27. Guerra, *Visions of Power,* 42–44.

28. Emma Pérez, "Ocupémonos de las cosas esenciales porque han llegado los tiempos," *Bohemia,* January 18–25, 1959, 14, 15, 164; Emma Pérez, "De Usted también diremos algo," *Bohemia,* June 21, 1959, 58, 99.

29. Emma Pérez, "Ocupémonos," 15.

30. Emma Pérez, "De Usted también diremos algo," *Bohemia,* February 1, 1959, 26; Pérez, "Fidel Castro tiene sus propios métodos," 30–31, quotation on 31.

31. Castro was in São Paulo and Brasilia between April 30 and May 1 and in Rio between May 5 and 7.

32. Emma Pérez, "De Usted también diremos algo," *Bohemia,* May 31, 1959, 121.

33. Emma Pérez, "De Usted también diremos algo," June 21, 1959, 58, 99.

34. Emma Pérez, "Debemos hablar a la vez de Reforma Agraria y de Reforma de la enseñanza—Fidel Castro," *Bohemia,* June 21, 1959, 58–60, 91–92.

35. Emma Pérez, "De Usted También diremos algo," *Bohemia,* October 4, 1959, 46, 124.

36. Tama Lea Engelking, "Crossing Borders with Colette's *Gigi,*" *French Review* 93, no. 3 (2020): 102–15, esp. 107.

37. See, among others, Silke Knippschild, "Seduction and Power in Postclassical Reception: Traditions and Trends," in *Seduction and Power: Antiquity in the Visual and Performing Arts,* ed. Silke Knippschild and Marta García Morcillo (Bloomsbury, 2013), 311–23; Joan W. Scott, "La teoría francesa de la seducción," in *La fantasia de la historia feminista* (Omnívora, 2022), 231–64.

38. William G. Kelley Jr., "Rhetoric as Seduction," *Philosophy and Rhetoric,* no. 2 (1973): 69–80.

39. Emma Pérez, "De Usted también diremos algo," *Bohemia,* April 3, 1959, 59. Pérez's

first article in *Bohemia* was specifically about television. "¿Está Usted a favor o en contra de la TV?," *Bohemia*, August 7, 1955, 62–75.

40. Rivero, *Broadcasting Modernity*; Lambe, "The Medium Is the Message."

41. Guerra, *Visions of Power*.

42. Emma Pérez, "Nuestro vino"; Emma Pérez, "De Usted también diremos algo," *Bohemia*, March 29, 1959, 51.

43. "El cubano sabe que la historia es lo que los hombres hacen. En nuestro país lo único que cuentan son los hechos," *Bohemia*, April 12, 1959, 58–60, 111, 59.

44. Emma Pérez, "Simón Bolívar, el seductor," *Bohemia*, March 8, 1959, 58–60, 101. Castro visited Venezuela from January 23 to 27, 1959.

45. Emma Pérez, "Simón Bolívar."

46. Emma Pérez, "La revolución ha contraído el compromiso de ganarse hasta el respeto de sus enemigos," *Bohemia*, June 28, 1959, 46–48, 137–38; Emma Pérez, "De Usted," *Bohemia*, June 28, 1959, 46, 121, respectively.

47. Emma Pérez, "La revolución," 47.

48. Teun A. van Dijk, "Discourse and Manipulation," *Discourse and Society* 17, no. 3 (2006): 359–83.

49. Espeche, "Between Emotion and Calculation."

50. Emma Pérez, "De Usted también diremos algo," *Bohemia*, July 21, 1959, 58, 99.

51. Emma Pérez, "De Usted también diremos algo," *Bohemia*, August 16, 1959, 46–48, 98; Emma Pérez, "De Usted también diremos algo," *Bohemia*, November 8, 1959, 44.

52. Emma Pérez, "Ahora sí podemos detener la enorme campaña de descrédito organizada contra Cuba," *Bohemia*, March 1, 1959, 42–44, 126.

53. Emma Pérez, "Ahora sí," 126.

54. John Andrew Gustavsen, "Tension Under the Sun: Tourism and Identity in Cuba, 1945–2007" (PhD diss., University of Miami, 2009).

55. Amalia Cabezas, *Economies of Desire: Sex and Tourism in Cuba and the Dominican Republic* (Temple University Press, 2009), 44.

56. Rachel Hynson, "Count, Capture, and Reeducate: The Campaign to Rehabilitate Cuba's Female Sex Workers, 1959–1966," *Journal of the History of Sexuality* 24, no. 1 (2015): 125–53.

57. Emma Pérez, "¿Por qué interesan los escritores? ¿Por sus libros o por sus vidas?," *Bohemia*, March 29, 1959, 50–53, 111, 122; Emma Pérez, "La novelista ahogada: Virginia Woolf," *Bohemia*, September 20, 1959, 36–38, 100–101, 108–9.

58. Scott, "La teoría francesa de la seducción."

59. Sergio Andricaín and Antonio Orlando Rodríguez, "Apuntes sobre la censura de autores y libros de literatura infantil y juvenil en Cuba (1960–1985)," MeowBlog, September 15, 2022, https://cuatrogatos.org/blog/?p=8146, https://www.in-cubadora.com/2022/09/20/sergio-andricain-antonio-orlando-rodriguez-apuntes-sobre-la-censura-de-autores-y-libros-de-literatura-infantil-y-juvenil-en-cuba-1960-1985/.

60. René Zavaleta Mercado, "Revolución en Cuba. Los fusilamientos o la impunidad

sistemática," *La Nación*, January 31, 1959; *René Zavaleta Mercado. Obra completa* III, vol. 1, ed. Mauricio Souza Crespo (Plural, 2015), 208–10.

61. René Zavaleta Mercado, "Revolución en Cuba: Monstruos y teléfonos cubanos," *La Nación*, February 1, 1959; *René Zavaleta Mercado* III, 1:210–12.

62. Espeche, "Between Emotion and Calculation."

63. "Coronel retirado que se pone pesado como adalid de una libertad en la que no cree," *La Nación*, October 3, 1959; "Continentalmente calumnia a la Revolución un informe de la sip," *La Nación*, October 10, 1959, in *René Zavaleta Mercado* III, 1:356–60.

64. James Dunkerley, *Rebelión en las venas: La lucha política en Bolivia, 1952-1982* (Plural, 2003): 113–56; Kevin Young, "Purging the Forces of Darkness: The United States, Monetary Stabilization, and the Containment of the Bolivian Revolution," *Diplomatic History* 37, no. 3 (2013): 509–37.

65. Mauricio Souza Crespo, "Apuntes sobre la obra de René Zavaleta Mercado 1957–1974," *Ahora sé por qué hubo quienes pensaban que conocer es recordar . . . René Zavaleta Mercado. Obra Completa* I (Plural, 2015), 12–17; Diego Giller, "Zavaleta Mercado, René," *Diccionario biográfico de las izquierdas latinoamericanas*, 2022, https://diccionario.cedinci.org/zavaleta-mercado-rene/.

66. Jerry W. Knudson, "The Press and the Bolivian National Revolution," *Journalism Monographs* 31 (November 1973).

67. Luis Tapia, "En el nacionalismo revolucionario: periodismo político," in Luis Tapa, *La producción de conocimiento local: historia y política en la obra de René Zavaleta Mercado* (Muela del Diablo, 2022), 42–55.

68. Zavaleta Mercado, "Revolución en Cuba: Monstruos y teléfonos cubanos."

69. Vanni Pettinà, "The Shadows of Cold War over Latin America: The US Reaction to Fidel Castro's Nationalism, 1956–59," *Cold War History* 11, no. 3 (2011): 317–39.

70. Zavaleta Mercado, "Revolución en Cuba: Monstruos y teléfonos cubanos."

71. Zavaleta Mercado, "Revolución en Cuba. Los fusilamientos o la impunidad sistemática."

72. Zavaleta Mercado, "Revolución en Cuba: Monstruos y teléfonos cubanos"; Renata Keller, "The Revolution Will Be Teletyped: Cuba's Prensa Latina News Agency and the Cold War Contest over Information," *Journal of Cold War Studies* 21, no. 3 (2019): 88–113.

73. Guerra, *Heroes*.

74. Herbert L. Matthews, "Cuban Rebel Is Visited in Hideout," *New York Times*, February 24–26, 1957; Jules Dubois, "First Castro Interview! Cuban Leader Tells Tribune His Plans for Civilian Rule," *Chicago Tribune*, January 4, 1959, 1–2.

75. "Jules Dubois, Colaborador de Bohemia," *Bohemia*, February 1, 1959, 6.

76. Jules Dubois, "What I Know About Castro," *Chicago Tribune*, February 8, 1959, 1, 7.

77. Dubois, "First Castro Interview!" 1, 2, 41; "Always Expected Victory, Says Raul Castro," *Chicago Tribune*, January 6, 1959, 1.

78. "Foreign," *Chicago Tribune*, October 25, 1959, 4.

79. Jules Dubois, "Las ejecuciones en Cuba," *Bohemia*, February 1, 1959, 6, 167.

80. Jules Dubois, "El Grandísimo espectáculo de Cuba," *Bohemia*, August 9, 1959, 9.

81. "Por la convivencia democrática," *Bohemia,* September 12, 1959, 80; "En Cuba," *Bohemia,* October 25, 1959, 82–83.

82. "The Deprivations of Mr. Dubois," *Chicago Tribune,* October 7, 1959, 12.

83. Juan Alberto Boza, "Las espadas mediáticas del anticomunismo Intelectuales y periodistas en la Guerra Fría latinoamericana," *Épocas. Revista de Historia* 18 (2018): 145–75, esp. 145–55.

84. Jules Dubois, *Fidel Castro: Rebel, Liberator or Dictator?* (Bobbs-Merrill, 1959); Jules Dubois, *Freedom Is My Beat* (Bobbs-Merrill, 1959); Jules Dubois, "A Lesson Not to Be Forgotten," *Bohemia,* February 15, 1959, 110.

85. Dubois, *Fidel Castro,* 8, 19, 241; Dubois, "What I Know About Castro," 1, 7; Jules Dubois, "Fidel Castro, Romulo Betancourt y la libertad," *Bohemia,* March 8, 1959, 108.

86. Jules Dubois, "Agencias de noticias auspiciadas por gobiernos," *Bohemia,* April 26, 1959, 108–14.

87. Daniel M. Braddock, "Dispatch from the Embassy in Cuba to the Department of State," no. 1159, April 14, 1959, Department of State, Central Files, 737.001/4-1459, https://history.state.gov/historicaldocuments/frus1958-60v06/d278.

88. Ariel Goldstein, *Nacionalismo, populismo y propaganda entre Argentina y Brasil* (IEALC, Editorial El Colectivo, 2023).

89. Jules Dubois, "Cubans Ban Red Efforts to Get Key Posts," *Chicago Tribune,* May 6, 1959, 1; Jules Dubois, "La conspiración comunista," *Bohemia,* May 10, 1959, 118.

90. Memorandum of Conversation, June 10, 1959, Department of State, Central Files, 737.00/6-1059. Confidential. Drafted by Wieland, available at https://history.state.gov/historicaldocuments/frus1958-60v06/d317 (accessed July 11, 2025).

91. Quotations from Dubois, "El Grandísimo espectáculo de Cuba," 95; see also Lambe, "The Medium Is the Message," 228.

92. Perón participated in a coup in 1943. He was elected president in 1945 and would govern for two terms until another coup in 1955 removed him from power. Mirta Varela, "Peronismo y medios: control político, industria nacional y gusto popular," *Red de Historia de los medios,* http://www.rehime.com.ar/escritos/documentos/idexalfa/v/varela/Mirta%20Varela%20-%20Peronismo%20y%20medios.pdf (accessed April 28, 2025).

93. Jules Dubois, "Reds Step Up Drive for Latin America," *Chicago Tribune,* April 12, 1959, 8.

94. Jules Dubois, "Get the Whole Story from the Man the Cubans Want to Kill," *Chicago Tribune,* November 21, 1959, 11.

95. Ernesto Guevara, "Discurso en la concentración ante el Palacio Presidencial," October 26, 1959, in Ernesto Guevara, *Obras escogidas,* Centro de Estudios Miguel Enríquez, Archivo Chile, 145–47, quotation on 147.

96. Keller, "Revolution Will Be Teletyped," 90.

97. Cindy Forster, "Not in All of America Can There Be Found a County as Democratic as This One: Che and Revolution in Guatemala," in *Che's Travels: The Making of a Revolutionary in 1950s Latin America,* ed. Paulo Drinot (Duke University Press, 2010), 210–44.

98. Jules Dubois, "Castro Moving to Dictatorship, Dubois Reports," *Chicago Tribune,*

October 25, 1959, 1; Jules Dubois, "Castro Calls 1,000,000 Anti-US Rally," *Chicago Tribune,* October 24, 1959, 1, 2.

99. Dubois, "Castro Moving to Dictatorship," 1.

100. John H. Thomson, "Castro Like Mad Hitler, Dubois Says," *Chicago Tribune,* November 11, 1959, 1.

101. Jeff Goodwin, James Jasper, and Francesca Polletta, "Introduction: Why Emotions Matter," in *Passionate Politics: Emotions and Social Movements* (University of Chicago Press, 2001), 1–24.

SEVEN

Revolutionary Roses
on the Cane Field

*Staging Cuban Women
in Socialist China, 1960–1965*

SIWEI WANG

Wearing his iconic black beret, Che Guevara stood before the smiling crowd at the Beijing Airport in November 1960. In a firm voice, he praised revolutionary solidarity between the People's Republic of China and the Republic of Cuba, two revolutionary states that had emerged after years of guerrilla struggles against foreign colonizers and bourgeois governments: "Comrades and friends of the great people of China, today we come with deep satisfaction to fulfill an official mandate of our government and our people's friendship."[1] In the following days, he traveled around China and visited factories, communes, and schools. As the minister of industries of Cuba, he persuaded the Chinese government to sign economic contracts to support the Cuban Revolution. The most significant among them was China's importation of one million tons of Cuban sugar every year.[2] The decision was mutually beneficial: China's sugar production had not recovered from the negative impact of the Great Leap Forward, and Cuba needed to export sugar to break the economic blockade imposed by the United States.[3]

More important was the exchange of experience concerning building an independent sugar industry on the ruins of colonialism. On November 25, 1960, Che paid a special visit to the Neijiang sugar factory in Sichuan Province, which had a centuries-old sugar industry.[4] Established in 1956, Neijiang was the first modern sugar factory whose equipment was entirely designed and made in China. During the Great Leap Forward, which promoted rapid industrial development, it also developed multiple techniques for utilizing sugarcane to produce other products such as wine and paper.[5] It is easy to imagine why such an achievement attracted Che, as Cuba was eager to nationalize its sugar industry, which relied heavily on American machines and technology. It required nationwide mass mobilization within Cuba and technical and economic support from the whole Socialist Bloc.[6] Sugar, as a symbol of revolutionary friendship within the socialist camp, entered into the everyday life of Chinese families and marked the beginning of the honeymoon period of the Sino-Cuban relationship in the 1960s.

Chinese news coverage of Che contained two symbolic images of the Cuban Revolution in socialist China: the bearded guerrilla rebel with a black beret and Cuban sugar. Even now Che's heroic image and the taste of Cuban sugar are the most impressive memories of Cuba for people who grew up in this era. For decades Chinese fans have traveled to Latin America in search of Che's footprint.[7] In 2000, Chinese dramatists Zhang Guangtian and Huang Jisu created a play about Che Guevara to commemorate his revolutionary spirit, which aroused a series of debates among the Chinese intellectual circle about the legacy of radical leftism in the twentieth century.[8] When I was traveling in Cuba in the spring of 2019, I met a group of Chinese tourists outside the American writer Ernest Hemingway's house in Havana. While drinking sugarcane juice bought from a street vendor, they talked about their childhood experience of eating Cuban sugar in the sixties. The taste of Cuban sugar was their most indelible memory of the solidarity between Afro-Asian Latin American people.

However, the role of women in the Cuban Revolution, the travels of Cuban women to socialist China, and women's contribution to Sino-Cuban anti-imperialist solidarity in the 1960s have been downplayed over time. Similarly, the scant scholarly literature on the history of the Sino-Cuban relationship mainly focuses on male-dominated governmental diplomacy.[9] In this chapter, I recover these broader transpacific encounters by arguing that bearded guerrillas and heroic male peasants were not the only idealized actors that symbolized the Cuban Revolution in China in the 1960s. Chinese media and transnational feminists also emphasized the role of women in the national revolution and in anti-imperialist struggles to mobilize the Chinese audience's identification with the Cuban Revolution. Using new archival sources based in China, this article explores the 1962 Chinese adaptation of the Cuban play *Cañaveral* (Cane field) as a case study to analyze how Chinese and Cuban dramatists worked together to build the image of Cuban women as militant, active revolutionaries with spontaneous political consciousness.[10] The play's content, and the behind-the-scenes negotiations over its gender representations, provide insight into the transnational dialogue that took place across the socialist Global South, spurred by the Cuban Revolution.

Sino-Cuban Friendship in the Cold War

Chinese interest in the Cuban Revolution did not begin in 1959. *People's Daily,* the official newspaper of the Chinese Communist Party, had been following the Cuban Left's struggles even before the foundation of the People's Republic of China in 1949. The Cuban Communist Party (Partido Socialista Popular, PSP) and the Chinese Cuban leftist organization Grand Alliance of Overseas Chinese in Cuba Protecting Democracy (Alianza Nacional de Apoyo a la Democracia China, 古巴华侨拥护民主大同盟) were two major institutions that had enthusiastically supported the PRC government.[11] Moreover, a few Latin American leftist intellectuals who were pioneers visiting China in the early 1950s, such as Cuban writer Nicolás Guillén, Chilean writer Pablo Neruda, Chilean artist José Venturelli, and Brazilian writer Jorge Amado, were active in connecting China and the broader Latin American leftist community through the world peace movements.[12]

In addition, two visits by Cuban leftist leaders played an important role in building the foundation for the Chinese audience to identify with Cuba as part of a broader anti-colonial and anti-imperialist Afro-Asian Latin American community. One was Edith García Buchaca's attendance at the 1949 Asian Women's Congress in Beijing as the president of the Democratic Federation of Cuban Women (Federación Democrática de Mujeres Cubanas, FDMC).[13] The other was Nicolás Guillén's visit to China with Jorge Amado in 1952 as representatives of the World Peace Council.[14] As the earliest Cuban intellectuals to visit socialist China, they proposed for the first time the issues of national liberation and women's liberation as common themes facing both Cuba and China.

After the success of the Cuban Revolution, the PRC government responded immediately with enthusiastic support. For their part, Chinese journalists quickly sought to establish more direct access to the island. According to the memoir of Pang Bing'an, the former Chinese correspondent in Cuba, while he was traveling with the Chinese acrobatic troupe that was touring in Latin America, he witnessed how people celebrated the victory of the Cuban Revolution in the streets of Uruguay on January 2, 1959. In March he met the founder of Cuba's Radio Rebelde, Jorge Enrique Mendoza, and broadcaster Violeta Casals in Santiago, Chile. With the support of the Chilean artist José Venturelli, he and another Chinese journalist, Kong Mai, flew to Cuba on April 13. Soon after, they established a branch of the Chinese official media, Xinhua News Agency, in Havana, aiming to provide firsthand reports about the ongoing Cuban Revolution that transcended the coverage dominated by the two superpowers.[15]

On September 2, 1960, Fidel Castro announced to the world in the First Declaration of Havana that Cuba would become the first Latin American country to establish a formal diplomatic relationship with the People's Republic of China.[16] This direct connection was important not only for the Chinese understanding of the Cuban Revolution but also for strengthening identification with ongoing revolutionary struggles throughout Latin America. The establishment of a formal diplomatic presence in Havana allowed the Chinese to build connections with many other Latin American intellectuals who traveled there.[17] In her study of the Chinese translation of Latin American literature, Teng Wei points out that the victory of the Cuban Revolution in 1959 directly spurred a peak in Chinese-Latin American translation. An anti-imperialist revolutionary culture centered around Cuba has become the mainstream impression of Latin America for the Chinese public that has persisted to this day.[18]

In the Chinese narrative, the year 1959 marked another peak of anti-colonial struggles in Asia, Africa, and Latin America. Cuba and Congo were often put together as representatives of nationalist revolutions.[19] Although Cuban leaders would not declare the revolution to be socialist until 1961, it was still considered a radical national liberation movement that was representative of other nationalist movements in Asia, Africa, and Latin America. Liu Simu, the associate editor of *Jiefang Daily*, reported on the nature of the Cuban Revolution in 1961 after the Bay of Pigs invasion. In his report, he argues that the Cuban Revolution was distinct from other national independence movements because it had gone through a long-term armed struggle in the countryside and gained wide support from the people, the majority of whom were peasants, through land reforms.[20] In an interview with Chinese journalists in 1959, Che Guevara explained that land reform was key to the success of the Cuban Revolution, successfully mobilizing peasants who had been suffering from the country's unequal land distribution (latifundia). Therefore, Guevara said, the Cuban Revolution "is not a movement of a small number of people or just a few leaders. Our revolution is a liberation movement of the people; the people are the power behind this revolutionary movement."[21]

Those reports highlighted the similarities between the Chinese and Cuban Revolutions as both achieved national independence from a semi-colonial state through armed struggle, land reform, and people's war. This interpretation also laid the foundation for China to include Cuba in its blueprint of an Afro-Asian-Latin American anti-imperialist camp as Chinese relations with the Soviet Union came under strain. Especially during the Cuban Missile Crisis, China expressed firm support for the armed resistance of the Cuban people against imperialism, opposing the Soviet proposal for peaceful coexistence with imperialism.[22] Although Chinese-Cuban relations would eventually be ruptured by the Sino-Soviet split, in which Cuba sided with the Soviets, Chinese leaders celebrated the Cuban

FIGURE 7.1. Stills from a brochure for the Chinese documentary film 战斗的古巴 (Cuba in Battle, 1960) produced by China Central Newsreel and Documentary Film Studio. Brochure printed in Beijing by China Film Press, 1961.

Revolution in the early 1960s as a kindred national liberation movement and revolutionary state in the Global South.

This political interpretation of the Cuban Revolution also influenced its cultural dissemination at the grassroots level in China. News reports of land reform in sugarcane plantations after the Cuban Revolution were often accompanied by a historical explanation of how Cuba's sugar industry led to its poverty under Spanish and American colonialism, how the nationalization of the sugar industry was essential for Cuba to overcome its underdevelopment and achieve national independence, and how militant peasants defended the sugarcane fields from clandestine American attacks. Nicolás Guillén contributed many poems that popularized the symbolic meaning of sugarcane in its transnational circulation. The Chinese translations of his poems such as "Caña" (Cane) and "Mi Patria es Dulce por Fuera" (My country is sweet outside) were popular among Chinese writers, artists, and intellectuals. Cuba's past, present, and future were condensed into one symbol: sugarcane. The image of sugarcane peasants wearing straw hats while holding a machete or gun to protect the cane field also became a classical symbol of the revolutionary Cuban people.

The popularity of sugarcane as a theme of literature and art reached a peak in 1961 and 1962 during the Bay of Pigs invasion and the Cuban Missile Crisis. The Chinese government organized a series of cultural activities to support the Cuban Revolution, including poetry recitations, film screenings, "living newspapers" (street performances based on news events), plays, songs, and woodcut prints, as well as a series of translations of Cuban literature and political writings by Castro and Guevara. The symbol of militant sugar workers implied the fundamental transformation of Cuba from an oppressed people to an anti-imperialist power. It functioned as an important lesson for ordinary Chinese people to connect their own experiences with what they learned from news media: the imported Cuban sugar they ate every day was inseparable from Cuba's colonial history and its contemporary struggle against American imperialism. Only through recalling the past's sufferings could they sense today's happiness. The bitterness and sweetness of the sugar reminded the Chinese people of their anti-colonial and anti-imperialist experiences since the Opium Wars in the nineteenth century. It also associated them with their ongoing socialist construction to conquer underdevelopment through agricultural reform and modernization. True internationalist solidarity could be established through such deep identification with each other's colonial experience and struggle for national independence. Through such education, new knowledge of Latin America was produced and circulated among the Chinese masses.

Women's Solidarity Across the Pacific: Anti-imperialist Solidarity and Women's Liberation

Chinese solidarity with the Cuban Revolution often referenced the shared experiences of guerrilla struggle, agrarian reform, and empowerment of the peasantry, but ideals about women's revolutionary participation and liberation were also important. Indeed, transnational connections between Chinese and Cuban women's liberation movements had already been established through anti-imperialist peace movements in the 1950s. In her study of Cuban women's participation in the Hands Off Korea Campaign (1950–51), Michelle Chase points out that anti-imperialist solidarity campaigns had already played an important role in the development of transnational links between feminists across the Global South before the Cuban Revolution. For example, Edith García Buchaca's attendance at the 1949 Asian Women's Congress in Beijing profoundly impacted her comprehension of the deep bonds between women's liberation and anti-imperialism, anti-colonialism, and socialist revolution. Chinese women's active participation in political campaigns, military forces, the workforce, and cultural events was inspiring for her.[23]

FIGURE 7.2. Cover of the catalog for an exhibit, 古巴革命摄影展览 (Photography exhibition of the Cuban Revolution), displayed in Beijing, 1963. Published by All-China Journalists Association, China Photographers Association, and Chinese-Cuban Friendship Association.

After the Cuban Revolution, the Chinese government invited several female leaders to visit China. Their presence further impressed Chinese audiences with the importance of women's contributions to the revolution. For example, Melba Hernández and Haydée Santamaría, who were the only two women in the attack on Moncada Barracks in Santiago de Cuba on July 26, 1953, visited China in the early sixties. At Melba's welcome dinner on July 30, 1962, Cuban ambassador Oscar Pino Santos explained to Premier Zhou Enlai how Melba and Haydée had challenged Fidel Castro's gender preconceptions by showing him that women were able to fight along with male guerrilla soldiers in the attack on Moncada Barracks.[24] Other leaders like Violeta Casals, who visited China as the leader of the Cuban Women's Delegation in 1959, also gave talks on Cuban women's participation in national liberation since the nineteenth century.[25] These talks revealed that Cuban leaders were conscious of emphasizing women's role in the revolution and challenging the gender boundaries within the revolution in its global circulation.

The Cuban revolutionary government also worked to shape global impressions of the Cuban Revolution by organizing a large photo exhibit that toured socialist countries including China. The exhibit, which included some five hundred photos showing the process of the Cuban Revolution from 1952 to 1962, opened in Beijing in 1963. On the catalog's cover page, Fidel Castro's profile floats like a virtual background above a multiracial group of women wearing militant costumes and holding guns. While identifying Castro as the spiritual leader of the Cuban Revolution, the image also foregrounds female guerrilla soldiers as a revolutionary power and a symbol of national liberation. As shown in the cover photo, and in some of the photographs in the exhibit, women's liberation and their active presence in nationalist, anti-imperialist struggles as well as the construction of socialism were common themes in representations of the Cuban Revolution in China.

Chinese women delegates also visited Cuba and brought back their firsthand observations of the Cuban Revolution. On September 22, 1962, Guo Jian, a militant feminist who had joined the CCP and participated in national liberation since the 1930s, represented the All-China Women's Federation at the First National Congress of the Federation of Cuban Women (Federación de Mujeres Cubanas, FMC) in 1962. She was deeply moved by how Cuban women actively supported national defense against the US imperialist invasion and economic blockade. Both working women and stay-at-home wives were mobilized as volunteers to guarantee the logistics supply for soldiers who battled at the front line. The FMC, Guo says in her report, had expanded from 17,000 to 376,000 people. Within a short amount of time, it developed more than three thousand branches in different factories, cooperatives, and other organizations nationwide. In addition, she also visited a Cuban peasant woman's house on a people's farm near Playa Larga. The woman, who used to live in huts before the revolution, showed her the new house constructed by the revolutionary government. She told Guo that the Cuban people would defend their country from American imperialism. Through her contact with Cuban women, as well as representatives from other Latin American countries such as Venezuela and Colombia, Guo confirmed Cuban women's contribution to national liberation against imperialism and the FMC's impressive power of mobilization.[26]

Wu Quanheng, another communist feminist who was the president of the All-China Women's Federation, also visited Cuba in 1962 and 1963. In her travelogue, she showed how the Cuban Revolution brought women liberation in all social realms, such as improved education and employment opportunities. She told a story of a nineteen-year-old Cuban girl who worked at the office of the Bureau of Tourism. The girl served in a militia from 6:00 a.m. to noon every other day. When she was not working, she studied during that period. On Sundays, she often participated in volunteer labor in the fields. She told Wu that her family used to rely on support from a rich uncle. Now she was able to support her family by herself through work and study. In another village, Wu met a Cuban woman who married a Chinese man from Guangdong Province. The woman told her how they suffered from racism before the revolution. Now all their children served in militias that defended their country.[27] The visit made Wu believe that women's liberation was inseparable from national liberation. On January 14, 1963, she gave a speech at the Congress of Women of the Americas, held in Havana. Appraising Cuban women's courage to defend their country from US imperialist invasion, Wu emphasized that American imperialism was the root of all the pains, poverty, hunger, unemployment, shortage of land, discrimination, and oppression. "In the battle for women's liberation, Chinese women know from their own experience that women's liberation, their equal rights, and children's happiness are inseparable from the struggle for national independence and democratic freedom." She said, "At the same time, the history of women's movements in various countries has proved that national independence is an important guarantee of women's liberation."[28] Wu's talk posited anti-imperialist national liberation as the shared material basis for the liberation of women all over the world, which further enhanced the mutual identification between Chinese and Cuban women.

In the 1960s, the narrative of revolutionary Cuban women in China was mainly focused on three images: guerrilla soldier, peasant, and volunteer teacher. Che Guevara's article "Lidia," which was written in commemoration of the sacrifice of the peasant woman Lidia Esther Doce Sánchez during the struggle against Batista, was translated into Chinese.[29] The Chinese writer Qin Mu also published the article "Four Cuban Peasant Women" in *People's Daily*, written during his visit to Cuba in 1962. The article praised the brave women who were killed by the invaders during the Bay of Pigs invasion.[30] After Cuba launched the literacy campaign in 1961, Daura Olema García's report *Maestra Voluntaria* (Volunteer teacher) was translated into Chinese by diplomats Huang Zhiliang and Liu Jingyan, who were stationed in Cuba.[31] Focusing on the experience of a female volunteer teacher in the literacy campaign in rural areas, the report highlights women's active agency in the social transformation of Cuban society after the revolution. The image of revolutionary Cuban women was deeply rooted in the socialist memory of many Chinese who grew up in this era. Decades later, the Chinese writer Zhang Chengzhi remembered how he had imagined the sacrifice of a brave Cuban female guerrilla soldier when he sang the Cuban song "El Mambí" along with other youths during the Cultural Revolution.[32]

Staging Feminist Anti-Imperialism from Cuba to China

As we have seen, depictions of the Cuban Revolution in China were not restricted to male guerrilla leaders and political and economic reform; Cuban and Chinese women also praised Cuban women's participation in the revolution and noted that women's liberation and national liberation were intertwined. At the same time, the Chinese portrayal of women in the Cuban Revolution reflected local dynamics that closely resonated with its own ongoing gender revolution. The Chinese performance of the Cuban play *Cañaveral* (Cane field), which was staged in multiple cities across China in 1962, provides an example of the way anti-imperialist Cuban women's voices were articulated to the Chinese audience at the popular level. In the process of adaptation, Chinese dramatists enriched the gender representation within the original play by highlighting women's spontaneous political consciousness and active agency in the Cuban Revolution.

In 1962, the Tianjin People's Art Theatre performed *Cañaveral* to celebrate the forthcoming third anniversary of the Cuban Revolution. It was a three-act play written by the Cuban director Paco Alfonso in 1950. Set on an American-owned sugarcane plantation before the Cuban Revolution (between 1950 and 1958), the story focuses on the sugarcane peasants' union struggle led by Fico and Juan Cuabas against the American imperialists who owned the plantation and their local agent Don Lucas, who studied in the United States and works as a manager of the plantation.

Featuring peasant dialect and realistic themes, *Cañaveral* was a play that had emerged in dialogue with the communist-led labor movement in Cuba. Its director, Paco Alfonso, was the founder of Teatro Popular (1942–45), which aimed to create national plays for the masses, the majority of whom were illiterate and marginalized by elite culture. Teatro Popular was developed out of the street theater brigades (*brigadas teatrales de la calle*) that arose in the late 1930s. Under the support of the Cuban Workers' Federation (Confederación de Trabajadores de Cuba, CTC), which was then led by the PSP, the group was able to provide free performances for workers in streets, unions, tents, or plazas. However, anti-communist political forces put their theater activities to an end in 1945.[33]

Despite the short life of Teatro Popular, Alfonso continued to create works concerned with the life of workers and peasants of African descent. *Cañaveral*, in his own words, reflected the Cuban government's suppression of unions and prosecution of union leaders like Jesús Menéndez.[34] In 1950, *Cañaveral* won the National Theatre Award in the competition initiated by the Cuban Ministry of Education. However, the Cuban government forbade its public performance due to its explicit revolutionary and communist content.[35] As a result, the cultural society Nuestro Tiempo, which had a close relationship with the PSP, presented the play publicly in the form of a dramatized reading with its actors.[36] According to Alfonso, the play finally premiered on stage at the underground theater in Havana on February 20, 1959, as a tribute to the victorious revolutionary army led by Fidel Castro. After being performed sixty times, the play attracted the military leader Camilo Cienfuegos's attention. With his support, the play was able to launch a national tour to mobilize the masses and raise funds for the army. When the play was translated into Chinese in 1961, it was then touring all Cuban sugar factories at the suggestion of the National Institute for Agrarian Reform in support of the ongoing agrarian reform.[37]

There is no published record as to the reason this particular play was selected to be translated and performed in China. But apparently Paco Alfonso, who was working at the Chinese State Administration of Foreign Experts Affairs (外国专家局) in Beijing, recommended this play to Ying Ruocheng (英若诚) when the new revolutionary regime of Cuba successfully defeated the Bay of Pigs invasion, carried out by American-trained Cuban exiles in 1961. Ying Ruocheng, who was one of the most influential dramatists as well as a founding member of the Beijing People's Art Theatre, translated the play into Chinese based on the English translation of the original script.[38] The Chinese name *Gan Zhe Tian* (甘蔗田) was inspired by the Chinese translation of the Cuban poet Nicolás Guillén's 1930 poem "Cañaveral" (Cane field).[39] In the same year, *Play* (剧本) published the script of *Cañaveral*, which was accompanied by Alfonso's introduction of its historical background. *Chinese Theatre* (戏剧报) also invited Alfonso to write an article that delineated how Cuban dramatists paved the way for national drama under Spanish colonialism.[40]

To celebrate the third anniversary of the Cuban Revolution, Tianjin People's Art Theatre's director Fang Chen (方沉) decided to stage the play. As a dramatist and actor who had been participating in CCP's underground theater since the 1940s, Fang had rich experience in directing proletariat drama and playing non-Chinese characters on stage.[41] While they were preparing for the performance, Ying accompanied Alfonso and his wife María Ofelia Díaz, who played the role of Soledad in the original play, to Tianjin and participated in the rehearsal process.[42] Alfonso wrote a new epilogue especially for the Chinese audience when he was in Beijing. The epilogue was immediately translated by the Spanish group at the China National Radio (中央人民广播电台西班牙语组) from Spanish to Chinese in November 1961. However, the epilogue was neither formally published nor performed in the end.[43] After its premiere in Tianjin in early January 1962, the play traveled to Shenyang and Beijing. It was shown to the public and foreign ambassadors, officials, and important figures in the Chinese cultural field such as Xiao San (萧三).[44] Motivated by the enthusiastic atmosphere, Zhu Duanjun (朱端钧), who joined the League of Chinese Left-Wing Dramatists (中国左翼戏剧家联盟) in the 1930s, organized teachers at Shanghai Theatre Academy (上海戏剧学院) to perform the play to the public in Shanghai. Devoted wholeheartedly to the play, he published an article in *Shanghai Drama* (上海戏剧) to share the experience with other dramatists.[45] The article also attracted many other local theater troupes interested in performing the play.[46] Overall, the play received nationwide attention in the enthusiastic wave of supporting the Cuban Revolution in the early 1960s.

FIGURE 7.3. A production photo of *Cañaveral* shows Fico's family (*from left to right*: mother Soledad, son Ñico, father Fico, and daughter Solita). All the actors were Chinese. Cane Field Archive, Tianjin People's Art Theatre, Tianjin, China.

However, to the surprise of the Chinese audience, the play did not fulfill their expectations with a direct representation of guerrilla wars led by heroic figures like Guevara and Castro. Nor did it show the exotic landscape and culture of their imagination: wide sugarcane plantations, big straw hats, guitars, and tropical music.[47] Instead, it told a more difficult story about the failure of the sugarcane peasants' union struggle against American imperialism and its local agents before the revolution. Moreover, the peasants' struggle is not represented directly on the stage but rather indicated through conversations. At the center of the stage are two ordinary peasant houses where peasant women (particularly Fico's wife Soledad) occupy the domestic space and deliver political speeches. Unlike the popular image of male sugarcane peasants holding a machete to protect the cane field as a symbol of the new Cuban nationality, *Cañaveral* touched on the gender dimension of the Cuban Revolution by focusing on women peasants as anti-imperialist subjects. The female protagonist Soledad impressed many Chinese critics as the most ideal representative of Cuban nationality and Cuban women.[48]

Focusing on the two peasant huts, the stage setting determines that all political conflicts are presented in the domestic space, usually defined as private and feminine. At the beginning of the first act, there are only four characters on stage: the mother Soledad and her daughter Solita are preparing to cook in Fico's hut, while the peasant Felipe and his wife Valeria are quarreling in their hut. The domestic space seems to have no relation to any politics outside at first. However, it is soon occupied by union politics after Soledad's son Ñico returns with the bad news that the sugar factory is going to use armed guards to suppress the union. Moving away from housework, Soledad begins with her first long monologue that denounces the latifundio system and sugar industry: "Look around you ... What do you see? The cane! ... Always the cane! ... It goes on forever, and men are left with the hunger and misery that it leaves!" Soledad ruminates on the fate that awaits her son. "Ñico ... What will he become? I have delivered one more machete to cut the cane! Like Fico, his father, he will be one more arm in that sea that grows and dries up, drowning us all! Instead of cane and sugar ... it is blood that goes to the North!"[49]

By comparing sugar to blood, her angry speech points out directly the cannibalistic nature of the sugar economy: just like the factory swallows the cane year by year, American capitalists will drain all the blood from the bodies of Cuban peasants. The production process from cane to sugar represents American capitalism's extraction of surplus value from Cuban peasants' labor. As the primary crop cultivated, it only leaves an endless cycle of poverty and hunger for the Cuban people. Soledad's monologue provokes a scream from the madwoman Florita, whose voice comes from the sugarcane forest toward the front stage: "Blood! ... Blood!" Soledad explains that Florita's father left his blood among the cane, which became sugar and flows to the North (referring to the United States). Then Florita appears at the front of the stage and walks into Soledad's hut with a monologue, exclaiming: "His blood ran out of the canes, and he stained the green bush and the white sugar ... ! They killed him ... ! They killed him! ... Cane and blood ... Cane and blood! *Vieja,* the bald eagles are flying, flying again like that day ... !"

Florita's scream reinforces the association between the four visual symbols: green cane, white sugar, red blood, and black bald eagles (representing American imperialism). Echoing Soledad's speech, her scream further strengthens its affective power through such horrific symbols. They fill the audience's imagination with the invisible violence behind the scenes and foreshadow the imminent murder of Fico. Moreover, her movement between the forest and Soledad's hut at the front of the stage crosses the boundary between the domestic space and the outside world and connects them by bringing the political conflicts behind the stage to the front. At this moment, the play reaches its first emotional climax that arouses sentiments against American imperialism both on and off stage.

In *Cañaveral*, Soledad and Florita's voices play an essential role in articulating Cuban women's call for anti-imperialist solidarity. Unlike the traditional image of madwomen and housewives, they are not isolated from social politics but speak out against imperialism as representatives of oppressed women. Soledad, in particular, represents the gendered ideal of a peasant woman and a revolutionary mother who unites her family to continue their struggle after Fico's death. Such a character echoed the Chinese news media's narrative of revolutionary Cuban women like Mariana Grajales Cuello, who fought along with her son General Antonio Maceo, the general of the Cuban Army of Independence, against Spanish colonizers in the late nineteenth century.[50] As wartime narratives, the international anti-imperialist women's movements often resorted to revolutionary motherhood to build universal emotional bonding among women of different cultural backgrounds and strengthen their identification with each other. As Michelle Chase states in her study of the Cuban women's campaigns' strategic association of women as mothers or future mothers, such references to motherhood were not necessarily apolitical or conservative.[51] This strategy also helped the Chinese actress to perform female characters in foreign dramas in this period. Director Fang assigned Yan Fei (严斐), a famous actress who had been performing realist drama since her first show in the leftist Cai Chusheng's film *Fifth Brother Wang* (王老五, 1937), to play the role of Soledad. At the beginning of rehearsal, Yan had difficulties identifying with the character because there was a lack of motivation for her political consciousness. Other actors advised her to understand this character from the perspective of a mother's love for her family.[52]

Yet the Chinese dramatists were not completely satisfied with the play's depictions of women and thus made efforts to revise the female characters in the play. Fang had a conversation with Alfonso about the condition of peasant women in Cuba. In his notes, he summarizes Alfonso's explanation of the female characters in *Cañaveral*,

> In the past women did not do any labor work [in the fields]. For example, Soledad is very progressive, but she does not strive for labor work and believes in superstition. Valeria is a harebrained woman. Her life is too boring. Therefore, she wants to look for sustenance. Regla is the one who wants to keep the pot boiling. Justina is also a person who has no ambition. Women do housework as good wives.[53]

The conversation reveals that Alfonso's original design of the female characters was relatively simple. Situated within an ongoing gender revolution in Chinese society, the Chinese dramatists were not satisfied with a flattened representation of these female characters. They hoped to flesh out female characters with reasonable motives stemming from their position as women oppressed by the semicolonial society. This was particularly evident concerning the representation of the negative character Valeria. As Felipe's wife, Valeria is presented as a woman who leaves her husband at home and maintains a sexual relationship with Don Lucas in the original play. In the end, she gives birth to a child and is expelled from the plantation. Alfonso disliked this character and thought that her fate was a result of her misbehaving. Such a depiction of Valeria risked the danger of representing her as a degenerate woman with loose morals similar to the stereotyped image of a mixed-race Cuban woman in popular culture. Unlike Alfonso, Chinese dramatists were inclined to understand the emptiness in her heart and interpret her miserable fate as a result of the structural problem of Cuban society.[54]

Moreover, the Chinese dramatists were inclined to portray Cuban women not as accessories to the male revolutionaries but as actively and consciously involved in the revolution. For example, director Fang instructed Yan to avoid being too sentimental and control her tears in the third act. In doing so, it would illustrate Soledad as a militant revolutionary woman with a strong will and resilience to fight against imperialism.[55] In the new epilogue that Alfonso wrote for the Chinese audience, perhaps to satisfy local expectations, Soledad's home was converted into a secret shelter for the guerrilla soldiers by 1959. She, Solita, and Ñico were busy delivering messages, raising money, and sending arms to the insurgent army in the mountain.[56] The domestic space became a real revolutionary space for political action, and women transformed from negative subjects under suppression to active political actors in the revolution.[57]

The Chinese dramatists' revision of the gender relations within the play was not a coincidence. In her discussion of Chinese feminism in the socialist period, Wang Zheng reveals that feminists utilized anti-imperialist protests to advocate gender equality and mobilize women to join women's liberation movements. For example, Chinese filmmakers like Chen Bo'er and Xia Yan attempted to construct the image of an oppressed woman with a resistant agency rather than a mere victim waiting for salvation from male revolutionaries. This largely challenged the gender norms in the prerevolutionary visual culture. On the other hand, she states, the tension between class and gender in the process of filmmaking limited the discussion of gender oppression within a proletariat space. The priority of class struggle and anti-imperialism gradually excluded the possibilities of a further gender revolution within the socialist revolution.[58] The result was the formation of a unanimously flattened image of powerful revolutionary heroines that failed to challenge gender oppression within the multiple systems of oppression.

We can see a similar dilemma in the Chinese adaptation of *Cañaveral*. Despite the Chinese dramatists' efforts, women's liberation was not brought up in the performance as an essential part of the national liberation in the Cuban Revolution. Moreover, the close connection with anti-imperialist mobilization also caused this play and the entire cultural representation surrounding the Cuban Revolution to be significantly affected by the rapid change and division of the anti-imperialist alliance due to the Sino-Soviet split. The nationwide enthusiasm for performances of the play only lasted for a short period. After 1962, it gradually declined in prominence and was eventually largely forgotten.

Conclusion

By the mid-1960s, Chinese-Cuban relations were in crisis. Ironically, these pressures also changed the political significance of Cuban sugar. No longer a shared symbol of anti-imperialist empowerment, it now reflected the degraded relations between Cuba and its Soviet patron. In his conversation with the North Korean cultural delegation in 1964, Chinese Premier Zhou Enlai criticized the Soviet Union's policy toward Cuba as "a continuation of the past method of U.S. imperialism's economic monoculture, turning Cuba into a supply base for sugar, providing the Soviet Union with sugar to eat."[59] Sino-Cuban relations moved toward an open crisis after the trade conflict in 1966.[60] The conflict happened right before the Tricontinental Conference was held in Havana, which aimed to build Afro-Asian–Latin American solidarity around anti-colonialism and anti-imperialism. As China embarked on a turbulent ten-year Cultural Revolution in the same year, the fervent anti-imperialist internationalist culture gradually waned across all levels of society.

The cooler relations with Cuba and diminishing anti-imperialist sentiment also affected Che's heroic image. When Guevara returned to China in 1965, the Chinese news media showed extreme indifference toward his trip and did not openly mention the reasons for his visit.[61] After Guevara died in Bolivia in 1967, the Chinese government translated his *Bolivian Diary* for internal circulation among high officials, not for mass dissemination. The preface criticized his guerrilla warfare as "guerrilla-centered adventurism."[62] This disdainful pronouncement formed a sharp contrast with the Chinese government's previous discourse supporting the Cuban guerrilla war against imperialism and the excitement raised by Che's first visit roughly a decade earlier.

Despite the brevity and limited scope of this Sino-Cuban honeymoon period, however, it is worth noting how those interactions opened space for both Chinese and Cuban activists who attempted to integrate women's liberation as an essential part of anti-imperialist solidarity. While the two countries articulated similar conceptions about women's liberation as a constituent part of national liberation, their ideals were not identical. In the case of the Chinese performance of the Cuban play *Cañaveral,* we see how Chinese dramatists were conscious of revising the gender representation within the original play to emphasize the active agency of militant women in the Cuban Revolution in a way that resonated with Chinese audiences. These transnational conversations capture the way ideas about gender were incorporated into the global dissemination of revolutionary culture.

Notes

1. Embajada de Cuba en China, "El Che, a 60 años de su primera visita a China" [El Che, 60 years after his first visit to China], https://www.youtube.com/watch?v=zxlOYK-2a-E&ab_channel=EmbajadadeCubaenChina, accessed December 5, 2021.

2. "格瓦拉少校离京前夕向我国人民发表广播讲话 美帝国主义是我们的直接敌人 古巴人民将以牙还牙斗争到底" [Comandante Guevara delivered a radio speech: American imperialism is our direct enemy, Cuban people will fight fire with fire until the end], *People's Daily,* December 2, 1960.

3. The Great Leap Forward was a campaign that lasted from 1958 to 1962. According to Rebecca Karl, the campaign was based on Mao's theory of mobilizing the masses to achieve a great leap in industrial and agricultural production within a short time instead of the slow progress advocated by the Soviet Union. In this process, women's liberation was one of the key issues as women were encouraged to contribute their labor to all fields of production. The campaign was controversial because its deliberate exaggeration of production data led to blind confidence in the transition to communism throughout society, disregarding the unreasonable waste of natural and social resources. As a result, a tragic great famine struck nationwide from 1959 to 1961. Rebecca E. Karl, *Mao Zedong and China in the Twentieth-Century World: A Concise History* (Duke University Press, 2010), 101–7.

4. "格瓦拉少校在内江参观" [Comandante Guevara visited Neijiang], *People's Daily,* November 26, 1960.

5. Kuang Song, 遇见格瓦拉 [Encountering Guevara] (University of Electronic Science and Technology of China, 2014).

6. Radoslav Yordanov, "Bittersweet Solidarity: Cuba, Sugar, and the Soviet Bloc," *Revista Histórica de América* 161 (2021): 215–40.

7. For example, Kuang Song, a professor from the Southwestern University of Finance and Economics, traveled to Cuba, Bolivia, and Argentina and visited the places where Che had been. After this trip he published two books: 遇见格瓦拉 [Encountering Guevara], and 切·格瓦拉故乡行：蓝色阿根廷 [Trip to Che Guevara's homeland: Blue Argentina] (University of Electronic Science and Technology of China, 2017).

8. On the controversies over the drama, see Claire Conceison, *Significant Other: Staging the American in China* (University of Hawai'i Press, 2004), 177–90.

9. Yinghong Cheng, "Sino-Cuban Relations During the Early Years of the Castro Regime, 1959–1966," *Journal of Cold War Studies* 9, no. 3 (2007): 78–114.

10. The archive pertaining to *Cañaveral* was accessed with the generous support of Li Yang, the director of the Tianjin People's Art Theater in 2021. The theater has its own archival room that preserves complete documents of the plays that had been performed, which is the tradition of all People's Theaters since the foundation of the PRC. I also owe special thanks to Professor Claire Conceison and actor Yang Lixin for giving me the opportunity to learn the history and performance training of the People's Theaters in China.

11. "古巴共产党大会电中国人民致敬" [The Communist Party of Cuba sends greetings to the Chinese people], *People's Daily*, December 2, 1948; "古巴民主妇联向中国母亲们致敬" [The Cuban Women's Democratic Federation pays tribute to the mothers in China], *People's Daily*, July 9, 1949; "统一美洲华侨民主组织古巴华侨拥护民主大同盟易名美洲华侨新民主同盟召开大会宣言拥护中央人民政府" [The United Chinese Democratic Organizations of the Americas, the Cuban Overseas Chinese in Support of the Democratic Alliance for Greater Unity, have changed their name to the New Democratic Alliance of Overseas Chinese], *People's Daily*, March 4, 1950. The name of Alianza had been changed many times. According to historian Kathleen López, it was called the Alianza Revolucionaria Protectora de Obreros y Campesinos Chinos de Cuba (古巴华侨工农革命大同盟, Chinese Cuban Revolutionary Alliance Protecting Workers and Peasants). Its leader, José Wong, was born in Guangzhou in 1898 and arrived in Cuba in the early 1920s. In 1929, he began publishing the first Chinese-language leftist newspaper in Cuba, 工农呼声 (*Grito Obrero-Campesino* [Call of the Worker and Peasant]), which was the primary version of *Kwon Wah Po*. He was active in the Anti-Imperialist League and connected with the members of the Cuban Communist Party. In 1930, he was murdered. For the history of Alianza, see Kathleen López, *Chinese Cubans: A Transnational History* (University of North Carolina Press, 2014), 198–99, 222–23, 226–28.

12. On the Latin American writers' participation in the world peace movement, see Jorge J. Locane, "On the World Peace Movement and the Early Internationalisation of Latin American Literature," in *Culture as Soft Power: Bridging Cultural Relations, Intellectual Cooperation, and Cultural Diplomacy*, ed. Elisabet Carbó-Catalan and Diana Roig Sanz (De Gruyter, 2022), 297–318.

13. Michelle Chase, "'Hands Off Korea!': Women's Internationalist Solidarity and Peace Activism in Early Cold War Cuba," *Journal of Women's History* 32, no. 3 (2020): 64–88.

14. Nicolás Guillén, "古巴人民争取和平与独立解放的斗争——一九五二年二月七日在中国人民外交学会欢迎会上的报告" [Cuban people's struggle for peace and independence liberation: Report at the Welcome Party of China People Diplomacy Academy], *People's Daily*, February 19, 1952.

15. Bing'an Pang, 亲历古巴——一个中国驻外记者的手记 [My personal experience in Cuba: Notes of a Chinese correspondent] (Xinhua Publishing House, 2000), 126.

16. Pang, 亲历古巴, 257–59.

17. Pang, 亲历古巴, 247–53.

18. Wei Teng, 边境"之南:拉丁美洲文学汉译与中国当代文学 *(1949-1999)* [South of

the border: Translation and Latin American literature in contemporary literature (1949–1999)] (Peking University Press, 2011), 15–18.

19. Fu Ke and Hong Gao, "中国人民全力支持古巴刚果人民" [Chinese people gave full support to Cuban and Congolese people], *People's Daily*, January 26, 1959.

20. Simu Liu, "Report About the Current Condition in Cuba," 1961, A73-1-433-1, Shanghai Municipal Archive.

21. William E. Ratliff, "A New Old Che Guevara Interview," *Hispanic American Historical Review* 46, no. 3 (1966): 288–300, https://doi.org/10.1215/00182168-46.3.288. The original title of the interview is "土地改革—古巴革命的矛头和旗帜—威·格瓦拉访问记" [Land reform—the spearhead and banner of the Cuban Revolution: Interview with Che Guevara]. The interview was published in *World Knowledge* on June 5, 1959.

22. "保卫古巴革命" [Defend the Cuban Revolution], *People's Daily*, October 31, 1962; "英雄的古巴人民必胜" [Heroic Cuban people will win], *Red Flag* 21 (1962): 1–3.

23. Chase, "Hands Off Korea!" 72–75.

24. Mu Yuan and Boqing Wang, "欢迎你,'七·二六'的女英雄——周恩来总理同参加攻打蒙卡达兵营的女战士梅耳巴会见记" [Welcome, female hero of 26th of July Movement: Record of Premier Zhou Enlai's meeting with Melba, the female fighter who participated in the assault on Moncada Barracks], *Guangming Daily*, July 30, 1962, 3.

25. Violeta Casals, "古巴革命中的妇女" [Women in the Cuban Revolution], *People's Daily*, July 27, 1959, 5; Boqing Wang and Zhiheng Yu, "岛国风暴" [Storm on the Island Country], *People's Daily*, July 25, 1959. Chinese writer Qin Mu also published the article "Four Cuban Peasant Women" in *People's Daily*. The article appraised the brave women who were killed by the counterrevolutionary army in the Bay of Pigs invasion. Mu Qin, "古巴四农妇" [Four Cuban peasant women], *People's Daily*, August 6, 1961, 8. There was also a translation of Che Guevara's memoir of the Cuban woman Lydia who sacrificed her life while transporting arms and messages in the guerrilla war, which was published in the literary collection *Qizhi ji* (Flag collection). Ernesto Che Guevara, "丽迪雅" [Lidia], in 旗帜集 [Flag collection] (Shanghai Literature & Art Publishing House, 1963), 112–16.

26. Jian Guo, "英雄的古巴妇女" [Heroic Cuban women], *Women of China* 12 (1962): 5–6, 28.

27. Quanheng Wu, "古巴散记" [Sketches of Cuba], *Women of China* 9 (1962): 20–21.

28. "我妇女代表在哈瓦那举行的美洲妇女代表大会上说中国人民与古巴人民同命运共呼吸古巴胜利证明人民是最强大的美帝国主义是可以击败的" [Chinese woman representative said at the Congress of Women of the Americas in Havana that Chinese people shared the same fate and breathe the same air as Cuban people. Cuba's victory proves that], *People's Daily*, January 14, 1963.

29. Guevara, "丽迪雅" [Lidia], 112–16.

30. Mu Qin, "古巴四农妇" [Four Cuban peasant women].

31. Daura Olema Garcia, 志愿女教师 [Volunteer teacher], trans. Huang Zhiliang and Liu Jingyan (Writers Publishing House, 1964).

32. The song was composed by Luis Casas Romero in 1912. The name "Mambí" refers to the soldiers who fought against Spain in the Cuba War of Independence (1895–98).

According to Zhang, he and other educated youth did not know the meaning of *mambí* despite the wide popularity of this song. They mistook it for a song of the Cuban Revolution during the Cultural Revolution. Chengzhi Zhang, "芒比" [El Mambí], May 20, 2016, http://m.wyzxwk.com/content.php?classid=14&id=364111.

33. Rosa Ileana Boudet, "Teatro Político: Carlos Montenegro, César Rodriguez Expósito y Paco Alfonso," in *Teatro cubano: Relectura cómplice* (Eds. de la Flecha, 2011): 181–83; Rine Leal, *Breve historia del teatro cubano* (Editorial Letras Cubanas, 1980), 123–26; Aymée Ma. Borroto Rubio, "Paco Alfonso: el teatro como arma," *Periódico Cubarte,* January 14, 2021, http://cubarte.cult.cu/periodico-cubarte/paco-alfonso-el-teatro-como-arma/; Navidad González Freire, *Teatro Cubano (1927–1961)* (Ministerio de relaciones exteriores, 1961), 85–86.

34. Paco Alfonso, "甘蔗田" (Cane field), *Play,* no. Z3 (1961): 128. Jesús Menéndez was a Black union leader who led the "sugar differential" struggle after World War II and was assassinated by the captain Joaquin Casillas in 1948. Por Pedro Rioseco, "Jesús Menéndez, el lider sindical asesinado por defender los obrerors," *Contraloría General República de Cuba,* January 21, 2024, https://www.contraloria.gob.cu/noticias/jesus-menendez-el-lider-sindical-asesinado-por-defender-los-obreros.

35. José Antonio Portuondo, *Historia de la literatura cubana II* (Letras Cubanas, 2003), 635.

36. Paco Alfonso, *Yari Yari. Mamá Olúa; y Cañaveral* (Torres y Rodríguez impresores, 1956), 107.

37. Paco Alfonso, "致中国读者" [To Chinese readers], trans. Sun Dalai, *Play,* no. Z3 (1961): 129.

38. There is no record of which English translation of *Cañaveral* Ying Ruocheng used or how he got the English copy.

39. Wang Yi, "【1962年1月13日】天津人艺在京演出《甘蔗田》—剧史里的党史（二八六）" [(January 13, 1962) Tianjin People's Art Theatre's performance of *Cane Field* in Beijing: CCP's history within theater history (286)], 剧史里的人 [People in theater history], Wechat Public Account, https://mp.weixin.qq.com/s/X7X4bNwdgfaEQ7B1Lu-TXA, accessed March 17, 2022.

40. Paco Alfonso, "古巴戏剧(历史片段)" [Cuban theater (fragments of history)], *Chinese Theatre,* no. Z4 (1961): 33–36.

41. Han Wuxi, "追忆方沉导演" [Commemorate director Fang Chen], Tianjin People's Art Theatre Wechat Public Account, https://mp.weixin.qq.com/s/q_cMAr6HP6n-sRGCWGLmmA, accessed March 17, 2022.

42. Wang, "【1962年1月13日】天津人艺在京演出《甘蔗田》—剧史里的党史（二八六）" [Tianjin People's Art Theatre's performance of *Cane Field*].

43. Fang Chen only briefly mentioned that he decided to give up the epilogue because it could not be unified with the previous plot. "组织文艺界座谈记录(天津市文化局、天津文联、天津剧协)" [Minutes of symposium with people from the circle of art and literature in Tianjin (Tianjin Municipal Bureau of Culture, Federation of Literary and Art Circles, Tianjin Dramatists Association)], February 15, 1962, no. 12, Cane Field Archive, Tianjin People's Art Theatre, Tianjin, China.

44. Xiao San, "革命的玫瑰花—古巴名剧《甘蔗田》观后感" [Revolutionary Red Rose: Review of the famous Cuban play *Cane Field*], *Chinese Theatre* 2 (1962): 3–4.

45. Zhu Duanjun and Ye Tao, "《甘蔗田》演出的几点解释和处理" [Some explanations and preparations of the performance of *Cane Field*], *Shanghai Drama* 12 (1962): 6–9, 31.

46. For example, Sichuan and Hubei provincial drama troupes had staged *Cañaveral* as well. Wang, "【1962年1月13日】天津人艺在京演出《甘蔗田》—剧史里的党史(二八六)" [Tianjin People's Art Theatre's performance of *Cane Field*].

47. Chen Fang, "导演意见" [Director's opinion], 甘蔗田档案 [*Cane Field* Archive], Tianjin People's Art Theatre, Tianjin.

48. Wenyuan Yao, "革命的'红玫瑰花'—读《甘蔗田》" [The Red Rose of Revolution: Review of *Cane Field*], *Shanghai Drama* 11 (1962): 8–10, 25; Mo Chen, "硬骨头和贱骨头—谈古巴话剧《甘蔗田》" [Hard bones and cheap bones—review of the Cuban play *Cane Field*], *Chinese Theatre*, no. Z8 (1961): 10–13; Xiao, "革命的玫瑰花" [Revolutionary Red Rose].

49. Paco Alfonso, *Yari Yari*, 125–26.

50. Mai Kong and Bing'an Pang, "战斗的古巴妇女" [Cuban women are fighting], *People's Daily*, March 12, 1960.

51. Chase, "Hands Off Korea!" 70.

52. "艺术总结" [Summary of Performance], *Cane Field* Archive. All translations from the archive are by the author.

53. "场记 (一)" [Field Record I], November 11, 1961, *Cane Field* Archive.

54. "记录(二)" [Record II], November 2 and December 7, 1961, *Cane Field* Archive.

55. "记录(二)" [Record II], December 7, 1961, *Cane Field* Archive.

56. "甘蔗田尾声" [Epilogue of *Cane Field*], *Cane Field* Archive.

57. Unfortunately, the Tianjin People's Theater decided to give up the epilogue because it was hard to coordinate with the previous scenes on the stage. "组织文艺界座谈记录" [Record of Symposium with People from the Circle of Art and Literature in Tianjin], *Cane Field* Archive.

58. Zheng Wang, *Finding Women in the State: A Socialist Feminist Revolution in the People's Republic of China, 1949–1964* (University of California Press, 2017), 189–90.

59. Memorandum of Conversation between Premier Zhou Enlai and the Korean Cultural Delegation, April 18, 1964, Wilson Center Digital Archive, PRC FMA 106-01434-01, 5–16, trans. Stephen Mercado, https://digitalarchive.wilsoncenter.org/document/119082.

60. "古巴总理菲德尔·卡斯特罗二月六日发表的反华声明" [The anti-China statement made by Cuban Prime Minister Fidel Castro on February 6], *People's Daily*, February 22, 1966.

61. "古巴社会主义革命统一党代表团格瓦拉等同志到广州" [Guevara and other comrades of the United Party of the Cuban Socialist Revolution arrived at Guangzhou], *People's Daily*, February 3, 1965.

62. Che Guevara, 切·格瓦拉在玻利维亚的日记 [Che Guevara's diary in Bolivia] (SDX Joint Publishing House, 1971).

FAMILY, CHILDHOOD, AND DAILY LIFE

EIGHT

The Paradoxes of Paradise

Memories of Exile and Family Life in Revolutionary Cuba, 1972–1990

TANYA HARMER

Beatriz Torres arrived in exile in Cuba in January 1974. Having crossed the Andes with her fifteen-month-old son two weeks after the Chilean coup on September 11, 1973, and fearing for her safety in Argentina amid growing repression, she asked the Cuban embassy in Buenos Aires for asylum. Once granted, she and her son flew seventeen hours, in an Argentine air force Hercules jet to Havana. Cuban officials and doctors met exiles at the airport, offering medical checks, food, and drink. Recounting her arrival more than four decades later, Beatriz struggled not to cry. The Cubans gave exiles everything, she explained: "work, guaranteed studies, training in every sense, respect, dignity, political parties continued to function. They gave us the houses with everything installed." When I asked about the journey to Cuba with a young child, Beatriz circled back to her son witnessing an armed raid in Chile. Then, without hesitation, she jumped to what Cuba felt like by comparison: "paradise ... *paradise,* paradise."[1]

During our two-and-a-half-hour conversation, Beatriz's emphatic depiction of Cuba as paradise would nevertheless morph into a more complex testimony. She never wavered from expressing profound gratitude. However, inconsistencies, frustration, and discomfort peppered her narrative as she remembered navigating her vision of an egalitarian revolutionary society alongside everyday inequalities and discrimination relating to gender, race, and sexuality she witnessed. What had it been like to live "la revolución"—as Cuba's continuing state-led socialist project was known—I asked. It meant grasping "the complexity," she explained:

understanding that no "revolution by decree, neither the French, nor any, changes human beings from one minute to the next, and a century may pass and there may still be tensions ... in everyday life ... on the ground. ... Paradise doesn't exist, at least I don't know it."[2]

These seemingly contradictory ideas of Cuba, first as paradise and then as a revolutionary state unable to create a utopia, are not unique to Beatriz's story. By the mid-1970s, *la Revolución* was more than a decade old. The initial fervor, idealism, and mobilization of the post-1959 years had waned. The island's "revolutionary offensive" in the late 1960s with its emphasis on moral incentives and voluntary sacrifice had also given way to institutionalization and material rewards. It was precisely at this transitional moment that thousands of exiles from the Southern Cone arrived. Although numbers are hard to verify, the largest groups came from Uruguay (c. 1,200) and Chile (c. 3,000–5,000). As examples of long-term *mass* migration to the island, these groups differed from smaller contemporaneous exile communities such as Argentine left-wing leaders and their families. Without a Chilean or Uruguayan embassy in Havana, exiles from these countries were also freer than their Argentine counterparts (who were under embassy surveillance) and were eventually integrated into everyday life in ways other exiles were not.[3] Seeking refuge from right-wing military dictatorships, exiles—particularly on the so-called revolutionary Left such as Uruguay's National Liberation Movement—Tupamaros (Movimiento de Liberación Nacional-Tupamaros, MLNT) and Chile's Revolutionary Left Movement (Movimiento de Izquierda Revolucionaria, MIR)—anticipated Cuba would provide military training and support for revolutionary struggles back home. However, these expectations often proved illusory. Most exiles remained on the island, building exilic lives that lasted more than a decade. Witness to the Cuban state's shifting parameters and expectations, they worked, studied, raised families, made friends, and, for those who arrived as children or were born on the island, grew into adolescence.

Chilean and Uruguayan exiles' perspectives therefore offer an interesting lens through which to explore what Isabella Cosse and Michelle Chase have called the "messy realities" of Cuban revolutionary programs.[4] Narrative tensions, like those in Beatriz's account—particularly regarding issues of gender, family, and sexuality—are revealing. Combining awe, gratitude, (veiled) criticism, and disagreement, they illuminate both the promises and the problems of state efforts to shape society. As historians like Rachel Hynson and Emily Snyder observe, the island's post-1959 history was characterized by a multipolar process involving top-down social engineering projects and negotiated adaptation to them. "Accommodation and resistance were not opposite, mutually exclusive responses," Hynson argues, "but rather complementary responses to the expanding power of the state."⁵ This was certainly true for exile families, which found a complex sense of belonging in Cuba, responding to state-led expectations of revolutionary citizenship, informal quotidian solidarity, and their own preconceived ideas of what life on the island would be like.

When it came to family life, the Cuban state prescribed that the revolution should take priority. However, it made significant changes, with varying success, as to how and why this should happen. During revolutionary operations and internationalist missions, Cubans' family life, relationships, and love had to wait. Even so, Emily Snyder observes that Cubans often "carved out spaces for affections and sex within revolutionary projects."⁶ At a more day-to-day level, *in Cuba*, couples were expected to build revolutionary families around a "legally formalized or judicially recognized marriage" as the "elementary cell of society."⁷ Two-parent families, sanctified by marriage, were nevertheless "far from typical," and, as Hynson notes, regulating the private sphere had mixed success.⁸ In the 1970s, the "intense and systematic institutionalization" of politics, society, and culture subsequently included new efforts to sculpt family life, comprising the Maternity Law (1974), Family Code (1975), and Code of the Child (1978).⁹ Together, these laws advocated women's "liberation from exploitation, isolation, and deficient class consciousness" through paid employment.¹⁰ As Elise Andaya notes, bringing hundreds of thousands of women into the workforce also helped with labor shortages and productivity goals.¹¹ Meanwhile, the number of university students during the 1970s increased sixfold. Half of all students by the mid-1980s studied part-time in the evenings alongside work. By 1990, the majority (57 percent) of students were also women.¹² Families had new access to household appliances, alleviating traditionally perceived women's work, freeing them to build socialism outside the home.¹³ Additionally, as the director of Cuba's Círculos Infantiles described, state childcare gave each woman the "opportunity to realize herself totally as a human being." Together, these provisions formed a so-called reproductive bargain, whereby the government provided the means for women to "liberate themselves."¹⁴ In the 1980s, women overwhelmingly reported gaining independence and self-esteem through paid employment and education, less reliant on male breadwinners or dependent on marriage to run a home. Helen Safa also noted an "erosion of the *casa/calle*" divide that had gendered private and public spheres.¹⁵

These developments notwithstanding, memoirs and histories of revolutionary Cuba identify a significant "tension between tradition and change."¹⁶ Childcare and family planning needs, for example, were often higher than supply, and women resisted regulatory control of reproductive rights.¹⁷ Despite top-down efforts to challenge machismo, patriarchal norms persisted in workplaces, and women were unequally represented in government.[18] And while women juggled revolutionary obligations on multiple fronts, men's domestic responsibilities rarely changed.[19]

This, then, was the context for Beatriz Torres's comments on a state's inability to change society by decree. Rather than equality and uniformity in line with the 1975 Family Code's prescriptions for a two-parent family with biological children, legalized by marriage, former exiles recounted inconsistencies, single-parent households, collective experiments, extended kinships, and social parenting. Indeed, examining how solidarity toward exiles—from the government and "el pueblo"—was channeled through and within the familial sphere reveals the Cuban state's ambitions, flexibility, and imperfect reach. In a period known for its institutionalization and codification of the private sphere, the state only partially conditioned exiles' quotidian life. And individuals proved adept at negotiating, modifying, and, often, making up for inadequacies of its directives.

Of course, exiles did not arrive as passive objects to be molded into revolutionary citizens. They were also shaped by their political affiliations and their party's instructions. Within Chile and Uruguay—as across the Southern Cone—ideas about family, sexuality, and gender were evolving and contested throughout the 1960s locally and because of transnational influences. Second-wave feminism, greater access to education, and labor market demands had changed women's self-perception and their roles, bringing more women into work, study, and political life. Moreover, as Cosse argues, the traditional patriarchal nuclear family "was part of the structures that revolutionaries sought to change."[20] The "construction of the 'new man'" in Cuba, meanwhile, had tangible impacts within revolutionary circles, opening "countless conflicts that marked militants' daily life and subjectivity" with "deep political" significance. Particularly on the revolutionary Left and among younger generations, militants debated monogamy, whether to have children, and women's roles within revolutionary organizations. And yet, although there were differences between parties and circumstances, the more engaged in armed operations or facing right-wing repression, the more conservative and rigid party directives about gender, sexuality, and revolutionary morality often became. In the context of resistance and revolution, party structures deemed sexual liberation and free love, already at odds with entrenched Catholicism and Marianism, unsafe, disloyal, and selfish.[21]

In practice, though, these prescriptions often proved aspirational, with many remembering their revolutionary years as a time of intense romantic relationships and promiscuity.[22] As Cosse notes, "The whirlwind of political events and the risks" revolutionaries "faced daily, including the possibility of dying or being forced to resort to violence, placed militants in extreme situations, lending new meaning and urgency to their amorous relationships."[23] Paula, a member of the

Communist Youth, remembered that men used this context to their advantage ("Let's do it, tomorrow we might die!") with women feeling they should conform.[24] Simultaneously, women would challenge the idea that they should play secondary, noncombatant roles after having children.[25]

The question here is how exile in Cuba affected such ideas and practices. Drawing primarily on oral history interviews with former exiles, this chapter probes Chilean and Uruguayan recollections of family life on the island. Using oral histories is of course complex; memories are fallible and change depending on context. In the case of exile in Cuba, taboos and trauma related to the Cold War and ongoing sensitivities surrounding revolutionary operations meant that some interviewees were also guarded. However, with archival access limited in Cuba, oral histories provide invaluable records of an otherwise silenced past. As historians have long since recognized, their value is more significant than recounting facts, with omissions and paradoxes revealing as much as what is said.[26] They are also essential for historicizing "refugeedom"—offering "a refugee-focused approach" and making "the displaced more visible as purposeful agents by locating them on their own terms."[27]

Following rank-and-file Chilean and Uruguayan exiles in Cuba, this chapter is structured in four parts. The first two trace the early years of exile, when Chileans and Uruguayans arrived in varied configurations. In these years, the rupture of exile and the exigencies of the moment provided space for a degree of experimentation and collective familial formations.[28] These sections examine these alternative structures, focusing on clandestine MLNT camps, known as *colonias*, and female MIR militants on the island with children. There were other collective experiments, notably the MIR's Proyecto Hogares, where children of those destined for operations in Chile were left with *padres sociales* (adoptive parents). However, because that was later and has received more attention, and because Cosse's chapter explores the implications of a similar Argentine experiment, it is not examined here.[29] Parts three and four then move on to the longer-term process of the socialization of exiles. They explore governmental directives' effects on exilic experiences, focusing on the 1975 Family Code's intention to "strengthen" the "family" and ensure "absolute equality of rights between men and women" in the domestic sphere, professional life, and education.[30]

Entrega total: Tupamaro Colonias in Cuba

Young Uruguayan and Chilean exiles on the revolutionary Left had particular, if conflicted, opinions about gender and family when they arrived in Cuba. If one idea united them and their Cuban hosts, it was the idea of total commitment (*entrega total*) to revolution and the prioritizing of "collective" over "individual will."[31] Implied in the positionality of Tupamaros and Miristas on the island was the expectation that family aspirations be postponed.[32] Where children were present, collective arrangements or the Cuban state relieved militants of individual parental responsibilities so they could commit to their revolutionary duties. However, when it came to gender equality and regulating private lives, MLNT and MIR militants pushed boundaries.

Young Tupamaros were possibly the extreme example of exiles who were expected to offer themselves completely to the revolution. Following an agreement between Fidel Castro and the MLNT leadership, exiled Uruguayan militants began arriving in Cuba from 1972 with the expectation of training to return clandestinely to Uruguay. As former participants have explained, transferring to Cuba, mostly from a first exile in Chile, was designed to save lives and to "keep people's spirits up" with a possible route home.[33] Numbers grew after a meeting of exiled Tupamaros in Chile in February 1973 attributed the organization's previous defeats, at least in part, to inadequate class-consciousness and political formation. The MLNT leadership with Cuban support believed it could proletarianize members through manual labor and political (re)education. Although participation was voluntary, at least initially, it therefore had a similar logic to other instances of "redemptive labor" in revolutionary Cuba.[34]

The colonias' design intentionally regulated life and work. By late 1973, approximately five hundred Tupamaros were undercover on the island, assuming different Latin American identities and separated into prearranged semi-clandestine colonias, comprising thirty to fifty people in their late teens and early twenties.[35] Conditions varied but whether in large houses or big sheds/warehouses (*naves grandes* or *galapones*), militants were divided into dormitories for men and women with bunk beds.[36] These arrangements discouraged cohabitation, making intimacy complicated by design. Laura, who arrived with her husband, remembered that some exceptions existed where couples had their own rooms.[37] However, personal lives were supposed to be on hold. As with internationalist revolutionary ventures during the 1980s that Snyder examines in this volume, falling in love was akin to "inherently challenging the revolutionary government's definition of love as self-sacrifice for collective rather than personal goals."[38] Pregnancies were also discouraged. Indeed, the Cuban government supplied the contraceptive pill to all women. Decades later Laura and her friends questioned this; at the time they took what they were given.[39]

Cuba's Ministry of the Interior, and more precisely the office within it responsible for Cuba's revolutionary policies in Latin America, which became the Cuban Communist Party's Americas Department under Manuel Piñeiro, provided supplies to the colonias. In addition to contraceptive pills, they contained toiletries, clothing, and food, including cooked meals from "industrial kitchens."[40] (One rural colonia also received two cows for milk supplies.)[41] These provisions fostered a radical experiment in egalitarian living, free from cooking and purchasing daily household supplies. Remaining chores such as cleaning or washing were divided equally. "In our microworld, equality was very important," Fernando Mazzeo explained.[42] Where children were present, or babies born, about which more below, colonias generally organized "collective care" with rosters so all parents could work.[43] Former colonia members were quick to discount the idea that such arrangements had been motivated by "feminist" concerns.[44] As Gabriela Gonzalez-Vaillant found, former Tupamaros recalled the concept of "feminism" as "frivolous," a distraction from liberation through class struggle.[45] Margaret Randall, who observed Cuban society as a privileged North American exile on the island, similarly notes that the Cuban state "considered feminism an imported bourgeois notion that would ultimately divide the working class" despite sometimes being "feminist in practice."[46] Rather than the result of feminism or Cuban instructions, then, colonia participants described aspirations to equality as "natural"—something they were disposed to when they arrived.[47]

Collective arrangements focused inhabitants on work and study. And women were insistent on fulfilling the same tasks as men, even when carrying fifty-kilo bags of cement mix that weighed more than they did.[48] As Olga Estévez explained, "We worked hard, very hard. But we wanted this ... As women we felt strong ... empowered." Known as "the skinny ones" (*flaquitas*), women wanted to return Cuba's support: "If we joined the guerrillas, it was because we believed we could do certain things. Obviously, there were things of force majeure related to men: muscles, blood, and whatnot. But everything we could do, we did ... What's more, we volunteered to do it. Hardheaded."[49] Women's attitude within the colonias built on gender relations within the MLNT before exile. Notably, in urban guerrilla operations in Uruguay, for example, female Tupamaros, accounting for 27 percent of the organization by 1972, had assumed military roles traditionally reserved for men. As Gonzalez-Vaillant argues, women's route to inclusion—and ultimately equality—within the MLNT required them to "mimic" men, "de-gendering" themselves by assuming conventionally masculine roles.[50] This pattern was then replicated in the colonias, where women asserted equality through labor. The Cuban men who worked with colonias were initially hesitant to accept this and were "protective" of the women, Olga remembered, but were persuaded: "They had had women in the guerrilla [campaign against Batista], [but] not like us, which was something else. And they told you: Hey girl, you can't handle that. And let's go, yes, I can. ... There we were doing it. And they learned to value us."[51]

Exiles' autonomy disrupted the colonias' controlled environment in other ways. Interviews and memoirs reveal that inhabitants had romantic and sexual relationships regardless of guidelines.[52] "Life goes on and people had to live their youth," Olga reasoned. For intimacy, participants improvised, sleeping in construction sites or taking turns using "marital rooms."[53] Although prohibited on the pretext of endangering future missions to Uruguay, some Tupamaros also dated Cubans. (One Uruguayan met a Cuban girlfriend when he went to the dentist where she worked in reception.)[54] Colonia members also became pregnant. Although abortion was still to some extent stigmatized on the island, and not freely legal until 1979, women were expected to terminate pregnancies.[55] Decades later, Laura tried, hesitantly, to make sense of this:

> It was prohibited, you could not get pregnant. . . . It was a responsibility [to be in the colonias]. . . . You were not legal, you had to. . . . We were asked, prohibited of course, I mean . . . but we were asked, women [were asked], not to become pregnant and if you became pregnant it was well seen that you [had] an abortion, like I did. . . . Some of us accepted, some of us, some of *them* . . . accepted [this] because they thought it was part of our contribution to the revolution or that the Cuban Revolution was being so generous with us so if they asked . . . but some people felt that we had a right to build our family.[56]

The MLNT and the Cubans were jointly responsible for regulating reproductive rights. Crucially, children could complicate clandestine missions to Uruguay.[57] One colonia's residents called an urgent plenary when a couple became pregnant to collectively decide whether the pregnancy should proceed.[58] As Laura's testimony reveals, the Cubans also issued specific guidelines not to get pregnant, which echoes similar instructions in other regulated settings on the island.[59] Certainly, pregnant women could not receive guerrilla training, and some hid their pregnancies, using a waist strap, to continue. As a former MLNT militant told Gonzalez-Vaillant, having children in this context was considered "antirevolutionary."[60] How babies born to Uruguayans, living clandestinely in Cuba, would be registered was also complicated. Raquel and Augustín, for example, were advised to register their daughter as Ecuadorian.[61] Those who had children gave birth at the Navy hospital, where colonia members also received medical attention. It was a privileged position, Laura reflected; they received clandestine care through "special channels."[62]

Compared to the majority of colonias, comprised of single adults or (at least initially) childless couples, there was one colonia for young families, who had previously been unable to travel to Cuba, precisely because children complicated training and revolutionary missions. After the Chilean coup forced them into exile in Sweden, however, Cuba's "criteria" changed.[63] Thus the Escuelita ("little school") colonia was formed for around twenty adults and their children as a collective home in a large prerevolutionary mansion. The colonia's adults were picked up in the morning in trucks to work at seaside resorts east of Havana, although, interestingly, a gendered labor division appears to have been more pronounced in this family-focused colonia, with men working in maintenance, construction, and sanitation, and women in painting. Childcare was nevertheless shared. Despite problems with noise preventing their daughters from sleeping, Raquel and Augustín recalled an idyllic extended family of children playing in the garden. "They were like siblings," Augustín explained, "with the same characteristics.... It was wonderful for us and for them."[64]

Prioritizing the Revolution: Miristas and Their Children in Alamar

The colonias' collective experiments jarred with the Cuban ideal of nuclear families, sanctified by marriage, as the ideal revolutionary familial formation. However, they were not the only alternative arrangement afforded to exiles. In 1975, Mirista women and their children received most of an apartment bloc in Alamar, a new housing complex east of Havana built in the early 1970s, housing fifteen thousand residents.[65] This *edificio de los chilenos* (Chilean building or D-2 by its address) was considered a radical experiment to allow women to militate and contribute to anti-dictatorial resistance.[66]

It was somewhat inevitable that Miristas did not arrive as two-parent families. Detention, disappearance, and death separated parents. The MIR's initial instructions to its members not to seek asylum were gendered, stipulating that women and children were exceptions: they were to be protected while men fought for the resistance. As a younger party with regard to militants' age and its foundation, there were also few established Mirista families. Militants often broke with their own families to join the MIR, signaling rupture before exile. Women within the organization regarded themselves as more liberated than counterparts in other parties and aspired to political equality. Yet men still dominated its leadership and operations.[67] Manuel Cabieses, in charge of the MIR in Cuba, for example, lived in D-2 and, as María Inés Ruz remembered, was nominally there to look after the women and children in the building. He attended to their needs with the "best intentions." But this was unmistakably a patriarchal authority women had to ask permission from and report to.[68]

Cabieses also assigned Mirista women work within the MIR's infrastructure.

Despite having the chance to study briefly, for example, María Inés represented the MIR at the Chilean Committee of Solidarity with the Antifascist Resistance (Comité Chileno de Solidaridad con la Resistencia Antifascista), an exile-run office comprising Chilean left-wing parties. Later, she worked for an office known as "tareas cerradas" (closed tasks), a secret project with multiple teams supporting Mirista operations, and as the MIR's local leader in Alamar.[69] Manuel Llorca, meanwhile, remembered his mother working in a women-run office on D-2's ground floor with its own darkroom. Women were also tasked with analyzing foreign newspapers, while their children devoured publications' sports pages, and cartoons.[70]

To fulfill this work, D-2's women shared chores like shopping and childcare. As a collective experiment this was "a kind of utopia," María Inés remembered, but it was only partially successful. Her abiding memory of its failure is walking home in the searing heat, laden with shopping for the whole building, and looking up to see her young son, supposedly under another woman's care, straddling the balcony of their fourth-floor apartment.[71]

School-aged D-2 children were meanwhile sent to a boarding school called Solidaridad con Chile in Miramar, in western Havana, to allow their mothers to work for the resistance and to protect them from the trauma of repression and exile.[72] Opened by Fidel Castro in 1974, the school was distinctive: children were mostly Chilean but there were other South Americans and, increasingly in the late 1970s and 1980s, Central Americans. Ambassadors' children, and some Cubans, including the daughters of athletic champions and singers, such as Silvio Rodríguez and Pablo Milanés, attended. The school had a small cinema, an orchard, a swimming pool, and sports grounds. In many ways, it was the epitome of the state's commitment to children's rights to "rest, recreation, cultural needs and interests."[73] Mixing representatives of Cuba's revolutionary elite and prized international guests, it was a privileged space, designed to forge an internationalist revolutionary generation.

Indeed, the state's role in caring for children of exiles—and the centrality children played in its self-conception of revolutionary solidarity—was noteworthy in Cuba.[74] As well as relieving parents, boarding schools were embraced as a way to immerse children in a collective world and shed individualism.[75] Emblematic of a new commitment to residential education, the Escuelas Secundarias Básicas del Campo mixed secondary school–aged children from different backgrounds, engaging them simultaneously in agricultural labor and traditional education to instill a revolutionary ethic.[76]

Some children who attended Solidaridad con Chile nevertheless have conflicted memories that relate, at least in part, to the subordinate place they assumed in their parents' priorities. Camila Krauss was only four when she started boarding and remembered crying secretly because, already at this age, she understood crying was "weak." In time, she adjusted and has happy memories of watching films and making friends, but she resented boarding so young.[77] Manuel's memories were similarly fraught: it was "very hard" (*bien fuerte*) and "sad," he explained, before recognizing the school's "extraordinary" facilities in the same sentence.[78] Many enjoyed the sense of belonging and camaraderie the school offered, including traveling together weekly to and from school.[79] On weekends in Alamar, children then played together while their mothers (or parents, where fathers were present) attended political meetings, volunteered, or studied.[80] As Manuel remembered, "There was a lot of detachment from children.... People were making the revolution and children took second place."[81]

This prioritization of the revolution remains a complex topic in families decades later. It is something that Camila's mother, María Inés, has thought a lot about. As a young widow with two small children, she had not realized she had a choice when it came to sending her daughter to boarding school. When, later, she discovered a fellow exile had kept her children at a local primary school, she reproached herself for not doing the same. But as a new exile and a fervent Mirista at the time, she recalled doing what Cuba's authorities and her own party advised without question.[82] A Uruguayan exile living in Santiago in the late 1970s would also regret sending her young baby to nursery. Hailed as a marvel of state provision, taking babies as young as forty-five days old to daycare became an obligation for those juggling work and parenthood, especially for exiles separated from extended family.[83] Daycare staff were known affectively as aunties—part of a makeshift state-sanctioned family. But this substitution sat uneasily with her decades later. "It doesn't seem right to me, but it was the only way to give them a place where they could be and we could continue our tasks."[84]

Some second-generation exiles also resent the cost of their parents' prioritizing revolutionary commitments. Soledad Guyer, a child of Uruguayan exiles, believes children shouldered large "sacrifices" for the revolution. Like others, she recalls her mother—rather than her also-working father—asked this of her. A single parent of two living in Guantánamo, committed to obtaining a degree in livestock engineering more than a hundred kilometers away at the University of Granma (Bayamo) on weekends, her mother left Soledad and her brother with neighbors for days or took them with her and left them in offices in Bayamo while she studied.[85] Tania, the child of Uruguayan Communist Party militants, regrets not having more time with her parents now that she is a mother herself. She lived at home but remembers her parents were always working (as an electrician and an accountant) or in meetings and volunteering "to return the solidarity Cuba had given them. This was the commitment they had—making revolution was important, it was also part of their social life."[86]

These tensions, between the political, professional, and personal, underlay Cuba's vision of socialist modernity in the 1970s and 1980s. However, if, initially, exiles' encounters with family life in Cuba were eclectic and varied, the majority gradually integrated into Cuban society. As exiles configured their lives to fit expectations, they also forged alternative kinships and support structures that gave them a sense of home, extended family, and belonging.

"Un Cubano Más": Integrating into Cuban Society

In the mid-1970s, two major changes occurred within Uruguayan and Chilean exile communities. First, the Chileans who had arrived en masse from 1973, older professional Uruguayan Tupamaros not deemed suitable for the colonias experiment, and Uruguayan Communists who arrived from a first exile in Argentina in 1975–76, were gradually housed in their own apartments. Before this, Chileans and Uruguayans had mostly lived in beach resorts or Havana's hotels as a solution to mass, unplanned exile. Families therefore lived in improvised spaces, reflecting the rupture of home, sharing hotel rooms. Children treated hotel buildings as theirs, running down corridors, visiting hotel kitchens, and regarding staff as extended family.[87]

Then, gradually, in accordance with Fidel Castro's request in mid-November 1973 that workers donate one apartment in every building that so-called microbrigades constructed to Chilean refugees, exiles moved into their own homes.[88] Housing shortages meant this took time.[89] Many exiles and their children lived in hotels for two years.[90] Some waited longer. One Uruguayan family, for example, lived in two different hotels and a collective exile house for four years before receiving an apartment.[91]

When exiles were housed, they were distributed to Havana's surrounding districts like Alamar or around the island, where they were integrated into communities, generally occupying one apartment per block as Fidel had envisaged.[92] A second stage of exile thus began, defined by psychologists Ana Vásquez-Bronfman and Ana María Araújo as the processes of "transculturation" and adjustment.[93] Moving into furnished apartments, exiles were expected to live "como un cubano más" (like any other Cuban). This meant using a ration book and adapting to less meat and fewer vegetables than was usual back home.[94] It also meant adjusting to family life in new spaces. For larger families, the apartments—standard two-bedroom units designed for nuclear families typical of new Cuban building projects—proved complicated.[95] Andrea Pellegrín, for example, shared a bedroom with her adolescent brother and sister for the first time, which was problematic when they all started dating.[96]

Political leaders in the exile community were nevertheless afforded different treatment. Ariel Ulloa, for example, a senior-ranking member of Chile's Socialist Party before the coup, with close contacts in the Americas Department, was given a house in a residential district of Santa Clara for Interior Ministry and armed forces personnel. It was small, he recalled, but "beautiful . . . paradise." Like apartments exiles received, it was furnished with kitchen appliances and a TV. However, it also included extra comforts such as a telephone, which was considered "very important" (apartment blocks generally had one per building). It also had a patio with mango and banana trees, and they received avocados from their neighbor's tree, which allowed them to offset fruit and vegetable shortages other exiles described as part of Cuban life.[97]

The second major change in the mid-1970s was the end of the Tupamaro colonias experiment in 1976. This was partly in response to MLNT divisions. At the First Congress of the Cuban Communist Party in 1975, Fidel Castro had also underlined a new allegiance to the Soviet Union and peaceful coexistence, thereby distancing Cuba from regional guerrilla insurgencies. As Castro announced, "Latin America is not now on the immediate eve of global changes that could lead, as in Cuba, to sudden socialist transformations."[98] Although the culture of *guerrillerismo* was never renounced completely, and despite continuing support for armed operations in Latin America, especially through long-term training for Communist Party cadres and in relation to Central America, it was no longer central to Cuba's relationships with regional left-wing parties.[99] Colonia members were henceforth offered the choice of leaving Cuba or relocating around the island. For approximately a hundred Uruguayans and their children who stayed, "legalization" on the island, as they understood it, allowed them to reassume their identities and integrate into society as *Uruguayans*.[100]

For Augustín and Raquel, who had gone from being exiled parents of a newborn in Chile and Sweden to a family of four in the Escuelita colonia, it meant living alone for the first time. In Cojímar, east of Havana, they juggled work, nighttime study for two years—to restart their psychology degrees, cut short first in Uruguay and then Chile—housework, and childcare. It was "a new experience," requiring adaptation. Meanwhile, Augustín and Raquel were relieved to reregister their second daughter as Uruguayan rather than Ecuadorian.[101]

Parenthood appears to have been common after the colonias. Partly, this related to age, but it also marked the end of revolutionary demands. No longer expecting to return immediately and clandestinely to Uruguay, having a family became possible. "There is a time for making war [*guerrear*], [and] there is a time for

The Paradoxes of Paradise 199

having children [*criar*]," Olga reflected. The decision to build families was also an acknowledgment that exile would be longer than expected. As Olga reasoned, "We all went about building our lives because we didn't know how long we were going to be there."[102]

As exiles grew families within Cuban communities, they were socialized in everyday forms of citizenship. As a UNHCR representative reported in 1978, Cuba's "ideological background" obliged every "able person" to work, and while there were some who objected, primarily because they did not want to be relocated outside Havana or because their salary in Cuban currency did not allow them to send enough money to family, it was something the majority embraced. Certainly, the UNHCR were unsympathetic to complaints: "There is little doubt that the condition of the refugees in Cuba is the best that refugees can have."[103] Former exiles remembered developing careers that would help them build a life in exile and post-exile in the Southern Cone. But they also recalled doing so out of gratitude to Cuba. As one exile explained, "Our total and absolute decision was to integrate ourselves absolutely into Cuban life," and work was "very important."[104]

Uruguayan and Chilean exiles, meanwhile, recounted seizing opportunities to study *in addition to* work. Having postponed degrees due to exile or not having the opportunity to study earlier, exiles in their mid-twenties tended to believe they were too old to be just students.[105] Flexible study programs developed in the 1970s were therefore attractive and, as they did across the island, they benefited women.[106] In this way, Raquel first, and then Augustín, took it in turns to finish their psychology degrees and work professionally on the island.[107] In Santiago, Fernando and his partner also shared childcare so they could study at night or on the weekends.[108]

Another common feature of family life—and citizenship—in Cuba involved active participation in neighborhood and civic projects. A legacy of the drive to forge the "New Man" in the 1960s, voluntary work was still taken seriously in the 1970s and 1980s.[109] Of course, "voluntary work" was also obligatory, evidence of revolutionary commitment monitored both by neighborhood revolutionary committees (Comités de Defensa de la Revolución, CDRs) and workplaces. There were instances when this expectation became onerous, particularly for women juggling work and homelife. When, on one occasion, Katy Ulloa, pregnant with her third child, did not cut sugarcane, her colleagues threatened to revoke her distinguished worker status.[110] But "voluntary" work also provided socialization, integration, and friendship. On "Red Sundays," from Guantánamo to Havana, communities and families participated.[111] Children painted railings, cleaned, or attended neighborhood gardens.[112] Leticia Cubas, who grew up in Santa Clara, fondly remembered participating in the Patrullas Click—young neighborhood patrols checking on electricity usage and encouraging savings by, for example, turning lights off.[113] With the shift to material incentives, hardworking "volunteers" in the 1970s and 1980s also won material rewards (such as washing machines and cars).[114]

Homelife was meanwhile more communal that many expected when they moved into individual apartments, with many remembering a Cuban propensity for open doors. Juan Saavedra and his partner, who moved to an apartment in Santa Clara after living in a semi-clandestine house in Havana with other Miristas during covert training, found open doors and neighborly proximity uncomfortable, especially after years of keeping their lives strictly private for the purposes of underground work.[115] As Soledad remembered, "Neighbors were part of your family."[116]

While exiles adapted to Cuban neighborliness, they lived the state's efforts to change the private sphere through its 1975 Family Code.[117] Yet, mirroring a general "ambivalence" on the island, they struggled to remember it.[118] This silence and their insights about gender equality more generally are telling of the code's simultaneous impact and irrelevance. Generational differences partly explain this inconsistency. Much as revolutionary leaders had envisaged, children imbibed the revolution's messages more than their parents. The Family Code was, as Elise Andaya has noted, a "pedagogical tool."[119] Camila, who grew up in Cuba, remembered the state's discourse empowering her.[120] Even so, the code's educational success had limits. Marina Cultelli, the daughter of MLNT exiles, remembered her Cuban boyfriend being shocked to see her father washing dishes.[121] Ingrained ideas were shared by women. A Uruguayan medical student vividly recalled a Cuban woman asking if he was gay because he washed his own trousers.[122]

Within their own homes, meanwhile, Uruguayans and Chileans did not recall state policies changing domestic life. Exiles either arrived sharing responsibilities, like Uruguayan former colonia members, or they maintained previous traditionally gendered roles (and those who practiced equality commented more on differences they encountered with Cubans). Despite the Cuban state's emphasis on joining the labor force, some women, primarily of an older generation and middle-class spouses of professional men, also never worked formally outside the home, remaining housewives in exile.[123] Not only does this show the limits of the Family Code, but it also reflects the autonomy certain exiles—likely due to class and status—had to reject requirements to work. (As Andaya notes, "Housewives were classified as unproductive citizens whose continued existence was considered both an economic drain on state resources and evidence of their inferior political consciousness.")[124]

Elsewhere, women continued pre-exile patterns of juggling work inside and outside the home, while their husbands were more politically and socially active. When Ariel was explaining his intense workday to me, his wife, Katy, declining to be interviewed but listening, interjected, reminding him that she had worked as intensely and *then* looked after their children and the house. While she did, he went on male-only fishing trips.[125] Tania, the daughter of Uruguayan communists, remembered her father being more politically involved—and absent from the home—than her mother, who was principally responsible for childcare. She is therefore skeptical of her parents' generation's claims of equality.

> The leaders were primarily men and the role reserved for women was to support them. Men, particularly of an older generation, will find it difficult to recognize there was no equality. They will say that there was and that women were fully incorporated into politics, but at the end of the day there was a sexual division of labor . . . in militancy and in the home.[126]

Opportunities and Paradoxes of Family Life in Practice

In a global context, continued gender inequality in 1970s and 1980s Cuba was by no means unique. However, for some exiles, reality chafed against the revolutionary equality they had imagined. Although grateful for opportunities to study and work, and despite state provision of education, childcare, and domestic services, parents tended to recall feeling overcommitted—and single mothers more so. To juggle opportunity and obligation, they also depicted family life as regularly reliant on, and integrated within, informal networks, private salaried help, and newly forged kinships—all recognized, informally at least, as Cuban societal norms at the time.

Isolina Lincolao's testimony reflects the complexities of institutionalizing equality and "liberation." In exile, while working on a cooperative farm in Triunvirato, Matanzas, she realized societal changes would be a long arduous struggle. With no kindergartens, older women or ad hoc collectives cared for children. Elsewhere, the town's culture was conservative, patriarchal, and formal, unlike the revolutionary society Isolina had imagined. "I'm talking about '74 . . . my eyes were like saucers [*ojos de plato*]," she recalled. "One of the technicians, a typical young communist, had a girlfriend. And he went to see her on Wednesdays and Sundays. And he had chaperones who were always watching. . . . It was like going back to the Middle Ages." "We thought it was all solved," she remembered of her dreams of Cuba in Chile. However, she encountered working women responsible for housework and childcare. "It was shocking," she remembered.

Women assumed it so calmly.... Of course, now they had water, they had bathrooms, they had some washing machines.... They were establishing common launderettes... but it wasn't easy.... There were the incentives to study but the ones who studied were the men.... I told them: you also have to go. And they looked at me smiling.... They considered it logical that the man, the husband, the head of the household should study.[127]

In 1975, Isolina moved to Santiago to live in a two-bedroom apartment with her Chilean single-parent friend, Beatriz, and Beatriz's son, whose story this chapter opened with. Housing single women with other family configurations was advocated by the Chilean exile community to make the most of available apartments.[128] It gave Isolina the opportunity to study architecture while working as a factory accountant. With Isolina sharing childcare, Beatriz also combined work at the Ministry of Culture with motherhood and study. As Beatriz recalled, exiles' female solidarity was important, and she, her son, and Isolina were "a family."[129]

In time, however, Beatriz left Cuba and Isolina began a relationship with a Cuban man. In 1980, they had a son. However, they never got married. As she worked and studied, he did no housework, had affairs, and soon ran off. She was thus left fulfilling the promise of female liberation through work and study as a single mother. Access to state day care helped but was insufficient because classes were at night.[130] She therefore had to find private childcare less than a month after her son's birth. When the Chilean dictatorship began allowing exiles to return in 1983, she then had to rely on her mother-in-law to obtain authorization from her son's father, who could legally veto such a move, to leave Cuba.[131]

Isolina's story illustrates the inherent tensions in Cuba's revolutionary gender politics. She took advantage of state-sponsored opportunities and enjoyed the benefits of autonomy that employment and education offered, but she relied on nonstate systems to do so. Simultaneously, at odds with the Family Code's expectations, she forged ad hoc families, with Beatriz, with a transitory Cuban partner, and as a single mother. She also came to realize, as with other Patria Potestad laws, that fathers still had power to determine children's future by blocking migration. (Until 1979, husbands' permission was also necessary for women to have an abortion.)[132]

Isolina's story also reveals the nonstate structures that plugged shortfalls in Cuba's "reproductive bargain." As Snyder writes, "The architecture of the revolution necessitated 'old' ways of organizing family."[133] For exiles, separated from relatives, alternative arrangements were vital. Fellow Uruguayans or Chileans often substituted, becoming "brothers [and] sisters."[134] Replicating Cuban adjustments to the state's gaps, exiled children frequently spent time with neighbors.[135] When

Tania's parents volunteered to harvest coffee, for example, a Cuban family looked after her.[136]

Indeed, neighbors became pillars of logistical and emotional support. Juan's discomfort at their proximity certainly dissipated: "They involved themselves in our lives . . . because we had a baby. . . . They took it upon themselves to take care of him, they took care of everything, everything, everything, everything, bringing us some fruit that we didn't have, so that the child had something to eat, right? [They offered us] enormous, enormous, enormous solidarity."[137] Rita and Marina Cultelli meanwhile affectionately spoke of their adoptive Cuban grandmother as being a central pillar of family life: "When my mother traveled to Mexico and Europe in the campaigns for my father's freedom, she always visited us, took care of us, watched out for us and offered us total security."[138] Children, like Rita, who attended boarding schools would also recall that friendships offset and substituted for family.[139]

Others inserted themselves into different kinships. Camila, for example, found inspiration in the underground rock scene as a teenager, thereby rebelling against exiled Chileans and officially sanctioned Cuban culture. The rockers became *hermanos* and she adopted their aesthetics and rituals, shaving her hair (a scandal in school and in Alamar) and spending Monday nights climbing to the top of buildings with an antenna to hear heavy metal US radio programs.[140] For not imbibing idealized revolutionary behavior, she was admonished at school and berated for "betraying" the sacrifices made by the island's revolutionary martyrs. However, Camila's close links to Cuba today are precisely because of this alternative kinship.

Final Remarks

Camila would have been one of the children the Cuban state worried about in the 1980s. As concerns regarding "delinquency" grew, the limitations of prescribing nuclear families and revolutionary citizens through work and civic duties became apparent. The island had more single parents, divorce, and abortions than ever before (43 percent of marriages ended in divorce by the late 1980s).[141] Despite growing independence and decision-making in the home, few men, married after 1975, contributed equally to domestic work (less than 5 percent) in 1989.[142] Cubans and exiles alike therefore lived the contradictions of the island's efforts to bring about a social revolution. As Beatriz's reflections at the beginning of this chapter suggested, this was not a unique Cuban problem; decrees rarely change societies—revolutionary or otherwise—overnight.[143]

Chilean and Uruguayan exiles' experiences in Cuba reveal the everyday realities of a state's efforts to sculpt society. They remembered life in Cuba as being a mix of opportunity and control, plentiful support, and scarcity.[144] When asked what they missed about Cuba, however, former exiles did not cite top-down revolutionary decrees or institutionalized laws of equality. While expressing gratitude for material provisions, education, and career opportunities, they mostly cherished the alternative, informal sense of belonging they had forged thanks to neighbors, friends, communities, kinships, and adopted family members. It is entirely possible that *without* the state's social engineering projects—and their limitations—these alternative kinships would never have existed. The combined architecture of aspirations and reality, in short, led exiles to carve out their own family constructs and relationships with *el pueblo* as they strove to navigate revolutionary citizenship. It was also the absence of *el pueblo* that returnees noted as being so alienating in post-dictatorial Chile or Uruguay. To Andrea, at least, Chilean society seemed "backward," lacking Cuba's "social and community consciousness."[145]

Notes

1. Author's interview with Beatriz Torres Abelaira, video chat, May 13, 2021.

2. Author's interview with Beatriz Torres Abelaira.

3. The 1,200 Uruguayans comprised 500 MLNT and 700 PCU militants, though it is unclear whether figures include dependents. Paola Parrella Meny and Valentina Curto Fonsalías, "En Cuba, experiencias con muchos contrastes," in *El Uruguay del exilio: gente, circunstancias, escenarios,* ed. Silvia Dutrénit Bielous (Trilce, 2006), 189. Estimates of Chileans in Cuba from author's interviews with Camilia Krauss, video chat, August 5 and 13, 2021.

4. Michelle Chase and Isabella Cosse, "Revolutionary Positions," *Radical History Review* 136 (2020): 5.

5. Rachel Hynson, *Laboring for the State: Women, Family and Work in Revolutionary Cuba, 1959–1971* (Cambridge University Press, 2020), 23.

6. Emily Snyder, "Internationalizing the Revolutionary Family: Love and Politics in Cuba and Nicaragua, 1979–1990," *Radical History Review* 136 (2020): 57–58, quotation on 60.

7. Ley no. 1289, Código de la Familia, 1975, https://oig.cepal.org/sites/default/files/1975_ley1289_cub.pdf, accessed April 30, 2025.

8. Hynson, *Laboring for the State,* 2, 21.

9. Emily J. Kirk, Anna Clayfield, and Isabel Story, eds., *Cuba's Forgotten Decade: How the 1970s Shaped the Revolution* (Lexington Books, 2018), 1.

10. Hope Bastian Martínez, "Cuban Women and the State: Women's Lives in the 1970s and the New Reproductive Bargain," in Kirk et al., *Cuba's Forgotten Decade,* 118, 123, 127; Helen I. Safa, *The Myth of the Male Breadwinner: Women and Industrialization in the Caribbean* (Westview, 1995), 128.

11. Elise Andaya, *Conceiving Cuba: Reproduction, Women, and the State in the Post-Soviet Era* (Rutgers University Press, 2014), 25; Bastian Martínez, "Cuban Women and the State," 121.

12. Rosi Smith, "The 'Three Ps' (Perfecting, Professionalization, and Pragmatism) and Their Limitations for Understanding Cuban Education in the 1970s," in Kirk et al., *Cuba's Forgotten Decade*, 137; Lois M. Smith and Alfred Padula, *Sex and Revolution: Women in Socialist Cuba* (Oxford University Press, 1996), 89–91.

13. Bastian Martínez, "Cuban Women and the State," 117, 122.

14. Clementia Serra as quoted in Marvin Leiner, *Children Are the Revolution: Day Care in Cuba* (Penguin, 1978), 15; Bastian Martínez, "Cuban Women and the State."

15. Safa, *Myth of the Male Breadwinner*, 30, 139, 154, 162; Margaret Randall, *To Change the World: My Years in Cuba* (Rutgers University Press, 2019), chap. 4, Kindle.

16. Smith and Padula, *Sex and Revolution*, 158. See also Randall, *To Change the World*, chap. 7.

17. Andaya, *Conceiving Cuba*, 43–44. See also Randall, *To Change the World*, chap. 3.

18. Safa, *Myth of the Male Breadwinner*, 143; Andaya, *Conceiving Cuba*, 42–43; Randall, *To Change the World*, chap. 7.

19. Bastian Martínez, "Cuban Women and the State," 117; Smith and Padula, *Sex and Revolution*, 147, 158.

20. Isabella Cosse, "Childhood, Love and Politics: The Montonero 'Nursery' in Cuba During the Cold War," *Journal of Latin American Studies* 55, no. 1 (2022): 9.

21. Isabella Cosse, "'Infidelidades': Moral, revolución y sexualidad en las organizaciones de la izquierda armada en la Argentina de los años 70," *Instituto de Desarrollo Económico y Social: Practicas de Oficio* 1, no. 19 (2017): 12 (quotations), 18.

22. Author's interview with Roberto, London, January 31, 2023.

23. Cosse, "Childhood, Love and Politics," 9.

24. Author's correspondence with Paula Riquelme, February 16, 2023.

25. Cosse, "Childhood, Love and Politics," 10; Tamara Vidaurrázaga Aránguiz, "Mujeres en rojo y negro. Reconstrucción de memoria de tres mujeres Miristas (1971–1990)" (MSc diss., Universidad de Chile, 2005), 150–54.

26. Alessandro Portelli, "What Makes Oral History Different," in *The Oral History Reader*, ed. Robert Perks and Alistair Thomson (Routledge, 2015), 52–53.

27. Peter Gatrell, Anindita Ghoshal, Katarzyna Nowak, and Alex Dowdall, "Reckoning with Refugeedom: Refugee Voices in Modern History," *Social History* 46, no. 1 (2021): 2–3.

28. For a comparison of collective living experiments in exile, see Alejandro Paredes, "El quiebre de la cotidianeidad en la niñez chilena exiliada en Mendoza, Argentina (1973–1989)," *Estudios de Filosofía Práctica e Historia de las ideas* 24 (2022): 11.

29. See *El edificio de los chilenos*, dir. Macarena Aguiló and Susana Foxley (Magic Lantern Films, 2010). For the Guardería, see Cosse, "Childhood, Love and Politics."

30. Código de la Familia, 1975, Articles 1, 24, and 28.

31. Gabriela Gonzalez-Vaillant, "The Tupamaros: Re-Gendering an Ungendered Guerrilla Movement," *NORMA: International Journal for Masculinity Studies* 10, nos. 3–4

(2015): 306; Lillian Guerra, *Patriots and Traitors in Revolutionary Cuba, 1961–1981* (University of Pittsburgh Press, 2023), 122.

32. On rejecting motherhood as a militant, see Ana Casamayou in Clara Aldrighi, ed., *Memorias de insurgencia: historias de vida y militancia en el MLN-Tupamaros 1965–1975* (Ediciones de la Banda Oriental, 2009), 290.

33. Parrella and Curto, "En Cuba," 191; Hugo Wilkins in Aldrighi, *Memorias de insurgencia*, 266–68.

34. Hynson, *Laboring for the State*, 12; Guerra, *Patriots and Traitors*, 121–36.

35. Author's interviews with Fernando Mazzeo, video chat, April 29, 2021; Olga Estevez, Whatsapp, May 22, 2021; "Laura" (pseudonym), video chats, April 15 and May 6, 2021; "Augustín and Raquel Rossetti" (pseudonyms), video chat, June 30, 2021. See also Parrella and Curto, "En Cuba," 191. On extreme secrecy and hidden identities, see Guerra, *Patriots and Traitors*, 105.

36. Author's interviews with Mazzeo, Laura, and Daniel Muzio Lladó, video chat, July 22, 2021. See also Parrella and Curto, "En Cuba," 191.

37. Laura interviews.

38. Snyder, "Internationalizing the Revolutionary Family," 66. On postponing love for the revolution in Cuba, see also Guerra, *Patriots and Traitors*, 40, 56.

39. Laura interviews. The state also provided contraception to boarding schools, acknowledging that it could not prevent sexual relationships. Author's interview with Gregory Randall, video chat, June 10, 2021.

40. Mazzeo and Laura interviews. See also Parrella and Curto, "En Cuba," 199.

41. Muzio interview.

42. Mazzeo interview.

43. Estevez and Laura interviews. One colonia appears to have had a more traditional outlook on childcare, with one woman taking overall responsibility. See Muzio interview.

44. Estevez interview.

45. Gonzalez-Vaillant, "Tupamaros," 296. On the Chilean revolutionary Left's rejection of "feminism," see Hillary Hiner, "'Memory Speaks from Today': Analyzing Oral Histories of Female Members of the MIR in Chile Through the Work of Luisa Passerini," *Women's History Review* 25, no. 3 (2016): 397.

46. Randall, *To Change the World*, chap. 7.

47. Mazzeo, Estevez, and Laura interviews.

48. Laura and Estevez interviews.

49. Estevez interview.

50. Gonzalez-Vaillant, "Tupamaros," 296, 302, 305.

51. Estevez interview (quotation); Mazzeo interview. Roberto in his interview discussed Cubans' initial skepticism that Mirista women could undertake the same military training as men.

52. Snyder, "Internationalizing the Revolutionary Family," 57.

53. Mazzeo and Estevez interviews.

54. Mazzeo interview.

55. On stigmatization, see Hynson, *Laboring for the State*, 262–63.

56. Laura interview.

57. Estevez interview; Casamayou in Aldrighi, *Memorias*, 296.

58. Darío Croc Ures, *La colonia tupamara en Cuba: un testimonio* (Argumento, 2019), 165. The "plenary's" outcome is unclear. However, the debate in closed-party environment resembles the reaction women who became pregnant during the MIR's operations faced. Author's interview with María Inés Ruz Zañartu, video chat, September 5, 2021.

59. Christine Hatzky, *Cubans in Angola: South-South Cooperation and Transfer of Knowledge, 1976-1991* (University of Wisconsin Press, 2015), 211.

60. Gonzalez-Vaillant, "Tupamaros," 305. On leaving training once her pregnancy was discovered, see Casamayou in Aldrighi, *Memorias*, 296.

61. Rossetti interview.

62. Laura interviews.

63. Rosetti interview; Wilkins in Aldrighi, *Memorias*, 272.

64. Rossetti interview.

65. Margaret Randall, *No se puede hacer la revolución sin nosotras* (Casa de las Américas, 1978), 121.

66. Not to be confused with D-22, which housed Proyecto Hogares, later called the "Edificio de los chilenos" in Aguló and Foxley's film. Mario Santucho's children also lived with adoptive parents in D-2.

67. Hiner, "Memory Speaks from Today," 393.

68. Ruz interview.

69. Ruz interview.

70. Author's interview with Manuel Llorca Jaña, video chat, June 24, 2021.

71. Ruz interview. A similar memory of a mother's terror seeing their child on a balcony came up in author's interview with Andrea Polanco, WhatsApp, April 16, 2021.

72. Leiner, *Children Are the Revolution*.

73. Llorca interview. Article 13, Code of Childhood and Youth (1978), as quoted in Anne Luke, "Within the Revolution, Everyone: Cuba, Youth, and Interrogating the 1970s Paradigm," in Kirk et al., *Cuba's Forgotten Decade*, 231–32.

74. Cosse, "Childhood, Love and Politics," 13.

75. Rosi Smith, "Three Ps," 134; Hatzky, *Cubans in Angola*, 15.

76. Bastian Martínez, "Cuban Women and the State," 122–23. On child labor as a means of forging loyalty and fulfilling economic goals, see Guerra, *Patriots and Traitors*, 243–48.

77. Krauss interviews.

78. Llorca interview.

79. Author's interview with Cecilia Millán, video chat, July 19, 2021.

80. Krauss interviews.

81. Krauss and Llorca interviews.

82. Ruz interview.

83. Leiner, *Children Are the Revolution*, 5, 13.

84. Estevez interview. For reflections on parental choices, see Randall, *To Change the World,* chap. 3; Roberto interview.

85. Author's interview with Soledad Guyer, video chat, August 9, 2021.

86. Author's interviews with "Tania," video chats, June 25 and September 9, 2021.

87. Author's interview with Sonia Daza Sepúlveda, Mexico City, 18 March 18, 2013; Torres interview. For a discussion of the impact of living in hotels on exiles' family life, see Paredes, "El quiebre de la cotidianeidad."

88. Tanya Harmer, *Beatriz Allende: A Revolutionary Life in Cold War Latin America* (University of North Carolina Press, 2020), 229. On this promise extending to Uruguayans, see Parrella and Curto, "En Cuba," 194.

89. Between 1959 and 1988, the Cuban state built 500,000 housing units (16,000 a year) but this fell short of needs. Smith and Padula, *Sex and Revolution,* 14.

90. Daza and Torres interviews.

91. Author's interview with José Enrique Pommerenck, video chat, May 6, 2021.

92. Author's interview with Juan Saavedra, video chat, May 12, 2021; Estevez, Torres, and Guyer interviews.

93. Ana Vásquez-Bronfman and Ana María Araújo, *La maldición de Ulises: repercusiones psicológicas del exilio* (Editorial Sudamericana, 1990), 23, 30–31.

94. Author's interview with Andrea Pellegrín, video chat, October 13, 2020; Laura, Rossetti, and Saavedra interviews.

95. Andaya, *Conceiving Cuba,* 34.

96. Pellegrín interview.

97. Author's interview with Ariel Ulloa, video chat, May 5, 2021.

98. Fidel Castro Ruz, *Informe del Comite Central del PCC al Primer Congreso* (Departamento de Orientación Revolucionaria del Comité Central del Partido Comunista de Cuba, 1975), 228.

99. See Anna Clayfield, "Militarized by Moscow? Re-examining Soviet Influence on Cuba in the 1970s," in Kirk et al., *Cuba's Forgotten Decade,* 71–85.

100. On numbers, see Wilkins in Aldrighi, *Memorias,* 277; author's interview with Hugo Wilkins, Havana, November 8, 2022.

101. Rossetti interview.

102. Estevez interview.

103. Memorandum, Hugo Idoyaga, UNHCR Regional Representative for Northern Latin America to UNHCR Representative in France, July 13, 1978, fonds 11, series 2, box 73, UNHCR Archives, Geneva. On work obligations in Cuba, see also Guerra, *Patriots and Traitors,* 225.

104. Ulloa interview.

105. Author's interview with Isolina Lincolao Lobos, Whatsapp, June 1, 2021.

106. Guyer, Estevez, and Lincolao interviews.

107. Rossetti interview.

108. Mazzeo interview.

109. Snyder, "Internationalizing the Revolutionary Family," 54.

110. Ulloa interview.

111. Guyer interview.

112. Millán and Llorca interviews.

113. Author's interview with Luis and Leticia Cubas, video (Montevideo, Uruguay), July 8, 2021.

114. Saavedra interview; Andaya, *Conceiving Cuba*, 38.

115. Saavedra interview.

116. Guyer interview.

117. Andaya, *Conceiving Cuba*, 32–33; Smith and Padula, *Sex and Revolution*, 154.

118. On ambivalence in Cuba, see Andaya, *Conceiving Cuba*, 37.

119. Andaya, *Conceiving Cuba*, 37. On generational differences, see also Safa, *Myth of the Male Breadwinner*, 127, 135–38.

120. Krauss interview.

121. Author's interview with Rita and Marina Cultelli, video chat, May 25, 2021. On the scandal of girls doing their boyfriends' laundry in the Escuelas Secundarias Básicas del Campo, see Smith and Padula, *Sex and Revolution*, 87.

122. Author's interview with Nestor Luzardo, WhatsApp, April 24, 2021.

123. Author's interviews with Ricardo Elena, video chat, July 3, 2021; Gonzalo Serrantes, video chat, June 17, 2021; Pommerenck.

124. Andaya, *Conceiving Cuba*, 28.

125. Ulloa interview.

126. Tania interviews.

127. Lincolao interview.

128. Memorandum: "Pauta de acción del Comité para los meses futuros," enclosure, Francisco Fernández, president, Comité Chileno, to Arturo Espinoza, director general, ICAP, March 11, 1975, Carpeta 1, Documentos Históricos del Comité Chileno Antifascista, Centro de Documentación de ICAP, Havana, Cuba.

129. Torres interview.

130. Regarding inflexible childcare to meet needs, see also Safa, *Myth of the Male Breadwinner*, 126.

131. Lincolao interview.

132. Andaya, *Conceiving Cuba*, 42–43.

133. Emily Snyder, "Gender, Power, and Female Revolutionaries," *Latin American Research Review* 58, no. 3 (2022): 8.

134. Estevez interview.

135. Padula and Smith, *Sex and Revolution*, 135.

136. Tania interviews; also Guyer and Polanco.

137. Saavedra interview.

138. Cultelli interview.

139. Cubas and Cultelli interviews.

140. Krauss interview.

141. Smith and Padula, *Sex and Revolution,* 160, 164; Safa, *Myth of the Male Breadwinner,* 30.

142. Marjorie Sue Zatz, *Producing Legality: Law and Socialism in Cuba* (New York: Routledge, 1994), 93–94; Safa, *Myth of the Male Breadwinner,* 137, 163; Andaya, *Conceiving Cuba,* 37.

143. See also Randall, *To Change the World,* chap. 9.

144. Cubas interview.

145. Polanco interview.

NINE

Between Two Empires

Youth, Identity, and Consumption in 1970s and 1980s Cuba

ALEXIS BALDACCI

Debates over consumption in Cuba in the late 1970s and early 1980s were shaped by transnational flows that situated average Cubans in the middle of the Cold War power struggle between East and West. On the one hand, the Soviet-sponsored World Festival of Youth and Students (WFYS) brought almost twenty thousand young people to Havana in 1978, putting Cuban youth and Cuba itself on the international stage and facilitating connections between Cubans and their peers from the Socialist Bloc. On the other hand, firsthand accounts of lifestyles in the United States from more than a hundred thousand exiles returning home for family visits in 1978–79 offered new insights that often clashed with how Cuban media had long portrayed life in exile. The Mariel boatlift, which brought more than 120,000 Cubans to the United States for the first time in 1980 as refugees from communism, derailed the brief thaw in Cuban-US relations and further complicated the political, economic, and cultural implications of consumption and material goods.

This chapter examines public discourse on material and consumer cultures to explore the extent to which the meaning of the revolutionary project, for individuals and on the international stage, was malleable and contested in this period. Both macro- and micro-level processes, including everyday encounters with visitors from the socialist and capitalist worlds and the Mariel exodus itself, revitalized ongoing debates about the rights and responsibilities of the individual in a collectivist society, the function of material things and modes of self-presentation in everyday life, (un)official constructions of Cuban identity, and the implications that consumption had for young women and men in this period. Economic conditions, including the US trade embargo and Cuba's role in the Soviet-led Comecon (Council for Mutual Economic Assistance), shaped the terms of these debates by determining what was available to consumers; yet contemporary sources—especially the Cuban press, which expanded in this period—reveal that for both Cuban leadership and youth these issues transcended economics with relevance for culture, politics, and identities. The new realities of life outside of Cuba, be it in Moscow or Miami, sometimes shook Cubans' confidence, if not in the revolution itself, then in revolutionary leaders whose inconsistencies were laid bare by increasingly visible inequality in a supposedly classless society and failure to live up to the goals and ideals that they themselves had stipulated.

The Revolution Enters a New Era: The 1970s

The Cuban economy changed significantly in the 1970s, with ramifications for both the realities facing Cuban consumers and how state representatives conceptualized and framed consumption in the context of ongoing revolution. Reeling from the public failure of the Ten Million Ton Harvest, Cuban leaders faced overwhelming evidence of widespread discontent and economic failure, including rates of absenteeism approaching one-third of the labor force.[1] Their economic response centered on intensifying Soviet influence in economic planning and oversight in the first years of the 1970s, a process that culminated in Cuba's integration into Comecon in July 1972.[2] In addition to the ramifications for trade, Cuba's entry into Comecon also marks the adoption of a new economic strategy marked by increased reliance on Soviet models, advice, and aid, which fostered economic development, including advances in industrialization and the mechanization of agriculture. This new strategy expanded prosperity, allowing the state to meet some of its most pressing needs and alleviate the more strenuous demands placed on consumers' time, creativity, and taste buds. The period from 1971 to 1975 saw an average economic growth per capita of 13 percent, which was astronomical compared to the figures of 1.2 percent for the period from 1963 to 1965 and -1.3 percent for 1966 to 1970.[3] In addition to stabilizing the economy, the pragmatic approach of the 1970s—a significant departure from the idealism and grand schemes of the 1960s, including the Ten Million Ton Harvest—made an expansion of consumerism possible, as the less ambitious economic development to be achieved with Soviet aid would not be built solely through Cuban efforts and therefore did not require so much capital accumulation within the island. Yet Cuba did not become a consumer's paradise during the 1970s and 1980s, despite the nostalgia that many Cubans today have for the era. The expansion of consumerism was always a balancing act between addressing state goals, working within the economic confines of central planning and trade orientation toward the Soviet Bloc, and mediating popular complaints, with popular complaints generally the lowest of these priorities.[4]

As the shifts in economic policy outlined above reveal, Cuban leaders' approach to revolution was far from static. The state's approach to culture and freedom of expression also changed over time. We might conceptualize these changes as cycles of opening and closure in which stricter, top-down mandates in the realms of ideology, politics, and economics alternated with looser moments in which policymakers were more attentive to bottom-up notions of what a true revolution should look like. In the spheres of artistic and intellectual culture, the repression of the early 1970s has been remembered as the Quinquenio Gris.[5] Yet in her analysis of the political institutions of this period, Carollee Bengelsdorf argues that many of the political changes initiated in the 1970s were aimed less at stifling discontent than at "channel[ing] discontent, to redefine the space for its expression within a framework molded, in the end, by the same paternalism that had haunted the 1960s."[6] Similarly, the spheres of popular and consumer culture came to be characterized by a greater openness to the Cuban people's understanding of their lives and the meaning of the revolution within them. Yet this economic, political, and popular cultural opening was not without limits. Flashpoint moments that challenged Cuban leaders' understanding of the popular legitimacy of their project or endangered Cuba's standing on the international stage caused the boundaries of acceptable self-representation through fashion to narrow considerably with ramifications for official and unofficial constructions of sexuality and political and gender identification. These threats could be short-lived, such as the 1980 Mariel boatlift, which as discussed below complicated but did not completely derail these processes, or more enduring, such as the Rectification of Errors and Negative Tendencies campaign announced in 1986, which marked an effective end to the openness in material and consumer culture initiated by the new economic policies from 1972 on.[7]

In the context of this economic opening, styles that were widely condemned in the press and by officials in the 1960s—particularly the casual youth clothing associated with the West—were increasingly adopted by a generation of Cuban youth that had been raised in a revolutionary context. Debates about internationally popular styles, and even the propriety of young people desiring to be fashionable in the first place, continued, but they were increasingly debates about how to reconcile the fashions to Cuban reality and values rather than official mandates to eliminate them altogether. Yet given the strict intellectual and artistic mandates of the period, ongoing economic challenges despite marked improvements, and memory of the dire political ramifications of these styles less than a decade before, the terms and outcomes of these debates were anything but clear-cut. As María A. Cabrera Arús has argued, the economic improvements of the 1970s led to changes in the "discursive frameworks through which goods, real and imagined, circulated in the island's popular culture." Increasingly, state actors sought to emphasize the abundance brought about by revolutionary policies as a socialist achievement, and yet, these "visions of plenty ... sat uneasily with a lingering emphasis on radical egalitarianism and unity." The result was "a consumer landscape characterized by ambiguity as much as cohesion."[8] Building on Cabrera Arús's arguments, I argue that transnational factors also contributed to this ambiguity by highlighting alternatives with regard to access to goods and the possibilities for their meaning within the Cold War competition between socialist and capitalist systems.

The late 1970s and early 1980s can help us understand these processes due to the unique transnational exposure experienced by Cuban youth in this period. As a result of the WFYS, hosted in Havana in 1978, and the family visits of Cuban exiles living in the United States, youth in Cuba were exposed to international styles more extensively in the late 1970s than perhaps in any other period since the triumph of the revolution. These encounters could and did have unintended consequences. The WFYS was a biennial event sponsored by the Communist Parties of the Soviet Union and other countries, designed to promote international peace and friendship. Yet as Pia Koivunen and Juliane Fürst have shown, there were often (in Koivunen's words) "contradictions between the aims of the festival organizers and the reality during the fortnight-long celebrations." At these moments, "the socialist system became vulnerable," and the unofficial and unsanctioned interactions between the thousands of gathered young people, who came from the socialist, capitalist, and nonaligned worlds, could lead to the spread of countercultures as well as official cultures.[9]

The family visits, by contrast, were a manifestation of the brief thaw in relations between Cuba and the United States under the Carter administration. They represent the important role of human rights concerns, particularly familial reconciliation, in the tentative rapprochement between the two hostile powers. Unlike the WFYS, which was a strictly organized event with an obvious ideological function, it is harder to access what cultural and political impact Cuban policymakers anticipated from the family visits. One outcome in the economic and fashion sphere was that many young Cubans gained new access to US fashions, unleashing further debates about appropriate self-expression and identity in a revolutionary context. For many Cubans, a T-shirt was undoubtably just a T-shirt. Yet for others, a T-shirt could be a form of "sartorial disobedience" and a means of expressing worldviews that ran counter to official narratives.[10] The youth countercultures that grew in the period of openness of the late 1970s soon took on sinister and dire proportions as the Mariel boatlift left officials reeling.

By the mid-1970s, leadership faced the quandary of inculcating revolutionary values among a new generation of Cuban youth who did not have direct memories of pre-1959 Cuba. Following the First Congress of the Communist Party in 1975, officials sought to expand the press as a key means of ideological orientation and education regarding state initiatives and values. Given the particular importance of educating Cuban youth, the "Thesis on Mass Media," released during the Congress, emphasized the development of new publications targeting young people, including *Somos Jóvenes,* the first issue of which coincided with the Third Congress of the Young Communist League (UJC) and early planning meetings for the Havana gathering of the WFYS.[11] For Cuban youth, the press was to serve as a guide to revolutionary life, as journalists explained the law and revolutionary ideology and how they translated into the everyday lives of citizens.

In addition to other facets of revolutionary life, the press also explained the consumer economy, orienting people to new ways of accessing goods and services, an important function in this period when the consumer economy was a site for experimentation and reform. This is significant, because even in the 1970s and 1980s—the era of the "fat cows," remembered for its relative abundance—the consumer economy was frequently a focus of complaints and source of discontent among Cuban citizens.[12] Strikingly, these complaints figure prominently in magazines of this period alongside "visions of plenty," utopic images of a socialist modernity already achieved, painting a picture of a consumer landscape that was at best ambiguous and at worst contradictory.[13] While designed to orient Cuban youth, these contradictions created space in magazines for critique of state policies, confusion over these policies, and deviation in how average citizens interpreted and internalized these policies, sometimes intentionally, as an educational exercise, and sometimes unintentionally. Transnational factors, including perceived ideological and cultural affiliation with either of the Cold War superpowers, were a crucial factor in determining the bounds of acceptability with regard to consumerism. Like leaders, young Cubans in this period often looked to the socialist world as their allies and peers, and analysis of youth fashion reveals a desire to showcase Cuba as a source of socialist modernity on par with those peers.

Encounters with the East: The Allure of Socialist Modernity

While popular remembrances of the late Cold War period often focus on the allure that Western styles, like blue jeans, had for socialist youth, the socialist world was equally, if not more, significant as a frame of reference for Cuban youth who were interested in fashion. Socialist alternatives to goods produced in the capitalist world were always preferable from an ideological standpoint as well as an economic one. As discussed below, US-produced goods were ideologically suspect due to the United States' oppositional stance to the Cuban Revolution, and purchasing goods from other nations in the capitalist world required hard currency, unlike acquiring goods from the socialist world. In addition, items from top fashion houses in France and Italy maintained a negative association with prerevolutionary class inequality. A poem published in *Mujeres* magazine captures the economic and ideological imperatives to buy socialist:

> This woman never knew
> if Christian Dior
> was better than Moscow Red
> but she knew that Moscow was a friendly name.[14]

While by 1980, the year that the poem was published, Christian Dior must have been very hard to come by in Havana, let alone elsewhere on the island, the poem implies that a patriotic woman would always choose a Soviet-produced item over an alternative produced in the capitalist world, even if it meant sacrificing style and quality.

After joining Comecon in 1972, Cuba coordinated its clothing industry with the Soviet Bloc countries. This involved cooperation through trade and information exchange through training programs. Throughout the early 1980s, for example, over six thousand Cuban girls were sent to Czechoslovakia and an additional two hundred to Hungary for two-year programs in which they could earn certificates in weaving, spinning, or machine repair. After the two-year course, which included language instruction as a first step, the girls spent two years working in a Czech or Hungarian factory to translate knowledge into experience.[15] Beginning in 1970, the Comecon countries also participated in annual fashion shows known as "The Culture of Dress and Costumes" (*La cultura del vestir y el vestuario*) which fashion experts from each country attended to showcase new designs and determine what would be mass-produced in the coming years. Each country presented a central collection and an accessory, usually targeting a gender-specific age group, and the results of the meeting were a guiding force for the scientific-technical and economic collaboration that established fashion norms throughout the socialist world. Cuba began participating in 1979, which is another example of Cuban youth's heightened exposure to transnational trends in the period under review in this essay.[16] Each country had a specialty that contributed to trade cooperation through Comecon: Hungary and Romania specialized in female accessories, Poland in youth clothing, Bulgaria in men's suits, and Cuba in beach and summer clothing.[17]

Cuba performed well at these events, winning international recognition for its achievements in fashion within the socialist world, with these accolades widely reported in the Cuban press. Despite rampant complaints about the poor quality and design of the clothing available to Cuban buyers, particularly with regard to youth fashions, the Cuban collection dedicated to youth fashions for the ages thirteen to seventeen was so well received that it was chosen for international representation after the event.[18] The coexistence of international acclaim for Cuban youth fashion with widespread discontent among Cuban youth resulted from the fact that these fashion shows, despite receiving considerable press attention, were significantly removed from Cubans' daily reality. A major mitigating force was the lag built into the economic system. The Culture of Dress and Costumes event for 1984 set norms to guide production of items that would not arrive in stores until 1986—a full two years away—leaving no flexibility to incorporate citizen input or fashion trends that might emerge in the intervening years.[19] This delay was not due to the complexities of international cooperation and trade. The lag between fashion design and production on the domestic level was also two years. Due to the coordination involved in a planned economy, clothing production schedules had to factor in every step from cotton harvests to cloth production, resulting in an inflexible system of production in which state responses to citizen complaints, when they did come, could not possibly have a concrete effect on what was available in stores for a full two years.[20] Plus, economic planners took a utilitarian approach to fashion that emphasized production numbers over quality and appeal, with the result that every Cuban citizen might have multiple pairs of shoes, for example, but not a single pair they considered usable due to aesthetic, quality, or production issues.[21]

In addition, it was one thing to produce high-quality clothing items in limited numbers for international exposition and another to mass-produce these items and make them available to the population in the quantities necessary to satisfy demand. As a result, the products that were exhibited to international acclaim at the Culture of Dress and Costumes events had very little to do with the products available in Cuban stores and closets, beyond perhaps serving as inspiration for homemade clothing. In 1982, the Culture of Dress and Costumes event was held in Budapest, and the Cuban delegation brought guayaberas of various designs.[22] A

FIGURE 9.1. The "comfortable, elegant, cool, sober, and at the same time, youthful" styles that the Cuban delegation showcased during the 1978 World Festival of Youth and Students. Published in *Somos Jóvenes*, circa 1978.

guayabera is a short-sleeved, button-down shirt with collar, usually decorated with stylized pleats or pockets on either side of the buttons. The style is traditionally worn by men and has long been popular in the Spanish-speaking Caribbean and associated with Cuban nationalism. Despite historic associations with the landowning and professional classes, the style was briefly "valorized for its nationalist symbolism in the Revolution's first years" before falling out of fashion due to associations with the prerevolutionary past. By the 1970s, the style was "experienc[ing] a definite revival," including state campaigns to produce them more cheaply and sell them in the parallel market stores.[23] Scarcity continued despite initiatives to create variations that suited both men and women in the mid-1970s, attempts that must only have been further invigorated by the decision to dress both male and female members of the Cuban delegation to the 1978 WFYS in guayaberas.[24] Yet the very same year that the Cuban delegation highlighted an updated variation of this traditional garb on the international socialist stage, Cuban youth were still suggesting that the fashion industry "should revitalize the guayabera," reflecting that what the Cuban fashion industry exhibited to the socialist world for display was not what they presented to the nation for purchase.[25]

Analysis of the guayabera is particularly revealing for understanding Cuban youth's frustration with the consumer economy in this period. It was a style with serious political chops. It had been associated with Cuban nationalism at various times in Cuban history, including in the early years of the revolution and, most recently, in the decision to dress the Cuban delegation to the WFYS in guayaberas. Yet even as Cuban industry failed to satisfy demand, the Cuban press highlighted the style, and it was a favored choice in portraying Cuba on the international stage, particularly to audiences of socialist allies present at the WFYS and the Culture of Dress and Costumes events. The widespread frustration was rooted, then, in the disconnect between the representation of a socialist modernity achieved in Cuba, highlighted through revitalized nationalist styles, and the reality for consumers of continued hardship.[26] In this case, Cuba's vanguard of leaders and WFYS delegates were far from the only ones interested in proudly displaying prevailing notions of national identity through dress. Socialist modernity as showcased on the international stage was appealing not just for Cuban leaders and international audiences but for Cuban youth more broadly, who were unable to reconcile this idealized form of national dress with the options available to them as consumers. Further contributing to this tension, the reality of socialist modernity available only to a select few clashed with the radical egalitarianism that was at the heart of Cuban revolutionary ideology.

The gulf between the image of Cuba that political, economic, and cultural leaders sought to portray on the international stage and the reality faced by Cuban consumers was a major source of discontent and disillusionment for many young Cubans. Yet there is clear evidence that the state was concerned with youth opinion in this period of openness with regard to fashion and consumption. The Institute for the Investigation and Orientation of Consumer Demand (ICIODI) was founded in April 1971 to oversee and shape the consumer economy in accordance with information they gathered through surveys, interviews with consumers and administrators, data collection on production and consumption, and even undercover visits to stores and restaurants to evaluate customer service.[27] They disseminated this information through a number of publications, including the popular magazine *Opina,* which began publication in 1979. In addition, magazines targeting youth specifically, like *Somos Jóvenes* and *Muchacha,* held and published group interviews that give insights into popular perceptions of the consumer economy.

In March 1982, Juan Carlos Rangel, social psychologist and researcher with the Bureau for Fashion Orientation, sat down with thirty-eight young people to interview them about the state of fashion in Cuba. The group of interviewees included twenty-five students from universities in Villa Clara, Guantánamo, La Habana Province, and the city of Havana, as well as thirteen workers from the province of Matanzas. A student from Villa Clara criticized the fashions published in *Muchacha,* which sometimes featured cloth that was not available for purchase in Cuba either through the ration or *por la libre.* By doing so, she argued, *Muchacha* was setting unrealistic expectations that required creative substitutions to achieve rather than orienting tastes in line with reality. As the student herself put it, "The people invent," out of necessity, inspired by material austerity and not desire or some deep-seated Cuban predilection for creativity. A *trabajadora* from Matanzas mentioned an even more damning difficulty, at least in terms of the state's initiatives to better orient the population using the state press. Journalists could spout practical advice until they were blue in the face, but it would not make a difference because Cubans struggled to access the magazines themselves: Fashion "orientation is scarce," she explained to Rangel. "*Muchacha* does not arrive frequently; *Somos Jóvenes* either; you see *Mujeres* sometimes, but not much. Some of us buy *Opina,* but there is only one page on fashion."[28] The statistics back her perception up: by 1980, just 10 percent of Cuban consumers reported using the Cuban media as a source of fashion inspiration, compared to 28 percent who reported turning to foreign magazines.[29]

In trying to understand the boundaries of acceptable complaint and critique in this period as well as how Cuban youth understood their everyday choices within the transnational framework of the late 1970s and early 1980s, it is notable that much of what appears in the press are critiques that the state was not living up to its own stated commitments and goals. Contrary to leaders' fears that Cuban youth would be seduced by the fashions of the West, as discussed below, the interview subjects instead reveal an unmet desire for a Cuban alternative. Openly critiquing the Eurocentrism they perceived in the fashion inspiration available to Cuban youth, the young people interviewed by Rangel denied the desire to emulate foreign trends, especially those associated with the West.[30] They did, however, seek to compete with them. The revolutionary response to the popularity of foreign trends, at least among youth who supported the revolution and understood fashion to be a political matter, was a call to action. In the openness of this period, complaint and critique, even protest, were acceptable so long as they remained within certain bounds, critiquing the system for not living up to its own stated goals rather than asserting alternatives or attempting to challenge the system altogether.

Encounters with the West: The Seduction of Capitalist Consumption

The West, and the United States specifically, cast a large shadow over Cuban youth culture in this period. While the socialist world provided acceptable models for competition and emulation, the capitalist world proved a more complex and dangerous model. The slippery concept of ideological diversionism is particularly revealing of how fashion could be a battleground over political loyalty and identity. It was an ambiguous concept at any given moment and was complicated further by changes over time in how political leaders defined ideological diversionism and enforced mandates against it. In the 1960s, trends associated with youth culture in the United States, particularly the use of sandals and form-fitting pants by men and miniskirts by women, were considered serious political crimes that could land male offenders in labor camps during enduring campaigns against "homosexualism" or "intellectualism."[31]

These extreme associations between clothing styles, gender and sexuality, and social and criminal malaise persisted into the early 1970s. In a 1972 speech before the Ministry of the Interior (MININT), Raúl Castro referenced a speech that Fidel Castro had given in Bulgaria just months before to explain why communist youth must resist the temptations of ideological diversionism. As Fidel had explained, while capitalist countries offered much materially, they offered nothing in the spiritual and moral realms, nor did they outline a "path" for their youth, resulting in an annual rise in crime, hopelessness, drug addiction, and mental disturbance in societies centered on meaningless material pursuits. This formulation stipulated a binary, with socialist societies associated with morality on one end and capitalist societies associated with material goods and moral decay on the other. Gender and sexuality, particularly the perceived association between Western styles, homosexuality, and anti-revolutionary political beliefs, played a major role in how political leaders conceptualized the threat that materialism posed to society.[32] As Fidel explained, the fashions in capitalist societies were so extreme in defying the natural order of things that "in many of these cases you cannot even distinguish between boy and girl."[33] These speeches reveal the extent to which rigidity and repression were the norm with regard to fashion and consumption at the start of the period of opening outlined in this essay. The economic and political changes that began in 1972 facilitated changes in popular culture as well, and by the early 1980s, less than ten years later, the international tide of casual, unisex youth clothing in the form of T-shirts, jeans, and sneakers had arrived in Cuba to stay. It was welcomed with enthusiasm, particularly among youth, tempered by suspicion concentrated among officials.

FIGURE 9.2. A cartoon published during the family visits pokes fun at outlandish foreign styles and their prestige among Cuban audiences. The tags on the man's sunglasses and belt say, "from outside," and his shoes say, "not made here." The quotation reads "you were right to leave the tags visible, so people know that it is all foreign clothing; otherwise you would look ridiculous." Published in *Opina*, December 1979.

FIGURE 9.3. A protester in demonstration against those who sought to leave Cuba as part of the Mariel boatlift holds a sign with a stylized cartoon of two male defectors. The cartoon reflects common stereotypes equating ideological diversionism with foreign fashion and the transgression of gender and sexual norms. Published in *Muchacha*, April 1980.

Comparison of figures 9.2 and 9.3 reveals just how flexible the mandates against materialism and ideological diversionism could be. Both come from a period in which international styles had become sufficiently pervasive that their association with dangerous ideological diversionism had softened; yet the differences between the moral and political contexts that frame the two cartoons reveal continued ambiguity with regard to both official stances and popular acceptance of such styles. At flashpoints when stakes were particularly high, such as during the 1980 Mariel boatlift, the portrayal of Cuban youth's adoption of and admiration for foreign styles shifted from silly and laughable to dark and tragic, associated with criminality and betrayal of the nation. Norms regarding gender and sexuality played a particularly important role at these flashpoint moments.

As illustrated by the political cartoon in figure 9.2, foreign clothing items held immense prestige in Cuba, especially as access expanded due to clothing brought by the returning exiles via the family visits of the late 1970s, discussed below. Even clothing items that might be considered excessive or ridiculous in the context of Cuban fashion norms could be perceived as stylish when their international origins were clearly established. Revolutionary dictates about appropriate male fashion had, since the 1960s, centered on reinforcing traditional images of masculinity by rejecting styles that were considered effeminate and associated with ideological diversionism. The skin-tight pants, platform shoes, and ostentatious belt and sunglasses worn by the figure in the cartoon all clearly showcase their foreign provenance, either through the tags, which the wearer has left attached for precisely this reason, or, in the case of the pants, by the small figure of Mickey Mouse, which reinforces a connection with the United States specifically. Without these foreign indicators, the wearer would look ridiculous, as the commentator notes. Even more than that, because all of those styles had associations with homosexuality in the Cuban revolutionary context, he might face political condemnation as well as other forms of social or even legal censure. The foreign origins of the clothing, clearly on display, seemingly removed the association with gay identity, however, because it was assumed that the wearer was motivated by the prestige of foreign styles rather than his own underlying gender or sexual identity. Thus, his outfit was considered appropriate only because of its foreign pedigree.

By contrast, the illustrations on the sign held by protestors in figure 9.3 feature very similar fashions—heeled boots, round sunglasses, and a wide belt. The foreign origins of the clothing are reinforced by the design on one man's shirt, which states, "I love you USA." In the context of the demonstrations against those who sought to leave Cuba in 1980, however, these fashions carry different meanings. This cartoon, when used to demonstrate public support for the Cuban state and condemn those who sought to leave Cuba, interprets fashion and individual choices of self-presentation as political statements and moral failings, going well beyond humorous notions of good or bad taste. The signs held by other protestors echo the official discourse of the time, as Cuban political leaders characterized those who sought exile in 1980 as "lazy," "lumpen," and "scum."[34] These images are therefore indicative of how macro-level events, like the Mariel boatlift and the Cuban state's response, could and did change the terms of debate about individual, micro-level choices, like deciding what to wear. The cartoons were published less than one year apart, which also reveals how quickly and radically the meaning assigned to material goods like clothing could shift, and the massive implications of that debate with regard to an individual's ability to be accepted as part of communities at the local, national, and transnational levels.

Analysis of the voices of average Cubans, which shape press coverage through letters to the editor and group interviews, reveals the extent to which these were true debates, rather than a one-way process in which representatives of the state mandated from the top down. Letters to the editor of *Muchacha*, the Federation of Cuban Women's youth magazine, in response to a piece published on societal debates about the value of fashion, illustrate how some young Cubans attempted to stake their own claims to revolutionary identity and authority during this period by taking the state script on diversionism with regard to youth fashions and running with it. Yet these young readers also expressed deep-rooted confusion, often unintentionally, thereby undermining the political and ideological stance they sought so fiercely to defend. It leads one to wonder to what extent the lack of clarity with regard to the crime of ideological diversionism must have undermined its legitimacy in the eyes of citizens. If you cannot even define a crime, how bad can it be?

In the fall of 1980, one reader, Tania Amador, wrote to editors from Cienfuegos to offer her strong and considered opinions on everything from skirt length to the appropriate uses of jeans and tall boots in Cuban contexts. It is clear from the letter that fashion was a favorite topic of hers, and that she had thought deeply about the applicability of suspect Western styles, like jeans and boots, to the revolutionary context; however, her letter is most significant for its lack of clarity about the relationship between ideological diversionism and fashion. Tania ends the letter by questioning whether the two were, in fact, the same thing. The response from editor Silvia Bota clarified that the two were not necessarily the same, but that fashion is one of the "very subtle means" used by "reactionary sectors of contemporary society" to "penetrate the minds of those who are not sufficiently prepared in the political-ideological order." Following the official stance of revolutionary leadership since the 1960s, Bota thus characterized fashion as a powerful force that must be carefully harnessed. She offered an example that was meant to clarify but actually obscured more than it revealed. After discussing how inappropriate it would be for a Cuban to wear a US Army T-shirt, given the history of US interventionism in the island's affairs and the anti-imperialist stance of the revolution, she then extended this comparison to all T-shirts with logos promoting transnational corporations in the entire capitalist world, as "symbols of consumer society."[35] No wonder young Cubans like Tania Amador were deeply confused about the political and ideological implications of their fashion choices: this comparison equates T-shirts with US foreign policy and the divide between the socialist and capitalist worlds, revealing the complex interplay between local fashion choices and transnational flows. On the one hand, in the two years before this exchange between Amador and Bota, the family visits had radically increased Cubans' access to goods from capitalist nations, and on the other, by 1980 the ongoing Mariel boatlift had derailed the brief thaw between Cuba and the United States and radically increased Cold War hostilities.

In a roughly one-year period in 1978 and 1979, more than 120,000 exiled Cubans visited Cuba.[36] A December 1978 article in *The Washington Post* highlighted the material influx that accompanied the first of these visitors: "Hundreds of exiles, most with pockets and suitcases bulging, visit [Cuba] monthly." The returning exiles brought a wide range of gifts for friends and family on the island, from consumer items like Western clothing to durables like small appliances, inundating the island with goods from the capitalist world for the first time in decades. Ideological tensions on the island, like those within the exile community, were thrown into sharp relief by the visits, as "hard-line revolutionaries" refused the goods provided through familial connections with the United States.[37] The choice to accept these gifts was a deeply personal one, and that some made the decision to reject them reveals the extent to which many Cubans did internalize state discourse about the dangers that consumption of Western goods posed for ideological diversionism. Much like Tania Amador in her letter to the editor of *Muchacha,* these hard-liners were staking out their own stance on consumer goods that harkens back to state discourses of the more closed era of the 1960s.

As people caught up with one another and took stock of their lives, a new frame of comparison emerged. Restrictive travel policies and state control over the media had long limited Cubans' horizons to the socialist world. Films, TV shows, and magazines imported from the Soviet Bloc as well as Cuban media's preferential coverage of the Second World painted pictures of life in the heart of communism. Suddenly, these pictures were accompanied by new, living, breathing images of life in the United States, transmitted by Cubans who shared a culture, despite the enormous cultural changes wrought by the revolution, and a history with those who had remained on the island. People could not help but compare their lives in Cuba with those of their loved ones in the United States, and some began to question the meaning of the revolution. As one man later remembered, the family visits shook reality as he knew it: "Within himself, for the first time, the Cuban started to think 'if these are common workers, and they can travel and spend money bringing us things, then it is because things are not so bad there. What's bad is what we have here.'"[38] Concerns like these represented practical reflections on the material culture of everyday life as well as, in many cases, reconsideration of the core ideological tenets of the revolutionary state's value system, including its emphasis on shared sacrifice and the collective over the rights and opportunities of the individual.

State representatives' response to these visits were complex, too. While individual revolutionaries may have felt an ideological compulsion to reject the goods, the state itself welcomed the influx of resources with open arms by implementing a number of measures to facilitate the process. Exiles were required to travel under the aegis of the state tourism apparatus and purchase package deals that they rarely used because they preferred to spend time in the homes of loved ones.[39] A weeklong visit from Miami could cost up to $1,500 for exiles staying in the private homes of family members, over four times the cost of a weeklong stay at comparable Caribbean tourist destinations. Thus, the Cuban state's temporary embrace of the exile community must be understood in terms of the "new, more cynical function" that the community acquired "for the Cuban state [in this period,] as bearer of hard currency."[40] This approach paid off, at least in the short term. María Cristina García cites a figure published by the *Miami Herald* claiming that by April 1979 the exile visitors had already injected $150 million in hard currency into the Cuban economy.[41] A February 1979 speech in which Fidel Castro reassured members of the Cuban Communist Party that "the revolution does not sell itself for a plate of lentils" reveals that some state representatives harbored ideological concerns about this openness to capitalist goods and dollars, much like the individual hard-line revolutionaries cited in the article above; however, at the level of policy, economic concerns trumped ideological ones.[42] The revolutionary state embraced and sought to maximize the influx of cold, hard cash.

To further promote exile spending, on May 1, 1979, the Cuban state updated customs laws to restrict the goods that visitors could bring into Cuba.[43] For those interested in acquiring additional gifts for friends and family, they also expanded a series of stores—the so-called *diplotiendas*—that had been created to serve foreigners living in Cuba, who prior to the start of the family visits were primarily diplomats. An unintentional result of this policy was increasingly visible material inequality, a phenomenon that up to this point had been largely confined to the gap between members of the privileged political class and everyone else. From the perspective of leaders, the expansion of the diplotiendas in this period was less about fomenting inequality, which ran contrary to the egalitarian ideals that guided domestic economic policy, than it was about providing the state with much-needed hard currency to make purchases on the international market to supplement their preferential trade deals with Comecon. Shoppers made purchases at the diplotiendas with Cuban pesos, yet to do so they were required to present a document stating that the pesos had been acquired through the exchange of hard currency. These documents attested at the point of purchase to the infusion of hard currency into the Cuban economy.[44] Further augmenting this process, the exchange rate that visitors paid for pesos was downright predatory: $100 US netted 75 Cuban pesos in this period.[45]

Even members of the privileged political class stood to gain from access to the diplotiendas through visiting family members. Despite her North American origins and the other material advantages that she acquired through her status, the law barred Lorna Burdsall along with all other Cubans then living on the island from the diplotiendas.[46] When her mother took advantage of the new travel opportunities to visit her daughter in 1978, she used the "foreigner's store" to purchase two high-demand items that were characteristic of the system's offerings: a seventy-dollar Japanese vacuum cleaner and jeans for her grandson, who struggled to find clothing that fit him at the stores accessible to Cubans. Goods like these eased the strain of scarcity for Burdsall's family by making domestic labor quicker and easier and meeting the need for comfortable, stylish youth clothing. The politically privileged like Burdsall, who had been married to a high-ranking official in the Cuban state security apparatus and who was a member of the cultural elite through her dance and choreography, gained even greater access to goods through the family visits, and in cases like hers, inequality compounded inequality.

As historian Michael Bustamante has written, both the goods that visiting exiles brought with them and, while in Cuba, their privileged access to goods that were off-limits to Cubans generated an "implicit challenge to some of the ingrained narratives Cubans had long heard about socialist accomplishments and the Revolution as history fulfilled."[47] At the same time, while political considerations colored these trends in consumption at both the macro and micro levels, for many young Cubans, accessing and wearing these styles was less about making a political statement and more about making a fashion statement. One Cuban remembers feeling proud to strut down Obispo Street in Old Havana in the fall of 1979 wearing a "Manhattan" shirt—a loudly patterned, short-sleeved button-down—that his great-aunt had brought him on her visit from West Palm Beach, Florida, despite the polyester's unsuitability for the Cuban climate.[48] The trends established in these years showed serious staying power. In 1980, T-shirts were exploding in popularity among young men and women, with one of Cuba's most prestigious youth publications going so far as to declare it the year of the T-shirt.[49]

In the midst of this social clamor for T-shirts, *Muchacha* editor Bota's response to Tania Amador's letter conflates the desire for this new, hip, and comfortable style with implicit support for US imperialism through the embrace of consumerist values. This leap in logic was unlikely to have been on the minds of teenagers actively seeking the styles, except as a result of the efforts of state representatives like Bota, which publicly cast T-shirts as questionable. The use of foreign logos, which is at the heart of Bota's rejection, remained controversial and debated; yet once more the heart of the issue seems to be less an obsession with the West and more an unmet desire for a Cuban alternative. Given the shortcomings of the domestic fashion industry, particularly with regard to keeping up with youth fashions, the variability of individual tastes, and the widespread desire for a less homogenous clothing supply, it is likely that the decision to wear a shirt with a foreign logo had more to do with access to a T-shirt—all the better if it was somehow unique—than a desire to make a political statement. Through the early 1980s, Cuban youth and organizations like ICIODI sought to reconcile the demand for T-shirts with state-sanctioned ideological values by calling for Cuban-produced T-shirts with slogans specific to Cuban youth and revolutionary identity.[50] The impact of these initiatives on consumer reality was severely limited, however: a national survey—the results of which were also published in the press—found that in the first half of 1985, a full five years into the national T-shirt craze, 81 percent of people were unable to purchase women's T-shirts, despite continued mass demand.[51]

Clearly, the high expectations for Cuban fashion held by both state and citizens were a source of disappointment to both producers and consumers because they created standards that Cuban industry could not meet. So why did the state continue to cultivate such expectations through press pieces, fashion spreads, and expositions that prescribed bourgeois tenets of good taste? Why not attempt to shape a new revolutionary ideology around clothing, one that was divorced from class-based notions of taste and emphasized functionality over all? Given the Cuban exceptionalism that the state embraced on many other fronts, including lauding its own political efforts at home and abroad as vanguard expressions of a future world, it does not seem far-fetched to wonder why the state did not try to build a future fashion for itself, one that would remove some of the pressure to devote scarce resources to the production of clothing and accessories, pressure that the state itself created in the visions of socialist modernity that were published in the press in this period.

Conclusions

The period from 1972 to 1986 was marked by openness in state policies surrounding the consumer and service economies. New economic policies resulted in economic growth and improved, if still imperfect, conditions for consumers. Officials created new means for accessing consumer opinions and facilitating public discourse about the role of consumption in a revolutionary society. At the same time, consumer goods and practices were still shaped by previous eras in which they had been associated with ideologically suspect behavior. The resulting consumer landscape was a minefield that the press sought to help young Cubans navigate, though the end result was more often ambiguity than clarity. Transnational forces shaped this ambiguity, particularly in the late 1970s due to the exposure that Cuban youth had to visitors to the island from both the socialist and capitalist worlds.

Yet this ambiguity and relative openness could and did snap shut at flashpoint moments that challenged Cuban leaders' understanding of the popular legitimacy of their project or endangered Cuba's standing on the international stage, such as the Mariel exodus. Lillian Guerra has analyzed Mariel in terms of moments of "realization," particularly among young Cubans, of the existence and impact of a "national security state that dictated particularly appropriate narratives about the past and present, while erasing and denying others."[52] The material and consumer economies, and the way that Cubans experienced them, in this period offer opportunities to explore the ability of average people to shape these narratives based on how they understood the successes, failures, and meanings of the ongoing revolutionary project that determined so many aspects of their lives, from state policies to the clothes on their backs. The voices from this period reveal the extent to which Cuban youth both internalized and shared state initiatives with regard to the pursuit of socialist modernity, while also seeking greater accountability in the meaningful pursuit of those goals.

Notes

1. Carollee Bengelsdorf, *The Problem of Democracy in Cuba: Between Vision and Reality* (Oxford University Press, 1994), 99.

2. Comecon was founded by Soviet leaders in 1949 to counter mutual aid associations established in capitalist Western Europe following World War II. The organization originally encompassed the Soviet Union and the Eastern Bloc, but expanded into Asia and the Caribbean as membership was extended to Mongolia, Cuba, and Vietnam over the course of the 1960s and 1970s. The basic contours of the economic history in this section were

garnered from Carmelo Mesa-Lago, *Cuba in the 1970s: Pragmatism and Institutionalization* (University of New Mexico Press, 1978), which includes a detailed examination of not only the economic changes made by the Cuban state in its turn from idealism in the early 1970s but also the changes made in the realms of government, social organization, and diplomacy.

3. Mesa-Lago, *Cuba in the 1970s,* 57.

4. See Alexis Baldacci, "Consumer Culture and Everyday Life in Revolutionary Cuba, 1971–1986" (PhD diss., University of Florida, 2018).

5. See, for example, Carlos A. Aguilera, ed., *La utopia vacia: Intelectuales y estado en Cuba* (Linkgua, 2009).

6. Bengelsdorf's analysis focuses on the creation of new political institutions, such as the Popular Power system, to "give the people direct control over an entire spectrum of issues that had evoked daily discontent." *Problem of Democracy,* 104.

7. The Rectification of Errors and Negative Tendencies Campaign was the Cuban state's response to the fiscal and ideological crisis sparked by economic and political changes in the Soviet Union. The campaign included a marked reemphasis on "ideological purity" and an ideological return to the anti-materialism of the 1960s, though scholars are divided on the extent to which economic policy in the period was actually anti-market and economically irrational. See Susan Eckstein, "The Rectification of Errors or the Errors of the Rectification Process in Cuba?" *Cuban Studies* 20 (1990): 68.

8. María A. Cabrera Arús, "The Material Promise of Socialist Modernity: Fashion and Domestic Space in the 1970s," in *The Revolution from Within: Cuba, 1959-1980,* ed. Michael J. Bustamante and Jennifer L. Lambe (Duke University Press, 2019), 191.

9. Pia Koivunen, "Overcoming Cold War Boundaries at the World Youth Festivals," in *Reassessing Cold War Europe,* ed. Sari Autio-Sarasmo and Katalin Miklóssy (Routledge, 2011), 175, quotations on 186. See also Juliane Fürst, *Flowers through Concrete: Explorations in Soviet Hippieland* (Oxford University Press, 2021), 2, for a discussion of one young man's "conversion" to hippie culture at the 1968 Festival of Youth hosted in East Berlin.

10. María A. Cabrera Arús and Mirta Suquet, "La moda en la literatura cubana, 1960–1979: Tejiendo y destejiendo al hombre nuevo," *Cuban Studies* 47 (2019): 212. Cabrera Arús and Suquet use the phrase in their analysis of the fashion choices of the main characters in Reinaldo Arenas's "Que trine Eva."

11. Glabrera, "Tres éxitos y todos contentos," *Somos Jóvenes,* January 1982, 1.

12. See Baldacci, "Consumer Culture," chapter 3.

13. Cabrera Arús, "Materialist Promise," 191.

14. "Ella en la poesía," *Mujeres,* February 1980, 20–21.

15. "La música de los telares," *Somos Jóvenes,* July 1983, 36–37.

16. Untitled, *Muchacha,* October 1984, 8.

17. Hugo L. Sarduy, "En 1984 estará de moda," *Mujeres,* April 1983, 36–37.

18. "Tradición y armonia," *Muchacha,* November 1984, 3.

19. Untitled, *Muchacha,* October 1984, 8.

20. See Esther, "Tendencias para 1986," *Muchacha,* January 1985, 4–5; Daisy Martin, "Más a la moda," *Mujeres,* April 1981, 66–67.

21. Baldacci, "Consumer Culture," 115-18.

22. Sarduy, "En 1984 estará de moda."

23. Cabrera Arús, "The Material Promise," 197-198.

24. Chaley Reyes, "Variaciones sobre la guayabera," *Somos Jóvenes,* April 1976, 22-23; Cristina, "Asi viste nuestra delegación," *Somos Jóvenes,* no. 8, undated (1978), 30-31.

25. Cary, "Saber vestir es importante," *Somos Jóvenes,* March 1982, 4.

26. This lines up with María Antonia Cabrera Arús's arguments about fashion in 1970s Cuba: "'representational' nationalist fictions not matching everyday experience and aspirations" leading to discontent and popular nonconformity due to "contradictions in the *way* consumption was represented." "Material Promise," 202.

27. Eugenio R. Balari, *Los consumidores y el desarrollo del Sistema de abastecimiento en Cuba* (Instituto Cubano de Investigaciones y Orientación de la Demanda Interna), 19.

28. Cary, "Saber vestir es importante," 2, 3 (quotation).

29. "El vestuario e la moda," *Opina,* January 1980, 3-4.

30. Cary, "Saber vestir es importante," 3.

31. Lillian Guerra, *Visions of Power in Cuba: Revolution, Redemption, and Resistance, 1959-1971* (University of North Carolina Press), 245-55. According to Guerra, "Cuba's antihomosexuality campaign" began in 1965 and peaked in 1971, though discriminatory laws and hiring practices used to police men's sexuality and gender identity as threats of "social dangerousness" persisted for decades (245).

32. See Guerra's analysis of the use of fashion markers to "dehumanize homosexuals and male intellectuals" and identify them as enemies of Cuba's revolutionary process due to their association with the consumerism of the United States. *Visions of Power in Cuba,* 248, 250.

33. Raúl Castro, "El diversionismo ideológico," 25.

34. Abel Sierra Madero has analyzed how "extreme circumstances helped to activate the intersection of nationalism and sexuality all the more visibly," in his discussion of collective violence during the Mariel exodus. Abel Sierra Madero, "'Here, Everyone's Got *Huevos,* Mister!': Nationalism, Sexuality, and Collective Violence in Cuba During the Mariel Exodus," in Bustamante and Lambe, *Revolution from Within,* 246.

35. Letters to the Editor, *Muchacha,* November 1980, 68-69.

36. María de los Angeles Torres, *In the Land of Mirrors: Cuban Exile Politics in the United States* (University of Michigan Press, 2001), 97. María Cristina García notes that in 1979, roughly a hundred thousand exiles visited Cuba. See *Havana USA: Cuban Exiles and Cuban Americans in South Florida, 1959-1994* (University of California Press, 1996), 51.

37. Karen DeYoung, "Cuban Exiles Visit Home with Gifts 'Made in USA,'" *Washington Post,* December 21, 1978.

38. José García, *Voces de Mariel: Historia oral de éxodo Cubano del 1980* (Alexandria Library, 2012), 117.

39. García, *Havana USA,* 52.

40. de los Angeles Torres, *In the Land of Mirrors,* 97, 98.

41. García, *Havana USA,* 52.

42. This speech has been reconstructed from a variety of sources and quoted by Michael J. Bustamante in *Cuban Memory Wars: Retrospective Politics in Revolution and Exile* (University of North Carolina Press, 2021), 196.

43. Bustamante, *Cuban Memory Wars,* 201.

44. DeYoung, "Cuban Exiles Visit Home."

45. Burdsall Family Papers, c. 1930s–1970s, Cuban Heritage Collection (CHC), University of Miami, box 1, folder 13, February 1, 1978.

46. See Baldacci, "Consumer Culture," 55–58, for an analysis of how Burdsall's family connections (both in the United States and within the Cuban state intelligence apparatus) as well as her ability to travel internationally through her dance career resulted in material privilege that was out of reach for most Cubans in the 1970s and 1980s.

47. Bustamante, *Cuban Memory Wars,* 208.

48. Jorge Ignacio Domínguez, "La camisa es Manhattan, el resto es selva," *Tersites* (blog), September 15, 2011, http://tersitesexcathedra.blogspot.com/2011/09/la-camisa-es-manhattan-el-resto-es.html.

49. *Caimán Barbudo,* 1980, cover. Thank you to Mike Bustamante for the source suggestion.

50. See, for example, Armando López, "A lo cubano: la gradica en la ropa: solución joven," *Opina,* June 1980, 13–15; Lic. Clara Rey Mena, "¡Nuevo! Opina de modas," *Opina,* July 1984, 46–47.

51. Juan Opina, "El que tiene tienda que la atienda: Encuesta sobre la industria ligera resultados," *Opina,* November 1985, 3.

52. Lillian Guerra, *Patriots and Traitors in Revolutionary Cuba, 1961–1981* (University of Pittsburgh Press, 2023), 377.

TEN

"We Were Like a Bomb"
Child Refugees, Cuban Politics, and Argentine Revolutionary Organizations, 1970–2020

ISABELLA COSSE

It was ten o'clock at night on December 27, 1976. The passengers were landing in Lima on a flight from Argentina. In the foreground, we see Ana and María carrying a bag. Behind them is Marcela, thirteen years old, one of the youngest. There were seven girls: María Ofelia, sixteen, was the oldest, and María Emilia, eleven, the youngest, accompanied by Ofelia Paz Ruiz, the only adult. The photograph did not capture the avalanche of journalists surrounding them. It was not just any group. They were the daughters and nieces of Mario Roberto Santucho, commander of the People's Revolutionary Army (Ejercito Revolucionario del Pueblo, ERP), the armed wing of the Workers' Revolutionary Party (Partido Revolucionario de los Trabajadores, PRT), one of the Argentine guerrilla leaders most wanted by the military in the region. They had managed to capture him a few months earlier, on July 19, when he was about to leave for Cuba.

The military had launched the coup four months before, on March 24, determined to completely exterminate "subversion," a term that encompassed any opposition to the dictatorship. But it targeted the revolutionary organizations with a special ferocity, with methods that included illegal, clandestine, and inhuman forms of repression based on the kidnapping, torture, and murder of their militants who, in many cases, were sedated and thrown alive into the sea. According to the military, Santucho died fighting, but his family figured out that he was taken alive to one of the clandestine detention centers (Campo de Mayo). He was

FIGURE 10.1. The daughters and nieces of Roberto Santucho, the leader of the most important Marxist armed organization in Argentina, leave for Cuba after a year of asylum in the Cuban embassy, on December 27, 1976. Unknown photographer. Courtesy Biblioteca Nacional Mariano Moreno (BNMM), Argentina, Departamento de Archivos, Fondo Editorial Sarmiento. Archivo de Redacción Crónica, AR0093105.

accompanied by other leaders. Among them, two women—Liliana Delfino, Santucho's partner, and Ana María Lanzilotto (who was pregnant)—were kidnapped alive. None of their bodies were handed over to their relatives.[1]

Roberto Santucho had become the undisputed leader of the PRT in 1970 by winning an internal debate over whether to create an armed wing, influenced by the Cuban Revolution and the rise of protests in Argentina in the context of global 1968. According to him, this had created a prerevolutionary situation. At the same time, other revolutionary movements had arisen in the country whose legitimacy had grown due to constant military interventions and the weakness of democracy because of the proscription of Peronism, the main political force. The Peronist party had been banned since 1955, when a military coup had overthrown Juan Perón, during whose presidencies (1946–55) workers acquired social rights and became crucial actors in national politics.

The PRT had emerged in 1965 from the merger of Palabra Obera, a group with Trotskyist roots that had a strong presence in Buenos Aires (in the center of the

"We Were Like a Bomb" 235

country) and the Revolutionary Indoamerican Popular Front (Frente Revolucionario Indoamericano Popular), created in Santiago del Estero, a small and isolated city in the north of Argentina. There, the Santucho "clan," headed by Francisco, the paterfamilias, with his ten children, was a well-known elite family with a strong political calling. Gradually, almost all its members became committed to the PRT.[2] By 1976, when the girls arrived in Lima, the family had been decimated: several of the adults had been killed and the children were captured in a clandestine military operation in December 1975, three months before the March 24 coup d'état, and spent the next year living in the Cuban embassy before finally leaving for asylum in Cuba. The children were all captured together, gathered for a children's birthday party. The party included Roberto Santucho's three daughters with Ana María Villareal: Ana Cristina, Marcela, and Gabriela, fourteen, twelve, and eleven years old, respectively, and Mario, nine months old, Santucho's son with Liliana Delfino, together with Santucho's nieces María Ofelia (fifteen), María Susana (fourteen), María Silvia (thirteen), and María Emilia (ten), and their mother and Santucho's sister-in-law, Ofelia Paz Ruiz (the only adult). Esteban Abdón, four years old, son of a fellow militant, was also captured.

The children and teenagers were sent to a hotel—in a very confused episode that I can't reconstruct here—from where Ofelia managed to warn the family; the children were rescued by the ERP and taken to the Cuban embassy. The girls stayed in the embassy for a year. They left Buenos Aires in one large security operation; another one awaited them in Lima. The next day they left for Cuba. Yet the island was not unfamiliar for all of them—three of Santucho's daughters had already spent three months there in 1973, three years earlier. Their father had sent them, thinking it was the way to protect them as repression in Argentina increased by the day. They had lost their mother, Ana María Villarreal, shortly before. The navy had murdered her while she was in the isolated Trelew prison, along with eighteen companions. The guards woke them in the middle of the night, made them leave their cell, and shot them at point-blank range. Their cousins had also lost their father (Oscar Asdrúbal) in combat the previous year.[3]

Rather than starting from conventional political or diplomatic history, this chapter reconstructs the history of the Santucho children—the children and nieces of Roberto Santucho—to illuminate unexplored dimensions of Cold War alliances and, in particular, the relations between Cuba and the forces of the revolutionary Left.[4] From this angle, I study not only the policies or discourses surrounding children—as important precedents have done[5]—but also their own experiences, conceiving of them as protagonists, but underlying that their condition differs from that of the adults and according to their age and the power relations in which they were inscribed. In this way, I broaden the vision of politics by incorporating children as well as their fears, sufferings, and strategies, often relegated to mere anecdotes in previous works. And, in doing so, I incorporate them into the core of political conflicts and history itself.

Children are central to any construction of power. They are the adults of the future, and no state or institution does not recognize them. Hence, policies aimed at children are consubstantial to almost any political project and, at the same time, have implicitly and explicitly legitimized modern forms of power. The ways of doing so have varied because they are historical and changing. However, we can recognize that modern policies and legitimations present a paradox: they have conceived of children as innocent beings who deserve care and attention. At the same time, they have created increasingly sophisticated forms of management, subjection, and violence.[6] During the Cold War, this paradox crystallized with unparalleled force. The "hot" regions of that confrontation are pristine evidence of this: children suffered violence directly, systematically, and on a massive scale. The novelty was that this centrality of children was articulated to transnational dynamics with unprecedented strength and clarity.

The Cuban Revolution from its origin drove these transnational dynamics. Therefore, it is important to ask: What does the study of children tell us about the international strategies of the Cuban Revolution and its relationship with organizations of the Latin American Left? I argue that children, with their social, political, and emotional significance, illuminate a dark area, still scarcely explored, of those relations between Cuba and the revolutionary organizations: the contradictions opened by the redefinitions of Cuban foreign policy in the seventies and its relation to the armed road to revolution in Latin America.

With this idea in mind, I will focus on the refuge that Cuban revolutionary authorities granted to children of the Argentine guerrilla organizations in the seventies. Then, I will discuss the role that some of those children played later, as adults, in the current struggles for human rights in Argentina. I will do so based on memoirs and testimonies, which I complement with conventional documentation such as the press, intelligence reports, diplomatic correspondence, and documents of the organizations. My analysis recognizes that memories are marked by subjective and affective significance and that they vary according to the historical and personal context, as well as the framework of remembrance and the interlocution of the researcher.[7] This does not detract from their value. It requires paying attention to the conditions of the documents' production, as with any other source, and understanding their particularities, such as the sensitive condition of children's memories. The use of interviews is enriched by contrasting them with other sources, as I do in this text. I also pay attention to the significant clues, as Carlo Ginzburg would say, omitted by other approaches, to produce a new overview that uses and values the childhood experience, but that transcends it to contribute to the understanding of the political strategies and the violence unleashed and lived in the continent in that period, and its effects among subsequent generations.[8]

Specifically, I will analyze the political vicissitudes experienced by the children and Ofelia at the embassy, their departure from the country, and their arrival in Cuba. Then I will address the political, social, and emotional significance of that country in their lives. Finally, I will close with the role played by that legacy in contemporary Argentina through two significant events: first, the lawsuit filed by María Ofelia—the eldest of the group—against her kidnapper in 2021, and second, the recovery in 2023 of Daniel, the son of Julio Santucho and Cristina Navajas, who was born during her captivity, and whom his grandmother and brother, as part of the Grandmothers of the Plaza de Mayo (Abuelas de Plaza de Mayo), had been seeking for forty-six years.[9]

In the Embassy

On the afternoon of December 13, a group of seven girls and at least one adult woman arrived at the main gate of the Cuban embassy in Buenos Aires. They had been left there by the ERP group that had rescued them from the trap the army had tried to set to capture Roberto Santucho. They said, in desperation, "We are the Santuchos, open up, they are going to kill us," according to María Ofelia, the oldest of the girls, then age fifteen. When they saw a local police detail approaching, they squeezed together and pounded harder. They did not understand the delay. They thought the Cubans were waiting for them. The door finally opened. The clerk was puzzled. They begged him to let them in and, according to Ofelia (the girls' mother and aunt), he would not let them in. There was great uncertainty. It may not have been a long time, but for them, it was "a ton," according to Gabriela. Finally, a man ran down the hall, ordering, "Let them in, *chico*." "We went in all bunched up. When I was able to calm down, I found out that they didn't know we were coming."[10]

Asylum was a resource of enormous importance for the politically persecuted in the Southern Cone, and militants frequently approached embassies with their families and even left children there to seek asylum alone.[11] However, the Cuban embassy was reluctant to grant diplomatic asylum. Cuba had refused to grant asylum status to Cubans who had resorted to entering foreign embassies to leave the country. Therefore, accepting asylum seekers would have established a precedent that could work against them domestically.[12] There was another reason: Cuba's international strategy was at a turning point. After the death of Che Guevara, the disarticulation of the Tupamaros, and the defeat of Allende, the Latin American revolution seemed farther and farther away. There was a new correlation of forces in the region. In that context, diplomacy became crucial to avoid isolation and guarantee the survival of the revolution, as Tanya Harmer has pointed out.[13] It was a two-pronged strategy: on the one hand, to promote bilateral and economic relations that would encourage loans and exports to complement Soviet support, and on the other, to forge alliances in international organizations.

Cuba's isolation had begun to diminish. In 1970 it had reestablished relations with Allende's Chile; shortly thereafter, in 1972, with the English-speaking Caribbean states (Guyana, Jamaica, Barbados, and Trinidad and Tobago) and Peru, then with Panama; and in 1974 with Venezuela.[14] It was a "pragmatic" policy. It did not imply raising the banners of internationalism or global revolutionary ambitions (which now began to focus on Africa), but it had direct effects in the Southern Cone and on Cuba's relationship with Argentine revolutionary armed organizations. In Argentina, the return of elections and of Peronism to power in 1973 and the ensuing social and political mobilization opened an expectant panorama. The political maneuvering had not ended and, in this vertiginous situation, every decision mattered. For Cuba it was essential to have an embassy in Argentina. Fidel had cultivated a relationship with Perón, and there were strong ties between Cuba and different organizations of the revolutionary Left dating back to the times of the Sierra Maestra.[15]

A new stage was opened when Cuban President Osvaldo Dorticós signed, in 1973, the act of assumption of President Héctor Cámpora, the Peronist candidate and the delegate of Perón, who was prohibited from running himself. For Cuba, Argentina was a gateway to loans, exports, and imports. It was also key in geopolitical terms. Relations were reestablished and the Cubans installed the embassy. They began to deploy intense diplomacy and to reestablish Prensa Latina, the Cuban news agency, in Argentina. A few months later, the embassy was used to facilitate the departure of some Cubans who arrived in Argentina clandestinely after being forced to flee Chile after the coup there on September 11, 1973. Chileans and Uruguayan Tupamaros who were escaping repression in their own countries were also arriving. The Cubans explained that they supported them but could not shelter them. There was compartmentalization between diplomatic and secret tasks, explains Carlos Alzugaray Treto.[16] In other words, they could support them in certain cases, but not openly.

Cuba's diplomatic strategy called for cultivating relations with Peronism in power. In contrast, the ERP decided to continue the armed struggle when Peronism took over. It was directed, supposedly, against the armed forces, but not against the government, an elusive distinction. Soon after, the Peronist armed organization Montoneros took a similar position, acknowledging that Perón had veered to the far Right. The Cubans expressed their disagreement with this strategy to leaders of the Montoneros as well as the PRT. Santucho sent an ERP leader to ask the Cubans for military training to launch the rural guerrillas. Santucho instructed him to speak only with Fidel, because he knew that the proposal would not be well received by the leaders of the Cuban Communist Party, who supported the Soviet strategy of détente. The emissary discovered that Fidel did not agree with the proposal either. He told him that the armed struggle was not viable against a government that "maintained democratic forms" and even less so against one that enjoyed undisputed popularity, such as the Perón government, which came to power with 62 percent of the votes. Fidel explained that Cuban foreign policy had no "double-talk or ambiguity." They had established diplomatic relations with Argentina, which prevented any form of military support to guerrilla groups opposing the government.[17]

In 1975, the Cuban consul Carlos Alzugaray Treto used the same rationale as Fidel with Ofelia and the girls: they could not give them asylum because they had diplomatic relations with Argentina. According to María Ofelia, he told them that they could only stay that night and would have to leave the next day. She recalls that they were pampered and that, finally, they decided that they would not force them to leave. They would take the risk of allowing them to stay because they were children and in danger. The girls, conceived as unprotected and small despite being teenagers, put Cuban foreign policy in check. They were granted the status of guests of the ambassador.[18] The ruse was a solution that highlighted the contradictions between revolutionary solidarity and diplomatic pragmatism.

It wasn't an accident. The revolution was for the children, as Fidel said many times. Childhood was the future. Enlightenment, socialism, and Cuba's historical tradition (particularly the writings of José Martí) all coincided to make childhood a privileged arena of the struggle between revolutionary and counterrevolutionary forces. The conflict, as this book proposes, was decisively articulated, from the very beginning, on a transnational scale. Children were part of that conflict, and the refuge given to children was part of Cuban internationalism. The exiled refugee children embodied, like no other group, that transnational political community and identity. The sanctuary given to these children expressed concretely and symbolically the network of ties and solidarity that existed between Cuba and the revolutionary organizations.

We still know little about this policy. We would need Cuban archives to which I have not yet had access. But Cuba gave refuge to children in danger due to the political and military situation in their countries or with parents who were at risk or could not take care of them because of their militancy. Cuba's system of *becas* (boarding schools where young people lived from Monday to Friday) and summer camps facilitated the reception and care of these children. Gregory Randall, who arrived at the age of nine after the persecution of his mother, Margaret Randall, in Mexico, recalls that he integrated quickly and that seeing the suffering of the other children (many of them orphans or war wounded) made him relativize his own anguish.[19]

The experience of Roberto Santucho's daughters was not always positive. On the previous trip to Cuba, in 1973, Ana, Marcela, and Gabriela Santucho arrived (ages eleven, ten, and nine years old, respectively) after their mother had been murdered. Their father believed they would have an education, stability, a future, and safety there. They traveled there with older relatives. They stayed at the Habana Libre, the luxurious hotel that had once been a Hilton. They enjoyed eating in the dining room with impeccable napkins and were free to play among the other children, including Che Guevara's nephews. However, they did not want to be away from their family. They could not get used to the boarding school either. Marcela recalls how unfamiliar the Caribbean country felt, with its different cultural characteristics, and how difficult it was to get used to sleeping in a room with eight other students in bunk beds.[20]

Santucho decided to send his daughters to Cuba because he believed that there was no better context than the revolution to form the new generations, including his own children. This was distinct from the modern and bourgeois model of child-rearing (that of a nuclear family with great affective intensity) and also from the "psi" model centered on children's autonomy and the introjection of maternal and paternal "roles." On the other hand, it was connected to the family's own previous experience and that of Santucho himself, who had only lived with his daughters for short periods and who, as was customary in the north of the country and other regions, delegated the care of the girls to their grandparents for long periods. Within militant couples, it was the women who were often left in charge of the daily upbringing of children. Sayo, as the girls' mother was called, did so until she began to absent herself as her political responsibilities increased. Her daughters, although now understanding their parents, suffered from these decisions at various times in their lives.

In fact, six months after their arrival in Cuba, Ana, the eldest sister, made it clear that they no longer wanted to live there. For them, the island was not the utopia their parents imagined it to be. Supported by their aunt Mercedes, they got their way: they returned to Argentina in 1973. On their return they lived with their father and his new partner, Liliana Delfino. Initially it was hard for them to accept her, but she finally managed to win them over. Roberto, for his part, established a good bond with Diego, son of Liliana's first union with Luis

Ortolani, also a militant of the organization, who in 1972 had written in prison one of the few documents on daily life there. This document conceived the family as part of the political struggle and promoted the upbringing of the children in the operative houses together with their fathers, mothers, and other comrades.[21]

Without calling it an "operating house," Roberto and Liliana's life together, with their children, fell into that category. It was a political house. They did not live alone. Ricardo Silva and Josefa Demarchi, known as "the Totos" or Toto and Tota, lived with them too. Of humble origins, they were a couple somewhat older than Roberto and Liliana, and they had lost their eldest son who, like their youngest, was a militant in the ERP; the Totos had committed themselves to the organization. I imagine that the solution was devised by Liliana, who was a psychologist, faced with the situation that the girls had refused to continue living in Cuba and sensing that they needed their father's presence, and that the girls along with her own son needed someone to take care of them when she and Roberto could not be there. Like other militant couples, they decided to ask their compañeros, the Totos, to take care of them.[22] On the other hand, Latin American popular classes also had a long tradition whereby, in the face of their parents' difficulties, children were cared for by relatives, friends, or connections of varying degrees of closeness, or even in public or charitable institutions.[23]

During the year in the embassy, the girls lived through serious and frightening events. On December 23, 1975, the ERP attacked the military barracks in Monte Chingolo. It was a major defeat. The army took no prisoners but left more than fifty militants dead, many of them buried in an unidentified mass grave. The army had seven casualties.[24] In those dark days, the ERP's attack was used by the military to justify the coup, and there were new losses in the guerrilla organization. Roberto and Liliana spent Christmas with the Santucho family. A few days later, Mario and Diego (Liliana's children, whose fathers were Santucho and Ortolani, respectively) left for Cuba with the Totos. Diego says that Toto and Tota were very calm. For him, taking his first plane trip filled him with emotion. He was completely excited to go to Cuba because his mother had explained to him that it was the best place in the world and that they wanted to build a similar country in Argentina. She also told him that on the island there had been pirates (which he loved) and that there were beaches and music. "For me, Cuba is the island of adventure, and it has always been that way."[25] The trip was organized by the Cubans in Buenos Aires who, in a compartmentalized way, had contact with the armed organizations despite their formal diplomatic relations with the Argentine government.

We still know little about the links between the Cubans and the ERP. It is revealing that, according to the Cuban chancellor, the girls arrived at the embassy accompanied by Roberto Guevara, brother of Che Guevara, but María Santucho doesn't remember him. In diplomatic terms, with the ruse of describing the girls as guests of the ambassador, the Cubans tried not to strain relations between the two countries, which would have risked the loan granted by the Peronist government to Cuba in 1973. The embassy's efforts to get clearance for the girls' departure were slow.

In the meantime, the girls were housed on an entire floor of the embassy. The cook brought them food and made a beer chicken that Ana found delicious. They had a special relationship with Elda and Damián, two members of the Cuban delegation who watched over their health and safety. The girls were not allowed to open the windows or raise the blinds. Nor could they leave the apartment or go into the garden. They could only sunbathe on the terrace on weekends. The Cubans encouraged them to take classes. The ambassador, Emilio Aragonés, often brought them letters from Roberto Santucho. None of this attention erased the fact that they were locked up. The youngest girls, with their games, violated the security rules. They played at making phone calls and then hanging up. Only much later, one of them realized that they were communicating with the offices of the embassy itself. María Ofelia, the oldest of the cousins, had what she now recognizes as a panic attack. Her situation declined as the political climate deteriorated.[26]

The coup of March 24, 1976, did not come as a surprise; violence had been increasing between left- and right-wing organizations (which were part of the repressive forces) used to legitimize the military intervention that, in fact, had already started to destroy the revolutionary organization before the coup. The Cubans were prepared and knew the night before that it would take place. They had orders to resist. The embassy woke up surrounded by a detachment and tanks, as Ana recalls. The chancellor, Carlos Alzugaray Treto, in charge of security that night, went out to talk. The army detachment was part of a gendarmerie battalion from Tucumán, where repressive actions were carried out in anticipation of the coup, including a fierce attack on the ERP. The head of the detachment explained that they had orders to protect the embassy. Alzugaray Treto stated that he had no objections as long as they stayed outside the embassy, which was Cuban territory. It was a tense moment. Finally, the embassy managed to handle the situation and served sandwiches and Cokes to the entire detachment. They did this twice a day for the month that the checkpoint lasted.

Inside the embassy, tensions ran high. Ana remembers they constantly feared that soldiers would enter. The security alert was at its highest. Ofelia must have burned the letters Roberto had sent to her daughters. Ana regrets it to this day. A good part of the diplomatic staff returned to Cuba. Already, the revolutionary organizations were being destroyed by fierce repression. The Montoneros and the

PRT-ERP were trying to unify, and Santucho was scheduled to attend a meeting before leaving for Cuba. He continued to gamble on reversing the political situation through armed resistance when, in July 1976, he was discovered by an army detachment and was left for dead while trying to resist. The girls heard about it on the radio. Ana is saddened by the memory. Gabriela, the youngest, completely repressed the memory. María Ofelia, the eldest niece, stopped eating and dropped any affectionate interactions.[27]

Santucho's death occupied entire pages of the press. The armed forces took full advantage of this expected, difficult victory. Cataloging him as a "delinquent," "criminal," and "Marxist agent," they accused him of being responsible for the wave of violence. This was not a new discourse; it was typical of national security doctrine, which described Argentine revolutionary militants as foreigners and stateless persons, because this condition defined them as enemies of the nation. But now there was a greater emphasis on the idea of a continent-wide threat. This was no coincidence. In those months, Plan Condor was capturing hundreds of militants throughout the region. The article did not mention the kidnapping of José Urteaga, three years old, or of Liliana Delfino and Ana María Lanzilotto.[28]

Days later, a secret CIA cable mentioned that a ticket to Cuba had been found on Santucho's body. True or not, the claim is revealing. Whoever provided it, surely high commanders of the armed forces had an express interest in reinforcing the continental character of the dispute and its relationship to the US conflict with Cuba.[29] The Argentine press denounced Cuba for having indoctrinated and given training and refuge to the Argentine guerrilla groups. It also lambasted the "idyll between justicialism [Peronism] and communism" as a result of the resumption of diplomatic relations, ignoring the fact that the Argentine dictatorship had a trade agreement with Cuba including a loan of several million dollars.[30] That loan symbolized the triumph of pragmatic politics.

The mention of Cuba was strategic. "Santucho's wife, her parents, and her children by a former marriage are believed to be in Cuba," a secret CIA report stated. The information was only partly factual and was probably given captiously. The Totos were in Cuba with Diego and Mario (who turned one while in Lima waiting for the plane) and their grandparents. Liliana did not travel. She had been kidnapped. In the embassy the Cubans walked a dramatic tightrope between "pragmatic" politics and revolutionary internationalism. In August, Jesús Cejas Arias and Crescencio Nicomedes Galañeña, two of the employees who were in charge of assisting Argentine militants and Chilean and Uruguayan exiles, were kidnapped by repressive forces. Ana remembers having had contact with one of them. This situation further delayed the negotiations regarding the girls. Finally, the embassy seemed to obtain safe passage guarantees, perhaps forced by the meeting of the girls' grandparents with Pope Paul VI on December 15.[31] The girls once again gained the political upper hand: the military allowed their departure.

In these negotiations, the girls were conceived of as *children;* in this way, any potential association with the social and political dangers of adolescence—like the youths who embodied subversion in the military's discourse—was displaced. However, that did not make them any less dangerous. "We were like a bomb," says María Ofelia today. She was not exaggerating. They left the embassy in a huge security operation. Their car was followed by the wailing of police sirens escorting another car, which carried Cuban diplomats with their guns drawn. The Cubans felt they could not let their guard down.[32] When the caravan entered the airport's jurisdiction, it came under the control of the air force, the military body in charge of clandestine detention centers as well as the "death flights," in which kidnapped people were thrown alive into the sea. The tension was extreme. Upon arrival, the airport was full (a flight from Rome had just arrived). The girls were accompanied by a Cuban official and by two or three military men with FAL (light automatic) rifles and an officer who led the way to the counter. The Cuban diplomats were extremely careful. They knew that there was panic in the Argentine foreign ministry. One of the girls said that their names were mentioned on loudspeakers. The others think that this did not happen. Ana argues that it is not plausible that it was openly broadcast. And she is right. But the sense of complete exposure conveyed by that anecdote was absolutely real.

Cuba and After: Life as Politics

María Ofelia faces the camera and speaks calmly. Forty-five years after her kidnapping, in 2020 she is testifying in the lawsuit she filed against the intelligence chief who turned her in. She recounts the violence of those days, as well as before and after. She describes the effects it had on her body, her history, and that of her family. For this investigation, she carefully recounted her arrival in Cuba. She did not unpack her suitcases for three months. Living in Cuba meant leaving behind the struggle for the revolution that she—not only her father and uncle—had made her own at the age of fifteen. She did not want to give up. She weighed forty kilos. She arrived with what today she knows was "war menopause." She was treated by psychologists and by a doctor who was dedicated to studying the health effects of repression. They advised her to take advantage of the possibility of leading a "normal" life.[33]

Each experience was unique.

Ana, Marcela, and Gabriela were returning to a country they had wanted to leave three years before. They arrived after learning of their father's death while in the embassy in asylum. It was not easy for them. A month after arriving, Ana and Marcela had to start high school and return to the *becas*. Ana had started her freshman year in Buenos Aires, at thirteen years old; in Cuba she had to repeat the same grade, now two years older. "It was terrible," she recalls. She couldn't do anything about it. She was in the same classroom with her younger sister Marcela and one of her cousins.[34] She is now a psychologist. She has thought about the fact that they had stopped being isolated in the embassy and had to enter the *becas* where they would be alone, without family and with controlled outings.

Gabriela and María Emilia, who were younger, went to elementary school. Gabriela remembers, unlike her sister Ana, that she met her grandmother when she arrived in Havana. "It was a relief. Finally, a place where I know people." She adds that she always got along well with the "tutors"—that is, with "the Totos," she clarifies. "I adapted quickly to Cuba. I always adapted." Mario, Diego, and the Totos had arrived almost a year earlier. Mario has no memories of it. Diego always felt welcome and cared for. "All my life in Cuba I was happy, although, of course, there were bitter moments," he says with an emotional voice that I can feel through the screen. The routine life, which María Ofelia found it hard to get used to, was good for Diego. It was the end of instability. For him, even today, Cuba was security.[35]

Everyone I interviewed agreed on the happiness of the reencounter.

Diego only shares biological ties with Mario, but with Ana, Marcela, and Gabriela, they all consider themselves brothers and sisters. They also consider María Ofelia, María Susana, María Silvia, and María Emilia their cousins. Since Liliana and Roberto made their relationship official in 1974, says Diego, the two families had been united. There was no lack of conflicts, although he thinks they exist in any family. The affective fabrics of that "singular extended family," as he calls it, formed in little more than a year, were updated upon their arrival in Cuba. That affection, one felt at the time as well as retrospectively, is the legacy that makes his tragic story somewhat less cruel.

The Santucho family settled in a house in Miramar, one of the neighborhoods built by Havana's upper class and assigned by the Cubans to the ERP. Mario and Diego had lived there briefly with their grandparents and other militants, such as the leader Enrique Gorriarán Merlo, with his wife and daughters. Roberto Santucho and Liliana Delfino had left the Totos with the mission of raising their sons and daughters. They prioritized political ties over biological ones in defining the environment in which they would raise their children. The grandparents did not play a role in raising Diego or Mario. This role was played by the Totos. They managed to leave the Miramar house to bring up the children in a working-class environment, with the approval of the Cubans of the Americas Department, which oversaw relations with the Latin American organizations.

In the following years, the children and adolescents contributed to forging ties with Cuba. Sensitivity to children and internationalism softened tensions between Cuban leaders and Argentine exiles, who were stung by Cuba's maintenance of relations with the dictatorship and the scant show of solidarity with them. Around the same time, the leadership of the Montoneros settled in Cuba. They decided to leave Mexico after the Argentine military intelligence tried to kill some of its members there. By then there was already full awareness that children and babies were being kidnapped and tortured to extract information from their parents. For that reason, the Montoneros created a *guardería* (home) in Cuba to care for the sons and daughters of militants who planned to return to fight in Argentina. About thirty children went through the *guardería* and were taken care of by fellow militants (some of them couples) with Cuban support (according to Jesús Cruz, their liaison from the Americas Department, with the direct intervention of Fidel and Celia Sánchez). This institution allowed the militant couples (not only the men) to return to Argentina to fight against the dictatorship in the controversial counteroffensive that led to internal fractures, the disappearance of dozens of militants, and the dissolution of the organization.[36]

The "PRT kids" and the Montonero kids did not know each other. The compartmentalization was complete to the point that each organization was "attended" by different people from the Americas Department. However, the Santucho boys had a relationship with the exiled Argentine *colonia*. This small colony was made up of militants, many of them leaders, who arrived at different stages. There were the families of the "heroes" or the "clans" of the "Guevara," the "Timossi," the "Burgos," the "Masetti," families of the most important internationalists in the Cuban Revolution. Other less prominent families were already there; some of them arrived early, invited by Che, others closer to the coup, such as Juan Carlos Volnovich, a psychoanalyst, from the Peronist Left.

In Cuba, the Chilean and Uruguayan exiles were numerous. They comprised perhaps 3,500 and 1,200 people, respectively, according to Tanya Harmer (in this volume). But Diego heard from unofficial sources that the number reached ten thousand. On the other hand, the Argentinean exile community was very small. According to María Ofelia, the number of children did not exceed thirty in her ambit, which did not include those in the *guardería* because there was complete compartmentalization. All together they probably did not exceed two hundred people. This reduced number of Argentines was the result of Cuba's "pragmatic" policy to maintain relations with the Argentine dictatorship. In economic terms, this decision allowed Cuba to survive the blockade. The $200 million annual loan from the Peronist government, with Minister José Gelbard, was not interrupted.[37] It was not only useful for Cuba; it also allowed Argentina to diversify exports and place industrial goods (including automobiles, ships and shipping equipment, and agricultural and construction machinery). I have been unable to determine how much of this trade had taken place by 1976. But there were efforts by the dictatorship to expand everything that had been implemented. The foreign ministry organized official visits with the participation of businessmen and a strong follow-up after 1979. That year, for example, a hundred Fiat trucks were sold to Cuba, and there were expectations for the future sale of tugboats and tuna boats.[38]

In political and diplomatic terms, Argentina and Cuba forged an alliance in international organizations and forums. Thus, for example, Argentina supported Cuba's candidacy to the United Nations Security Council in exchange for support for its candidacy to the Commission on Human Rights at the UN Economic and Social Council.[39] For its part, the Argentine dictatorship tried to clean up its image in the face of international criticism of its human rights violations by offering to mediate in the conflicts unleashed in 1980 when a group of Cubans took asylum in the Peruvian embassy.[40] The foreign ministry even thought of offering to receive Cuban political prisoners in Argentina. The strategy did not materialize. But it would have championed the dictatorship as a champion of human rights when the Amnesty International report on the crimes committed by the Argentine military had just been published and the delegation of the Inter-American Commission on Human Rights was preparing to investigate Argentina.[41] How was this relationship possible? There was a tacit agreement. Cuba ignored the human rights violations in Argentina and Argentina kept economic and political negotiations open with Cuba.[42]

These tensions between Cuba and the guerrilla organizations were offset by the children who catalyzed Cuba's internationalist solidarity. Cuba furthered its internationalist aspirations through its solidarity efforts, associating such efforts with the feelings universally evoked by children. The combination was so powerful that it destabilized Cuba's tacit hands-off approach to the human rights violations of the Argentine dictatorship. In 1979, the Argentine embassy reported with alarm that Radio Reloj, a popular Cuban radio station, had mentioned the existence of a transnational exchange of political prisoners between the dictatorships of the Southern Cone and especially the appearance of two children in Valparaíso "presumably disappeared." The evening newspaper *Juventud Rebelde* highlighted news about such denunciations in different Latin American media.[43]

The news expressed the powerful connection of internationalism and the sensitivity toward children in which a large part of Cubans believed and, of course, the numerous media cadres such as those in charge of Radio Reloj and *Juventud Rebelde*. The attention given to refugee children catalyzed internationalist conviction. Diego felt loved by neighbors and comrades because of his family history of militancy, as happened to the Montoneros children. They had gone from living clandestinely and hearing on the radio that their father was labeled a criminal to publicly honoring his political trajectory. However, the Cubans did not promote the cult of Santucho, although he was known in the exile community.

There was no PRT-ERP project of collective care, unlike the homes organized by Montoneros, Movimiento de Izquierda Revolucionaria, and Frente Farabundo Martí. The Totos wanted the children to live like any Cuban. They felt comfortable in the popular neighborhood of Alamar, formed by a large group of buildings far from the center of Havana, in whose construction Santucho and other refugees who had fled from Rawson prison (after those who couldn't flee were killed in Trelew) had worked. Ofelia and her daughters settled in the same building as the Totos. Two Cuban and seventeen Chilean families lived there. A community was created in which they occupied a unique place. Toto was a *jodón,* a friend to all, exiles and Cubans. He used to take the children and their friends (many Chileans lived only with their mothers) to play sports and go to the beach. Tota, on the other hand, was more hermitic, but sensitive. Many classmates and friends would go to her to tell her their problems and projects. "She functioned as a sage or community psychologist," Diego says with emotion. They were, each in their own way, older parental figures than most of the other adult exiles.[44]

The ties created in this daily life were decisive. They allowed the circulation of knowledge about the new place (how to carry out paperwork, obtain identification, get access to local leaders), support and strategies to solve daily necessities, and emotional support. These practices, displaced from political narratives, gave rise to a community of belonging created from uprooting and the experience of persecution, and sustained in daily solidarities. In doing so, they had immediate political effects and, as we shall see, future ones.[45]

After Santucho's death, the PRT-ERP went into exile and in 1979 suffered a schism that would completely disintegrate it. Before that happened, the Totos carried out tasks. They organized study groups and classified cables for the Americas Department. Their house was visited by Argentines living inside and outside Cuba. Perhaps their closest circle was the "pro-Soviet" group in Cuba—that is to say, the wing that favored the policy of détente and giving priority to international solidarity, which included Julio Santucho and the siblings of Che Guevara (Roberto, Ana, and Martín Guevara). On the other hand, the Guevarist faction, in favor of the Third World liberation movement, led by Gorriarán Merlo, made its base in Nicaragua. At any rate, as Vera Carnovale argues, these positions were complex and were shaped by various factors.[46]

Argentine identity was present in the Alamar home and, as was often the case, knit together mentions of Argentina's history and situation with daily customs,

Tota's stews, and the rock music that Diego discovered in 1984. However, Argentinian identity coexisted with the "Cubanness" produced by growing up and living on the island and by personal decisions made in the case of Diego and María Ofelia. This process was not free of anguish. Latin American identity, nurtured by internationalism and the life shared with Chileans and Uruguayans, offered Diego a unifying belonging. María Ofelia, for her part, considered herself Cuban: "We talked like Cubans. I never mentioned my history." She did not want to be pitied. That Cuban identity became intertwined with Latin American identity: María Ofelia created with her future husband, Victor Casaus, a cultural center dedicated to Latin America, the Centro Pablo de la Torriente Brau in Old Havana, which they maintained for four decades.[47]

The Santucho children experienced their tragedy differently. Age affected the way they processed the losses and adapted to the new situation. Mario has a symbolic link with his biological parents, whose story he always knew and sometimes wants to explore further, but he recognizes the Totos as affective maternal and paternal figures. He believes that there was a "tragic and at the same time beautiful coupling" between the losses of the Totos' children and that of their parents, in which a new family was created. Diego was also in the "drifting canoe" that found its way to Havana. Let's remember that they were one and six years old when they arrived.[48] On the other hand, Roberto Santucho's older daughters (Ana, Marcela, and Gabriela) were teenagers. They had suffered, with full awareness, extreme situations of vulnerability, danger, and cruelty. Their orphanhood was complete. They ended up living in a country they had wanted to leave.[49] Each one found in her own way the affection and love that allowed them to rebuild their lives. It was not easy for any of them.

The history of political violence and the terror of military repression remain at the center of the political stage in Argentina. The Santuchos have returned again and again to the bloody experiences they went through. Gabriela was unable, for many years, to tell her children about it. The pain was too intense. It still is. The family and the sons and daughters of Roberto Santucho have demanded to know where his body is and to bury him. Forty years later, Ana, Marcela, and Gabriela managed to have their suffering—the emotional and psychological damage of persecution and marginalization—recognized by the courts. Some wounds cannot be healed, but the sentence has a symbolic and political character.[50]

Upon her return to Argentina, Ana Santucho began a long and difficult judicial process, beginning in 1996, and joined HIJOS, an organization of the children of the disappeared, who reclaim the remains of their parents' bodies. The details of this legal battle are beyond the scope of this article, but the case demanded a face-to-face confrontation with General Jorge Rafael Videla and other human rights violators. Her father's body was never found. But the case, which took place during the retraction of human rights policies in Argentina,[51] allowed her to obtain information and undertake a public denunciation in a painful process of elaborating her own history.[52]

In 2020, when the policies of the Kirchner governments had restored the state's commitment to human rights and thereby opened the possibility of trials against the military, María Ofelia decided to file a lawsuit against the head of counter-intelligence who was in charge of them when they were kidnapped. At the trial, she explained that she was testifying for the thirty thousand disappeared—for the comrades who had not been fortunate enough to survive and for their children— for her father and mother, for her family, daughters, and grandchildren, for the people who accompanied her in the denunciation process, and also for Cuba and the Cuban people. The trial was restorative. She was able to confront the military man who had held her hostage.[53]

In the dramatic history of these children, Cuba did not have the same meaning for each of them. For María Ofelia it was a place that allowed her to move forward. Only when the trial was over did she decide to return definitively to Argentina. Two years later, in 2023, Miguel Santucho (son of Julio, the youngest of the Santucho family, and Cristina, his wife, who disappeared while pregnant) sat in a press conference together with Estela de Carlotto, president of the Grandmothers of Plaza de Mayo, to announce that they had found grandson number 133. It was his brother, born in captivity. María Ofelia and Mario stood by his side.

Conclusions

The story of the Santucho children was far from unique. However, the savage repression against their family forced them to live in an extreme situation. The condition of children and adolescents moves us with their vulnerability and strength. But, above all, it shines new light on previously obscure areas that perhaps we would not have registered with the same intensity concerning adults. This insight makes it possible to glimpse the effects that this repression had on their lives and the different ways in which they were able to face the cruelty (physical and psychological torture) and the trials to which they were subjected.

Children played a central role in Cuba's international policy. The Americas Department prioritized the refuge, care, and security of the children of political militants of revolutionary forces from around the world. It continued to do so even when its policy prioritized economic opening and diplomatic transactions. In fact, the children's condition allows us to understand the tensions of Cuban politics at that crucial moment and the weight of internationalist ideology and the sensitivity toward children that facilitated the asylum of the Santucho girls and their departure from Argentina.

The story of the children and the Santucho family shows the intertwining of kinship and political relations and, at the same time, the attempt to create a new type of family. Roberto Santucho and Liliana Delfino decided that their sons and daughters would be raised in a family sustained exclusively on political belonging, struggles, and shared losses. The Totos, as foster mother and father and as guardians, were often on the margins of this story. But they played a role linking the small but important Argentine exile in Cuba and became a reference for Chilean and Uruguayan families. Their place was made possible at the intersection of the customary dynamics of child circulation and the radical creation of new families on the Left in the 1970s.

Uprootedness was the origin of the emergence of a family sustained by the daily cooperation ties in the colony of exiles from the Southern Cone. The "socialist homeland" offered shelter to these children of militants at risk of death. Life was not easy for those who had been orphaned and had gone through extreme cruelty and extreme experiences with full awareness. Half a century later, their story is still being played out in the courts of justice and in the streets of Latin America.

Acknowledgments

The author would like to thank Michelle Chase for the multiple exchanges and for her translation and to Nara Milanich for the conversations about the sad stories of child migration. Thanks to Lillian Guerra and the anonymous reviewers for their insightful comments and to the participants in the Workshop Infancias y Migración Working, July 2020, in the VI Jornadas de Trabajo sobre Exilios Políticos del Cono Sur en el siglo XX, Universidad Nacional de Mar del Plata, November 2023, and in the History Department Colloquium, University of New Mexico, January 2024.

Notes

1. Mario Santucho, "Quien entregó a mi viejo," *Crisis*, May–June 2024, 58–65. According to some versions, Liliana Delfino was also pregnant. But the family has not been able to confirm this. Email exchange with Mario Santucho, December 24, 2024.

2. The most complete book on the family remains María Seoane, *Todo o nada. La historia secreta y la historia pública del jefe guerrillero Mario Roberto Santucho* (Planeta, 1991).

3. "Parientes del extinto guerrillero Santucho siguieron viaje a Cuba," *El Comercio*,

December 29, 1976, n.p.; Marcela Eva Santucho, *Mario Roberto Santucho PRT-ERP. Organizador del contrapoder. Derecho a réplica* (Dunken, 2010), 121–29.

4. Tanya Harmer, *El gobierno de Allende y la Guerra Fría Interamericana* (Ediciones Universidad Diego Portales, 2013); Vanni Pettinà, *Historia mínima de la Guerra Fría en América Latina* (Colegio de México, 2018).

5. For Cuba the reference is Anita Casavantes Bradford, *The Revolution Is for the Children: The Politics of Childhood in Havana and Miami, 1959-1962* (University of North Carolina Press, 2014).

6. On childhood and the Cold War, see, especially, Anna Peterson and Kay Read, "Victims, Heroes, Enemies: Children in Central American Wars," in *Minor Omissions: Children in Latin American History and Society,* ed. Tobias Hecht (University of Wisconsin Press, 2002), 215–32; Ilene Cohn and Guy S. Goodwin-Gill, *Child Soldiers: The Role of Children in Armed Conflict* (Oxford University Press, 1994), 215–32; Isabella Cosse, "Childhood, Love and Politics: The Montonero 'Nursery' in Cuba During the Cold War," *Journal of Latin American Studies* 55, vol. 1 (2023): 1–26. On modern legitimation there are countless studies, but here I mention Martha C. Nussbaum, *Political Emotions: Why Love Matters for Justice* (Paidós, 2014).

7. Alessandro Portelli, "Lo que hace diferente a la historia oral," in *La historia oral,* ed. Dora Schwarzstein (Centro Editor de América Latina, 1991), 36–61. On children's memory and state and clandestine violence, see Jordana Blejmar, Silvana Mandolessi, and Mariana Eva Pérez, eds., *El pasado inasequible. Desaparecidos, hijos y combatientes en el arte y la literatura del nuevo milenio* (Eudeba, 2017).

8. Carlo Ginzburg, *Mitos, emblemas e indicios* (Gedisa, 1999).

9. The human rights group Grandmothers of the Plaza de Mayo has fought to identify and locate the four hundred children kidnapped by the dictatorship.

10. Seoane, *Todo o nada,* 266; author's online interviews with Carlos Alzugaray Treto, July 15, 2023; with María Ofelia Santucho, March 9, 2020; and with Gabriela Santucho, July 14, 2023.

11. For an overview of the field of exile studies, see Silvina Jensen and Soledad Lastra, eds., *Exilios: Militancia y represión* (Universidad de La Plata, 2014); in relation to asylum, see Leonardo Franco, *ACNUR y la protección internacional de refugiados en América Latina* (Editorama, 2004) and, especially, Silvia Dutrénit Bielous, *La embajada indoblegable. Asilo mexicano en Montevideo durante la dictadura* (Fin de Siglo, 2011).

12. Interview with Alzugaray Treto.

13. Tanya Harmer, *The Allende Government and the Inter-American Cold War* (University of North Carolina Press, 2011).

14. Dirk Kruijt, "Cuba and Its Ties with Latin America and the Caribbean, 1959–present," *Revista Uruguaya de Ciencia Política* 28, no. 1 (2019): 279-301.

15. Interview with Alzugaray Treto; Jesús Cruz interview in *Semillas de la Patria Grande: Jesus Cruz, cubano, revolucionario, peronista,* dir. Jorge Devoto and Leonardo Anolles (Manoso Contenidos Audiovisuales, 2022).

16. Interview with Alzugaray Treto.

17. Luis Mattini, *Hombres y mujeres del PRT: La pasión militante* (De la Campana, 2008), 279–85.

18. Interviews with María Ofelia Santucho and Alzugaray Treto.

19. Isabella Cosse, "Children of the Revolution: Generation Gaps in Socialist and Latin American Cuba. Interview with Gregory Randall," *Radical History Review* 136 (2020): 198–208.

20. Santucho, *Mario Roberto Santucho PRT-ERP*, 123.

21. Luis Ortolani, "Moral y proletarización," *Política de la memoria* 5 (December 2004): 93–102.

22. Online interviews with Diego Ortolani, May 17, July 5 and 19, 2023.

23. The bibliography is very extensive. See the pioneering study by Claudia Fonseca, *Caminos de adopción* (Eudeba, 1998).

24. Seoane, *Todo o nada*, 272–73.

25. Ortolani interviews.

26. Testimony of María Ofelia Santucho in the trial against Carlos Antonio Españadero, Tribunal Oral en lo Criminal Federal No 6 de la Ciudad Autónoma de Buenos Aires, November 11, 2020; Gabriela Santucho interview.

27. María Ofelia Santucho interview.

28. "Documentación clave del grupo descabezado," *Hoy*, July 23, 1976, folder AR00093116 "Santucho, Mario Roberto, terrorist. Su muerte 19/7/1976," BNMM—Archivo Crónica.

29. "Background to Operation Leading," July 21, 1976, Intelligence Information Cable, Report Class Secret, National Archive and Records Administration (NARA), accessed via Centro de Estudios Legales y Sociales (CELS).

30. "La esencial complicidad cubana," *La Prensa*, July 22, 1976, n.p., folder AR00093116, BNMM.

31. Blanca Rina Santucho, *Nosotros, los Santucho*, 101–9; Mario Santucho and Ortolani interviews; testimony of María Ofelia Santucho. The grandparents were Francisco Santucho and Manuela Juarez.

32. Alzugaray Treto interview.

33. Testimony of María Ofelia Santucho.

34. Author's interview with Ana Santucho, Buenos Aires, June 14, 2023.

35. Gabriela Santucho, Mario Santucho, and Diego Ortolani interviews.

36. Hernán Confino, *La contraofensiva: el final de Montoneros* (Fondo de Cultura Económica, 2022). On the institution to care for the children, see Cosse, "Childhood, Love and Politics."

37. See Isidoro Gilbert, *El oro de Moscú. Historia secreta de la diplomacia, el comercio y la inteligencia soviética en Argentina* (Sudamericana, 2007), 373–76.

38. Cable 673, from the Cuban Embassy to the Foreign Ministry, November 26, 1979, signed by Rafel Máximo Vázquez, Cables received and dispatched Cuban Embassy and others, 1979–1982 Section 71 Communications, box AH/0572, Archivo Histórico de la Cancillería, Argentina (hereinafter AHCA).

39. Cable 333/334, July 26, 1979, signed by Francisco Molina Salas, Department of International Organizations to Argentine Embassy Havana, box AH/0565, AHCA.

40. Consuegra Sanfiel, "Entre el pragmatismo y el consenso: los vínculos del gobierno cubano y la última dictadura argentina (1976–1983)," *Secuencia* 111 (2021): 1–26.

41. Secret, 719, From the Latin America Department of the Foreign Ministry to the Argentine Embassy in Cuba, January 9, 1979 (signature not legible), Section 71—Communications, Cables received and dispatched, c. 70, box AH/0565, 1979–1982–1988, AHCA.

42. Cables 359 to 362, Cuban Embassy, ca. July 29, 1979, signed by Rafel Máximo Vázquez, Cables received and dispatched Cuban Embassy and others, Section 71 Communications c. 70 a. 4, box AH/0572, AHCA.

43. Cables 359 to 362, AHCA; Vera Carnovale, "The PRT in Exile: Weapons, Communism and Human Rights," *Revista Historia* 15 (2014): 1–28.

44. Ortolani interviews.

45. Ortolani interviews.

46. Vera Carnovale, "PRT in Exile."

47. María Ofelia Santucho interview.

48. Mario Santucho interview.

49. Gabriela Santucho and Ana Santucho interviews.

50. "La justicia ordenó indemnizar a las hijas de Mario Santucho por su detención y muerte," *Infobae,* March 13, 2023, https://www.infobae.com/judiciales/2023/03/13/la-justicia-ordeno-indemnizar-a-las-hijas-de-mario-santucho-por-su-detencion-y-muerte/.

51. As embodied by the "Punto Final" and "Obediencia Debida" laws of 1986 and 1987, both overturned in 2005.

52. Ana Santucho began proceedings April 3, 1996. "Santucho, Mario Roberto s/ Ausencia por desaparición forzada," Juzgado de Primera Instancia en lo Civil y Comercial no. 1, a cargo de la jueza Dra Martina Forns, Secretaría no. 1 del Departamento Judicial de San Martín, Argentina. Email exchange with Ana Santucho, January 10, 2025.

53. Ailín Bullentini, "Cuando María Ofelia Santucho, sobrina de Roberto, le habló a su propio secuestrador," *Página 12,* February 5, 2021, https://www.pagina12.com.ar/321670-cuando-maria-ofelia-santucho-sobrina-de-roberto-le-hablo-a-s.

ELEVEN

Internationalizing
the Revolutionary Family

*Love and Politics
in Cuba and Nicaragua,
1979–1990*

EMILY SNYDER

On July 26, 1979, just one week after the Sandinista National Liberation Front (Frente Sandinista de Liberación Nacional, FSLN) overthrew the US-backed Anastasio Somoza dictatorship in Nicaragua, its leaders reestablished diplomatic relations with Cuba.[1] That same day, during a speech commemorating the twenty-sixth anniversary of the 1953 Moncada Barracks attack, Fidel Castro promised the new Sandinista government an internationalist brotherhood. Even as he acknowledged the island's financial and material constraints, Castro offered Cuba's wealth of human resources—all the medics, teachers, and advisers Nicaragua needed to carry out its revolution.[2] More than twenty-nine thousand Cubans responded, willing to go to Nicaragua.[3] They traveled to Nicaragua as *internacionalistas*—civilians who volunteered, usually for two years, to work on behalf of the revolution in health, education, construction, and the military—in addition to Cubans who went as experts, artists, and members of various solidarity brigades.[4] Internationalism, always part of the revolutionary project, became personal for Cuban citizens in the late 1970s and 1980s as thousands of them participated in efforts abroad.

Conversing with literatures on gender and the Cuban Revolution, gender and foreign policy, and Cuban revolutionary diplomacy, this chapter argues that Cuban ideas about gender, sexuality, and the family shaped internationalism to

Nicaragua and within Cuba. It examines the gendered dimensions of internationalism by tracing Cuban statist constructions of the New Family and the New Man, how Cubans and Nicaraguans navigated love and revolution by contracting transnational marriages, and Nicaraguan students' experiences on the Isla de la Juventud (Isle of Youth), a small island off Cuba's southern coast. In each of these sites of analysis, family functioned as an institution where the Cuban state's heteronormative attitudes toward marriage, childcare, and gender intersected with internationalism. But considering the family as an ever-changing space where social affinities and gender relations are formulated also demonstrates how internationalism gave rise to new relationships that challenged both the state's view of internationalism and that of the women and men involved.

Cuban internationalism sprang from a gendered political discourse that revolved around constructing the New Man and New Family. In the 1960s, Ernesto "Che" Guevara theorized that the New Man would be a new kind of individual, born of revolutionary struggle, who was willing to sacrifice himself for liberation projects, putting the needs of the collective above his own. He was anti-imperialist, (inter)nationalist, straight, heroic, and the model to which every socialist subject should aspire.[5] By the 1980s, the Cuban state prophesied that the revolutionary New Man could be made anew through internationalist efforts; duty and self-abnegation beyond Cuba's borders were paramount. From the early moments of revolutionary consolidation, the state had also cast the New Family as a mechanism to organize citizens' labor. The New Family consisted of a male head of house who worked a state-approved job outside the home and lived with his legal wife, whose labor—both reproductive and remunerative—the state controlled.[6] By the late 1970s, revolutionary ideals dictated that the New Family would labor to construct an international "revolutionary family" by privileging revolutionary love over romantic, individual love. Though internationalist missions conscripted women as participants alongside men, leaders simultaneously designed policies that emphasized women's domestic responsibilities. Families, most often women, filled in labor gaps internationalists left at home, such as childcare and housework.

Cuban internationalism in Nicaragua built on histories of solidarity with the Third World that Rafael Cesar and Michelle Chase examine regarding Angola and Vietnam, respectively, in this volume. It also relied on the institutional structures developed for managing cooperation with Angola, such as the State Committee for Economic Collaboration (Comité Estatal de Colaboración Económica, CECE). Collaboration with Nicaragua differed from Cuban efforts in Angola, however. The Angolan government paid for Cuban support and crafted trade agreements that benefited the Cuban economy.[7] In contrast, Cuba supplied its human resources to Nicaragua without compensation, signaling that Cuban leaders saw nonmaterial benefits of collaboration.[8] Beyond the fact that Nicaragua had far less to give materially, Cuba operated according to a hemispheric priority. The success of another leftist revolution achieved through armed violence in Latin America meant that Cuba finally had an ally and a base to continue agitating for revolution across Central America.[9] Nicaragua also offered Cuba a nascent revolution through which it could radicalize its own young generation and revitalize its ossifying revolution.

Nicaragua received the second-highest number of Cuban internationalists after Angola, despite unfavorable economic benefits. Official government figures report that approximately fifty thousand civilians went to Angola between 1975 and 1991.[10] To Nicaragua, Cuba sent 16,787 civilians between 1979 and 1990.[11] The majority were teachers; about two thousand worked in Nicaragua annually between 1980 and 1984. Officials selected volunteers who possessed teacher certification, at least three years of teaching experience, and "appropriate" moral and political consciousness.[12] This meant membership in the Communist Party or in the Communist Youth (Unión de Jóvenes Comunistas, UJC), as well as in less selective mass organizations. Internationalists to both Cuba and Angola were supposed to be loyal revolutionaries with a proven record of model work and behavior.

This chapter illuminates how Cubans and Nicaraguans navigated love and revolution within the context of internationalism. As such, it contributes to studies of social history on militancy and the family, as well as to emerging studies on the Cuban Revolution's 1980s and trans/international histories of the Sandinista Revolution.[13] Ultimately, mobility enabled by internationalist exchanges generated space for convulsive personal experiences, love within revolution, and new family dynamics.

Forging the Internationalist Family and Making the New Man

Internationalist missions depended on the labor of Cuban families, but the state's construction of the New Family changed over the course of the 1960s and 1970s. The family operated as a site of state formation, political contestation, and ideological conflict. In the messy years of revolutionary consolidation between 1959 and 1962, marriage, the politicization of youth, and new roles for women outside the home produced anxiety about the destruction of the family.[14] The state thus encouraged marriage and throughout the 1960s engaged in campaigns whose goals were to "(re)define the nuclear family and position this model as an apparatus through which citizens could be organized to serve the state."[15] By the late 1960s, Cuban leaders sought to pivot the New Family's labor outcomes by freeing women from the multiple burdens they shouldered at home, such as childcare and domestic labor, in order to allow them time to join the workforce, study, or otherwise engage in revolutionary work beyond the home. Services such as *círculos infantiles* (day cares) and *seminternados* (boarding schools for children to attend during the week) assisted with childcare, and worker cafeterias alleviated the burden of food preparation. However, maintaining these initiatives proved challenging. Revolutionary leaders did not prioritize dedicating economic resources toward these services that would help confront gender inequality and reduce the time women spent taking care of the home or involved in care work. Women's inequality was a material issue—one that the revolutionary leadership chose not to resolve. Instead, the FMC cast the solution to these problems to be within the family.[16]

The Family Code passed in 1975 was an attempt to legislate gender and domestic equality and alleviate women's "triple burden" of productive labor, reproductive labor, and political labor. It officially reinscribed the family as a partner in children's political and social development and called for men to share in work at home. The code also reinforced patriarchal norms by signaling the nuclear family as the preferred family structure. Legislating its way into the home, the state sought new ways to harness familial power and labor and define acceptable roles for revolutionary women.[17]

The New Family shared responsibility with the state for making the New Man, whose characteristics also shifted by the late 1970s. In the 1960s, Cuban leaders specifically defined the New Man as someone who participated in mass organizations, volunteered to cut sugarcane, and put the needs of the revolution before his own. In the 1970s, the new revolutionary generation came of age. Guevara had theorized that these youth would become "authentic revolutionaries," free from the "original sin" that plagued those who had been educated before 1959.[18] The new generation went to boarding schools, performed voluntary labor in the countryside, and were socialized under the revolution. But the heroism, hope, and immediacy of the early years of the revolution no longer marked everyday life.

Instead, staleness and monotony characterized revolutionary culture by the end of the revolution's second decade. Revolutionary glory lived in the past and the future would be brighter still, but the present was routine. In the 1970s, "commemoration was everywhere... but few new domestic milestones appeared worthy of state-sanctioned remembrance in the future."[19] Moreover, the new generation had not been witnesses to the historical narrative revolutionary authorities curated. Yet Fidel insisted that young people had a responsibility to sacrifice and achieve like the revolutionaries before them, and indeed, that "the new generations will have to be superior to the older generations."[20] With the revolution assumed "complete"—that is, having reached a certain level of material stability, achieved political institutionalization, and made significant strides in education and health care—revolutionary authorities turned abroad to radicalize Cuban youth.

Through internationalist missions, youth would participate in processes similar to those of the early Cuban Revolution. Fidel's revision of the New Man in 1980 engraved the centrality of internationalism to his construction. When the Sandinista newspaper *Barricada* asked Fidel to describe the main characteristics of the New Cuban Man, he defined it as "a man who can feel internationalism, that is, solidarity toward other peoples. A man who can feel solidarity toward his own brothers. A generous man, capable of sacrificing for others. . . . that is the New Man."[21]

The meaning of New Man solidarity thus expanded from sacrificing alongside a fellow Cuban to leaving Cuba to sacrifice on behalf of another revolution. By bringing revolution or helping solidify fledging governments in other recently liberated countries, Cubans performed their own transformation.

The New Man was predicated on rebel hegemonic masculinity, rooted in strength, courage, and virility, and defined in opposition to femininity and homosexuality.[22] But if the gay man was antithetical to the New Man, women played a key role in New Man ideology.[23] As New Women, they created New Men as mothers, served as examples in laboring for and sacrificing their bodies to the state, took care of the home, and maintained traditional feminine beauty.[24] Chase's chapter in this volume examines how Cuban leaders and press used the image of the revolutionary Vietnamese woman as a model for Cuba's own New Woman, which shows how the construction of the New Woman (and New Man) developed in relation to internationalist solidarity. By the mid-1970s, New Women not only participated in their own national liberation struggles but also went abroad as internationalists, and their participation played an important role in the Cuban state's construction of guerrilla masculinity. The opposition between revolutionary masculinity and a feminized counterrevolution became a recurring theme in the revolution's early years and reappeared in later discourses on Cuban internationalist teachers in Nicaragua.[25]

In 1980, the Cuban media cast the internationalist teachers sent to participate in the Sandinistas' Literacy Crusade as brave, masculine revolutionaries, in contrast to the cowardly, feminine, US-backed Contras. The figure of the female *internacionalista* established revolutionary/counterrevolutionary opposition by emasculating Contra men. For example, one magazine article told the story of a female teacher's success in inverting a Contra's plan to humiliate her. The Contra soldier, frustrated that she would not leave her students despite repeated physical threats, put a snake in her desk drawer in order to "make her look ridiculous" in front of her students.[26] However, a student tipped the teacher off. The teacher asked for a machete and, in front of the class, killed the snake "to the admiration of all the students, and later, of the pueblo." She displayed so-called masculine bravery by confronting the snake in public, turning the Contra's plan to feminize her (and by extension the Cuban missions) through humiliation on its head. Snakes in the Nicaraguan countryside were common, but Freudian notions of the snake as a phallic symbol underlaid the story and highlighted Contra emasculation. And using a female figure to represent a "battlefield triumph" followed the gendered logic that losses were psychologically greater when they came at the hands of women, thereby questioning the losers' masculinity.[27]

Other media also employed gender as a strategy to legitimate internationalists' moral and revolutionary cause while discrediting the counterrevolution. The Cuban television series *Por el mismo camino,* which aired in 1982, romanticized the manly sacrifice of the *internacionalistas* and wove the teachers' experience in Nicaragua into a readable narrative for the broader Cuban public. The accompanying graphic novel featured still shots from the show and dramatized the experiences of one group of teachers in Nicaragua. In the middle of the story, the teachers heard that the Contras had killed two Cuban teachers and four Nicaraguan students in Siuna. Tomás Borge, the Sandinista minister of the interior, delivered a condolence speech. He reported that the Cuban teachers had "died bravely, their clothes illuminated with sweat and mud from the road." In contrast, their attackers were "cowardly" and effeminate, wearing Christian Dior shirts and maintaining the "feminine smoothness of their lazy hands."[28] In this portrayal, sweat, grime, and bravery evidenced the Cubans' masculinity, while clean, designer clothes and soft hands feminized the imperialist enemy.

The story ends with the main teacher, Águedo Morales Reyna, assassinated by the counterrevolution.[29] Before knowing whether the assassinated teacher was Cuban or Nicaraguan, the Sandinista minister of agriculture, Jaime Wheelock, wrote a letter to Fidel Castro, which is reproduced as the final element in the book. He had just visited the site where Cuba was funding and building a new sugar mill—another token of internationalism—and upon leaving, he passed a lone Cuban woman walking along the road. He writes, "That one Cuban teacher simply carrying out her beautiful internationalist mission taught me that maybe more than others, Cuba and Nicaragua are called upon to hold onto life, hope, and the right to redemption for our people." But the citizens of Cuba and Nicaragua must pay for this "destiny" through the "high cost of sacrifice."[30]

These accounts portrayed Cuban teachers fulfilling gendered visions of the New Man in Nicaragua. State political discourse feminized the enemy, and final victory rested with the stronger, more masculine, and ultimately moral revolution. Revolutionary nationalism turned on the ideology that heteronormative masculinity would assure the revolution's endurance in the face of North American imperialist aggression.[31] The New Man was the standard of revolutionary masculinity, and in the 1980s, he was an internationalist.

Revolutionary Love and the Family

As masculine subjects, internationalists theoretically sacrificed personal needs, family, and love for the revolution and Nicaragua.[32] Death surely constituted the most dramatic (and final) menace with which Cuban volunteers contended, but sacrifice came in many forms. Internationalists faced physical, external discomfort: teachers traversed inhospitable terrain, forged through rain, climbed mountains, walked long distances, endured mosquitos, and survived with limited provisions.[33] In addition to physical discomfort, they made sexual sacrifices. In the 1980s, the revolution required surrendering up the body, and its sexual impulses, abroad.

Somos Jóvenes, a new Cuban magazine the government began publishing in 1977 to appeal to young people, discussed sexual sacrifice and what one should do about sex when away on an internationalist mission. One article responded to an anonymous letter from a male *internacionalista* who wondered if "lack of sexual contact for a prolonged time could affect one's health and if masturbation would bring consequences like impotency and other evils."[34] The editorial response debunked these myths, characterizing masturbation as a "normal physical process" that under no circumstances prevented men or women from reaching orgasm. However, the article went on to argue that "it is not correct to encourage masturbation, but rather to educate people in occasional abstinence." Because it had nothing to do with love, masturbation should only be an antidote to sexual emergency. The article left the dimensions of "emergency" unaddressed—and bypassed the possibility of forming relationships with locals altogether. Instead, the writer assured the young, sexually frustrated *internacionalista* that he could "be sure that each person has the capacity to be able to temporarily control their sexual tensions through activities that serve as distractions." In order to do this, he should focus on things that must be accomplished and direct his energy into chosen distractions, such as reading, writing, or a sport. In other words, the state used the same argument it deployed to repress homosexuality: masturbation was unproductive for personal development and, by extension, for the revolutionary project.[35]

Furthermore, according to government policy and media, an *internacionalista* should be willing to sacrifice human love and relationships for the revolution. Love cannot be divorced from history, politics, or power relations.[36] Love within the Cuban Revolution was no exception, and revolutionary love revolved around the public good and the nation rather than a bourgeois desire for private love and family.[37] Accordingly, internationalists' desire to volunteer their labor abroad superseded their desire to stay in Cuba with a partner; love for serving the revolution and broader humanity came before that for a partner.

A short story in *Somos Jóvenes* featured a young internationalist facing conflict and instructed readers about the relationship between amorous love and revolutionary love.[38] Isis, the heroine, is a young teacher preparing to leave for Nicaragua. She and her boyfriend, Iván, fight: he threatens to break up with her for leaving him and for putting herself in a position where she might be killed. However, Isis "didn't cry.... She imagined teaching her boyfriend about morality and consciousness, and she knew in the end he would give in, because he was revolutionary." And he does, reluctantly. Meanwhile, Isis forges ahead, bolstered by her father's communist sentiments and the memory of her mother, who died as a literacy worker in the Escambray Mountains during Cuba's Literacy Campaign in 1960. Significantly, Isis performs her socially expected labor of love as a woman through her relationship with Nicaragua as a member of a literacy brigade, rather than through a romantic partnership with a heterosexual man.

Cuba's revolutionary leaders promoted a particular version of love and, by extension, family. In the 1980s, *Mujeres* profiled men and women who subsumed relationships and intimacy with a spouse to the ideals of the revolution. One article exalted Asela and her husband, Orlando. They met while studying in Poland and spent the subsequent decade moving between jobs and places, taking turns caring for their two children or leaving them with grandparents. Asela gave birth to their second daughter in Poland while Orlando was in Havana; once she finished studying and returned to Cuba, Orlando left for Canada. When he returned, Asela got a job in Cárdenas, and Orlando continued to work in Havana. Then he went to Vietnam, and Asela considered going to East Germany. She says, "In the future, it might not be a training course in Germany, but an internationalist mission, who knows? Wherever they need our work, there we will be!"[39]

Mujeres then highlighted Cecilia and Antonio, who also traded off time in Cuba with their children (and each other) and time abroad in the USSR, Poland, and Canada. Like Asela and Orlando, they relied on their parents for housing and childcare and always managed to time their travels so that one of them stayed with the children.[40] Reflecting ideals of the New Family, the husband performed childcare responsibilities alongside his equally revolutionary wife. These families suggest that markers of the revolutionary family included long spans of separation from one's partner, prioritizing education and labor for the revolution over family life. Tanya Harmer's chapter in this volume shows that similar prioritizations imbued Chilean and Uruguayan exiles' lives in Cuba and how their choices affected their children, revealing the messy and sometimes painful personal costs wrapped up in this vision of family.

Internationalism also separated participants from their children. The press lauded leaving behind young children as one of the greatest "sacrifices" a woman could make. It represented both her revolutionary commitment and the importance of work to be done in Nicaragua. For instance, a *noticiero* (weekly newsreel) featured teachers convening and preparing to go to Nicaragua. The two internationalists who spoke first in the clip were women. One declared that upon arriving in Nicaragua, she was "prepared to do what is necessary." She explained, "In my case, I left my one-year-old boy with my mother, an elderly woman, and my husband. . . . If we are there for two years, my son will be three-plus years [old when I return], and he won't know me." Another woman in the circle of teachers spoke up next, saying that she also left a daughter, and that it had been very painful to leave her.[41]

Internationalist missions separated families, but extended familial labor, rather than governmental institutions, made such arrangements possible. One study of female internationalists confirmed that more than half of the five hundred women interviewed were mothers, with 73.7 percent leaving their children in the care of their parents or grandparents.[42] Going to Nicaragua, Cubans left their family behind but were promised that they would find a new revolutionary family.[43] Yet internationalist labor depended on care work that the Cuban government obscured, leaving women to either arrange childcare with extended family members or, in the case of an absent partner, shoulder the entire burden themselves.

Family complicated the state's neat portrayals of revolutionary love. According to the state's narrative, love for the revolution and belief in solidarity propelled Cubans to volunteer for missions, despite relationships at home. In reality, a variety of reasons motivated civilian internationalists. In the case of Angola, these included the younger generation's desire to participate in heroic campaigns, and the opportunity to leave the parental home, improve their social and professional standing, travel, and attain material benefits.[44] The internationalists who went to Nicaragua volunteered for similar reasons. And, for some women, the ability to join husbands motivated some to volunteer themselves.[45] Being selected as an internationalist was a competitive process, and these women were model citizens. At the same time, some leveraged their political cachet for personal reasons, strategically placing themselves with their male partners.

Working in Nicaragua as a couple led to strengthened marriages for some, and dissolution for others. Gladys Chántez Oliva went to Nicaragua as a teacher alongside her husband, a military adviser. She remembered sharing worries with him about their children and parents they left back in Cuba, and her satisfaction at being able to take care of him. Gladys affirmed that their time in Nicaragua working toward the same goal strengthened their marriage. However, Cuban officials' decision to evacuate women from Nicaragua after the United States invaded Grenada in 1983 negatively impacted other marriages. At the time, Guadalupe Espiñeira González, a doctor, was on mission along with her husband. They had a young daughter back in Cuba, and Guadalupe was sent home but her husband was not. The husband remained in Nicaragua and met a Nicaraguan woman, and Guadalupe ended their marriage.[46] Gendered revolutionary logic thus influenced the ability of partners to be together and foreclosed even that slim possibility after 1983, as Cuba sent only men to Nicaragua after Grenada. The decision to pull women from Nicaragua, especially those with children, also reinforced traditional gender norms that held childcare as a maternal responsibility.

State discourse and policies surrounding internationalist missions reveal connections between care work and ideas of the revolutionary family, as well as contradictions in gendered revolutionary logic. While revolutionary culture celebrated the labor of internationalists, it simultaneously obscured the labor required to make the missions function. Officials expected extended family members to take on the work of raising children while their parents volunteered for missions. Then, according to official discourse, women selected as internationalists performed New Womanhood by subsuming family responsibility to the revolution. Constructing the "revolutionary family" came first, as women left the labor of caring for children and husbands to [female] relatives in Cuba. But Cuban leaders' decision to bar women internationalists after 1983 revealed that the "revolutionary family's" primacy only superseded the nuclear family's to a certain point. Women could be loaned to construct the "revolutionary family," but only insofar as it was not dangerous, because their real responsibility was to raise children in Cuba.

Falling in Love on Mission: Marriage and Transnational Families

Internationalism relied on the labor of Cuban families, solidified or challenged marriages, and created *new* transnational families. Documents from the Cuban Ministry of Foreign Relations show internationalists demanding that the state recognize and facilitate marriages while they were on mission and facilitate family reunification after their departure. These *internacionalistas* and their Nicaraguan counterparts forged their own meanings of international solidarity, often challenging prescribed notions of "revolutionary love." Harmer's chapter in this volume shows how exiled Tupamaros in Cuba subverted state directives to put their personal lives on hold. Cubans in Nicaragua similarly challenged the state's sexless and loveless narratives about internationalist missions. Internationalists across Nicaragua carved out spaces for affection and sex within revolutionary projects as they fell in love, had children, created new families, and, in some cases, got married and emigrated.

Internationalists formed relationships despite the Cuban government's efforts to organize missions in a way that limited contact with locals outside of work. In order to cultivate a "together but separate ethos," Cuban doctors lived in spaces separate from Nicaraguans and were often prohibited from going anywhere alone.[47] The Cuban government feared defection and sought to keep its workers as isolated as possible. Emigration became even more politically charged after 125,000 citizens left Cuba for the United States in the Mariel boatlift of 1980, which signaled widespread loss of faith in revolutionary leadership.[48] Internationalist defections of avowedly vetted revolutionaries clearly challenged the Cuban Revolution's legitimacy. Emigration through marriage, however, occupied murkier territory: going through legal channels, internationalists retained their revolutionary credentials even though they no longer resided in Cuba. But, as discussed above, politics infused marriage, as Cuban leaders knew well.[49] Transnational love and marriage amended the Cuban Revolution's ideologies of revolutionary love. By falling in love, internationalists inserted eroticism back into the equation, and perhaps they saw themselves as shaping a new love, one that bound two revolutions together beyond solidarity and sacrifice.

Internationalist collaboration in Nicaragua created conditions and relationships that often facilitated marriage as a migration tactic. Internationalist emigration was primarily male.[50] By late 1982, a growing group of Cubans and Nicaraguans seeking to formalize their relationships compelled Cuban authorities to clarify the state's policies and processes governing marriage and migration. A "numerous group" of teachers had already married, and thirty more had plans to do so.[51] A 1976 law outlined the procedures for Cubans wishing to contract marriages abroad.[52] But the legal, technical, and ideological discussions around Cuban-Nicaraguan marriage in the 1980s reflect confusion over what the laws stipulated and which departments transacted marriages.

In October 1982, the Cuban ambassador to Nicaragua convened a meeting in Managua with representatives from each Cuban ministry that worked with or sent people to Nicaragua. The meeting clarified the government's rules and regulations for marriages and migrations. For Cubans to marry Nicaraguans, they needed to obtain an *hago constar* (affidavit) from the minister or the highest Cuban government official from the organization or institution they reported to in Nicaragua. The Ministry of Foreign Relations then authenticated this document, which needed to expressly state that "the formalization of the marriage does not affect the mission, work, or tasks that the interested party carries out, or is the reason they are abroad."[53] In other words, the signatories had to swear that they did not go abroad for the purposes of contracting a marriage, and thus defecting.

According to Julián López Díaz, the Cuban ambassador to Nicaragua, the most challenging aspect of allowing marriage was ensuring "militancy" and finding "definitive solutions" to ensure the marriages would "not affect the feelings and the will of the internationalist, of the revolutionary, of the communist."[54] Here, romance potentially threatened the internationalists' inner will and militancy, as if personal relationships and the sexuality they implied were direct threats to revolutionary sentiment. This requirement reinforced official Cuban views on revolutionary commitment and love. Marriages could only proceed if they did not detract from the revolutionary mission. Otherwise, internationalists had to sacrifice their affective ties.

Cubans also had to present the desire to marry before the last six months of their time in Nicaragua, as well as their birth certificate and a sworn declaration of relationship status, providing a divorce certificate, if applicable.[55] Fear of insincere marriage reigned. One Cuban official characterized transnational marriage as "very complicated," because in Cuba the "migratory procedures are *just like those of any other citizen who wants to abandon the country.*"[56] In the aftermath of the Mariel boatlift, when Cuban leadership feared desertion of the revolutionary project, the official's complaint insinuated that Cubans married Nicaraguans as a strategy to leave the country. This was not the desired outcome of internationalist missions but rather a subversive co-optation of Cuban informal diplomacy. Migration to another revolutionary Caribbean country also placed in question Cuba's revolutionary "expertise" and its ability to capture the loyalty of the younger generation.

Furthermore, marriage represented the only avenue a Cuban could use to bring a Nicaraguan partner to Cuba or return to Nicaragua.[57] Any other relationship arrangement, even one that involved children, afforded no travel rights to the couple. For an unmarried Cuban father to bring children back to Cuba, he had to recognize them through the consular office and obtain the mother's permission for the children to leave. This patriarchal policy likely deterred fathers from returning to Cuba with children born to them in Nicaragua, defaulting responsibility for offspring to the Nicaraguan mother unless the Cuban man chose otherwise. The Cuban state held fatherhood to be optional; motherhood, unavoidable.

The 1982 meeting outlining marriage and migration procedures concluded with resolutions to print the regulations for distribution to internationalist brigade chiefs and hire an assistant to help the chief of the consular office in Managua deal with the likely increase in marriage petitions.[58] However, bureaucratic inefficiency compounded Cuba's reluctance to sanction the emigration of those who were supposed to embody the archetype of the New Man. Cubans' relationships with Nicaraguans challenged the Cuban government's prohibitions on traveling to and from the island apart from in an official capacity. Traveling to Nicaragua to further a relationship during the 1980s was not itself outright illegal. Instead, the Cuban government produced "legal uncertainty" through the law—or enforced norms—in order to impede movement and maintain social control.[59] A marriage requirement, approval through the immigration office to leave the country, and flight ticket purchases in US dollars combined to complicate or make it nearly impossible for Cubans to travel to Nicaragua. Yet legal uncertainty also created space for Cubans to contest the law.

Over the course of 1986, the Nicaraguan embassy complained to Manuel Piñeiro, head of the Americas Department, about the problems arising from Nicaraguan-Cuban marriages and "requested that we [the department] worry about this matter, given the variety of cases being presented."[60] It highlighted the fact that Cuba had no official avenue to authorize its citizens' exits, which resulted in a "long and cumbersome" process, especially for doctors. Then, once Cubans completed the immigration requirements to leave, they had to buy their plane ticket to Nicaragua in US dollars—making the trip not only financially prohibitive but also technically illegal because the dollar was criminalized. The Cuban government allowed Nicaraguans to travel to Cuba by taking collaboration flights run by CECE for free and return to Nicaragua by paying for the ticket in Cuban pesos.[61] But the rules differed for Cubans. Cubana de Aviación charged Cubans USD $228 from Managua to Havana and USD $223 for the return—an exorbitant amount. The Cuban embassy in Nicaragua also begged Piñeiro to figure out a solution to ticket pricing, because they were "facing situations of this type daily."[62]

By 1987, Cubans denied by the National Bank of Cuba to pay their ticket to Nicaragua in pesos "did not accept this and went to the Department of Americas with passport in hand, seeking an answer to their problem, which is creating difficulties." Fed up, the head of the Nicaraguan Section called a meeting with the immigration office and the National Bank to sort out the inconsistency. The National Bank reported that it had "clear instructions" not to sell Cubans flights in Cuban pesos, so immigration agreed that it would not approve Cubans to leave the country if the bank did not approve the ticket sale in Cuban pesos. Officials hoped this would prevent "interested parties from going to the Department of Americas with the idea that it would approve the ticket sale in *moneda nacional* or authorize a free flight."[63] They also floated the desire to end the policy allowing

Nicaraguans to take CECE's flights for free, which would further restrict unofficial movement between Cuba and Nicaragua.

The letters Cubans wrote to Isidoro Malmierca, the minister of foreign relations, provide glimpses into the dynamics of transnational relationships, the marriage process, and citizens protesting policy. For example, Manuel Durán Legón, a teacher, had a baby with his Nicaraguan girlfriend during his time on mission. He was not able to marry her due to an incomplete divorce and lack of documentation, but after returning to Cuba and finalizing the divorce, he wanted to return to Nicaragua at the end of 1981. Durán asked Malmierca to give him "the opportunity to work another period as a teacher in that country [Nicaragua], during which I can personally resolve the case and bring my formalized family back [to Cuba]." Apparently, he had been told after returning to Cuba the first time that he would be able to return on a flight to Nicaragua without extending his mission. Failing that, the only way Durán figured he could get back to Nicaragua and carry out the immigration process was to volunteer to go back on mission. He felt it important that Malmierca know that his *compañera* and their son had to leave her parents' house, which was close to the Honduran border, because she had been "threatened with death by the genocidal Somocistas for having a son with a Cuban." She was waiting for Durán to get her, and thus the situation was urgent.[64]

It does not seem like Durán returned to Nicaragua in 1982, because he reappears in the archive in 1989, this time agitated. He wrote to Malmierca, "I continue wanting to go to see my son and want a response that clarifies my situation, and if possible, reassesses my case." He explained that he went through the process of obtaining permission to be able to visit his son back in 1982, securing a thirty-day travel authorization through the immigration office and a current passport. But when he attempted to purchase the flight, he was asked to pay in US dollars, which presumably impeded his visit. Indignant, he asked Malmierca, "How is it possible to require payment in dollars, if I am a Cuban worker who receives my salary in Cuban pesos? Is there a legal way by which a Cuban citizen can acquire the dollar?" Durán exposed the paradox of traveling to Nicaragua: the act itself was not illegal, but the only way to complete it was by breaking the law. He went further by arguing that "according to what I understand in the new penal code [1988], bank obstacles for these cases no longer exist." He wielded his credentials as a militant of the Communist Party and concluded that "from the humane and logical point of view, I think I am in the right and this is why I ask that my case be analyzed."[65]

Another internationalist, Juan Miguel Vésente, also sought Malmierca's help to reunite him with his Nicaraguan wife whom he married while on a mission.

After earning her degree in medicine, Vésente's wife solicited a residential visa for Cuba, but it was denied because she owed two years of social service to Nicaragua. She then asked for a visitation visa, but she "could not travel because they demanded the trip's payment in dollars, which made it impossible." Given the situation, Vésente asked if he could go to Nicaragua but pay for the trip in *moneda nacional*. Like Durán, Vésente appealed to Malmierca's sympathy, explaining that he had already endured eighteen months of a long-distance marriage, "plus two more years that I would have to wait for her to finish her social service . . . It's not easy at all [*no es nada fácil*]."[66] Malmierca's response is absent from the archive, but it seems unlikely that he approved Vésente's petition.

Marriages and relationships were a by-product of internationalist missions in Nicaragua, and also very human responses to an otherwise abstract political project. While the Cuban revolutionary government did not explicitly outlaw these relationships, it discouraged them through bureaucratic inconsistences and by impeding Cubans' ability to leave Cuba. Romantic relationships challenged revolutionary rhetoric about internationalist missions, which revolved around themes of self-sacrifice and the priority of the collective over the individual. The government was loath to lose some of its most necessary citizens to individualistic love. But love and sex existed alongside internationalism, and internationalists' desire to maintain emotional and physical connections with their partners and children endured well after the end of their mission.

Internationalism on the Isla de la Juventud

As Cuban internationalists went to Nicaragua, Nicaraguans came to Cuba to study. The Cuban Revolution's largest internationalist project unfolded in the form of boarding schools on the Isla de Pinos, renamed the Isla de la Juventud in 1978. In the 1970s, the *escuelas en el campo* concept defined the island and saw widespread installation. Escuelas Secundarias Básicas en el Campo (ESBEC, Secondary Schools in the Countryside), boarding schools spanning the seventh to ninth grades, operated on the premise that manual labor, usually agricultural, constituted an essential element of revolutionary education. Students studied for half of the school day and worked in the fields for the other half. Five to six hundred students lived in each school, placed throughout the countryside, for weeks or months at a time. In the early 1970s, the government stocked the schools with children from mainland Cuba. Beginning in 1977, however, Cuba "offered" schools on the island to foreign governments Cuba had relations with and that were in the midst of their own revolutionary struggle, such as Angola and Mozambique.

Nicaraguans arrived on the island just three months after the triumph of the

Sandinista Revolution in 1979 and populated ESBEC no. 53, Carlos Fonseca Amador, named for the founder of the FSLN. A second school, Amistad Cuba-Nicaragua, opened in March 1980. Many students in the early classes had participated in the revolution: 40 percent of the 515 students that came in the spring of 1980 fought with the FSLN to overthrow Somoza's dictatorship.[67] Cuban news outlets featured these children, highlighting both their revolutionary credentials and Cuba's role in training them for the next phase of Nicaragua's revolutionary consolidation.[68] Cuba would provide Nicaraguans with a different kind of revolutionary education, one earned not in battle but in the classroom and fields.

For all the triumphant press, many Nicaraguan students had trouble adapting to life in Cuba. Out of the first group of 603 students, 545 completed three years.[69] The Sandinista government gave students little preparation about what to expect and enforced minimal screening.[70] It only required parent permission and the ability to travel alone—which likely excluded women with children. One student remembered her physical education teacher inviting whoever wanted to study in Cuba to sign up.[71] Therefore, for many the transition from Nicaragua to the *escuelas en el campo* was radical.[72] In Cuba, students found themselves without their families and with different soap, different food, different schools, and different rules that restricted their movements. As a result of the labor and conditions in the schools, many students sought to leave the Isla and return to Nicaragua.[73]

Nicaraguans' maladjustment to Cuba's *escuelas en el campo* was widespread. In order to help his students, the director of Carlos Fonseca petitioned the FMC in the fall of 1979 to select local families to "adopt" a Nicaraguan student. The FMC called the program Madres Combatientes Internacionalistas (Combatant Internationalist Mothers), modeled off the preexisting Movimiento de Madres Combatientes por la Educación (Movement of Combatant Mothers for Education), which organized women to volunteer in local schools.[74] However, the labor required of FMC women on the island to help the schools function differed. Instead of working inside the schools or alongside teachers, the revolution's internationalism solicited their skills as mothers and caretakers. Nicaraguan students visited their Cuban families' houses on the weekends to be taken care of by a Cuban mom. She did laundry, cooked, and cared for the Nicaraguan student, providing them with a family and love.[75] The program was a resounding success; though it began with Nicaraguans, it spread to other schools and nationalities once students and administrators saw the benefits of connecting with local women and families.[76] Relationships forged between the Cuban families and Nicaraguan students were close, as some families brought their Nicaraguan student back to the mainland with them for vacations and kept in touch once their student returned to Nicaragua. Nicaraguan students who return to the Isla still seek out their Cuban families to visit and reconnect, attesting to how important local Cuban women were to their lives on the island.

Paralleling Cuban internationalism in Nicaragua, internationalist collaboration on the Isla de la Juventud also forged new families. Sex ratios within the schools likely informed sexual practices: males significantly outnumbered females in secondary and preuniversity schools, and the Carlos Fonseca Military Academy was exclusively male. Only 29 percent of the Escuela Amistad Cuba-Nicaragua's incoming 1980 class was female; by 1989, the gender disparity continued, with a 25 percent female enrollment at Amistad Cuba-Nicaragua and 30 percent at Carlos Fonseca.[77] Though students formed relationships within the schools, the uneven sex ratios ostensibly drove males to find partners outside of the schools. They dated women they met during their free time on weekends and through their sponsorship by families. Unsurprisingly, some of these relationships resulted in children.[78]

Nicaraguan students also got pregnant. In the early 1980s, protocol for pregnancy within secondary and preuniversity schools called for both the woman and the baby's father to be sent back to Nicaragua.[79] Abortion was not an option, and both parties lost their scholarships. As a result, some young women carried out their own abortions to avoid penalty.[80] After a few years, the Cuban state permitted students to obtain legal abortions and likely encouraged this option over either returning to Nicaragua or having the baby.[81] In at least two cases, Nicaraguan women neither returned to Nicaragua nor had abortions, instead carrying their pregnancies to term and giving birth on the island.[82] Officials had established a day care (*círculo infantil*) in La Fe, a suburb of Nueva Gerona, to accommodate other foreign students studying on the island who arrived already pregnant. The Nicaraguan mothers were able to drop their babies off for day care while they went to school. In another case, Illeana D'Carmen Espinoza got pregnant her last year of preuniversity, at age nineteen.[83] She was given the choice of abortion—after seeking "permission"—or having the baby. She chose to have the baby, graduated eight months pregnant, and returned to Nicaragua to give birth.

The Cuban state intervened when Nicaraguan female students became pregnant, but not when Nicaraguan men impregnated Cuban women. The state was responsible for the Nicaraguan students within the school, and it extended its patriarchal reach into the family and Cuban women's sexuality to include Nicaraguan women. For female Nicaraguan students, then, attending school on the Isla meant relinquishing some degree of control over sexuality to the Cuban state. However, though state policy suggested that being a young, unmarried mother was incompatible with being a revolutionary student, some Nicaraguan women held otherwise. Though officials frowned on pregnancy, it seems that more space existed after secondary school for Nicaraguan women to choose to have their babies or access abortion. But the fact that female secondary students performed their own abortions in order to continue studying highlights the state's failure to provide sex education and birth control, the mutually exclusive categories of "mother" and "student," and the burdens state policies placed on young women.

Conclusion

Internationalism informed the core of Cuba's foreign policy strategy in the 1980s. As Cubans left the island for years to complete missions, internationalist projects affected broad swaths of the population. This chapter has examined the gendered logics of Cuban internationalism in the 1980s and demonstrated how mobility gave rise to new relationship dynamics. In Cuba, revolutionary sacrifice and the constructions of the New Man evolved to emphasize an internationalist volunteerism, albeit an internationalism predicated on guerrilla masculinity. Yet Cuban women also participated as internationalists, despite—and sometimes because of—family. Once in Nicaragua, many Cubans fell in love, inherently challenging the revolutionary government's definition of love as self-sacrifice for collective rather than personal goals. By soliciting marriages, Cuban internationalists compelled leaders to clarify emigration policy and confront their revolutionaries' desires. And, as Cuba sent internationalists to Nicaragua, Nicaraguan students came to study on the Isla de la Juventud. They navigated everyday difficulties in boarding schools with the help of Cuban women. In both Cuba and Nicaragua, internationalist collaboration created new, transnational relationships and families.

Cuban policies surrounding internationalism in both Nicaragua and Cuba illuminate state attitudes toward gender, sexuality, love, and care work. The Cuban state had always expected women to subsume love and family responsibilities to the revolution while still raising children and caring for the home. The onset of internationalist missions continued in this vein: leaving children evidenced women's revolutionary sacrifice. At the same time, Cuban leaders held care work to be women's responsibility, sending home internationalists with young children, recruiting women on the Isla de la Juventud to adopt foreign students, and leaving the offspring of unmarried Cuban fathers in the care of their Nicaraguan mothers. Ultimately, women's labor constructed the revolutionary family with little governmental support.

Assessing internationalist collaboration between Cuba and Nicaragua also reveals the Cuban leaders' continued emphasis on heteronormative and legally "legitimate" nuclear families. They envisioned a de-eroticized revolutionary family bound by ideology, work, education, and neat national boundaries, rather than romantic love, sex, offspring, and transnational families. But internationalism created space for new relationships and individuals to shape their own experiences abroad, challenging both the state's lingering emphasis on familial legitimacy and individual views of revolutionary love. Considering Cuba's internationalism with the Sandinista Revolution through the lenses of gender and sexuality exposes the internal logic of the Cuban Revolution, its transnational dimensions, and the intimate consequences of foreign policy in the private lives of citizens. This approach wrestles with what it meant to Cubans and Nicaraguans to leave, be left, and navigate inter/transnational cooperation.

Notes

1. Emily Snyder, "Internationalizing the Revolutionary Family: Love and Politics in Cuba and Nicaragua, 1979–1990," in *Radical History Review* no. 136, pp. 50–74. Copyright 2020, MARHO: The Radical Historians' Organization, Inc. All rights reserved. Republished by permission of the copyright holder, and the Publisher. www.dukeupress.edu.

2. Fidel Castro, "Discurso del XXVI aniversario del asalto al Cuartel Moncada," *Granma*, July 26, 1979, 3.

3. Marta Rojas, "El aula verde," *Cuba Internacional* 10 (1981): 13.

4. *Internacionalista* was a professional term referring to a category of Cuban collaborators who completed years of service.

5. Che Guevara, "El socialismo y el hombre en Cuba (1965)," in *Che Guevara Presente: Una antología mínima*, ed. María del Carmen Ariet García and David Deutschmann (Ocean Press, 2004).

6. Rachel Hynson theorizes the New Family in *Laboring for the State: Women, Family, and Work in Revolutionary Cuba, 1959–1971* (Cambridge University Press, 2020), 2.

7. Cristine Hatzky, *Cubans in Angola: South-South Cooperation and Transfer of Knowledge, 1976–1991* (University of Wisconsin Press, 2015), 194, 152.

8. Internationalists who went to Angola were not aware that the Popular Movement for the Liberation of Angola (Movimento Popular de Libertação de Angola, MPLA) was paying the Cuban government for their labor. It is possible that the Sandinistas paid for some of the services and personnel supplied by Cuba, but evidence suggests that cooperation with Nicaragua was not economically beneficial to Cuba. See Ricardo Cabrisas to Luis Carrión, "Protocolo sobre el intercambio comercial," May 12, 1988, Personal archive of Michel Vazquez de Oca; Vazquez de Oca, interview by author, Havana, Cuba, December 16, 2017.

9. Andrea Oñate, "The Red Affair: FMLN-Cuban Relations During the Salvadoran Civil War, 1981–92," *Cold War History* 11, no. 2 (2011): 133–54.

10. The actual number probably falls between 44,000 and 49,000. Hatzky, *Cubans in Angola*, 153–55.

11. Angel García Pérez-Castañeda, "El internacionalismo de Cuba en la colaboración

económica y científico-técnica: Esbozo histórico de un cuarto de siglo de la Revolución Socialista Cubana 1963-1988," cited in Hatzky, *Cubans in Angola*. I suspect both Angola's and Nicaragua's statistics are inflated due to the reports' summation methods: The Ministry of Education lists the number of collaborators per year and then totals them, and it is unclear if people who spent more than one year abroad were accounted for. See Jorge Batista Girbau, "La colaboración educacional cubana en Nicaragua," unpublished report, Biblioteca del Ministerio de Educación, La Habana, Cuba (n.d.): 13; Nancy Jiménez Rodríguez, *Mujeres sin fronteras* (Editoria Política, 2008), 97.

12. Jiménez Rodríguez, *Mujeres sin fronteras*, 97.

13. Isabella Cosse, "Infidelities: Morality, Revolution, and Sexuality in Left-Wing Guerrilla Organizations in 1960s and 1970s Argentina," *Journal of the History of Sexuality* 23, no. 3 (2014): 415-50; Heidi Tinsman, *Partners in Conflict: The Politics of Gender, Sexuality, and Labor in the Chilean Agrarian Reform, 1950-1973* (Duke University Press, 2002); Michael Bustamante and Jennifer Lambe, eds., *The Revolution from Within: Cuba, 1959-1980* (Duke University Press, 2019).

14. Michelle Chase, *Revolution within the Revolution: Women and Gender Politics in Cuba, 1952-1962* (University of North Carolina Press, 2015), 170-208.

15. Hynson, *Laboring for the State*, 2. These efforts included controlling women's biological reproduction, promoting marriage, reeducating sex workers, and controlling men's informal labor.

16. Alexis Baldacci, "Consumer Culture and Everyday Life in Revolutionary Cuba, 1971-1986" (PhD diss., University of Florida, 2018), 82-83, 87.

17. Baldacci, "Consumer Culture," 23, 123-58.

18. Guevara, "El socialismo y el hombre," 235; Lillian Guerra, *Visions of Power in Cuba: Revolution, Redemption, and Resistance, 1959-1971* (University of North Carolina Press, 2012), 230-35.

19. Michael Bustamante, "Anniversary Overload? Memory Fatigue at Cuba's Socialist Apex," in Bustamante and Lambe, *Revolution from Within*, 235.

20. Original quote in Bustamante, "Anniversary Overload?" 226.

21. "Fidel entrevistado por Barricada: Nadie puede discutir papel de vanguardia a sandinistas," *Barricada*, July 29, 1980, 3.

22. Lorraine Bayard de Volo, *Women and the Cuban Insurrection: How Gender Shaped Castro's Victory* (Cambridge University Press, 2018), 90.

23. Emilio Bejel, *Gay Cuban Nation* (University of Chicago Press, 2001); Sierra Maduro, "El trabajo os hará hombres: Masculinización nacional, trabajo forzado y control social en Cuba durante los años 60," *Cuban Studies* 44 (2016): 309-49.

24. Lillian Guerra, "Gender Policing, Homosexuality and the New Patriarchy of the Cuban Revolution, 1965-70," *Social History* 35, no. 3 (2010): 275-79; Baldacci, "Consumer Culture," 21.

25. Bayard de Volo, *Women and the Cuban Insurrection*.

26. Bravo, "Una bella misión," *Cuba Internacional* 9 (1983): 41-43.

27. Bayard de Volo, *Women and the Cuban Insurrection*, 212.

28. Nilda Rodríguez Torres, *Por el mismo camino* (Editorial Gente Nueva, 1982), 47.

29. On the assassination of the real Áquedo Morales, see "Dispuestos miles de cubanos," *Cuba Internacional* 2 (1982): 3.

30. Rodríguez Torres, *Por el mismo camino*, 94–95.

31. Abel Sierra Madero, "El trabajo os hará hombres," 315–16.

32. Fidel Castro, *Fidel Castro y la religión: Conversaciones con Frei Betto* (Siglo Veintiuno Editores, 1988), 261–63.

33. Rodríguez Torres, *Por el mismo camino*, 46–47; "Cuba y Nicaragua marchan juntas hacia el futuro," *Cuba Internacional* 12 (1981): 3; José Benitez, "El maestro cubano de Waspado Central," *Cuba Internacional* 12 (1981): 11.

34. Caridad Carrobello, "Por favor no publicar mi nombre," *Somos Jóvenes* 90–91 (1987): 42–43.

35. Sierra Maduro, "El trabajo os hará hombres."

36. Carrie Hamilton, *Sexual Revolutions in Cuba: Passion, Politics, and Memory* (University of North Carolina Press, 2012), 74.

37. Krissie Butler, "Deconstructing an Icon: Fidel Castro and Revolutionary Masculinity" (PhD diss., University of Kentucky, 2012), 62–65.

38. Mercedes Santos, "Floreciéndole a la vida," *Somos Jóvenes* 42 (1983): 32–33.

39. Heidy González Cabrera, "Esa muchacha aparentemente frágil," *Mujeres* 19, no. 12 (1979): 8–10.

40. González Cabrera, "Juntos, todo resulta fácil," 62–63.

41. Noticiero no. 945, November 22, 1979, Archivo Fílmico de Arte e Industria Cinematográficos, Havana, Cuba (ICAIC).

42. Jiménez Rodríguez, *Mujeres sin fronteras*, 14.

43. "Maestros cubanos en Nicaragua," *Cuba Internacional* 1 (1980): 5.

44. Hatzky, *Cubans in Angola*, 93.

45. Niurka Pérez Rojas, interview with author, February 24, 2018, Havana, Cuba.

46. Jiménez Rodríguez, *De las mujeres*, 214–15.

47. Kristin Anderson, "Health Care Reform in Sandinista Nicaragua, 1979–1990" (PhD diss., University of Texas at Austin, 2014), 205.

48. María Cristina García, *Havana USA: Cuban Exiles and Cuban Americans in South Florida, 1959-1994* (University of California Press, 1997), 59; María de los Angeles Torres, *In the Land of Mirrors: Cuban Exile Politics in the United States* (University of Michigan Press, 1999), 113.

49. Hynson, *Laboring for the State*, 91–148.

50. Scholars have primarily studied love and migration in relation to female sex workers during the Special Period. See Florence Babb, "Sex and Sentiment in Cuban Tourism," *Caribbean Studies* 38, no. 2 (2010): 93–115; Amalia Cabezas, *Economies of Desire: Sex and Tourism in Cuba and the Dominican Republic* (Temple University Press, 2009); Coco Fusco, "Hustling for Dollars: *Jineterismo* in Cuba," in *Global Sex Workers: Rights, Resistance, and Redefinition*, ed. Kamala Kempadoo and Jo Doezema (Oxford University Press, 1998), 151–66.

51. Dirección Jurídica, Reunión en la Embajada de Cuba en Nicaragua, October 29, 1982, p. 3, box 2, folder 1982, Nicaragua, Archivo Central Ministerio de Relaciones Exteriores de Cuba, Havana, Cuba (ACMINREX).

52. Dirección Jurídica, Circular No. 27/76, December 10, 1976, box 2, folder 1976, Nicaragua, ACMINREX.

53. José Viera Linares to Héctor Rodriguez Llompart, p. 1, box 2, folder 1982, Nicaragua, ACMINREX.

54. Julián López Díaz and Daniel Herrera Pérez to José Machado Ventura, August 20, 1982, box 2, folder 1982, Nicaragua, ACMINREX.

55. Dirección Jurídica, Reunión en la Embajada de Cuba en Nicaragua, 3–4. An earlier memo put the number at three months. Authorities enforced (or theoretically enforced) the *hago contestar* requirement after October 1982.

56. Dirección Jurídica, Reunión en la Embajada de Cuba en Nicaragua, 3–4, emphasis added.

57. Dirección Jurídica, Reunión en la Embajada de Cuba en Nicaragua, 4–5.

58. Dirección Jurídica, Reunión en la Embajada de Cuba en Nicaragua, 5–6.

59. Amalia Pérez Martín, "Entre la redención y la resistencia: El rol político y sociohistórico del derecho en Cuba posrevolucionaria," paper presented at "New Voices in Cuba Studies: Graduate Student Symposium," Harvard University, November 30, 2018.

60. Manuel Piñeiro to Isodoro Malmierca, September 9, 1986, box 4, folder 1986, Nicaragua, ACMINREX; José Raúl Vira Linares to Roberto González Caro, September 24, 1986, box 4, folder 1986, Nicaragua, ACMINREX.

61. Dirección Jurídica to Giraldo Mazola, 1, June 23, 1987, box 4, folder 1987, Nicaragua, ACMINREX; Manuel Munsulí Gómez to Manuel Piñeiro Losada, February 27, 1986, box 4, folder 1986, Nicaragua, ACMINREX.

62. Manuel Munsulí Gómez to Manuel Piñeiro Losada, 1, 2 (quotation).

63. Dirección Jurídica to Giraldo Mazola.

64. Manuel Durán Legrá to Malmierca, November 20, 1981, box 2, folder 1982, Nicaragua, ACMINREX.

65. Manuel Durán Legrá to Malmierca, April 15, 1989, box 5, folder 1989, Nicaragua, ACMINREX.

66. Juan Miguel Vésente to Malmierca, December 30, 1987, box 4, folder 1987, Nicaragua, ACMINREX.

67. Sergio Colina, "Otra ESBEC para estudiantes nicaragüenses abre sus puertas en la Isla de la Juventud," *Victoria,* April 10, 1980.

68. Reynaldo Escobar Casas, "Nicaragua: generación de la victoria," *Cuba Internacional* 3 (1980): 38–40; Cristina González, "Recuerdos de la batalla," *Somos Jóvenes* 20 (1980): 13.

69. "Trabajo investigativo: Sobre las escuelas internacionales en la Isla de la Juventud," 1986, box 11, folder 225, Archivo Histórico Municipal de la Isla de la Juventud, Nueva Gerona, Isla de la Juventud, Cuba (hereafter AHM).

70. Omar Morales to Malmierca, April 30, 1988, 3–4, Nicaragua, box 4, folder 1988, ACMINREX.

71. Johanna Malespin García, interview with author, Darío, Nicaragua, January 23, 2019.

72. Marlen Villavicencio Batista, interview with author, Nueva Gerona, Isla de la Juventud, Cuba, January 30, 2018.

73. Omar Morales to Malmierca, 3; Waldo Garrido Pérez, *Memorias y Reencuentros* (Bitecsa, 2011), 17, 21–24.

74. Garrido Pérez, *Memorias y Reencuentros,* 44–45; "Las madres combatientes," *Mujeres* 8 (1981): 58.

75. Alicia Cascaret, "Un nuevo combate: el estudio," *Mujeres* 20, no. 5 (1980): 21; Villavicencio Batista interview.

76. Villavicencio Batista interview.

77. Colina, "Otra ESBEC"; Luis Sires Pérez, Proyección del curso escolar 89/90, 7, box 16, folder 388, AHM.

78. Alejandro Hernández Solis, interview with author, Managua, Nicaragua, February 5, 2019.

79. Garrido Pérez, *Memorias,* 54; Villavicencio Batista interview.

80. Illeana D'Carmen Espinoza, interview with author, Rivas, Nicaragua, January 25, 2019.

81. Abortion policy changed over the years; deregulation by 1979 made it accessible and contributed to the [re-]creation of an "abortion culture." Danièle Bélanger and Andrea Flynn, "The Persistence of Induced Abortion in Cuba: Exploring the Notion of an 'Abortion Culture,'" *Studies in Family Planning* 40, no. 1 (2009): 13.

82. Villavicencio Batista interview.

83. D'Carmen Espinoza interview.

Afterword

AILYNN TORRES SANTANA

Gender and feminist studies have insisted for decades on the relevance of analyzing how concepts and policies regarding women, families, sexuality, sexual dissidence, and domestic life, as well as men, masculinity, and what is considered public life, are constructed, resisted, and hegemonized. Scholarship has also attended to how these issues impact states and societies, and are impacted by them. Today we know that the question of gender, sexuality, and everyday life in political projects and strategies of power is important for any process. That is the central question that this book takes up; it uses it to analyze Cuba, its political project, and the achievements of that project. It is not about the study of women as a social group that can self-referentially explain itself, but about gender relations as an arena of power that transverses the realm of the political, individual and collective bodies, families and the nation, power and the project of power.

Indeed, the Cuban Revolution built, from very early on, a political program toward gender relations and sexuality. This program was central to the deployment of the revolution inwardly and to its representation outwardly. It was also the framework through which different international links were established and through which conflicts were dealt with domestically. This volume's authors have a common interest in dissecting, from this angle, the irradiation of the revolution through its international, cultural, racial, and economic policies, and the consequences the resulting transnational encounters had for Cuba and its interlocutors. Therefore, through an analysis of Cuba, this book also contributes to our understanding of the Global South.

The eleven chapters in this book plus the introduction show that uncovering imaginaries of gender and sexuality—as represented, narrated, practiced—is fundamental to understanding post-1959 Cuba. The essays recover the politics that made such programs possible and study the experiences of the subjects in their family and daily life. From this perspective they weave together social and cultural histories—with all their dilemmas and problems—of a specific period: the Cold War, and, more centrally, the Cuban sixties and seventies, a crucial period for understanding the channels through which power was institutionalized after the triumph of the revolution in 1959, and when the contradictions that the revolutionary fervor of the sixties had tempered began to reemerge, and new ones rose.

In synthesis, this collection shows, first, that the revolution's politics of gender and sexuality were central to the post-1959 process. It accounts for the ways in which these operated as a political device to mobilize labor and social support, to reproduce its own and/or its allies' political project, to represent present needs and future possibilities. Thus, it is argued here at length that gender relations, sexuality, and the organization of everyday life give political content to actually existing political practices and events.

The analyses go a step further: they verify that policies on gender and sexuality were produced from above, but, at the same time, were deliberated in multiple social settings. In effect, the revolution defined its own versions of love, the family, women and men in the revolution, of marriage and heteronormativity; it constructed a framework of what was possible and considered virtuous in these realms. Having said that, it is necessary to add that revolutionary policies on gender and sexuality contained aspects that were difficult to reconcile, and which revealed, from their origins, multiple contradictions.

The texts in this book reveal those contradictions by highlighting the effort of the political leadership to bring together, in the same framework, competing ideals and practices. Thus we find traditional values on women, motherhood, the family, the couple, and sexual life alongside the necessary promises of emancipation for women; the suspension of personal and sexual life as a sacrifice for the revolution alongside the valorization of the family as a sociopolitical entity; the democratization of domestic life alongside the exaltation of maternal sacrifice; the search for manpower and political support from all sectors alongside open exclusions based on sexual orientation, ideology, or other characteristics; declarations on the end of racism and sexism, alongside racist and sexist political realities; diplomacy aimed at garnering support for other states alongside solidarity with revolutionary movements working to overthrow those same states; and much more. The contradictions inherent to the framework constructed "from above" produced, many times, "confused realities" that are evidenced here. Thus, the different chapters challenge a standard reading that explains post-1959 Cuban history as the result of a mantle of authoritarian power that was spread over the people who, at times, were able to resist it.

Feminist historiography has shown the weight of political power in the construction of genders and sexualities that inhabit the national *imagined community*. In this way, political power has intervened directly in women's bodies and has constructed regimes of representation in which they fit. This book returns to the question of what sexual and gender politics have to do with the deployment of authoritarian power, but it shows us a more complex picture: state interventions into gender relations and sexuality are both resisted and reproduced. The various social agents absorbed and transformed the framework of the possible. Sometimes they contested it; other times they adapted to it, reproducing it in their own voice as part of hegemonic consolidation.

And here I add one of the greatest virtues of the volume: its authors constantly reaffirm the importance of individual and collective agency as a vital component for understanding the messy overlapping structures, dynamics, representations, and narratives about Cuba. The analyses insistently ask why people do what they do and what ultimately transforms them—through the various themes that are touched upon here—into political subjects (and not only subject *to* politics). Agency is evidenced here in different ways. It is in the identification of the tensions between different actors (Cubans and external allies) and the frameworks offered by the island's leadership; in the justifications that people made to articulate their own sacrifices for a project that they understood transcended them; in the strategic use they made of the conditions of life in the country; in the multifaceted defense of the revolution; in the use of memory to reprocess for the present what happened in the fervor of the post-1959 decades; in the ways of circumventing institutional limits without dissenting from the greater project; in the codification in their own terms of what it meant to be an ally of the revolution, an internationalist, a revolutionary, a man or a woman of the time.

In this way, this book reveals multiple, complex, and contradictory layers of the Cuban Revolution through the analysis of its policies on gender and sexuality. And it also shows how consensus was produced within those layers. The analyses sketch a field of transformations and disputes that show gender conceptions as a "weapon of war" and as a field of struggle for exiled individuals and families, for children from Cuba or brought to Cuba, for organic intellectuals of the revolution (Cuban and foreign), and for the state. They show how, and in which registers of public discussion of the period, issues related to gender and sexual morality were persistent and important, and how their analysis informs the needs of institutionalized power in its processes of affirmation, restructuring, consolidation, or crisis.

The evidence regarding the gender and sexual programs of the revolution is connected in the different chapters with regimes of representation. The questions here are about how and with what images and meanings the state represented the revolution, women, homosexuals, internationalists, intellectuals, enemies, the family, and the future.

This book allows us to understand the expectations constructed by the revolution for different subjects and groups, and the tensions those expectations embodied. Women were expected to be mothers, combatants, internationalists, revolutionaries, volunteers, *brigadistas,* productive workers, caregivers, wives, leaders; they were expected to be self-sacrificing, loving, beautiful, and much more. This book shows that the disjunctures between each of these vectors of representation were played out in transnational conversations involving political processes such as those in Vietnam, Angola, China, and Latin American countries.

From the collective analysis offered here, it is possible to conclude that there was a certain plasticity in the ways women were represented—which adapted to circumstances and political needs—but also a clear continuity of the fundamental tension between conservative and emancipatory visions. The image of the traditional woman was constantly being questioned as well as reproduced—both, simultaneously. The essays preceding these pages contain abundant evidence of this.

Analyses in this vein also ask who has the power of representation, which voices are authorized to represent, and also who or what does *not* have the privilege of representation—that is, those whose racial belonging, sexual orientation, or any other identity is obliterated or marginalized from the framework necessary to articulate revolutionary power. As several analyses in the book show, a fundamental and persistent question was: Who is the "universal" human the revolution addressed? Who was its political subject?

The authors' reflections also advance along another axis: the relation between affect and politics. Several chapters recover emotion and thereby challenge the tradition that exalts reason at the expense of bodies. Here we find efforts to reinstate questions about how subjects constructed knowledge about their own feelings, and how and in what ways that knowledge was conditioned by social and normative structures or discursive regimes. In different ways, this book attends to the emotionality of public discourses that construct, for example, notions of seduction; it explores the affects that inhabit the construction of memory, representations, self-representations, and symbols produced within the framework of "affective economies." In other words, it is not a matter of understanding emotionality as a self-referential field but of analyzing, as is done here, the conditions of production of that emotionality *around* and *within* the revolution. Thus, we find in the book reflections on the circuits of distribution of those emotions embodied in symbols (the revolutionary woman, the New Man, the internationalist) and on the affective investiture of the revolution.

These intersections between affect, politics of gender and sexuality, and regimes of representation show us complex structures of discrimination and exclusion, but also powerful efforts at inclusion and democratization.

Scales of Time, Subjects, and Space

This is not a work only about the Cuban Revolution, although it starts with it and returns to it on most of its pages. It is a book that also develops a history of South-South relations during the Cold War. In that period, the place of the Cuban Revolution was prominent, and it is key to understanding intercontinental threads, regional processes, and national political dynamics in Latin America as well as in Asia and Africa. Thus, this book is a gateway, passing through the Cuban Revolution, to those conversations that translated global tensions, resolving some and sharpening others.

The analyses presented here share a key premise: no political process can be explained solely self-referentially. The Cuban Revolution cannot be understood without its fundamental ties to Nicaragua, Angola, China, Argentina, Uruguay, Vietnam, Mexico—the Global South. Nor can the participation of these countries in the Cold War be explained without Cuba. The same could be said about the Eastern European socialist camp, which is not a scenario dealt with in this work and remains a pending issue in the historiography on Cuba and the global historiography on socialism. The texts here make this absence noticeable and indicate it as a necessity for future research.

But what several analyses in this volume do is to show that Cuba was not only an inspiration, a symbol, and a real support for the democratizing political processes in other areas of the Global South, but that it was—and in many ways continues to be, as I argue below—a gateway for the discussion of more general issues in those other contexts. The debates on Cuba were key to establish boundaries between political sectors in different countries, based on their support or criticism of the revolution, and to raise and settle conversations about the Left, democracy, the inclusion of certain marginal groups, moral conservatism, and so on. Through these dialogues, the very idea of Cuban utopia was constructed. In that sense, the symbol of the Cuban Revolution is also the result of the transnational conversations that this book captures.

The macro-social scale—involving national states or more general political projects—is not the only one that matters. The chapters in this book move from the individual to the community, from families to states, from specific parties to the broader field of the Left, from couples and the nuclear family to the collectivization of life. And within each of these scales the analyses expand: they explore the implications of the radical transformation from citizen to exile, from heterosexual man to woman, from internationalism as a state project to internationalism as an individual project.

In balancing these various scales, the constant tension between the individual and the collective is vital. The valorization of the collective that the revolution and other political projects of the time produced ran up against personal projects and individual lives. This confrontation sparked negotiations between states, families, and individuals, and led to questioning and rethinking of the quality of sacrifice that was possible, just, and desirable in the name of the revolutionary project. The relationship between the individual and the collective continues to be an arena of political dispute for the Left. This book helps us think about its historicity.

Finally, on the question of sources: As I have said, this is a history book, but not the usual kind. At least some of the texts here are, strictly speaking, interdisciplinary. What makes them interdisciplinary are the methods they employ and the analytical imagination they use. We are before a work of social and cultural history with full awareness that time is a political experience and that the understanding of societies can only take place through collective effort. In fact, by doing so, this work is inspiring other necessary collaborations and questions—for example, combining cultural history with economic history and with more general redistributive issues. It raises questions about how those gendered subjects—those belligerent bodies that were represented, integrated, or exalted by the revolution—participated in the economic structures of the nation, in its productive life, in its material conditions of existence.

A Book on the Twentieth Century for the Twenty-First Century

When mass protests erupted in Cuba on July 11, 2021 (now known as 11J), old questions about socialism, the Left, and the future of the Cuban Revolution resurged. Does what happens now in Cuba matter at all to the Lefts in Latin America, the Global South, and elsewhere? Is the Cuban Revolution the past? Is Cuba still a utopia?

Before 11J, at least some of those questions seemed meaningless. The conversation about Cuba and the utopia embodied in its 1959 revolution was scarce in the panorama of issues of primary interest to the diverse Lefts in Latin America and the world. After 11J, the political and programmatic value of anti-capitalist alternatives regained importance. Questions about the vitality of the revolution were once again important. Global and regional Lefts once again debated how much of the revolution could still be found in Cuba, how and why Cuba is today the country it is, and the extent to which it embodies some kind of utopia. Cuba once again shaped transnational political conversations about what justice should be and what constitutes a plausible emancipatory horizon. More than six decades after 1959, these debates once again brought out allies and detractors within the global Left.

But internally, the situation has been different. The collective voice of the Cuban people asks less and less if any utopia survives in the real Cuba, the country that witnessed the protests of July 11, and in which resistance is the hallmark of daily life. The decades analyzed in this book do not seem to be a source of inspiration to think about a future that manifests, above all, as one of great uncertainty. While precariousness and inequality grow, the alternatives imagined are far from the vocabulary built in the sixties and seventies to describe the horizon of justice. However, part of the explanation of how we have reached this point can be found in the chapters of this book. And it is important to return to it, not only for intellectual reasons but also because of the importance of imagination and civic political sensitivity.

For the Cuban Revolution, that zenith event of the twentieth century discussed in the chapters that precede these pages, the principles of equality and justice were the guide. But history has not unfolded in a straight line. The route has been full of zigzags, contradictions, and diversions from the original goals. The most serious ruptures—including the current crisis—have replaced the narrative of utopia with one of disenchantment. Abroad, some today view Cuba with critical melancholy; for others it continues to be a place to return to amid the horror of the world. For Cubans it is more about the real and concrete country they find themselves in, more prosaic than the ideal, full of inequalities and discontents.

In 2021, the report of the Eighth Congress of the Communist Party of Cuba stated: "The moral authority of the single party that guarantees and represents the unity of the nation, emanates precisely from the exemplary fulfillment of duty and constitutional postulates, as well as high ethical, political and ideological qualities, in close connection with the masses."[1] The jargon and gestures of political power today differ, in tone and substance, from what we have read in this volume. They denote a gap between the utopia of justice and the reality of inequality and scarcity, between power and ideals. Politics now plays out on different terrains from those evoked by the political leadership.

This book asks many times where the crux of the dispute has been. The answers are multiple: sometimes it was in the body that transitioned its gender identity; sometimes in the family broken by political violence, exiled, and welcomed in Cuba; sometimes in the community that collectivized the care of children; sometimes in state institutions; sometimes in the field of representation; sometimes in the obliteration of anti-racist radicalism and sometimes in its exaltation. The same question continues to have total relevance for history and for the present: Where is the crux of the political dispute in Cuba today?

Note

1. Central Report to the Eighth Congress of the Communist Party of Cuba, available at https://cubaminrex.cu/es/node/4462.

CONTRIBUTORS

ALEXIS BALDACCI is assistant professor of history at Rockford University. Her research and teaching focus on questions of citizenship, power, gender, and equity. Her current book project, *I, the Revolution: Austerity, Identity, and Desire in Cuba, 1971–1991*, analyzes consumer and material cultures to explore the nature of political participation in Cuba and the popular legitimacy of the revolutionary project.

FELIPE CARO ROMERO (he/him) holds a PhD in Latin American History. His research is focused on LGBTQ+ movement history and political radicalism. His forthcoming book *La Conquista de los Corazones. Historia de la protesta LGBTIQ+ en Colombia, 1979–2019*, tackles the history of the first forty years of LGBTQ+ protest in Colombia, one of the first studies of its kind.

RAFAEL CESAR is an assistant professor of Spanish and Portuguese at Princeton University, where he teaches the history and literature of Portuguese-speaking Africa, Brazil, and the Caribbean, with a special focus on race. His current book project, tentatively titled "Fictions of Racelessness: The 'Latin American' Racial Imaginaries of Angola," explores the forging of a "politics of racelessness" in Angola through intellectual and political exchanges with Brazil and Cuba.

MICHELLE CHASE is associate professor of history at Pace University. She is the author of *Revolution within the Revolution: Women and Gender Politics in Cuba, 1952–1962* (University of North Carolina Press, 2015). She co–guest edited *Radical History Review* issue no. 136 (January 2020), "Revolutionary Positions: Gender and Sexuality in Cuba and Beyond," with Isabella Cosse, Melina Pappademos, and Heidi Tinsman. She is currently writing a book about transnational expressions of anti-Castro activism in the Cold War.

ISABELLA COSSE is an independent researcher at the Consejo Nacional de Investigaciones Científicas y Técnicas (CONICET) and professor at the Universidad Nacional de San Martín. She is the author of *Mafalda: A Social and Political History* of *Latin America's Global Comic* (Duke University Press, 2019), *Pareja, sexualidad y familia en los años sesenta* (Siglo XXI, 2010), and *Estigmas de nacimiento: Peronismo y orden familiar, 1946–1955* (FCE, 2006), among other books. She co-guest edited *Radical History Review* issue no. 136 (January 2020), "Revolutionary Positions: Gender and Sexuality in Cuba and Beyond," with Michelle Chase, Melina Pappademos, and Heidi Tinsman. She is currently finishing her book project tentatively titled "Love and Politics in the Cold War."

XIMENA ESPECHE is an independent researcher at the Consejo Nacional de Investigaciones Científicas y Técnicas (CONICET), member of the Centro de Historia Intelectual at the Universidad Nacional de Quilmes, and professor at the Universidad de Buenos Aires. Her book *La paradoja uruguaya. Intelectuales, latinoamericanismo y nación a mediados del siglo XX* was published in 2016. Her current research is about battles for information in the Cold War in Latin America.

ROBERT FRANCO is an assistant professor of history at Kenyon College. He specializes in the history of Mexico with a focus on gender and sexuality, disability rights, and social movements. Franco's forthcoming manuscript, tentatively titled "Revolution in the Sheets: The Sexual Politics of Tolerance in Mexico," examines the long and fraught relationship between sexual politics—such as abortion and sexual liberation—and left-wing parties in Mexico. His work can be found in the *Journal of the History of Sexuality, Radical History Review,* and *Journal of Latin American Cultural Studies.*

TANYA HARMER is an associate professor in the Department of International History at the London School of Economics and Political Science. She is author of *Allende's Chile and the Inter-American Cold War* (University of North Carolina Press, 2011) and *Beatriz Allende: A Revolutionary Life in Cold War Latin America* (University of North Carolina Press, 2020). Her current research examines the memories, legacies, and trajectories of Southern Cone exiles in Cuba during the 1970s and 1980s.

SARAH J. SEIDMAN is the Puffin Foundation Curator of Social Activism at the Museum of the City of New York, where her exhibitions include *Activist New York; Changing the Face of Democracy: Shirley Chisholm at 100; King in New York; Raise Your Voice: An Art Installation by Amanda Phingbodhipakkiya;* and more. She is coeditor of *Armed by Design: Posters and Publications of Cuba's Organization of Solidarity of the Peoples of Africa, Asia, and Latin America (OSPAAAL)* (Common Notions, 2025) with Lani Hanna, Jen Hoyer, Josh MacPhee, and Vero Ordaz, and is completing a book on the connections between the Black liberation movement and the Cuban Revolution.

EMILY SNYDER is the Mellon Research Fellow in American History at the University of Cambridge. Her book, *Caribbean Internationalisms: Revolution and Reaction in Cuba, Nicaragua, and the United States,* is under contract with University of California Press. She earned her PhD in Latin American history from Yale University in 2021, and her dissertation won the George Washington Egelston Prize and the Edwin W. Small Prize. Her work can be found in the *Radical History Review* and *The Americas.*

AILYNN TORRES SANTANA is a professor in the Sociology and Gender Studies Department of the Facultad Latinoamericana de Ciencias Sociales (FLACSO, Ecuador). She edited and contributed to the books *Derechos en riesgo en América Latina: 11 estudios sobre grupos neoconservadores* (Fundación Rosa Luxemburgo / Desde Abajo, 2020) and *Los Cuidados: del centro de la vida al centro de la política* (FES-ILDIS, 2021). She has published many articles about gender inequalities, feminisms, and anti-feminist politics in Latin America and Cuba.

SIWEI WANG holds a PhD in East Asian Languages and Cultures (EALAC) from the Institute for Comparative Literature and Society (ICLS) at Columbia University. Her research focuses on the cultural and political connections between China and Latin America since the late nineteenth century. She is currently conducting research as an independent scholar.

INDEX

Page numbers in *italics* refer to illustrations.

Abdón, Esteban, 236
Abortion, 272–273, 278n81
Abt, John, 74
Adorno, Theodor, 70
Afonso, Teresa, 23–24, 29
Africa: decolonization, 5; Portuguese colonies, 3; racism within, 28; tribal concepts, 22. *See also* Angola; Congo-Léopoldville
African Americans: activism, 68; Afro hairstyles, 78; Black Panther Party (BPP), 68, 77, 100. *See also* Davis, Angela Y.
Agencia Latina, 153
Agricultural labor, 58–60
AIDS crisis, 104, 107
Alamar housing complex, 195–198
Alexander, Franklin, 67, *68*, 71, 74, 79
Alexander, Kendra, 67, *68*, 71, 79, 83
Alfonso, Paco, 172–173, 176–177
Allende, Salvador, 108
Almendros, Néstor, 103
Alzugaray Treto, Carlos, 239, 240, 243
Amado, Jorge, 165
Amador, Tania, 225–226, 229
Ana Betancourt Award, 83–84
Andaya, Elise, 189, 201
Angola, 6; Cuban guerrilla fighters in, 22; historiography, gender and class biases, 18–19; liberation struggle and Black internationalism, 33–34; nationalism, 19–20; Natives Group, 28; Operación Carlota, 26–27, *27*; trade agreements with Cuba, 257; War of Independence, 17, 21. *See also* Rodrigues, Deolinda
Angolan Voluntary Refugee Assistance Corps, 22
Another Country (Baldwin), 32
Aptheker, Bettina, 75
Arafat, Yasser, 124
Aragonés, Emilio, 243
Araújo, Ana María, 198
Arauz, Rita, 107
Arbenz, Jacobo, 152, 154
Arenas, Reinaldo, 102–103, 105
Argentina: Argentine militants, children of, 8; Cuban embassy, 238–239; exiles from, 234–236; guerrilla organizations, 237; homosexual movement, 99–101; Perón, 153; revolutionary groups, 3
Armed Forces of National Liberation (Venezuela), 47
Asdrúbal, Oscar, 236
Asian Women's Congress (Beijing, 1949), 165, 168
"As in Vietnam" campaign, 58–60, *59*
Astudillo, Felix Pita, 82
Asylum seekers, 238–239. *See also* Exiles

Baldacci, Alexis, 8, 9
Baldwin, James, 32, 35, 74
Barbudos (bearded rebels), 81
Barricada (Sandinista newspaper), 260

Batista (Fulgencio Batista) dictatorship, 148, 150
Bay of Pigs invasion, 95, 166, 168
Beale, Frances, 74
Beech, Keyes, 73
Beijing People's Art Theatre, 173
Beltrán, Felix, 76–77
Bengelsdorf, Carollee, 214
Berlin Wall, 127
Betancourt, Ana, 83–84
Biota, Silvia, 225–226
Black Americans. *See* African Americans
Black Cubans: slavery, legacy of, 26
Black internationalism, 33–34
Black liberation movement, 6, 74
Black Panther Party (BPP), 68, 77, 100
Black Power Movement, 72
Black Scholar (journal), 68, 74
Bohemia (magazine), 143, 144, 145–146, 149, 151–152
Bolívar, Simón, 145, 147
Bolivia: *La Nación*, 143; revolution, 149
Bolivian Diary (Guevara), 178
Borge, Tomás, 261
Bornot, Telma, 67, 68, 75
Bota, Silvia, 225–226, 229
Bradford, Anita Casavantes, 5
Brazil: homosexual movement, 104–106; media ecosystem, 153; *Lampião da Esquina* (magazine), 94
Burdsall, Lorna, 228
Bureau for Fashion Orientation, 221
Bustamante, Michael, 4, 228

Cabieses, Manuel, 195–196
Cabrera Arús, María Antonia, 215, 232n26
Cai Chusheng, 176
Cámpora, Héctor, 239
"Caña" (Guillén), 167
Cañaveral (Alfonso), 164, 172–178, *174*
"Canción para Ángela Davis" (Milanés), 74–75

Capitalism: anti-capitalism and African American activism, 84–85; anti-capitalism and women's liberation, 45, 61, 80, 81; and homosexual activism, 95; and individualism, 118; and sugar economy, 175; and Western consumerism, 3, 212–230
Cardenal, Ernesto, 104
Carlos Fonseca Military Academy, 271, 272
Carmichael, Stokely, 68, 70, 72, 77
Carnovale, Vera, 249
Caro, Felipe, 7, 9, 10
Carta a mi padre (Echeverría Gaitán), 118, 120
Casa de Las Américas, 95
Casals, Violeta, 165, 169
Casaus, Victor, 250
Castellanos, Tania, 74
Castillo Armas, Carlos, 152
Castro, Fidel: criticism of, 152–153, 154–155; on gender roles and clothing styles, 222; homosexuality, views concerning, 98, 115n67, 126; journalistic constructions of, 146–148, 150–153; *La Jornada* interview, 109–110; as masculine ideal, 141–142; photographs of, *55*, *67*, *68*, *80*; Prensa Latina, Cuban news agency, 152–153; Quang Tri Province visit, 49; Revolution, hypersexualization of, 144–145; seduction as political weapon, 142, 145, 146–149, 155; on socialism and Marxism, 95; Solidaridad con Chile school, 196; Soviet invasion of Czechoslovakia, endorsement of, 2; Soviet Union, relationship with, 199; on treatment of exiles, 198; Vietnam War, support for, 48; on women's battalion in Revolution, 56
Castro, Mariela, 109, 110
Castro, Raúl, 81, 109, 151, 222
Catlett, Elizabeth, 75, 82
Cejas Arias, Jesús, 244
CENESEX (National Center for Sexual Ed-

ucation), 109–110
Centro Pablo de la Torriente Brau, 250
Cesar, Rafael, 6, 9, 257
Chántez Oliva, Gladys, 264–265
Charcot-Marie-Tooth disease, 117
Chase, Michelle, 7, 9, 168, 176, 188, 257
Che-Lumumba Club (CPUSA), 70–71
Chen Bo'er, 177
Cheri (Colette), 146
Chicago Tribune (newspaper), 144, 151
Children: roles in revolutionary contexts, 236–238, 240, 251–252. *See also* Family structures
Chile: Chilean Communist Party, 108; Committee of Solidarity with the Antifascist Resistance, 196; coup, 199; exiles from, 6, 188, 191, 247; Revolutionary Left Movement (MIR), 188, 191
China. *See* People's Republic of China
Cienfuegos, Camilo, 172
Cienfuegos Squad, 23, 37
Círculos Infantiles, 189
Clare, Eli, 130
Cleaver, Eldridge, 68, 72
Clothing styles, 214–219, *219;* Bureau for Fashion Orientation research, 220–221; foreign influences, 222–225, *223;* guayabera, 219–220; impact of, 225–226; T-shirts, social significance of, 216, 226, 228–229
Code of the Child, 189
Cohen, Irene, 23, 28, 29
Cold War: Africa as theater of, 22; children's roles, 237; Cuba-China relationship, 165–168; larger context of, 283–284; manipulation and propaganda, 148; mass media during, 142–143
Colette, 141, 146–147
Colombia: homosexual movement, 103–104; Revolutionary Armed Forces (FARC), 108, 124
Colonialism: anti-colonial movements, 17, 40, 96–97, 166–168; criticism of, 32–33, 34–37, 70; decolonization movements, 5; Portuguese policies, 19–20; sugar production, 163, 167; violence in Angola, 24
Colonias (MLNT camps), 191, 192–193, 199; pregnancy discouraged in, 192, 194
"Colorblindness," 17. *See also* Racelessness
Comecon (Council for Mutual Economic Assistance), 213, 230–231n2; and training for Cuban girls, 217–218
Come Out (U.S. magazine), 98
Comité Cubano de Solidaridad con Vietnam, 45, 49; delegation to Vietnam (1965), 52–53; and labor issues, 57–59, 59; and women's liberation, 56
Comité de Familiares de Presos Políticos, 122
Comité de Solidaridad con Angela Davis, 75
Comité Estatal de Colaboración Económica (CECE), 257, 268–269
Committee of Solidarity with the Antifascist Resistance, Chile, 196
Committees for the Defense of the Revolution (CDR), 77–78
Conga Against Homophobia and Transphobia, 110
Congo-Léopoldville: guerrilla fighters, training of, 21–22, 28; race relations within, 36
Congress of Women of the Americas (1963), 170–171
Consumer culture, 3, 212–230; *diplotienda* stores, 227–228. *See also* Capitalism
Contraceptives, 192
Contras, Nicaragua, 260–261
Cosse, Isabella, 8, 9, 188, 190
CPUSA (Communist Party USA), 67, 69–70; Angela Davis on Cuba, 83; Che-Lumumba Club, 70–71
Cruz, Jesús, 247
Cruz, Viriato da, 20, 25–26

Index 293

Cuba in Battle (documentary film), *167*
"Cuba Libre" statue, 76
Cuba magazine, 78
Cuban Committee of Solidarity with South Vietnam. *See* Comité Cubano de Solidaridad con Vietnam
Cuban Committee to Free Angela Davis, 78–79
Cuban Missile Crisis, 166, 168
Cuban Revolution, impact and legacy, 284–286
Cuban Workers' Federation (CTC), 172
Cubas, Leticia, 200–201
Cultelli, Marina, 201, 204
Cultelli, Rita, 204
"The Culture of Dress and Costumes," 217–219, *219*
Czechoslovakia, invasion of, 2

Dang Thi Thanh, 55
Davis, Angela Y.: and Black liberation movement, 70; Cuba, first visit to (1969), 70–73; Cuba, increasing links with, 73; education and formation, 69–70; false charges against, 73; and gender, perceptions of, in Cuba, 78–83; legacy and impact, 67–69, 84–85; photographs, *68, 80*; as symbol of persecution, 68, 73–79, *76*; travels after acquittal (1972), 79–80; UCLA controversies, 73
Davis, Fania, 73–74
Day of the Heroic *Guerrillero* (Che Guevara), 104
D'Carmen Espinoza, Illeana, 272
De Almeida, Roberto, 31, 32, 38–39
De Ambiente (Colombian magazine), 94
De Andrade, Mario, 30
De Carlotto, Estela, 251
Decolonization. *See* Colonialism
Delfino, Liliana, 236, 241–242, 244, 246, 252
Demarchi, Josefa, 242

Democratic Federation of Cuban Women (FDMC), 165
Democratic Republic of Vietnam (DRV), 47–48
Dialectics of Liberation Conference (1967), 70
Díaz, María Ofelia, 173
Diplotiendas, 227–228
Disablism, 119–120, 123, 130
Doce Sánchez, Lidia Esther, 171
Dorticós, Osvaldo, *55,* 79, *80,* 239
Dos Santos, Engrácia, 23–24, 29
Dubois, Jules, 142, 143–144, 150, 151–155
Durán Legón, Manuel, 269

Ebony magazine, 32
Echeverría, Rodolfo, 122
Echeverría Gaitán, Irina Layevska, *129; Carta a mi padre,* 120; Charcot-Marie-Tooth disease and disability, 117; Che Guevara, resemblance to, 119, 127–129; Che Guevara as substitute father, 123–124; childhood and family background, 121–124; designated male at birth, 118–119; disability and identity, 123, 124–125, *125,* 128; father, relationship with, 123–124, 132; gender affirmation and New Woman ideal, 129–132; gender assignment, 120; gender identity, 120–121, 124, 129–132; impact and legacy, 133; New Man and Che Guevara, 127–129; New Man and gender identity, 119–121; New Woman, 131–132; overview, 117–119; PRT (Revolutionary Workers Party), 127; transition and medical care, 124–127
Ejército Revolucionario del Pueblo (ERP), 234, 239–240, 242
11J protests, 284
El Machete (newspaper), 122
El Otro (Colombian magazine), 94
"El socialismo y el hombre en Cuba" (Che Guevara), 118

"Entre la Arcilla y la Obra" *(Granma)*, 82
Eón Inteligencia Transgenérica (Aeon Transgender Alliance), 129
Escuelas en el campo concept, 270–271
Escuelas Secundarias Básicas en el Campo (ESBEC), 196, 270–271
Espeche, Ximena, 8
Espín, Vilma, 44–45, 53, 57–58, 60–61, 81–82, 109
Espiñeira González, Guadalupe, 265
Estévez, Olga, 193–194
Exile and Pride (Clare), 130
Exiles: from Argentina, 234–236; children and teenagers, 236–237, 240–241; and *diplotienda* stores, 227–228; exiled Cubans visiting Cuba, 215–216, 226–228; integration into Cuban society, 198–202; Roberto Santucho extended family, 238–245; study programs, 200

Family Code (1975), 3, 83, 189, 190, 191, 201, 259
Family structures: in *colonias*, 192–193, 199–202; and Cuban internationalism, 257; during Cuban Revolution, 188–190, 202–205; Mirista women, 195–198; transnational families, 265–270. *See also* New Family
Fang Chen, 173, 176–177
FARC (Revolutionary Armed Forces of Colombia), 108, 124
Fashion. *See* Clothing styles
Federation of Cuban Women (FMC), 17, 22, 44, 68, 80–82, 271; Angela Davis, support for, 75, 80; Family Code, 83; First National Congress, 170; second congress (1974), 83–84
Femininity: Angela Davis, portrayals of, 78; Echeverría Gaitán's displays of, 120, 123, 128; ideals of, revolutionary, 51, 55, 260
Feminism: in *colonias*, 193; Cuban rejection of US feminist movement, 81–82; feminist historiography, 281; second-wave, 45, 56, 190; women's emancipation, 60–61. *See also* Women's liberation
Ferrer, Yolanda, 57–58
Fidel Castro: Rebel, Liberator or Dictator? (Dubois), 152
Fifth Brother Wang (film), 176
First Congress of Culture and Education (1971), 98–99
First Declaration of Havana, 165–166
First National Congress of Culture and Education (1971), 96, 97
First National Congress of the Federation of Cuban Women, 170
FNLA. *See* Frente Nacional de Libertação de Angola (FNLA)
Fonseca Amador, Carlos, 271
"Four Cuban Peasant Women" (Qin Mu), 171
Franco, Robert, 7, 9, 10
Freedom Is My Beat (Dubois), 152
Frente de Liberación Homosexual, 99–100, 101
Frente Homosexual de Acción Revolucionaria, 102
Frente Nacional de Libertação de Angola (FNLA), 21, 23, 25
Frente Revolucionario Indoamericano Popular, 236
Friedan, Betty, 74
Front for Homosexual Liberation, Argentina, 99
FSLN. *See* Sandinista National Liberation Front (FSLN)
Fürst, Juliane, 215

Gaitán, Yolanda, 122
Garcia, Angelina D., 78, 84
García, María Cristina, 227
Garcia, Torres, 2
García Buchaca, Edith, 165, 168

Gay Latino Alliance, 107
Gay liberation, 97. *See also* Homosexual movement
Gays for the Nicaraguan Revolution, 107
Gelbard, José, 247
Gendered roles: Angela Davis in Cuba, 79–84; and clothing styles, 222; in *colonias*, 201–202; in Cuban Revolution, 279–282; in political strategy, 4; sex ratios within schools, 272–273. *See also* Femininity; Masculinity; Women
Geyer, Georgie Anne, 73
Gigi (Colette), 141, 146–147
Ginsberg, Allen, 95–96, 99
Ginzburg, Carlo, 237–238
Gleijeses, Piero, 5
Global South: in context of Cold War, 283–284; revolutionary and transnational movements, 5–7, 9, 47, 168; socialism in, 51–52, 121; use of term, 10n1
Gómez, Sara, 82
Gonzalez-Vaillant, Gabriela, 193
Gorriarán Merlo, Enrique, 246
Grajales Cuello, Mariana, 81, 176
Grand Alliance of Overseas Chinese in Cuba, 165
Grandmothers of Plaza de Mayo, 251
Granma magazine: Angela Davis, coverage of, 78, 82; "Sisters in Arms" series, 53–54
Gran zafra (great harvest) campaign, 71, 85
Gray Years (Quinquenio Gris), 3, 71, 214
Grupo Lambda, 101, 102
Gualdino, Josefa, 29
Guatemala: Rebel Armed Forces, 48; revolution in, 143, 154
Guerra, Lillian, 3, 230
Guerrillerismo, 199
Guevara, Ana, 249
Guevara, Ernesto "Che," 22, 154; Agostinho Neto, meeting with, 22; *Bolivian Diary*, 178; commemoration of death, 104; "El socialismo y el hombre en Cuba," 118; *Ink* magazine, 98–99, 99; on land reform, 166; "Lidia," 171; and New Man, 257; "Socialism and Man in Cuba," 121–122; on Vietnam War, 48; visit to China (1960), 163–164
Guevara, Martín, 249
Guevara, Roberto, 243, 249
Guillén, Nicolás, 165, 167, 173
Guo Jian, 170
Guyer, Soledad, 197

Hands Off Korea Campaign, 168
Harlem Black Women to Free Angela Davis, 74
Harmer, Tanya, 6, 8, 9, 47, 247, 263–264, 265–266
Hatzky, Christine, 5
Havana, Cuba, as revolutionary hub, 6, 47
Healy, Dorothy, 71
Helsinki, Finland: World Festival for Youth and Students, 70
Hemingway, Ernest, 164
Hernández, Melba, 45, 49–50, 50, 58, 169
Heroínas de Angola (Jiménez Rodríguez), 23–27, 24
HIJOS (Hijos e Hijas por la Identidad y la Justicia contra el Olvido y el Silencio), 250
Historia reciente, 5, 11–12n9
Historiography: feminist, 281; innovative methods, 5–6; of marginalized groups, 69
Ho Chi Minh trail, 48
Homeward Bound (May), 4
Homosexuales (Black Panther bulletin), 100
Homosexual Front of Revolutionary Action, 101
Homosexuality: illegality in Cuba, 96, 104; intolerance of, 2–3; viewed as weakness, 95
Homosexual Liberation Movement of Colombia (MLHC), 104

Homosexual movement, 93–111; after Cuban Revolution, 106–108; global nature of, 93–94; homophobia in Cuba, 94–96; homophobia in Cuba, Argentinean and Mexican responses, 99–103; homophobia in Cuba, Colombian and Brazilian responses, 103–106; homophobia in Cuba, global response to, 96–99; Mexico, 125–126; overview of Cuban Revolution's treatment of, 93–94; Pride parades, 103; ties with other leftist organizations, 97; twenty-first century, 109–110
Homosexual Work Commission, 126
Huang Jisu, 164
Huang Zhiliang, 171
Hynson, Rachel, 5, 188–189

"Imagined community," Cuba as, 281
Improper Conduct (documentary film), 102–103
Ink (English magazine), 98–99, *99*
Institute for the Investigation and Orientation of Consumer Demand (ICIODI), 220, 229
Institutional Revolutionary Party (PRI), 122
Inter-American Commission on Human Rights, 248
Inter-American Press Association (IAPA), 144, 150
Internationalism: Black, 33; Cuban, 240; Isla de la Juventud, 270–273; and New Family, 262–265; transnational families, 248, 265–270
International Lesbian, Gay, Bisexual, Trans, and Intersex Association (ILGA), 109
International Women's Day, 64n52, 75
International Women's Year Conference (1975), 60–61
International Year of the Woman (1975), 83
Isla de la Juventud (Isle of Youth), 79, 257, 270–273

Isla de Pinos, 270. *See also* Isla de la Juventud (Isle of Youth)

Jackson, Esther Cooper, 70
Jackson, George, 72, 77
Jackson, James, 70
Jiefang Daily (Chinese newspaper), 166
Jiménez, Orlando, 103
Jiménez Rodríguez, Limbania, 17, *29; Heroínas de Angola,* 23–27, *24; Heroínas de Angola* contrasted with Deolinda's diaries, 39–40; racial context, understanding of, 28–30; on racism, 36–37; research in Angola, 39
July 11, 2021, protests, 284
Juventud Rebelde (Young Communist League newspaper), 248

Kamy Squad, 23, 27, *29,* 37
Keller, Renata, 154
Khrushchev, Nikita, 4
King, Dr. Martin Luther, Jr., 32, 35
Kirchner government policies, 251
"Kitchen debates" (Khrushchev and Nixon), 4
Koivunen, Pia, 215
Kong Mai, 165
Korean War, 142
Krauss, Camila, 197

Labor issues in Vietnam, 57–60
La Jornada (Mexican newspaper), 109–110
Lambe, Jennifer, 4
Lampião da Esquina (Brazilian magazine), 94, 105–106, *106*
La Nación (Bolivian newspaper), 143, 150
Land reform, 166
Lanzilotto, Ana María, 235, 244
Latifundia (landed estates and land distribution), 166
Latin American Student Congress (1966), 47

League of Chinese Left-Wing Dramatists, 173
Lecumberri prison, 122, 123
Lemebel, Pedro, 108
Liberation, women's vs. national, 56, 170–171
Limonta, Mayda, 78
Lincolao, Isolina, 202–204
Literacy Campaigns, 260, 263
Liu Jingyan, 171
Liu Simu, 166
Llorca, Manuel, 196
López Díaz, Julián, 267
Los Angeles Times (newspaper), 73
Lucas, Don, 172, 177
Lumsden, Ian, 111, 115n67
Lumumba, Patrice, 21
Ly Van Sau, 50

Maceo, Antonio, 81, 176
Madres Combatientes Internacionalistas, 271
Maestra Voluntaria (Olema García), 171
Malmierca, Isodoro, 269–270
Mambisas (women independence fighters), 80–81
"Manifiesto (Hablo por mi diferencia)" (Lemebel), 108
Marcuse, Herbert, 70
Mariel boatlift, 102, 103–104, 212, 214, 266; *marielitos*, 102–103, 104; opposition to, 223, 224
Marriage: and New Family, 263–265; and transnational families, 265–270. *See also* Family structures
Martí, José, 76, 145, 240
Martín Álvarez, Alberto, 47
Marulanda Vélez, Manuel, 124
Marxism: sexual conservatism, 95; and Tricontinentalism, 46
Masculinity, 7; Che Guevara and masculinist politics, 133; hegemonic, 260. *See also* Gendered roles; New Man ideology; Patriarchal frameworks

Masetti, Jorge R., 153
Massamba-Débat, Alphonse, 21
Matanzas, Cuba: "Cuba Libre" statue, 76; rebellion in, 26
Maternity Law, 189
Mattachine Society, 96
Matthews, Herbert, 151
May, Elaine Tyler, 4
Mazzeo, Fernando, 193
Mbundu people (Angola), 20
Mederos, René, 59–60, 59
Memory, role in historical scholarship, 5, 11–12n9, 119–120, 281
Mendoza, Jorge Enrique, 165
Menéndez, Jesús, 172
Merlo, Gorriarán, 249
Mestizaje within MPLA (Angola), 30
Mexican Communist Party (PCM), 103, 122, 125, 126–127
Mexico: homosexual movement, 101–103, 125–126; Mexican Revolution, 122; Zapatista Army of National Liberation, 115n62
Miami Herald (newspaper), 227
Migration: to Cuba, 188; Cuban, to US, 102, 266; and marriage, 267–268
Miguéis, Matias, 26
Miguel, José, 26
Milanés, Pablo, 74–75, 196
Military Units to Aid Production (UMAP), 95–96
Ministry of the Interior (MININT), 222
"Mi Patria es Dulce por Fuera" (Guillén), 167
MIR (Movimiento de Izquierda Revolucionaria), 188, 191, 195–196
Miristas, 192; Mirista women, 195–198
Mitchell, Charlene, 70–71
Mobutu, Joseph, 21
Moncada Barracks attack (1953), 153, 169, 256
Montenegro, Carlos, 145
Montoneros (Peronist organization), 240, 243–244, 248–249; *guardería*, 247

Morales Reyna, Águedo, 261
Morante, Raphael, 77
Morir de pie (documentary film), 118
Movimiento 22 de Abril (M-22), 108
Movimiento de Liberación Homosexual de Colombia (MLHC), 104, 114n45
Movimiento de Madres Combatientes por la Educación, 271
Movimiento Nacionalista Revolucionario (MNR), 143
MPLA (Movimento Popular de Libertação de Angola), 17; capture of women by FNLA (1967), 23; and Che Guevara, 22; Cienfuegos Squad, 23; and Deolinda Rodrigues, 19; emergence of, 20; factionalism, 26; FNLA as rival movement, 25; *mestizaje* within, 30; opposition to, 21; race relations within, 25–26, 33–35
Muchacha (Federation of Cuban Women magazine), 220, 221, 225, 226, 229
Mujeres (FMC publication), 56, 75, 217, 221, 263–264

National Association of Colored Women's Clubs, 33
National Bank of Cuba, 268–269
National Center for Sexual Education (CENESEX), 109–110
National Congress on Culture and Education, 2
National Council of Negro Women, 33
National Institute for Agrarian Reform, 173
National Liberation Front (NLF), 44, 47–48; awarded foreign embassy status, 49; Comité messaging, 50; delegation to Vietnam (1965), 53
National Liberation Movement—Tupamaros (MLNT), 188, 191
National United Committee to Free Angela Davis (NUCFAD), 74
Navajas, Cristina, 238
Neruda, Pablo, 165

Neto, Agostinho, 20, 22, 26, 28, 36
New Family, 257, 259; and internationalism, 262–265; transnational families, 265–270. *See also* Family structures
New Man ideology, 7, 58, 59–60, 117, 257; Echeverría Gaitán, appropriation of, 119; *hombrecito* (tough man) ideals, 123; and internationalist family missions, 258–262; New Man and New Woman, 118; women's roles, 260–262; and work projects, 200. *See also* Masculinity
Newton, Huey P., 68, 77, 100
Ngô Đình Diệm, 47
Ngo Thi Tuyen, 55
Nguyen Thi Binh, 54, 55
Nguyen Thi Dinh, 44, 53, 54–56
Nguyen Van Troi, 50, 53
Nicaragua: Contras, 260–261; and Cuban concepts of gender, sexuality, and family, 256–274; New Man and internationalist missions, 258–262; Nicaragua Revolution (1979), 3; Sandinista National Liberation Front (FSLN), 107, 124; Sandinista Revolution, 6, 10, 270–271; trade and resources, 257–258; and transnational families, 265–270
Nicomedes Galañeña, Crescencio, 244
Night of the Gardenias, 108
Night of the Three Ps, 105–106
19th of April Movement, 108
Nixon, Richard, 4
Non-Aligned Movement (NAM), 47
Noth, Juliane, 51
Nuestro Mundo, 99
Nuestro Tiempo, 172

Oikabeth (lesbian organization), 101, 102
Olema García, Daura, 171
Operación Carlota (Angola), 26–27, 27, 39
"Operation Truth," 147, 149, 150
Opina (magazine), 220, 221

Index 299

Orden Playa Girón (Order of the Bay of Pigs), 79
Organization of Latin American Solidarity (OLAS), 70
Organization of Solidarity with the Peoples of Africa, Asia, and Latin America (OSPAAAL), 57, 75, 76
Organization of the Angolan Woman (OMA), 17, 22
Ortega, Daniel, 124
Ortolani, Diego, 241, 242, 244, 246, 247, 249, 250, 254
Ortolani, Luis, 241–242
Ovimbundu people (Angola), 21

Padilla, Heberto, 2
Padilla Affair (1971), 2
Paim, Lucrécia, 23–24, 29
Palabra Obera, 235–236
Palestine Liberation Organization (PLO), 124
Pang Bing'an, 165
Partido Socialista Popular (PSP), 82
Pasolini, Pier Paolo, 105
Patria Potestad laws, 203
Patriarchal frameworks, 267; in Angola, 30; and New Man, 118
Patrullas Click, 201
Paul VI (pope), 245
Paz Ruiz, Ofelia, 234, 236
PCM. *See* Mexican Communist Party (PCM)
Pellegrín, Andrea, 198–199
Penal Code, Cuban, 96, 104, 109, 269
People's Daily (Chinese Communist Party newspaper), 165, 171
People's Republic of China, 163–179; Che Guevara's visit (1960), 163–164; Cold War era relationship with Cuba, 165–168; Cuban photo exhibit, *169*, 169–170; Cultural Revolution, 178; feminist anti-imperialism, 171–178; Great Leap Forward, 163–164, 179n3; sugar importation from Cuba, 163–164; women's solidarity, 168–171; Xinhua News Agency, 165
People's Revolutionary Army (ERP), 234
Pepetela (Angolan writer), 38
Peralta, Braulio, 126
Pérez Téllez, Emma, 141, 142, 143, 144, 145–149
Perón, Juan Domingo, 100, 153, 235
Peronism, 239–240
Phan Thi Quyen, 53
Piñeiro, Manuel, 192–193, 268
Piñera, Virgilio, 106
Pino Santos, Oscar, 169
Plan Condor, 244
Pons Rabasa, Alba, 120
Popular Movement for the Liberation of Angola. *See* MPLA (Movimento Popular de Libertação de Angola)
Popular Socialist Party (PSP), 82, 172
"Por Ángela" (Castellanos), 74
Por el mismo camino (television series), 261
Portugal: African colonies, 3; Angolan war of independence, 21; decolonization, resistance to, 21; settlement in Angola, 20
Pregnancy within boarding schools, 272–273
Prensa Latina, 54, 143, 150, 152–153, 239; criticism of, 153–154
Prensa Libre, 154
Propaganda: Castro's use of, 148; criticism of in Cuba, 154–155; Nazi-Fascist, 142; revolutionary pedagogy, 142–149; seduction as political weapon, 142, 145, 146–149, 155
Provisional Revolutionary Government (PRG), 49
Proyecto Hogares (MIR), 191
PRT. *See* Workers' Revolutionary Party (PRT)
"Psychological war," 142, 152

Qin Mu, 171
Queer rights, 93. *See also* Homosexual movement
Quinquenio Gris (Gray Years), 3, 71, 214

Racelessness, 6, 17; Cuban politics of, 18; MPLA's image of, 39
Racism: addressed in *Heroínas de Angola* (Jiménez Rodríguez), 25–26; in Cuba, 68–69; within Cuban Revolution, 72; Cuba's mission in Africa, 28; Deolinda Rodrigues in racial context, 28–30; racial violence, 32; "reverse racism," 36; white persons, pejorative words for, 31
Radio Rebeide, 165
Radio Reloj, 248
Randall, Gregory, 241
Randall, Margaret, 193
Rangel, Juan Carlos, 220–221
Rebel Armed Forces (Guatemala), 48
Rectification of Errors and Negative Tendencies Campaign, 214, 231n7
Refugees. *See* Exiles
"Reverse racism," 36
Revolutionary Armed Forces of Colombia (FARC), 108, 124
Revolutionary Indoamerican Popular Front, 236
Revolutionary Left Movement. *See* MIR (Movimiento de Izquierda Revolucionaria)
Revolutionary Workers Party. *See* Workers' Revolutionary Party (PRT)
Reyes Guzmán, Nélida, 127, 129, 132
Ricardo Franco Front, 108
Rivera, Diego, 122, 124
Roberto, Holden, 21, 28, 30
Robertson, Carole, 70
Rodrigues, Deolinda, 17, *29;* background and overview, 19–23, *20;* diaries, contrasted with *Heroínas de Angola,* 39–40;

diaries, publication of, 17, 31, 39; impact and legacy, 38–40; in racial context, 28–29; racial violence, views on, 31–35; racism, diary entries concerning, 37–38; revolutionary consciousness, 32–33; as symbol after death, 23–30; universalism, views on, 35–38
Rodríguez, Limbania. *See* Jiménez Rodríguez, Limbania
Rodríguez, Silvio, 75, 196
Rojas, Marta, 45, 52, 53, 58; "Sisters in Arms" series *(Granma),* 53–54
Romances (FMC publication), 75, 78
Rostgaard, Alfredo, 75–76, *76*
Ruz, María Inés, 195, 197

Saade, Lira, 109–110
Saavedra, Juan, 201
Sánchez, Celia, 81, 247
Sandinista National Liberation Front (FSLN), 107, 124, 256, 271
Sandinistas: Literacy Crusade, 260; Sandinista Revolution, 6, 10, 270–271
San Francisco Examiner (newspaper), 73
Santamaría, Haydée, 81, 169
Santería (Afro-Caribbean religion), 26
Santucho, Ana Cristina, 234, 236
Santucho, Gabriela, 236
Santucho, Julio, 249
Santucho, Marcela, 234, 236
Santucho, María Emilia, 234, 236, 246
Santucho, María Ofelia, 238, 240, 243, 245, 247, 250, 251
Santucho, María Silvia, 246
Santucho, María Susana, 236, 246
Santucho, Mario, 236
Santucho, Mario Roberto, 234–235
Santucho, Miguel, 251
Santucho, Roberto, 236, 238; death of, 244; life with Liliana Delfino, 241–242

Santucho extended family, 236–237; cooperation with Cuba, 240; lawsuit (2020), 245–246, 250–251; life in exile, 241, 243–251
Savimbi, Jonas, 21
Seduction as political weapon, 142, 145, 146–149, 155
Seidman, Sarah, 7
Sexism, double, in Angola, 30
Sexuality, 7; *internacionalistas,* sacrifices of, 262–263; masturbation, 262; women's roles during Cuban Revolution, 190–191. *See also* Gendered roles
Shakur, Assata, 68
Shanghai Theatre Academy, 173
Sierra Madero, Abel, 95, 232n34
Sierra Maestra (newspaper), 145
Sierra Maestra (revolutionary headquarters), 56, 81
Silva, Ricardo, 242
Silveira Cabrera, Cecilia, 78
"Sisters in Arms" series *(Granma),* 53–54
Slavery, legacy of, 22, 26, 85
Snyder, Emily, 6, 8, 9, 188–189, 203
"Socialism and Man in Cuba" (Guevara), 121–122
Soledad Brothers, 73
Solidaridad con Chile school, 196–197
Solidarity campaigns: New Man solidarity, 260; support for Angela Davis, 68–69, 74–77; support for China, 164; support for Cuban Revolution, 125–126; transnational, 6–7, 69, 97, 101, 196, 240, 248; women's support for China, 168–171. *See also* Vietnam
Solidarity Committee with Angela Davis, 75
SOMOS (Argentinean magazine), 94, 100–101, 106
Somos Jóvenes (youth magazine), 216, 220, 221, 262–263
Somoza, Anastasio, 256

Soviet Union: Comecon (Council for Mutual Economic Assistance), 213; dissolution of, 119; homosexuality, attitudes toward, 95; influence on Cuban economic planning, 213; invasion of Czechoslovakia, 2; "peace" as foreign policy emphasis, 49
Special Period (economic crisis), 127
Steinem, Gloria, 74
Stonewall riots, 96–97
Stride Toward Freedom (King), 32
Student Nonviolent Coordinating Committee (SNCC), 68
Students for a Democratic Society (SDS), 97
Sugar industry, 46, 163–164; *Cañaveral* (Alfonso), 172–178, *174;* and colonialism, 167; sugarcane as artistic theme, 167–168; Ten Million Ton Harvest, 46, 58, 213

Tacueyó Massacre (1984), 108
Teatro Popular, 172
Television, Castro's use of, 147
Téllez, Dora María, 107
Teng Wei, 166
Ten Million Ton Harvest (sugar), 46, 58, 213
Territorial Troop Militia, 56
Testimonio literature, 118, 119–120. *See also* Echeverría Gaitán, Irina Layevska
Third Congress of the Young Communist League (UJC), 216
Third International (workers' organization), 95
Third World Women's Alliance, 73, 74
Tianjin People's Art Theatre, 173
Tlatelolco Massacre (1968), 102, 121–122
Torres, Beatriz, 187–188, 190
Tourism, 148, 227
Tran Buu Kiem, 50
Transnational families, 265–270. *See also* Family structures

Transsexuality, 120–121; transgender movements, 129–130. *See also* Echeverría Gaitán, Irina Layevska
Trauma, 245–246; racial violence, 32
Tribalism, 27; FNLA's influence, 25; tribal concepts in Africa, 22
"Tricontinental" alliance, 5, 7
Tricontinental Bulletin, 57
Tricontinental Conference (1966), 44–45, 47, 55, 64n52, 178; Vietnam War, support for, 48
Tricontinentalism, 45–46, 51
Tricontinental magazine, 27, 75–77
T-shirts, social significance of, 216, 226, 228–229
Túpac Amaru Revolutionary Movement, 108
Tupamaros, 188, 192, 193–194, 198, 199
26th of July Movement, 45, 47, 49, 81–82

Ulloa, Ariel, 199
Ulloa, Katy, 200
Unión de Jóvenes Comunistas (UJC), 258
Union for the Total Independence of Angola (UNITA), 21
United Nations, 248; Decade for Women (1975–1985), 83; UNHCR (High Commissioner for Refugees), 200
United States: exiled Cubans visiting Cuba, 226–228; impact on youth fashion, 222–225, *223;* repression and imperialism, 75, 171; Venceremos Brigades, 97. *See also* CPUSA (Communist Party USA)
Universalism: Che Guevara's views, 22; Deolinda Rodrigues' views, 35–38
University of California, Los Angeles (UCLA), 73
University of Havana, 79
Urteaga, José, 244
Uruguay: exiles from, 6, 188, 191, 192, 247; National Liberation Movement—Tupamaros (MLNT), 188, 191

Valdés Vivó, Raúl, *50,* 52–53, 58
Vásquez-Bronfman, Ana, 198
Vázquez Barrón, Arturo, 126
Venceremos Brigades, 71, 72, 73, 85, 97
Venezuela: Armed Forces of National Liberation, 47; Castro's visit, 147; Cuban relations with, 239
Ventana Gay (Colombian magazine), 94
Venturelli, José, 165
Vésente, Juan Miguel, 269–270
Videla, Jorge Rafael, 251
Vieira, Luandino, 38
Vietnam: Cuban Committee of Solidarity with South Vietnam, 45; Cuban-Vietnamese solidarity, 45–50; delegates to Tricontinental Conference (1966), 44; labor issues, 57–60; National Liberation Front (NLF), 44, 47–48; Provisional Revolutionary Government (PRG), 49
Vietnam War, 7, 48–53
Vietnam Women's Union, 52
Villareal, Ana María, 236
Violence: racial, 32; trauma, 245–246
Volnovich, Juan Carlos, 247
VWU (Vietnam Women's Union), 56, 58

Wang, Siwei, 7, 8, 9
Wang Zheng, 177
The Washington Post (newspaper), 226
Wheelock, Jaime, 261
Williams, Robert F., 68, 72, 77
Winston, Henry, 72
Women: Chinese and Cuban solidarity, 168–171; in Cuban workforce, 46; femininity, expectations of, 55–56; feminist anti-imperialism, 171–178; militant images of revolutionary women, 51–52, 80–81, 171; roles in Angolan liberation, 31; roles in *colonias,* 193–194; roles in Cuban Revolution, 25, 164; roles in New Man ideology, 260–262; roles in Nicaraguan Contras, 260–261; roles in

Women (*continued*)
  revolutionary movements, 24–25; "triple burden," 259; Vietnamese women, heroic model of, 44–45; Vietnamese women, solidarity with, 45–46; women's inequality, 259. *See also* Gendered roles
Women, Culture, and Politics (Davis), 85
Women, Race, and Class (Davis), 85
Women of Viet Nam (VWU magazine), 58
Women's International Democratic Federation (WIDF), 64n52, 74
Women's liberation: and national liberation, 56, 170–171; racial attitudes within, 74; Vietnam and Cuba, 52–57. *See also* Feminism
Women's Revolutionary Brigades, 81
Women's Strike for Equality March (1970), 74
Women's Union for the Liberation of South Vietnam, 44, 53
Workers' Revolutionary Party (PRT), 101, 103, 126–127, 234–236; PRT-ERP, 249
Workers Socialist Party (POS), 103
World Congress of Women (Helsinki/1969), 58
World Festival of Youth and Students (WFYS), 212, 215–216, 219–220
World Peace Council, 165
Wu Quanheng, 170–171

Xia Yan, 177

Yan Fei, 176–177
Ying Ruocheng, 173
Young, Allen, 98–99, 100–101
Youth culture, 212–230; Bureau for Fashion Orientation research, 221; and capitalist consumerism, 222–229; clothing styles, 214–220, *219*; guayabera as fashion, 219–220; Isla de la Juventud, 270–273; press, impact of, 216

Zapatista Army of National Liberation, 132
Zavaleta Mercado, René, 142, 143, 144, 149–151
Zhang Chengzhi, 171
Zhang Guangtian, 164
Zhou Enlai, 169, 178
Zhu Duanjun, 173
Zuleta, León, 104

Caribbean Crossroads:
Race, Identity, and Freedom Struggles

Edited by Lillian Guerra, Devyn Spence Benson, April Mayes, and Solsiree del Moral

More than any other region of the Americas, the Caribbean has been continuously defined by the push and pull between global white supremacy and Black liberation, colonial and anticolonial impulses, and the struggle for freedom against externally imposed economies and political systems. This series focuses on these varied and contradictory histories of the region with a particular focus on Cuba, Puerto Rico, Haiti, the Dominican Republic, and their transnational ties. Importantly, books explore the Caribbean as a racialized space and are not afraid to name the ways whiteness and Blackness work in the region.

Black Freedom and Education in Nineteenth-Century Cuba, by Raquel Alicia Otheguy (2025)

Cuba's Cosmopolitan Enclaves: Imperialism and Internationalism in Eastern Sugar Towns, by Frances Peace Sullivan (2025)

The Cuban Revolution and the New Left: Transnational Histories of Gender, Sexuality, and Family, edited by Michelle Chase and Isabella Cosse (2026)

www.ingramcontent.com/pod-product-compliance
Lightning Source LLC
Chambersburg PA
CBHW022026240426
43667CB00042B/1198